P9-ECV-980

Velvet Whispers

Other Books By Joan Elizabeth Lloyd

Black Satin

The Pleasure of JessicaLynn

Slow Dancing

The Love Flower

Velvet Whispers

by

Joan Elizabeth Lloyd

CARROLL & GRAF PUBLISHERS, INC.
NEW YORK

First Carroll & Graf edition 1999

Carroll & Graf Publishers, Inc.
19 West 21st Street
New York, NY 10010-6805

ISBN: 0-7394-0493-8

Manufactured in the United States of America

Velvet Whispers

Chapter 1

"Hi, Sugar." Liza's voice was soft and husky, not its usual speaking tone. "How's my man tonight?" She had also added just a hint of a southern accent, which softened and lengthened each word.

"I'm just great now that I can hear your voice, Liza."

Liza shifted the phone to her other shoulder and settled back into her overstuffed lounge chair in the small room that was her private space. "I'm so thrilled that you called."

"You knew I would. It's Tuesday, you know."

"I do know, but sometimes you are really naughty and disappoint me." She had already double-checked to be sure that the door was closed and locked and now she reached up and turned off the light. The room was now lit only by mid-evening moonlight shining through the window. She could close the blinds, but Liza liked the softening effect the moonlight had on her psyche. "I just hate it when you're naughty."

"I like being naughty with you, Liza," the man purred.

"Mmm," she purred back. "Maybe we should be naughty together. What should we do?"

After a slight pause, he said, "Let's take a walk in the woods."

"Good idea." Liza created her picture of him, walking beside her between tall trees, the air filled with the smell of pine. He was tall, with broad shoulders, long fingers, a broad chest, and narrow hips. Mentally she created his face, all planes and angles, with a firm jaw and soft lips. His eyes were deep blue with raven lashes that matched the long wavy black hair he wore gathered at the nape of his neck with a leather thong. "Yes, let's," she said. "Will you hold my hand?"

"Oh yes," the man said, his voice soft yet clear despite the miles between them.

"It's so cool here in the shade of the trees, but your hand is warm, and I can feel the heat travel up my arm warming all of me. Are you warm too?" She felt in the near darkness for the glass of wine she had placed on the table beside her chair and took a silent sip. As she always did, she felt a delicious tingle all over.

"You know I am," he said.

"It's so quiet here," she continued. She lifted her long hair from the back of her neck and draped it over the back of the chair. "Our footsteps are almost completely silent on the deep carpet of pine needles. I can hear a bird far away, its song faint and almost melancholy. The sky is so blue that it almost hurts my eyes. The breeze is cool, but the pockets of bright sun are warm and each time we walk from shadow to brightness, I turn my face up to the heat and feel it through my body."

"What are you wearing? Tell me how you look."

She already knew his preferences. "Well, you know that you're tall enough to tower over me. I like having to look up to see your handsome face. I'm wearing my hair in a single braid down my back, and there's only a slender black ribbon at the bottom holding it together. It will be easy to remove."

"And the rest of you?"

Liza could hear his breathing, now a bit heavy. "I'm wearing a peasant blouse of soft white cotton. It's been washed so many times that the fabric is almost transparent. And I have on that full, dark green skirt that I know you like so much and soft leather sandals. I'm afraid that I had so little time to dress this morning that I didn't put on anything underneath my clothes. It's a bit embarrassing."

"Oh, baby," the man said, "you know me too well."

"I'm afraid that from your height, you can see right down the front of my blouse. I can't help it if the cool wind makes my nipples hard. I hope you won't look."

There was a soft chuckle. "Of course I won't look," he said.

In her chair, Liza unbuttoned her blouse and slid her palm over her satin-covered breasts. In the dark she almost became the girl in the woods. "I'm so glad I can trust you that way. Let's walk for a ways. I know there's a small stream just over that little hill. If we're feeling brave, we can wade through the cold water to the big flat rock in the middle. It will be a nice place for us to sit and talk." She was silent for a moment, then continued. "Do you like it here? Of course you do. I knew you'd like this place. The sun is shining through the branches of the huge trees that line the stream and, as the wind blows softly, the sunlight sparkles on the smoothly flowing water. Shall we cross to that rock?"

"Oh yes. We really should."

"Good. But you wouldn't want to ruin your beautiful leather boots, would you? Sit down here on the bank and take them off. Shall I help you? Of course I should. I'll just unlace them. You know it's hard for me to keep my hands off your muscular thighs, but I'm a bit embarrassed and I really shouldn't touch you."

"It's all right. You can touch me." His voice was hoarse with excitement.

"Are you sure?"

His "Yes" was no more than a long-drawn-out sigh.

"Oh, your legs are so hard and tight and sexy," she said. "I love to slide just the tips of my fingers over your knees and then up your beautiful thighs. I want to touch that large bulge at the front of your pants, but I don't dare, so I'll stop my hands and just pull off your boots. Why don't you take your shirt off, too, so you can enjoy the warm sunshine?"

"Will you take your blouse off too?"

"Sugar, I knew you were a naughty boy." She paused. "You are so beautiful without your shirt. Your chest is hairless and so smooth. Your abdomen is rippled with muscles so hard, I just love to touch it." She laughed. "No, I shouldn't do that. Instead, I'm going to kick off my sandals and run through the water to the big flat rock out in the middle of the stream. Can you see it?"

"Yes."

"Ooh, it's hard to climb out of the water onto this rock. The stones in the stream are mossy and quite slippery. Okay, I've got a hold now. Good. I can sit on top. Mmm. The rock is almost hot from the sun. I've left wet footprints on the stone. Are you coming? I can see you standing there on the stream bank, so handsome and sexy. I'll pull my blouse off over my head if you want so you can see my large breasts. I'll just put it over here. Do you like the way I look?"

"Yes. I'm going to wade to your rock."

"I'm going to remove the ribbon from my hair. I run my fingers through it and pull my brown curls over my chest, but they don't quite keep my nipples from poking through.

They're so hard and tight. I guess it's from thinking about you and your gorgeous body." She sighed deeply. "I'm going to lie down on the warm stone. Oh yes. I can feel the heat against the bare skin of my back. Do you need any help climbing onto the rock?"

"Not at all. I like being here with you."

"It's good to have you here beside me now." She paused. "Oh, look. You've gotten the bottoms of your pants legs wet. Why don't you take your pants off and lay them out on the rock so they can dry? Come on, take them off. No one can see." She paused for a heartbeat. "There. Isn't that better? Oh, my," she said. "You're not wearing anything under those pants, you naughty boy. Lie down on your back and let the rock warm your tight buttocks. Shall I warm you too?"

"Mmm," his voice purred.

"Maybe I'll just cuddle against you with my breasts pressed against your chest. Can you feel my hard nipples against your smooth skin? The contrast between the cool breeze and the warm sun is so exciting. And we're here in the open. If any people come by, they'll know what we're doing. Do we care?"

"Of course not. We just care about each other."

"That's so wonderful. I love the feel of you. May I kiss you?"

"Oh yes."

"Your mouth is so soft, yet strong. Part your lips so I can taste you. You taste so good." She waited just a moment. "You don't know what I'm doing. I've got my fingers in the cold water and now I'm going to drip icy water on your swollen shaft. Oooh, that's cold. Shall I warm it with my mouth?"

"Oh, God."

"Your cock is so hard it's standing straight up, urging me to take it between my lips. When I open my mouth wide, I can barely take all of you. I'm doing my best to surround your cock with my hot, wet mouth and I can suck most of you inside. You taste so good. I pull you deep into my mouth, then draw back, over and over until that cock is so hard it's almost painful. Now I'm sitting up, watching you stare at my body. I know how much you want me. You want to grab me, but I know you won't. You're so patient and you let me set the pace."

"But I'm so hungry."

"I know and I'll bet that the cool air on your wet cock feels *sooo* sexy. Would you like to suck my nipples?" Liza sighed and pulled her bra cups down and pinched her own erect nipples. The picture in her head was making her really hot.

"I love sucking you," he said.

"Yes. Suck me. I'm going to climb over you so my big breasts hang over your mouth. Don't raise your head. Let me do it. I slowly lower my breast until the nipple brushes your lips. Now open your mouth. Yes, like that." She pinched again and felt the shards of pleasure rocket through her. "I love it when you suck me, but that's not enough for me now. I need you inside me. Your large cock will fill me so completely. I'm going to move lower and touch your rigid staff with my wet pussy. Then I'll spread my skirt so that it covers us both. No one can see the secrets we hide beneath the dark green cotton. I've got the tip of you against my wetness. Do you want to be inside?"

"Oh, God. Oh, God."

"Not too fast. I like it really slow. Millimeter by millimeter I lower myself onto you. My body's so hot and wet. Do you want to thrust into me? I know you do, but be patient. Let me go *sooo* slowly until you fill me completely. Yes, like that," she purred. Without changing her voice pattern, she unzipped her jeans and wiggled them down over her hips. Then she inserted her fingers between her thighs and rubbed her bottom against the soft leather of the chair. "Like that." She found her clit and rubbed. "Just like that. If we keep doing that, I'm going to come. Are you?"

"Yes," he said, his breathing now rapid and raspy.

"I'm raising up on my knees and then dropping suddenly onto your stiff cock. Over and over I raise and lower." She rubbed. "Just a few more times. Do it for me. Drive that big cock of yours into my hungry body." With the help of her experienced fingers, Liza came.

"Yes," the man said. "Just another moment." He paused, then groaned. "Yes," he whispered.

Liza panted, the telephone lying against her shoulder. "That was wonderful, as always, sugar."

"Yes, it was. Maybe I can call you again next Tuesday."

"I'll look forward to hearing from you."

A hundred miles away, the man hung up the phone then took a tissue and wiped the semen from his liver-spotted hand and his now-flaccid cock. As he stretched back on his bed he thought about his wife of forty-three years, now gone for more than two. *I used to be like that man in Liza's story,* he thought, *and Myra was like the woman, so hot and receptive. Oh, baby, I miss you so much,* he thought, *but Liza fills some of the emptiness and I know you wouldn't mind.*

Bless Liza.

Bless Velvet Whispers.

~

Alice Waterman rubbed the back of her neck, trying to loosen what had become a semipermanent kink. Had it always been there? she wondered. No, she suspected, only for the past few months, since her mother had taken ill. She glanced up and peered through the square opening above her desk as the office's outer door opened and closed. A man of about fifty crossed the waiting room and casually leaned on the sill of Alice's window. "Good morning, Mr. McGillis," Alice said, making sure both her voice and her face were cheerful. Dental patients were always a bit tense and she knew that her cheery attitude tended to relax them just a bit.

"Good morning, Alice. How are you this morning?"

"I'm fine. How about you?"

"I'm okay."

"How's your son? Did you hear about medical school?"

Mr. McGillis's face lit up. "It's so nice of you to remember. Yes, we're very excited. He was accepted to Johns Hopkins, of all places. We're going to miss him terribly, but it's his first choice and he's thrilled. We never expected him to get in, even with his terrific grades."

Alice made it a point to remember details about the patients' lives, further putting them at ease. "That's great news. Congratulate him for all of us." She winked. "And be sure he comes in for his checkup before he leaves."

"I will."

"Dr. Tannenbaum will be with you in just a moment. He's just finishing up with his previous patient." The woman whose painful molar was being filled had been almost fifteen minutes late and now Dr. Tannenbaum would be a bit behind all morning.

"No problem," Mr. McGillis said. "I'll wait as long as necessary. Years even."

Alice chuckled. "I'm sure it won't be that long." She flipped the switch that would turn on the doctor's "The Next Patient Is Waiting" light in the rear operatory. As she watched, Mr. McGillis took a well-thumbed magazine from the rack and settled into a soft upholstered chair. As Alice returned to her computer, her best friend, Betsy, one of Dr. Tannenbaum's dental assistants, settled into a chair beside her. "He's almost done." Betsy shook her head slowly. "That woman's going to be the death of me," she said, sotto voce referring to Mrs. Sutter, the woman with the painful molar. "First she's late and then she's irritated that we won't sit and chat. 'Let me tell you about my granddaughter,' she says. 'She's just started walking. . . .' Then she drags out about fifty pictures." When Alice failed to react, Betsy said, "Earth to Alice. Where are you?"

Alice refocused her deep brown eyes. "Sorry. I guess I'm really preoccupied this morning."

"I gathered that when you almost charged Mr. Cardova for a root canal when all he had was a cleaning. You never do that. Anything I can help you with?"

Alice and Betsy had been friends off and on since high school. Seated alphabetically, Alice Waterman and Betsy York had been relegated to the far back of the room, free to whisper and giggle, mostly about boys and the constant bulge beneath their social studies teacher Mr. Hollingsworth's trousers. "I'm afraid not," Alice said softly. Then she sighed, knowing that Betsy really cared. "It looks like my sister and I are going to have to put Mom in a nursing home." Alice's sister, Susan, was six years older, married with a teenaged daughter. Although their mother's illness had brought them a bit closer, she and her sister had little in common.

Betsy reached out and took Alice's small hand in her large one. "Oh, hon, I'm so sorry. Your mom's really that bad?"

"She keeps having more small strokes and she's really out of it. Sue called me last night and said that the doctor's recommending twenty-four-hour care. Sue can be home with her for a few days and she's got a friend who can baby-sit for a few weeks. We can pay her about twenty-five dollars a day and she'll be happy to earn it. But she can only do it until the first of May when she moves, so in about six weeks, we'll have no choice but to find a nursing home for Mom."

Alice thought about her mother, always a robust woman until four months earlier when she had her first "episode" as the doctor put it. She had collapsed in the kitchen of her New York City apartment. Sue, Alice's sister, had phoned and gotten no answer so, after several hours, Sue had called the police. Their "check on the welfare" visit had ultimately resulted in the superintendent opening the apartment door and the ambulance screaming Mrs. Waterman away.

After three more mini strokes the woman who had raised and cared for her two daughters was now in need of permanent care herself. Alice had visited her at her sister's house in Queens just last weekend, making the long drive south to spend time with the woman who was now only a shadow of the person she used to be. As Alice had walked into her niece's bedroom, now taken over by the seriously ill older woman, her mother had smiled just a bit and her eyes had softened. Alice had sat, holding her hand and talking to her for more than an hour, until her mother fell asleep.

Betsy's indigo eyes expressed her deep concern more than any words could. "Do you have a place in mind? I hear the Rutlandt Nursing Home down-county is really pretty good."

"We've been asking around since Mom's first stroke and Sue and I would love to have her there. It's halfway between us and would be so convenient for visiting. It's supposed to be first-rate, but it costs the earth." She sighed. She'd been over it and over it and there was just no way. "We'll just have to find something more within our price range. We're going out to look again this weekend." She pictured her mother sharing a gray-painted room with some other incapacitated woman, being patted on the head, fed and cleaned, but otherwise ignored. *No,* she thought, *I can't dwell on that.* Alice grinned ruefully. "I could always win the lottery."

Rutlandt had bright colors on the walls and nurses who cared, really cared. When she and Sue had visited, an elderly man was being wheeled to a waiting ambulance on a stretcher. One nurse kissed him good-bye. Kissed him like she cared. If they could only swing it. With a child of their own, Sue and her husband were only going to be able to add a small amount to her mother's Social Security and her late-father's pension and insurance payments. Alice could manage only a few dollars as well and neither family had any savings to speak of. With just a hundred dollars a week more, they could manage it. Sure, she thought. A hundred extra dollars a week. It might as well be a million.

"You don't ever play the lottery," Betsy said.

Alice returned to her friend. "Yeah. Makes it harder, doesn't it."

Despite Alice's sad news, Betsy grinned. "You never lose your sense of humor, do you?"

"I try to keep it light, but this really has me down." Alice glanced up and assured herself that Mr. McGillis was still reading his magazine. Then she combed her stubby fingers through deep-brown hair that she wore cut short so she needed to do nothing after her morning shower but rub it dry with a towel. The extra fifteen pounds she carried was evenly distributed over her five-foot-three-inch frame and, although she wore a size sixteen, her uniform, a loose, brightly patterned scrub top and white pants, covered most of the extra weight. "So many of those places are so awful; ugly places where people go who are already dead but their bodies haven't gotten the final message yet. It's just so depressing." She tapped her forehead. "Although she can't speak, Mom's brain's still alive and I hate to see her relegated to nothingness."

A "Green" light lit on the panel on the wall, indicating that Betsy could bring Mr. McGillis back into the operatory. "You know," Betsy said rising, "I might have a solution to your problem. Can you stop by my house right after work? It's time I filled you in on a little secret."

Alice had little time to wonder what Betsy was talking about, as Mrs. Sutter bustled out of the back room. "Wait till you see. I've got new pictures of Christine."

"That's wonderful, Mrs. Sutter. I can't wait to see them."

At five-fifteen, Dr. Tannenbaum closed his office and Alice and Betsy walked down the staircase and across the parking lot. "Don't forget," Betsy said, "you're going to stop by at the house."

"Okay," Alice said, rubbing the back of her neck. "I'll see you there." She climbed behind the wheel of her seven-year-old Toyota and started the engine. It was late March and the willow trees in Putnam County, New York, had just started to get that wonderful green glow that signaled the beginning of spring. It had been a particularly cold winter, and the season had yet to loosen its hold. The forsythia were still trying to bloom with just a few errant blossoms coloring the slender, leafless branches. Two-sythia her mother used to call them. Alice sighed and tried not to think about the older woman.

The weather forecaster on Channel 2 had said that the weekend should bring a dramatic rise in temperature. As she shifted into drive, Alice wondered whether she could drive down to Sue's and take her mother out, if only in a wheelchair. But where would they get one? Could they afford one? They must cost a fortune. Maybe through Medicare or maybe they could rent one.

"Stop it," Alice said out loud. "You're making yourself crazy." She turned up the volume on the radio and sang along with the Five Satins. "Show dote 'n showbee-doe. Show dote 'n showbee-doe. In the still . . ." By the time she pulled into Betsy's driveway behind her friend's new Buick, her spirits had lightened considerably.

The two women got out of their cars and walked up the well-tended front walk. "I can't wait for the azaleas," Betsy said. "It's like everything's holding its breath waiting for the temperature to go up."

"I know. The weatherman says this weekend."

"God, it's a hell-of-about time." She opened the front door and yelled, "I'm home."

Shouts of "Hi, Mom" were followed by three pair of feet pounding down the stairs. "Mom, Justin says that Mr. Marks is going to let him play third base this year. That's mine. Mr. Marks promised last spring he'd let me play third."

"Mom," another voice yelled, "can I go to the mall tonight? Everyone's going to be there."

"Mom," a third boy called, "can you quiz me on my spelling words?"

"Hold it!" Betsy yelled. "Alice and I need fifteen minutes of peace and quiet, then all things will work out."

"Oh, hi Alice," Betsy's three look-alike boys said almost in unison.

"Hi, guys. If you all need an extra chauffeur later, I can help."

"Thanks, Alice," Josh, Betsy's twelve-year-old, said.

"Okay, guys," Betsy said in her best motherly voice. "Is there anything that can't wait fifteen minutes? If not, shoo." She made pushing motions toward the staircase.

After several long-suffering sighs and a small amount of grumbling, the three boys disappeared back upstairs. "Now," Betsy said, making her way into the kitchen, "how about a soda?"

"Love it. I'm really dry." Alice dropped into a kitchen chair. "I've only been here five minutes and already your boys have me exhausted. How do you do it?"

"I haven't got a clue. They say that if a cowboy starts lifting a calf at birth and picks him up each day, eventually he'll be able to lift an entire cow. I think I'm lifting a cow now—or maybe three."

Betsy put two glasses of Diet Coke on the table and settled into the chair opposite Alice. "Now, let me tell you something about me you don't know. I hope you're not going to be mad that I've been keeping secrets but at first it didn't seem that important. Then it got bigger and I didn't know how to tell you."

"You don't have to tell me anything you don't want to, you know," Alice said. "But I must admit that you've got me curious. Do you rob banks in your spare time? Do you rent the boys out for white slavery?"

The corners of Betsy's mouth tried to curve upward, but didn't quite make it. She started to speak, then turned it into a deep sigh.

Alice reached over and took her friend's hand. "Hey. Whatever it is, it's not tragic. It will work out. Really."

Betsy clasped Alice's hand. "It's not like that at all. It's wonderful, the most fun I've ever had, but it's weird. I'm just not sure how you'll take it."

Alice took a swallow of her soda. "I'm really intrigued. Why don't you just spit it out?"

"I have another job one evening a week."

"Really, I never knew." Seeing Betsy's face, she knew there was more. "And . . ."

"I do phone sex."

"What?"

"I do phone sex. My name's Liza, or whatever the customer wants it to be, and I talk to them. You know, hot, erotic stuff."

"You're joking. What do you really do?"

Betsy withdrew her hand and sipped her Coke. "That's what I really do. I work one night a week for three hours and I average between two hundred and two hundred and fifty dollars."

"You're serious." Alice's mind was boggled. Betsy had always seemed so straight. So white-picket-fence. Three handsome boys and a great-looking husband. "What does Larry think about this? Does he know?"

"Of course he knows. Every Tuesday evening I disappear into the den, stretch out in the lounge chair, and take my calls. It works out well because the office is closed on Wednesdays, so if I run late, I can catch a nap the next day while the boys are at school."

"I have only a million questions. Do the boys know?"

"No. Of course not. They know I'm in phone sales, and that's enough. They know that on Tuesday evenings I work in the den and I'm not to be disturbed."

"How long have you been doing this? How did you start? How does it work? Do you have regular customers?" Alice leaned forward. "I mean, it just doesn't seem like you. I mean, phone sex. Shit. I'm babbling."

Betsy smiled softly. "How about this? Larry won't be home until late tonight. If you've got no plans for dinner, let's take the boys out for pizza at the mall and we can talk then. It will also give you some time to digest what I just told you. We can then send Phillip and Bran to the arcade for a while and Josh can spend time with his friends. While they're gone, I'll answer any questions you've got. Yes?"

"Sure." Alice shook her head as if trying to get puzzle pieces to fit. They wouldn't. Not a chance.

Ten minutes later, the five of them stood in Betsy's driveway. "Alice," Brandon, Betsy's nine-year-old said, "can I ride with you? You could test me on my spelling. And I've got to be able to use the words in sentences. You could come up with a story."

Alice had always believed that learning could be fun and she had developed a game with the boys. They would give her a group of words and she would come up with a story that used them all. They would hand the tale off, one to the other, each adding a paragraph wilder than the previous to try to stump the next storyteller.

"Sure, if that's okay with everyone else."

"I love your stories," Josh said. "Can I come too?"

"That sounds great," Betsy said. "Phillip, you can ride with me and we'll talk about third base."

Chapter 2

When they reached the mall, the two women parked next to each other and the boys piled out. "That was a great one, Alice," Josh said. "Phillip, you should have heard the story we did." He insinuated himself between his brother and his mother. "It was fantastic, Mom, with monsters and people on another planet." With Phillip in the lead, the three boys ran ahead toward Festival of Italy.

"Thanks for taking Josh and Bran. It gave me a chance to have a heart-to-heart with Phillip about the Little League team."

"You're welcome. I really enjoy your kids, and the stories we get into tax my creativity sometimes. Bran had the word *gravity* on his vocabulary list so we got into life on Mars. Each time one of the boys took a turn, the story got more fantastic."

"It's that imagination of yours that intrigues me." They walked through the mall entrance. "We'll talk about it later."

They sat down at a large table in the pizza parlor and, after considerable argument, agreed on a small pie with pepperoni and a small with half mushrooms, half extra cheese. "Don't let them get any mushrooms on my side," Brandon said. "Yuck."

"There will be none of that," Betsy said.

"Can we continue the story, Alice?" Brandon asked. "Maybe Josh can have a turn."

"Not me," Josh said, eyeing a table filled with other kids about his age. "Storytelling's too babyish for me."

"But, Josh," Bran said.

"It's all right, Bran," Alice said. "I understand completely. He doesn't have to join in unless he wants to. We can do a great story without him. Maybe we'll even let your mother take a turn."

"I'm getting to be a pretty good storyteller and Phil's terrific," Betsy said, rubbing Phil's hair. "Fill the kid and me in."

For the next half an hour the group tossed the tale back and forth, taxing their collective imaginations. After wolfing down three slices, Josh had moved to the table with his friends, but the other four were more than able to complete the fantastic story.

"So finally Morg got the ray gun and blasted everyone," Phil said. "Then he climbed back into his spaceship and headed for Earth."

"The end," Alice said.

"No," Bran whined, "don't make it end."

Betsy reached into her wallet and handed each boy a five-dollar bill. "How about you two go over to the arcade while Alice and I visit? We'll meet you at the main entrance in . . ."

"An hour?" the two boys chorused.

"Let's make it half an hour. In the meantime in case you need us, Alice and I will be sitting on the benches right outside the arcade. I want you two to stay together. If I see either of you alone, that will be the end."

"Make it forty-five minutes," Phillip said.

"Okay. Forty-five minutes it is." The two boys dashed off and Betsy walked over to Josh, bent down, and whispered in his ear. Then she stood, raised an eyebrow and her son nodded.

"Okay," Betsy said as she rejoined her friend. "We're clear until seven-thirty. How about we get cappuccinos and sit and talk?"

Hot, frothy coffee in hand, the two women found an unoccupied bench near the arcade and made themselves comfortable. "You've been mysterious long enough," Alice said, sipping her hot coffee. "Tell me everything."

"Do you remember when I was so depressed a few years after Brandon was born? I felt lousy about myself. I couldn't work with three boys and I felt like a slug."

"Yeah. That was a really bad time for you but you pulled yourself out of it, as I remember."

"I started working with Velvet."

"Velvet?"

"Velvet Polaski. Velvet Whispers. That's the agency through which I get the customers." Betsy hesitated. "This is really awkward. It's tough to tell your best friend that you've had a secret for six years. I'm not sure I know how you'll react to this whole thing even now."

Alice stared at her friend, wondering how you could be best friends with someone for almost fifteen years and not know something that seemed so important. Velvet Whispers. "Hey, I love you," Alice said. "You're my oldest and dearest friend. There's nothing you could tell me that would change that."

"I hope so. It all goes back to the night Brandon was born. I went into labor at about midnight but I didn't call you until the next morning. You had had the flu and were still a bit rocky, and maybe contagious. Remember? And of course Larry had to stay home with the two older boys."

"I do remember and I still feel guilty about it all. I should have baby-sat so that Larry could have been with you."

"Actually it was a blessing in disguise. I didn't mind being at the hospital by myself. After all, Brandon was my third and I hadn't had bad labors with the other two. I had a book so, for a while, between contractions, I read and watched the clock. At about 2:00 A.M., another woman came in and they put us together in one labor room, I guess to keep each other company. I think the labor-and-delivery area was really crowded and all the birthing suites were full. Nurses kept running in, checking on us and dashing out again."

Betsy sipped her coffee, then continued. "Anyway. This woman and I got to talking as we tried not to concentrate on the pains. What else was there to do, after all? Her name was Victoria, but everyone called her Velvet. The baby was her first and she was very nervous. Her husband was away on a business trip and, with no real family, I became the calm expert, the voice of reason. I helped her along, sort of told her what to expect. We got quite chummy, quite quickly. Between pains, there was a strange sense of intimacy. We talked about our husbands, my kids, like that."

Betsy's mind drifted back to parts of that strange conversation.

"Do you work?" Velvet had asked.

"With a two-and-a-half-year-old and a sixteen-month-old, I sure do."

"Sorry," Velvet said. "Dumb question."

"Actually, I did work before the boys were born. I'm a dental assistant." Betsy sighed. "I guess I miss it. When your world is populated by gremlins two feet tall who speak only single words, it gets a bit boring."

"I'll bet. I'm going to keep my job after the baby. I just can't give it up."

"What do you do?" Betsy asked.

"I'm in phone sales."

"What do you sell?"

Just then a contraction interrupted Velvet's conversation. When the pain subsided, she said, "I sell sex."

Betsy sat bolt upright. "Come again?"

"I have a phone-sex business. Men call and I talk to them. I'm really busy and I make quite a good living."

"You're kidding." Betsy looked at her new friend, and saw that Velvet was totally serious. "Okay. You're not kidding."

"No. I'm not. It started as a joke several years ago with some buddies of my husband's. They wanted to play a prank on one of their friends so they set me up to talk dirty to him. They thought it would be a lark, but, as they listened in, they realized that I was very good at it. Actually, I felt bad about it, playing such a joke, but he was a great guy and let me off the hook."

The two women stopped talking as Velvet had another contraction, making conversation impossible. When things calmed, Velvet continued, "I was so good at it that, secretly, one of Bob's friends kept calling, asking me to talk dirty to him. I did, and he paid me."

"He actually paid you?"

"Fifty bucks for half an hour. He said that's what he paid for other phone-sex lines and that I deserved every penny of it. He told someone, and they told others. Now I have men calling every night and I make a nice living. It's too bad I'll have to cut back now, with the baby and all."

Betsy turned to Alice. "So Velvet and I had our babies and crossed paths a few times that first year at the pediatrician's office. She loved motherhood and our babies both thrived. It was a couple of years later, when I was so depressed, that I ran into her again at the pediatrician's office." Betsy sipped her cappuccino. "We got to talking. Dr. Brewster was running late, as usual, so we had almost an hour to visit. It was quite a while before I asked her about the business."

When Betsy drifted off, Alice prodded. "And?"

"Business was booming and Velvet had hired another woman to answer calls but she was still having to turn away customers. When she heard that I was so down, she suggested that I give her business a try. I was horrified, of course, but, well, as time passed, the idea began to appeal to me somehow. I discussed it with Larry and he was all for it. Things between us have always been great and he thought I'd be good at talking dirty to men. He was also glad that I seemed to be perking up. A phone-based job wouldn't entail having to travel to work and he promised to take care of the kids one evening a week. Both the money and something to do were welcome."

People walked past their bench, but the two women were oblivious. "How did this Velvet know you'd be good at phone sex? Wasn't she taking a risk?"

"Actually she had a friend call me and be my first customer just to be sure, but after so many years on the phone, she's a pretty good judge of character."

"I couldn't have done it," Alice said, putting her coffee on the bench beside her.

"Needless to say, I was terrified, but after a few moments I guess I just got into it."

"Tell me about it," Alice urged.

"His name was Austin. Velvet had given me some reading to do, some ideas for how to talk to men. She'd also let me listen to her end of a few conversations. That made me feel better but I quickly learned that every call and every client is different."

"So Austin called you. Weren't you scared with him having your phone number?"

"She had given me his number and I called him at a prearranged time. Velvet pays me and covers my phone bill too."

"What about the real customers?"

"They call and give credit-card information to a router, who finds out what the client wants, then relays the call. Velvet doesn't take many calls anymore so she usually does that herself. Sometimes, if she's busy, one of us goes to her place and does it."

"One of us?"

"There are almost a dozen women working for her now. She pays us fifty dollars an hour for routing, and on the phone we get half of whatever Velvet charges."

"Wow. I never imagined."

"Neither did I that first time."

"Do you remember that first call?"

At that moment, Phillip dashed out of the arcade. "Mom, Bran's hogging the Duel of Death. It's my turn."

"You know the rules," Betsy said. "If you can't work out your problems, we're out of here."

"But Mom . . ."

Betsy raised an eyebrow and Phillip slunk back into the arcade. The two women clearly heard him yell, "Bran, Mom says . . ."

Chuckling, the two women returned to their conversation. "That first call," Betsy said. "How could I ever forget? I had told Larry all about it and he was incredulous, but willing to go along, especially since I was going to get paid. He said he'd put the boys to bed, then watch a ball game in the living room and that I should come down when I was done. I was supposed to call the guy at about eight so I locked myself in the bedroom at about seven-thirty and shook for half an hour."

Betsy sat in her small bedroom, alternately exhilarated and terrified. *What's the worst that can happen?* she asked herself. *So I make an idiot of myself. So I'm so tongue-tied that I can't speak at all. So what?* At exactly eight, she looked down at the small sheet of paper on which Velvet had written the number and reread it, although she had already memorized it. Velvet had said that she might want to extend the call as long as possible since she was being paid by the hour, but Betsy had rejected that idea. The call would last as long as it lasted and she'd make what she made. She wouldn't con anyone. When she had apologized to Velvet, the woman had laughed. That was her theory too.

Hands trembling, Betsy picked up the phone and dialed.

"Hello?"

Betsy had a naturally soft, slightly husky voice and Velvet had told her that she needn't change anything. "Hello. I'm glad I could call you tonight." She tried to sit on the edge of the bed, but found that she needed to pace while she talked.

"I'm glad you could too," he said. "My name's Austin. What's yours?"

"What would you like my name to be?" So far, so good. She was following the pattern she had set up for herself. The standard, as Velvet had told her, was to let the man lead the way as much as possible.

"I don't know. How about Mona?"

"Okay. Mona it is. What are you wearing, Austin?"

"Just jeans and a polo shirt."

"What color shirt? I want to be able to picture you."

"It's yellow."

"Is it tight, so I can see your chest and arms as the shirt hugs you?"

"Yes," he said with a sigh. "What are you wearing?"

Betsy was actually wearing a comfortable sweat suit, but she answered, "I'm wearing a tank top that's slightly too small for me, and a pair of shorts."

"Are you wearing underwear?"

"Oh yes, but we can take them off together." Betsy listened carefully to the sound of Austin's breathing as Velvet had suggested, to gauge how excited he was. So far, he was pretty calm. She settled on the edge of the bed.

"Do you have shoes on?" he asked.

Betsy toed at her sneakers. "I do, but I can kick them off so my bare toes can wiggle. Would you like me to do that?"

"Oh yes," Austin said. "I want to hear you kick them off."

Betsy used the toe of one foot to ease her sneaker off her heel then bent over and held the phone near the floor as she pushed it off and it dropped on the rug. "I'm afraid you didn't hear much," she said, "since there's a nice thick rug. Let me kick off the other one." Again she moved the phone so Austin could hear the thud. "Now I can wiggle my bare toes in the carpet. It's so soft." Betsy could hear Austin's sigh. Although Velvet hadn't told her so, Austin might like feet, she thought, filing the knowledge away. She'd done a lot of reading, hoping that nothing could surprise her.

"I like that. I'm going to kick my shoes off too. Hear that?" She heard the slap of shoe sole on hard floor.

"It sounds like you don't have a carpet there," she said. "That's too bad. If you did you could walk barefoot on the soft rug as we talk."

"I wish I could do that too."

"Here's an idea. Why don't you get a thick towel from the bathroom and spread it on the cold floor? Then we can both walk around as we talk."

Betsy could hear Austin's excitement. "What a great idea. Hold on." The line went silent. Betsy took a deep breath. So far, so good.

"He actually got a towel?" Alice asked. "How did you think to do that?"

"I haven't a clue. It just came to me. Most of my calls now are spontaneous. I have no idea from one moment to the next what direction they will take."

"I'm still flabbergasted."

"You know, me too. I still can't believe I do this, but it's so much fun now."

"Back then it must have been really scary."

"Believe me, it was."

Austin returned to the phone. "I'm back, and I have a towel on the floor. I can curl my toes, and it's so soft."

"Good. Let's walk as we talk." Betsy was momentarily tongue-tied and the silence started to drag. *What can I say now?* she screamed at herself. *I have to get to sexy stuff.* "You know," she said inspired, "it's really hot in my room here."

"It is?"

"Yes. I'd like to take my sweater off."

"You mean your tank top."

"Right." Dumb. Dumb. She took the piece of paper with the phone number on it and wrote *tank top and shorts. Barefoot.* "It's a knit top and it's red. Bright red. I love red. Do you? Can you picture my bright red tank top?"

"Yes, Mona, I can," he said, "but take it off. Tell me about your bra."

Betsy jotted the word *Mona* on her pad. It wouldn't do for her to forget the name Austin had given her. "Well," she said, trying to sound as if she was removing her clothing, "it's red too. And it's lace, with thin straps."

"Are your breasts big?"

She remembered that Velvet had suggested that she always have large breasts. "Do you like big breasts?"

"Yes. I love tits that fill my hands."

"How would you like them to look?"

"Oh, they'd be white, with big, really dark nipples, and the nipples would be sticking out."

"How strange?" Betsy said. "You've just described me really well. I have a bit of a tan, but my tits are really white.

I never sunbathe topless since someone might see my boobs." *Yes,* she thought, *use those hot words.*

"Can I see them?" There was a long pause. "Please."

"I guess. Let me unhook my bra. I'm cradling the phone against my ear now so I can reach around and get at the hooks."

"It doesn't hook at the front? I like bras that hook at the front."

"Not this one, but if we talk again, I'll be sure to have one that hooks in the front. Maybe a black one next time."

Again Austin sighed. "Yes. A black satiny one that hooks in the front. Have you got your bra off yet?"

Betsy made a decision. "I can't quite manage it so I have to put the phone down to take it off. Will you wait for me?"

"Of course."

Betsy put the phone on the bed and pulled her sweatshirt over her head and removed her beige cotton bra. Being clothed felt like a cheat now. Her breasts were small and tight, but at least she was naked from the waist up. She picked up the receiver. "That's so much better. My tits felt like I was being strangled in that tight bra. Now these large white globes are free. Would you like to touch them?"

"Oh God, yes," Austin said, the pitch of his voice rising.

"Close your eyes and reach out your two hands, palms up. I'll lean over and fill your hands with my boobs." She paused, then continued, "Can you feel them in your hands?"

"Oh yes," he said, his voice tight.

"What else would you like to touch? Or would you like me to touch you?" *Can I pull this off?* Betsy wondered. *Touching yet not touching is really weird, but he seems to be enjoying it.*

"I'd like to take my shirt off. Would you rub your boobs on my chest?"

"Of course. Let me help you with your shirt. I'm holding

the front of your shirt and pulling it over your head. Is it all the way off now?"

"Yes."

"Good. Are you naked from the waist up now?"

"Yes."

She wanted to describe touching his chest, but she had no idea whether he was hairy or smooth. Her mind thrashed, trying to think how she could find out. "I want to rub my hands over your chest. How would that feel? Touch your chest and tell me."

"I don't know. Smooth, I guess."

"Yes, so smooth and warm. You feel almost hot. I love the way my hands slide over your skin. Would you touch me while I stroke you?" She stopped, then said, "My breasts are so heavy and feel so . . ." She fumbled for a word. "Satiny. Look at your dark hands on my white skin. That's so sexy it makes me hot. You've got great hands, you know."

"Yeah," he said.

"Now kiss me, lover. Press my hot lips against yours. I'll slide my tongue into your mouth and press my tits against your naked chest. Mmm. I'm moving my body so my nipples rub against you while we kiss. They're getting really hard. You're so sexy."

Betsy turned out the light and stretched out on the bed. She slipped her free hand over her ribs, touching her skin and trying to describe what she was feeling. "I can feel your hard ribs beneath your skin, steel beneath smooth silk." She touched her lips. "Your lips are so soft and warm. Let me touch your tongue with mine."

She heard a long-drawn-out moan and knew she was doing fine so far. "I'm getting hot for you, Austin. Maybe I'll just step back and slide my shorts off." She wiggled out of her sweatpants and bikinis. "I'm naked now. Will you get naked for me?"

"Well, sure." She heard rustling and she assumed Austin was taking off his jeans.

"Are you naked now, baby? I want to see your gorgeous body."

"I'm not so gorgeous, you know," Austin said in a small voice.

"You're gorgeous to me because you're mine right now. Is your cock all hard?"

"Oh yes."

"Touch it and pretend that it's my hand. I'm touching your cock with one hand, wrapping my fingers around the hard shaft. Goodness," she said, "it's so big I can barely close my fingers around you, and it's so hard."

"Yes, it is. I wish I were touching you."

"If you were, here's what you'd feel. My pussy's covered with dark, crispy hair and if you weave your fingers through it, you can find out that I'm wet and hot for you. My cunt is steaming, waiting for your fingers. Rub me, baby. Rub my clit. Like that." Betsy rubbed her now-swollen clit with her finger, amazed at how hot the entire scene was making her. "You make me so hungry. I'm touching my pussy, dreaming that these are your fingertips. I'm sliding my hand farther back so I can slide my index finger into my cunt. Are you holding your cock? Rubbing it?"

"Oh God, yes."

"Get some baby oil so you can rub it faster while I push my finger into my pussy." She waited a beat, then said, "Now two fingers." She actually inserted two fingers into herself, loving the way it felt to be filled.

"God, Mona, you're making me so hot, I can't stand it."

"Oh, love, hold your cock in one hand and stroke it with the other. Pretend they are my hands, with long fingernails that I can use to scratch your skin." All the sexy women had long fingernails, didn't they? "Are you rubbing? Do more.

Make it feel *sooo* good. I'm rubbing myself and making my pussy feel so wonderful."

For a few moments, the phone line was silent as the two touched themselves. "Are you close, Austin?"

"Yes," Austin said, almost breathless.

"Me too," Betsy said, realizing that it was true. She removed her hand, thinking of Larry sitting in the living room. She'd have a surprise for him in a few minutes.

"I'm gonna come, Mona. Right here. You're making me come."

"Yes, my hands are so talented. Close your eyes now, baby," Betsy said. "Picture my mouth approaching the tip of your cock. Shall I suck it?" She made a few slurping sounds. Then Betsy heard a few gasps and an, "Oh, shit."

"You made me come. Just like that, you made me come."

Betsy was dumbfounded. She had actually made Austin climax. Phone sex. This was dynamite. "Was it good, lover?"

"Oh yes. I'm going to use that towel from the floor to clean myself up. I've got to go now. Can I call again next week?"

Holy shit, she thought. He wants to call again. He wants to spend real money next week. "Sure, baby. Mona will be here waiting for you."

"Bye for now," he said, still breathless.

"Bye." She flipped on the light. It was after eight-thirty. She'd been on the phone with him for almost forty minutes. She looked at the small piece of paper with Austin's phone number and the notes she had made. She added smooth chest, hard cock, and the word *suck*, which she assumed was what drove him over the edge. She'd be better prepared next time. She put the paper into her bedtable drawer.

She fumbled in her closet and pulled out an old peignoir, one she hadn't worn since before Phillip was born. She walked down the hall and glanced into the boys' rooms. All three were sound asleep.

She crept down the stairs and found Larry in the living room. "Wow, you look great. How did it go?"

"It was a blast," Betsy said. "Great money, and it's got fringe benefits." She knelt between Larry's knees and unzipped his fly, feeling him get instantly hard.

"What's this?"

"What does it look like?" She reached into the opening and pulled out Larry's erection, already rock-hard.

"It looks like some other guy made you hot."

Betsy looked into her husband's eyes. "I made me hot, and I want you. No one else. Just you." She rubbed the end of Larry's cock over her closed lips, feeling the slippery fluid already leaking out. "Want me?"

"You know it," Larry moaned. "I kept thinking about some guy getting his rocks off while you talked to him. It drove me crazy."

"It made me hot knowing he was coming, but he's not here. He's just a voice. On the other hand, you are here, now. And I want you." She kissed the tip of Larry's cock.

"You really got off on it."

"I did, and I want to take it out on you." She stood up, opened her robe and climbed onto the sofa on her knees, straddling Larry's lap. With little preliminary, she lowered her steaming cunt on his hard shaft. Using her thigh muscles, she raised and lowered her body, fucking his cock without his having to move.

It took no more than a few moments for him to come, spurting semen deep inside of her. Then he took his fingers and rubbed Betsy's clit until she came, the spasms rocking her entire body.

Silently, they cleaned themselves up, closed up the downstairs, and went up to the bedroom. Quickly they readied themselves for bed and, both naked, climbed between the sheets. "If anything about this bothers you, I won't do it again," Betsy said, prepared to give it all up if Larry wanted her to.

Larry thought about it for a minute, then said, "I was really jealous as I sat downstairs and thought about you on the phone with some other guy, but what followed was terrific. You're right. It doesn't matter how you get hot, as long as you work off your heat with me and no one else. I'm not ready to share your body."

"I have no intention of sharing my body with anyone but you." She slipped her arms around her husband's waist. "He wants to call me again next week, this time for real money."

"No shit. You must be good at it. What did you say?"

"You know," Betsy said, her tone serious, "somehow that's private and I don't think it feels right to tell you. But anytime you want me to talk dirty to you, I'll be delighted. You will, of course, have to pay." Betsy grabbed her husband's already hardening cock. "I know just how."

"Well," Betsy said to Alice, "Larry and I didn't get to sleep for quite a while." A wide grin split her face.

"That's amazing," Alice said. "I guess I'm not surprised, though. You were always good at everything you put your mind to."

"I don't know about everything, but I have more customers than I can handle, so to speak. I spend only one night a week on the phone, and can only take three or four calls."

"Have you ever seen any of these guys?"

"Nope. I wouldn't know them if they bumped into me in the food court. It's great that way. Anonymous. We can each imagine anything we want."

"Larry still isn't jealous?"

"Occasionally he needs reassurance, but I love him to pieces and in his heart he knows there's no danger at all."

At that moment Phillip and Brandon ran out of the arcade. "Mom," Phillip said, "can we have another dollar each? Please? You can take it out of our allowances."

"Please, Mom," Brandon chimed in. "We still have ten minutes. Please?"

"Let me," Alice said. She fished her wallet out of her pocketbook and gave the boys each a dollar.

"What do you say?" Betsy said as the boys darted off.

"Thanks, Alice," they said in unison, then headed back into the arcade.

"The boys think you're in phone sales. Don't you worry that they will find out?"

"Not really. It might happen, but we are careful. They know that Mom disappears every Tuesday evening into a room behind a locked door. It's the only time doors are locked in our house, so they know it's important. Most of the time, Larry takes them out for dinner and a movie so I have more privacy. It really works out fine since Larry and the boys get to spend quality time together each week. He helps them with homework, then puts them to bed while I'm locked in the den. I paid for that room, you know. With my earnings."

"If you do so well, why do you continue at Dr. Tannenbaum's office?"

"I like the work and with three boys to put through college, every cent is important."

"If you don't mind me asking, how much do you make?"

"Velvet charges $2.99 per minute and I get half."

Alice did some quick calculations. "That's ninety dollars an hour."

"Not many calls last an hour, but yes, that's what it adds up to."

"Wow."

"Yes, wow. You could do it too."

Alice barked a laugh. "I could not."

"Of course you could. You're a great storyteller and that has to mean you've got a great imagination. Just think about it. It would solve all your money problems. I can introduce you to Velvet and you can discuss it, no commitment."

"I don't think so."

"Why not?"

"Because."

"Good answer." Betsy glanced at her watch. "It's almost eight and Larry will think I've absconded with the boys." She took the last few gulps of her coffee. "Nah. He knows that if I ever abscond, I'll leave the boys here so I can have a little quiet." She stood up, tossed her cappuccino cup in the trash and picked up her pocketbook. "I'm going to find my two darlings, then get Josh and get out of here. Alice, think about what I told you and I'll see you at work tomorrow."

"Hmm," Alice said. "You know, I'll think about it."

Chapter 3

Alice watched Betsy stride into the arcade and emerge minutes later with her two protesting boys. The three turned and waved. Weakly, Alice waved back, shaking her head. Betsy. A phone-sex person. *I wonder what you call them,* she thought. *Phone sluts?* Betsy was not a slut. She was the nicest human being Alice had ever met. But this?

Alice stared unseeingly at the front of the arcade. *What's wrong with phone sex? She never meets the guys she talks with. She's never been unfaithful to Larry and Larry knows all about it. If he doesn't mind, why should I?* She shook her head again. *Now she wants me to do it too. Ridiculous.*

Alice sipped the cold remains of her cappuccino, then stood and dropped the cup into the trash. Phone sex. Me? Not a chance. But half of $2.99 a minute. Ninety dollars an hour. With just an hour or two, she could manage to have her mother stay at Rutlandt. Could she do it? She shook her head. Not a chance.

Slowly, Alice wandered the mall, gazing into store windows, not really seeing any of the items. Her mind was whirling, both with Betsy's revelation and with the idea that she could make some real money that way. *Even if I could,* she said to herself, *who knows whether I'd be good at it. Good enough to attract regular customers. Could I talk about sex? What the hell do I know about good sex. Ralph wasn't worth much in the bedroom.*

She pictured her ex-husband, paunchy and dull, and over fifty now. *I still have no clue what ever possessed me.* Although Alice hadn't been pretty, Ralph Finch, a longtime family friend, had watched her change from girl to woman and had wanted her. As he told her, he found her innocence appealing, her intelligence fascinating, and her sense of humor delightful. He had little chance to meet and get to know women with his job as a long-haul truck driver so he had never married. Now it was time to have a wife and start a family and what could be better than someone he already knew well. Love? Passion? They would grow in time.

Her parents had been delighted with the idea and Alice really liked "Uncle Ralph." So, the day after Alice's high school graduation, they were married in the living room of the Waterman home.

The marriage was a bore. Alice worked as the receptionist for an obstetrician while Ralph drove his long-haul truck. They were apart for long periods of time and slowly Alice realized that she was happier when Ralph was not around. When he came home, he enjoyed watching TV, eating the massive amounts of food that Alice cooked to fill him up, sex, and not much else.

Evenings, with Alice beside him on the sofa, they watched sitcoms. As the evening progressed, Ralph would drape his arm around Alice's shoulder and fondle her breast. Then he took her hand and put it on his crotch. "It's been a long time, girl. See how ready I am?"

Usually Alice wasn't nearly ready but, feeling it was her job to satisfy her husband, she allowed Ralph to lead her into the bedroom. She undressed and, after coating his cock with K-Y Jelly, he pushed it into her. "I'll never understand why you don't get wet," he said during almost every session. "Maybe you should ask that doctor you work for."

She asked and was told that everything about her physiology was normal. "You might suggest that your husband take his time," the doctor had recommended. She hadn't mentioned that to Ralph.

After almost three years of marriage, Ralph arrived home one day from two weeks on the road. He set his suitcase beside the door and walked slowly into the bedroom, with Alice following. "Honey, I'm really sorry about this, but I'm leaving. There's someone else."

"What?" Alice had been completely unaware that he had any problem with their marriage. She dropped onto the edge of the bed and grabbed a tissue from the box on the bedside table.

"In L.A.," Ralph continued. "She's my age and hot to trot. She loves to do all the things that you don't. She loves *The Cosby Show* and *Golden Girls* and she's great in the sack, if you know what I mean. You just never seem to enjoy it." Alice merely stared, unable to get a word in edgewise, even if she'd had anything to say. "Anyway," Ralph said, "we've been seeing each other each time I drive to the coast. Her grown son just moved out and she wants me to move in with her. I'm gonna do it." As Alice stared, Ralph began to throw the rest of his clothes into their only other large suitcase. "You need someone younger anyway. You need to have some fun."

"I need?" Alice choked past her thick throat.

"Sure. You need a young stud. I know you're not happy."

"What do you care about what I need? This has nothing

to do with me. You've found someone better." She hovered between anger and panic.

"Listen. I'm not saying this real well, but it's for the best for both of us." He pulled something from his back pocket. "I went to the bank and took a thousand dollars from our savings account. Here's the passbook." He handed her the slim leather book. "There's almost seven hundred dollars left. Use it to get a divorce. I won't contest anything."

"I put most of that money in there," Alice shrieked. "How dare you take that money so you can move in with that, that woman."

Ralph tossed his few remaining shirts and sweaters into the suitcase. "I've got a load outside and it's going to L.A. I'm not coming back."

"What about the apartment? What about my family?"

"Your job will cover the rent and I really don't care about your family."

"My dad's your best friend. At least call him and explain."

"No time. You tell him whatever you want. Tell him I'll write from the coast."

"Don't bother."

Alice had cried for several days, then she had gotten along surprisingly well. Their first Christmas apart, Ralph had sent her a card with a picture of a decorated tree standing in the middle of a beach. He'd signed the card Ralph and Missy. Alice had dropped it into the garbage. Her parents had been supportive and as helpful as they could be and life quickly took on a new character.

She worked, dated occasionally, and spent increasing amounts of time with Betsy and her family. She felt as close to Larry and the boys as she did to her own family. They had all stood beside her at her father's funeral, celebrated at her sister's wedding, and they spent every holiday together. Now she realized that she hadn't known them. Not by a long shot.

Alice wandered aimlessly around the mall and found herself in front of Victoria's Secret. She gazed in the window at a display of bra and panty sets in vibrant jewel tones. *Sure. Me. Think like a sexpot. Right. Never happen. But the money would be so nice.*

She drove home on automatic pilot, her mind still reeling from Betsy's revelations. As the door to her apartment closed behind her, Alice leaned down to scratch Roger, her brown tabby cat, behind his ears. Always noisy, Roger *merrowed* and rubbed his sides along her legs. "And hello to you," she said. "You'll never believe what I found out today."

Merrow.

She picked up Roger and settled on the sofa with him on her lap. She told the cat everything that Betsy had confessed to her. When he *merrowed* again, Alice said, "Right. I know. You're surprised too."

The ringing of the phone startled them both. Roger dug his claws into Alice's thighs and darted into the bedroom. *No one ever calls me this late.* Worried that it might be her sister with bad news about her mother, she answered, "Hello?"

It was Betsy's voice. "I thought I'd call and make sure you're not shocked or mad at me or something. You don't hate me?"

"Betsy, you know I don't hate you and I'm not mad. Shocked, maybe a little, and maybe just a bit sad that you didn't tell me sooner."

"I didn't know how you'd take it all. You always were a bit . . ."

"A bit what?"

"Sorry. That didn't come out right. Listen. Let me say it this way. Everyone in the world except me, and maybe Larry, thinks that you're a bit of a prude. I know that beneath that straight exterior, there's someone who's willing and able to give the sexy side of life a try."

"A prude? People think I'm a prude?" She slumped back on the overstuffed tan sofa, the one on which Ralph used to watch TV.

"People who don't know you like I do might think you were, well, the old-fashioned spinster type. But you're not, and I know it."

"Spinster type?" Roger jumped onto Alice's lap and she began to scratch him behind his ears. She looked down. Cat, well-worn tan sofa, empty house. Spinster type.

"I wouldn't butt into your life for anything, and you know that. It just seems to me that you've stopped living before you ever started." When Alice gasped, Betsy continued, "Now don't get all defensive and just listen for a moment. I never meant to start this, but maybe it's time I did. After Ralph left, you closed yourself off. You shut everything that was womanly away. You work, hang out with us, and you know we love you, but you need a social life."

"You mean a man."

"Or men, yes. That's what I mean. Have you ever had good sex? I remember Ralph, and I doubt it. I know what's under all that bullshit you've built around yourself. I remember the hours we used to talk about boys. You had wants and needs back then. You used to fantasize about Ponch and John on *CHiPs,* just like the rest of us. Remember those cruises we used to plan on *The Love Boat*? You got Gopher and I got, oh, what was the name of the cute guy who took the pictures?"

Alice chuckled and put her feet up on the coffee table. "Ace. He was only there at the end. I do remember. We used to spend long evenings talking when we were supposed to be doing social studies."

"So what happened to her?"

"Who?"

"The you who used to be so alive?"

Alice was silent. She'd never heard Betsy talk this way. "I like my life."

"Spending time with my kids? I have never pushed you and I'm not going to start now. I do want you to think about all this, though, and consider that this job, if it works out, may be a way to find your sexual self without any risk. It's just the phone."

"If I'm such a spinster type," she said, bitterly, "why the hell do you think I'd be any good at this phone stuff?"

"Because I know you better than you know yourself. There's a real woman under there, with hot erotic fantasies and dreams. This would be the perfect outlet. You're a natural storyteller. Even the boys know that. You could use that talent and create erotic fantasies for nice, frustrated men who just want someone to talk dirty with."

Alice tried to keep the pain out of her voice. "I really don't think so but I understand all this a bit better now."

"Alice, don't be hurt. You know how much I care about you. I love you like a sister. Please, think over all I've said and I'll see you in the morning."

The morning. How would she face her friend? She'd have to. If she lost Betsy, who did she have? She gazed at the blank TV screen. Wasn't that the point Betsy was trying to make? "Yeah. I'll see you in the morning. Night."

"Night, babe." The phone went silent in her hand. Slowly she replaced the receiver on the base, picked up the cat, and walked slowly into the bedroom, turning off lights as she went. She flipped on the bedroom light and looked around. The room was pretty much unchanged from the day that Ralph left, nearly ten years earlier. Actually from long before that since Alice had moved into Ralph's apartment after they were married. She looked around. Heavy wooden furniture that had been Ralph's. Faded blue bedspread and blue denim drapes that she had made from an old sheet their first winter together. Dull gray carpet with a nail-polish stain beside the bed. It was pretty dismal but she seldom really saw it.

Mindlessly Alice turned on the TV, already tuned to *Headline News*. "God, Roger," she said, dropping onto the bed still holding the cat, "maybe Betsy's right. *Headline News*. It's nine-thirty and I'm watching *Headline News*. If it were Tuesday, Betsy would be on the phone to God-knows-who talking about God-knows-what." She scratched the cat under his chin. "You're the only man in my life. Prude. Spinster type. Shit."

Throughout the night, Alice tossed and turned, unable to get her conversations with Betsy out of her mind. The following morning, feeling cranky from lack of sleep, she arrived at Dr. Tannenbaum's office. Betsy was already there dressed in a light purple scrub top and matching pants, her brown hair pulled back with two gold barrettes. "Morning," Betsy said, sounding disgustingly cheerful. "You look like shit."

"I didn't get much sleep." Alice pulled off her coat, revealing a cartoon character–print scrub top and jeans. She wore only lipstick and there were faint purple circles underneath her eyes.

"I was afraid of that." Betsy took Alice's coat, hung it up then hugged her friend. "I'm sorry. I replayed the discussions we had. My diatribe, actually, and I'm afraid lots of it didn't come out quite the way I intended."

Alice hugged Betsy then stepped back. "You know, I thought it all through, too, and I have to admit that lots of what you said made sense." She smiled. "I hate it when you're right."

"Right how?" Betsy's expression was wary.

"I do need a life. I'm not sure whether I need the one you're offering, but it's certainly worth a bit more thought and I really do need the money."

The two women walked into the reception room and sat

down. "I'm really sorry for a lot of what I said," Betsy said.

"It's the way you feel."

"Yes, but I don't want to push you. You don't have to do anything you don't want to do. If you want to talk more about it, let me know, but I promise that I won't mention it again."

"You won't have to. I'll wager I won't be able to think about anything else." The door opened and the two women looked up. "Good morning, Mrs. McAllister," Alice said to the morning's first patient. "How's your lovely new grand-baby?"

Over the next few days Alice spent a great deal of time talking to her sister. Her mother's condition had stabilized and even improved a bit and Sue's friend was working out well as a daytime caregiver. They had applied to Rutlandt and two or three second-best nursing homes, hoping for admission by May first. If Rutlandt came through, they'd have to figure out how to pay for it, or turn it down in favor of the less-expensive place.

The following Tuesday evening, Alice sat in her living room, holding Roger and trying to picture Betsy on the phone with her customers. *Where would I even start? I can't talk dirty. I'm not even sure what guys like. I certainly didn't know what Ralph liked. Guys like women who know how to perform oral sex. Ralph used to joke about it. "Too bad you don't give head, girl," he used to tell her. Why didn't he ever let me try?*

Since Dr. Tannenbaum's office was closed on Wednesdays, Alice ran a few errands in the neighborhood, but continued to dwell on Betsy's phone business. Bizarre pictures whirled in her head. Betsy with shiny flame-red lipstick, her pursed lips near the receiver. Men with no faces but large ears, listening, talking, touching themselves. There were moments when she thought she might be able to do what her best friend did, but there were hours when she knew she couldn't.

Thursday morning, Alice arrived at work before Betsy and expectantly waited for her friend. "Morning," Betsy said, breezing in despite a freezing March drizzle that had soaked Alice's coat and made driving hazardous.

"How'd it go Tuesday evening?" Alice asked, watching Betsy hang up her heavy coat. "I kept thinking about you."

"It went great. It almost always does."

"Almost always?"

"Oh, occasionally it's difficult to get on the same wavelength with someone new," she said, walking into the empty reception area. "You have to use some charm and skill to find out what turns them on."

"How did you learn all that?" Alice asked, feeling more daunted than ever.

"Time, and lots of calls. And Velvet's a great help. She's been doing this for almost fifteen years and she knows all the tricks."

"Where do you start? I mean how do you know what will turn someone on?"

"I get lots of those shrink-wrapped magazines and read them from cover to cover. I particularly read the stories and the ads for phone sex. You'd be amazed what you can learn from what the publishers of those magazines think men like. I assume they're right since the magazines sell."

"I could do that, but I'd feel like a fool going into a store and buying *Penthouse* or *Playboy*."

"Why? Nice folks read them, you know. Now, of course, there's the Internet. You can find thousands of stories out there. I browse occasionally for new ideas and, along with the pictures of naked men and women, there are lots of pieces of good, erotic fiction out there." Maureen, the dental hygienist, walked in and hung up her coat. After the usual good mornings, she walked into the operatory area and the two women lowered their voices.

"That's a good idea. Maybe I'll do that and see whether I could say some of that stuff."

"You know, Velvet has a large number of guys who phone regularly. I wonder whether anyone likes the reticent, shy type who'll say the naughty words only reluctantly." Betsy's eyes glazed over momentarily. "That might be appealing actually."

"Really?"

"I don't know. Look, if you think you want to do this, I'll give Velvet a call and ask. I'd want you to meet her anyway."

That night, Alice signed on to her Internet account and went searching. She found several stories that seemed like they might be good so she printed them out. When she was done, she went into the bedroom with a beer. Roger curled up beside her as she started to read.

Without a Word
by Silent Sal

Michelle lay somewhere between sleep and wakefulness, listening to the upstairs neighbors stomp around their bedroom getting ready for bed. She glanced at the clock. Almost 2:00 A.M. *I shouldn't get too angry since it happens so seldom,* she told herself. *They're such nice people, they probably just aren't thinking.*

She felt her husband, Bill, scramble out of his side of the bed and wander to the bathroom. The door closed, the light went on, and then later it went out again. In a few minutes he was back in the warm cocoon and, with a yawn, Michelle leisurely climbed out of her side and padded to the bathroom.

Several minutes later, slightly chilled from the cold night air, she climbed back under the thick quilt, thinking how glad she was that unlike Bill, she could go to the john in the middle of the night without having to turn on the light. As she snuggled her chest against Bill's large, warm back, she had a few fleeting erotic flashes. Well, she reasoned, if she fell back to sleep, she'd awake refreshed.

Wait a moment, she told herself. *Why should I go back to sleep? I have the desire and Bill's right here. Why not do something about it?*

She had never been particularly bold about lovemaking, leaving most of the first moves to her husband. Bill was almost always the initiator of sex, but why shouldn't she be the aggressor from time to time? She cuddled more tightly against his back and felt her nipples harden in response to her wandering thoughts. Was he still awake? She'd find out quickly enough.

She stroked Bill's arm, just enjoying the feel of the short, wiry hairs that covered his skin. She seldom took the time to enjoy touching her husband so she spent several minutes stroking his arm, hands, and fingers. Then she reached around and flattened her palms on Bill's chest and stroked the smooth surface. When her palms contacted Bill's small nipples, she rubbed them, then used a short fingernail to scratch the tiny nub into life. Amazed, she felt it harden beneath her finger. She wiggled her hips so her pubic bone rubbed against Bill's tailbone and realized that she was getting wetter. Bill hadn't said anything or reacted in any obvious way, but Michelle became aware of a slight hoarseness to his breathing. *He's awake all right. He's playing possum so I'll continue, so he must be enjoying what I'm doing.*

She slid her palm down to Bill's waist and felt his abdominal muscles contract. With her cheek against his back, she could hear and feel his breathing quicken. When he tried to turn over, she held on, enjoying her position behind him. Slowly Michelle slid her palm down his belly and suddenly his cock, hard and throbbing, bumped against the back of her hand. Seemingly content now to remain on his side with his wife in charge, Bill gasped and lay still.

He's so horny, she thought, *and I did that.* It was a revelation. She knew in her mind that he would enjoy it if she took the lead occasionally, but she had always been hesitant. *What if I do it wrong or he thinks I'm being silly or he's not in the mood?* Worried, in the past, when she had considered making the first move, she had demurred. *Well,* she thought, *he is obviously enjoying this. Maybe I can do it more often.* She quieted her thoughts and concentrated on the feel of Bill's body. As her palm caressed his belly, the back of her hand caressed his hard cock.

She kissed his back and licked a wide stripe. Then, unable to get enough of his skin into her mouth to nip him, she scraped her teeth along his spine. She knew full well that he wanted her to grasp his cock, but she resisted the urge, teasing him. She knew that he wouldn't ask, leaving her to set the pace, unwilling to disturb the mood. He was enjoying the silence, the dark, the slight mystery and anonymity of it all as much as she was.

Michelle squirmed, feeling Bill's skin against her now-heated body. Her belly against his back, her thighs against his ass cheeks, her breasts against his shoulder blades, she moved like a cat in heat. God, he felt so good.

Then she did it. She grasped Bill's cock and held it tightly. She had held his cock many times before, to guide it into her waiting body, but she'd never actually rubbed it to climax. Could she do it? She wanted him inside of her, but this was too intriguing to resist. Although it was scary, she wanted to try. She held him tightly and felt his whole body tense. Her entire body was in tune with his and she was aware of his every reaction to what she was doing. She held fast, pulling her hand upward toward the tip of his erection. The end was already wet with his pre-come and she used the tip of her index finger to rub the lubricant around the head of his penis.

As she did so, she felt his body tighten still more and his hips moved almost involuntarily. *God, this is so good,* she thought again. She squeezed again and pulled her hand downward toward the base of the hard rod, using his body's own lubricant to ease her way. Again to the tip and more fluid.

Soon his cock was slippery and she could slide her hand up and down in a slow rhythm. Feeling braver, she stopped and decided to explore a bit. She slid one finger up and down the underside of Bill's cock, then slid farther down and touched his balls. The moan she heard and felt was all the reassurance she needed. It was a bit difficult to reach, but she ran the pad of her finger over the surface of his sac. Did she want him to turn over so she could do more? No, she realized. If he lay on his back she'd be tempted to climb on top of him and she really wanted to see whether she could bring him to climax without intercourse.

She returned her attention to his cock and stroked, first toward the tip, then downward to the base. She heard air hiss out between Bill's teeth. His cock took on a life of its own and moved beneath her hand. Bill sighed, then groaned softly.

Michelle flattened her hand on the underside of his cock, pressed it against his abdomen and rubbed. She felt him pulse, then his hips jerked and his cock twitched against her palm. He came, silently, his entire body throbbing against her. Her hand was now covered with his sticky come and some of it dripped onto the sheet. Wordlessly, Bill grabbed a corner of the top sheet and wiped the goo from her hand and his abdomen.

Still silent, he turned and pushed her onto her back. His mouth found her hard, erect nipple, and his teeth caused shards of pleasure to rocket through her already aroused body. His mouth alternated between her nipples until she was almost crying with need. Unwilling to break the silence, she pushed against Bill's shoulders, urging him to use his hands to finish her off. She heard a slight chuckle, then he slithered down beneath the covers and locked his mouth on her now-needy pussy. His tongue flicked over her clit, then lapped up the fluids that had collected between her swollen inner lips.

Now almost crazy with lust, Michelle tangled her long fingers in her husband's curly hair and held his face tightly against her need. A finger pushed inside her channel and, as he licked, he drove first one then two fingers in and out of her hot pussy. Her belly clenched and her legs trembled. It was only moments before she came, spasms echoing through her body as flaming colors flashed behind her eyes. Almost unable to catch her breath, she gently pushed Bill's face aside and he slid up and cuddled against her. In almost no time, they were both back to sleep.

In the morning, Michelle awoke to find Bill propped on his elbow, watching her. "I had the most wonderful dream," he purred.

"You did?" she said, a grin spreading across her face.

He leaned over until she could feel his warm breath on her face. "I dreamed that a sexy woman held me and stroked me in the middle of the night until I came. She didn't say anything, but I could have sworn it was you."

"I had a wonderful dream too. Some sexy man used his very talented mouth to make me come."

"Hmm. Matching dreams. I wonder whether that has some significance?"

"I think it does. I certainly think so."

Alice put the pages beside her on the bed and lifted Roger onto her lap. That woman had had her doubts too. She hadn't been sure how to touch her husband, but she had done what felt good to both of them. Why hadn't she ever done anything like that? Her sex life had been a bust and she hadn't done anything to make it better. She hadn't known anything, but how was she supposed to have learned? Ralph had never told her what to do, never even suggested. She had been a failure as a wife, but didn't Ralph bear any of the responsibility? Wasn't it his job, if only a little, to help her, teach her? She had read several sex books their first year together and had tried to talk to her husband about their love life but he had always put her off. "Oh, girl, it's all right. I'm happy with things the way they are." But she hadn't been happy and she knew now that he hadn't been happy either.

So whose fault was it? Was she a prude who would never be any good at sex? No, and it wasn't her fault, nor was it Ralph's. And what about her life since? Hadn't she just given up? After Ralph left, she had her job, her family, and Betsy. Was that normal? She hadn't really dated, and she hadn't had anything resembling sex in what seemed like forever.

She sighed and said, "Roger, where am I now? Thirty-two years old. A spinster type who's never even lived." She dumped Roger onto the bed and strode into the bathroom. She closed the door and looked at herself in the full-length mirror. "Dumpy," she said. Face? Plain. She tucked her shirt into her jeans, sucked in her stomach and pulled a large gulp of air into her lungs. Figure? Ordinary. Overweight. Boobs? Average. Quickly she stripped off her clothes and looked at her naked body. "Underneath all those clothes there's nothing good." Thighs? Heavy. Belly? Rounded and getting rounder. Tits? Sagging. She lifted her arms, looked at the slight droop beneath her upper arms and sighed. She wandered back into the bedroom and pulled on the oversized New York Jets T-shirt she slept in. "You know, Roger, it's only phone sex. They'd never see me. I could look like a hippo for all anyone would know, and I could become anyone."

She crouched beside her bookshelf and found the collection of how-to sex books she had bought while she was married. She pulled one out and stared at the dust. *I could learn a lot. I remember that these had a lot of good ideas. I could do some reading and learn.* "I really could, Roger."

She climbed into bed and picked up the second set of pages she had printed from the Internet. One more before sleep. Maybe it would lead to good dreams.

Chapter 4

In the Hot Tub

It had been a terrible week for twenty-eight-year-old Eric La Monte. First, he and his girlfriend of almost a year had split. "I want some freedom," she had said, "some time to explore who I really am." Eric had sat on his side of the bed in their Palm Springs condo and watched her pack. Then he'd spent three days explaining her absence to his entire family and all his friends. Why? everyone asked. God only knows, became his litany. Finally, on Thursday, his district manager had arrived for a three-day surprise visit to the supermarket he managed. Sure, he thought later, everything could have been a lot worse on that front. He'd received only a few "needs improvement" warnings, but, all in all, it had been an awful week.

Now it was Saturday evening, and he was exhausted and alone. He lay on the bed and tried to sleep, but it was impossible. Every time he closed his eyes he thought about Marge or Mr. Pomerantz. Neither mental picture was geared to allow him to sleep. "Shit," he muttered climbing out of bed as the red numerals on the clock read 1:07 A.M. "I gotta relax." Although it was early summer, it was still over eighty degrees. The condo's hot tub and pool closed at eleven but he could easily climb the fence and lounge in the hot bubbling water for a while. "It'll help me unwind."

With just a towel around his loins, Eric walked to the fence around the pool, surprised to find the gate unlocked. Most of the lights were out, so he heard rather than saw that the bubbles were on in the tub. Through the mist, he saw a woman's gray head. Since much of Palm Springs's population was made up of retirees, Eric assumed that the person in the pool was some ancient specimen boiling the arthritis out of old bones at 1:00 A.M. "Shit," he muttered again. "Some old bitch is where I want to be." He remembered that, since he had assumed he'd be alone, he had not worn a bathing suit. "Fuck her," he hissed, striding to the edge of the tub, dropping the towel and climbing into the bubbling cauldron.

As he settled into the hot water, Eric looked through the dimly lighted mist at the woman sitting across the pool. She was not bad-looking, maybe only fifty or so, with flushed cheeks and wet, shoulder-length hair. Eric ignored her, cradled his head on the concrete rim, draped his arms over the edge, and closed his eyes.

"I thought I'd be the only one here at this hour," her soft voice said over the bubble noise. "I'm Carol."

"Eric," he grunted.

"Well," Carol said, "it's going to get a bit embarrassing in here in a minute or so. The timer on the pump has only a short while to go and I'm afraid I'm not wearing anything either. I usually reset the dial for a second go-around."

"No sweat," Eric said. "I promise I won't look if you want to extend the time."

"Thanks." Eric could hear the smile in her voice. Then

he heard her leave the water and quietly pad over to the controls. He heard the creak of the dials. He couldn't resist, so he opened his eyes and looked. Not bad, he thought. Not bad at all. She was slender and firm, with a slight droop to her bosom but in general not bad. Not Marge, of course but . . .

She padded back to the steps and slowly walked down into the heated water. "You're looking," she said, seeming unperturbed.

Eric slammed his eyes shut. "Sorry," he mumbled.

"I'm not," she said. "I like it when men look at me."

Eric opened his eyes again and saw that she was still standing, thigh-deep in the warm water. "You're not bad to look at," he said.

He watched as she slowly took a handful of heated water and released it over her right breast. Then another over her left. "I love the heat," she said.

Despite the debilitating effect of the hot water, Eric felt a stirring in his groin. "How come you're here after hours?" he asked, deflecting the conversation before his cock got embarrassingly hard.

"I couldn't sleep. I often come out here after midnight so I got a key from a particularly friendly security guard."

The way she said *particularly friendly* had Eric's ears perked. How friendly, he wondered.

"How about you?" she asked, lowering herself into the water beside him. "How come you're here tonight?"

"Couldn't sleep either," Eric said. He could sense her presence beside him although he couldn't actually feel her skin.

"I couldn't help but notice that Marge moved out."

"What do you know about that?"

"There's not much real privacy here. I hope it was your idea. Breakups can be so difficult."

"Actually it was hers," Eric said, closing his eyes. "I don't really want to talk about it." Suddenly Eric felt a hand on his leg.

"I'm sure you don't, Eric," Carol said. "It's tough."

The hand was kneading his thigh. It could be just a gesture of sympathy, he told himself, but it was having an effect on his cock anyway. *I've got to change the subject before I say something dumb.* "Are you married?" Was that a change of topic?

"Used to be, but we were divorced almost five years ago."

"That's tough," Eric said.

"Not really," Carol said, her hand still kneading the flesh of Eric's thigh. "I make do."

This is getting to be a bit too much, Eric thought. *She can't be doing what I think she's doing. This sort of thing doesn't happen. Not to me.* "Oh." Eric squeezed his eyes shut, trying to ignore the hand on his thigh. "Which unit is yours?" he asked.

"I'm in B-204. It's quite comfortable for just me."

The hand crept a bit higher, the fingers almost in his groin. "I'll bet it is," he croaked.

He felt her mouth close to his cheek. "I hope I'm not upsetting you," she said into his ear. Then she giggled. "Actually I hope I am." The hand found his testicles and one finger brushed the surface. "Am I?"

Eric opened his eyes and looked at the woman sitting next to him. There could be no misinterpreting her movements. She was seducing him. His arm was still on the edge of the pool. He draped it around her shoulders and pulled her closer. "Yes," he said, his mouth against hers, "you are. Is that what you want?"

Carol's tongue reached out and licked the sweat from Eric's upper lip. "Oh yes. I want to bother you a lot."

He kissed her then, pressing his wet mouth against hers, tasting salt and chlorine and her. His mouth opened and his tongue touched hers. So hot, deep, and wet. Her mouth seemed to pull him closer.

His hands found her breasts, soft, full, and floaty in the bubbling water. He had never played with weightless breasts before. They felt loose and incredibly sexy. Then he couldn't concentrate on anything, because her hand had surrounded his cock and now squeezed tightly. "God," she breathed, "you're so big."

She probably says that to everyone, he thought in the small part of his brain still capable of thought. It's such a cliché come-on line, but he went with it all. His cock was the biggest ever, and she wanted it.

He slid his hands to her waist and started to lift her onto his ready staff.

"Not so fast, baby," she purred. "I'm not nearly ready for you yet." She stood up and climbed out of the tub, beckoning him to follow. He was incapable of resistance. She straddled a plastic-webbed lounge chair, one foot on the concrete at either side. She patted the chair between her legs. "Here, baby," she purred and he sat facing her.

She lay back and smiled. "The air is just cool enough to feel good on my hot, wet body. Yours too?"

"Yes," Eric said, his hands scrambling in her crotch. She reached down and held her labia open. "Touch nice and soft right now," she said. "Rub in the folds. I like to be touched everywhere."

Eric had calmed a bit and was now able to think coherently. He slowly explored every crease between Carol's legs. He'd always been too hungry to pay much attention to Marge's body. Now he got to know Carol's. When he rubbed back toward her anus, she moaned and moved her hips. When he brushed her clit, she gasped. It was wonderful. She was telling him so clearly exactly what she wanted, without saying a word.

She was so wet, he noticed. Slippery juice oozed backward

and wet her puckered rear entry. He ran his finger around the opening and Carol trembled. Could he?

"I like what you're doing," she said, as if reading his mind. "You can do anything you like. I'll tell you to stop if I don't like it."

He had never just sat and touched a woman like this before, watching her face and body respond to his fingers. It was arousing, yet as hard as his cock was, he was also capable of waiting, enjoying the now and not rushing forward. He pressed his index finger against her puckered rear hole and marveled at how it slipped in just a bit.

"Oh, God," she hissed. "That's incredible."

Eric slipped the finger in just a bit more and watched Carol writhe. He used his other hand to stroke her clit, knowing that she was close to climax. Part of him wanted to plunge his cock into her, but another part wanted to finish her off just this way. He pulled the finger from her ass, then pushed it back in. Her juices were flowing so copiously that his hand was soaked, his finger wet enough to penetrate her rear hole. Slowly the digit slid farther and farther into her rear passage. Faster and faster he rubbed her hard nub.

When he thought she was ready, he leaned down and placed his mouth over her clit. He flicked his tongue firmly over the hard bud and felt her back arch and her hands tangle in his hair. "Yes, yes," she hissed. "Now."

He felt her come, felt the spasms in her ass, felt her cunt pulse against his mouth. He didn't move until he felt her begin to relax. "I want to fuck you," he said.

"I know," Carol said, panting, "but let's do this my way. Please."

Eric shrugged. He was beyond caring about the "how."

Slowly, Carol got up and moved Eric around so he was sitting properly on the chair, her body stretched out between his legs. "I love it this way," she whispered. Her hands cupped his balls and her mouth found his cock. She licked the tip, then blew on the wet spot. She licked the length of his shaft underneath, then each side. She kneaded his balls, then insinuated one finger beneath his sacs, reaching for his anus.

He closed his eyes. No one had ever touched him there and he wasn't sure he would like it. He did. It was electric. Shafts of pure pleasure rocketed down his cock as the familiar tightness started in his belly and balls. "I'm going to shoot," he said, his voice hoarse.

Carol lifted her head. "Oh yes. Do it, baby. Shoot for me." She took the length of him in her mouth as she rimmed his asshole.

He couldn't hold back and the jism boiled from his loins into her mouth. He opened his eyes and looked at her cheeks as she tried unsuccessfully to swallow his come. Small dribbles escaped from the corners of her mouth and wet his balls.

A few minutes later Carol took her towel, dipped it in the hot tub and tenderly washed Eric's groin. "I have to go in now," she said.

Limp, drained, and unable to move, Eric said, "I wish you'd stay."

"No you don't," she said, smiling. "You need to recover alone. But I'm here almost every night about one o'clock. Come back whenever you get lonely."

"Good night," Eric said. "I know I'll be here again soon."

"Oh," she said, opening the gate, "I hope so."

Eric watched her back and remembered thinking of her as an old bitch. *Gray hair indeed,* he thought. *The fire's still on in that sexy furnace. I'll never underestimate older women again.*

Alice put the pages on the bed-table beside her and flipped off the light. *I'm only thirty-two,* she thought. *I could learn. I really could. Then I'd be like Carol. I just need a little practice.* She yawned and was asleep almost instantly.

In her dream she was in a hot tub, naked. The water bubbled all around her, teasing and tickling. She looked around and all she could see were palm trees, thick and completely surrounding the tub, obliterating any houses and prying eyes. There was a man in the water with her, across the tub, an old man with thick white hair and a wizened face with deep wrinkles and smile lines. "Ralph?" she asked.

"No. He's gone," the man said. "I'm here with you."

"Oh," she said, the bubbles now causing steam to rise from the tub. What was she doing in a hot tub, nude, with some strange man? She moved to cover herself but realized that with all the bubbles, nothing could be seen below the water.

"It's your turn now," he said.

"My turn for what?"

"It's your turn for yourself."

"What does that mean?"

The man shook his head sadly. "If you don't know, well . . . It's really all up to you."

"You talk in riddles," Alice said.

"No, I don't. You don't want to hear."

"Do you mean I can do this? I should do this?"

"Only you know."

She rested her head on the edge of the tub and closed her eyes. Then his hands were on her, gently pinching her nipples, his teeth nipping at her ear. She lay, her arms stretched across the edge of the tub as his hands played with her breasts and his mouth teased hers. Then his hands were between her legs. She opened her eyes and looked down but she couldn't see what he was doing through the bubbles.

It felt good. He touched and teased, yet she couldn't quite feel where his hands were at anytime. It was just a general sensation of being touched everywhere. She felt her nipples harden and her pussy swell. She wanted. Needed.

Then she was awake, staring into the darkened room,

feeling the warmth of Roger's body pressed against her side. She was lying with her arms stretched out at the shoulder and she could almost feel the edge of the hot tub. As the dream faded, she turned on her side and went back to sleep.

The following morning, she was up before the alarm and at Dr. Tannenbaum's office before eight. The first patient was early and was already in the operatory when Betsy arrived. The two women had little time to talk throughout the busy morning. At about eleven, Alice snagged Betsy as she passed. "Lunch?" she asked her friend. "We haven't had lunch together in a few weeks. How about it?"

"You sound like a woman with a purpose," Betsy said. "Have you come to a decision?"

"I think so but I need to talk to you."

"Okay. How about the diner?"

"Done."

By one-fifteen Betsy and Alice were seated in a booth and had ordered club sandwiches and Diet Cokes. "I did some reading last evening and that led to a lot of thinking. I'd like to give it a try but I'll need lots of help."

"Don't worry about that. I hope you won't mind but I already talked to Velvet and broached the idea about you taking a few calls. She'll need to meet you and chat, but I think it will work out. Her business is growing every month and she was already thinking about hiring another girl or two. You'd fit right in."

"How does it work, logistically, I mean?"

"Velvet has a pretty advanced computer system. Someone calls. If it's a prearranged appointment, the call goes directly to the right phone. If it's not, the person talks to the router and the caller can ask for the woman he wants to talk to. If she's available, then the call goes through. If she's not, then the caller can wait, in which case they pay while they are on hold. If he doesn't want to wait for a specific woman or if the caller is new to Velvet Whispers, there's a queuing system so it's the next available person. Some girls need a place to be, so they work at Velvet's house. Others, like me, work at our own homes but between the computer and the phone company, everyone gets paid."

"How many girls does Velvet have?"

"It varies. It's usually around a dozen."

"I never realized that there would be so many people doing this stuff."

"And Velvet's only one of thousands of phone services all around the country."

"Does she really charge three dollars a minute?"

"It seems like a lot, but many services charge more."

"I can't get over it. My cut would be almost a hundred bucks an hour." That number had been bouncing around in her brain since Betsy first told her about Velvet Whispers.

"I know. It still amazes me. I get to keep half, the router gets paid, and Velvet gets the rest."

"That seems fair. Is this legal?"

"Sure. It's not prostitution. Just a phone call."

The two women stopped talking as the waiter brought their sandwiches and drinks. When he turned toward another table Alice leaned forward and, sotto voce, asked, "What if a guy refuses to pay?" What if she tried it and was a flop?

"Velvet and the girl involved take the hit, of course, and he never gets to call again. Most men really enjoy the service and wouldn't jeopardize it by not paying the bill. Actually for some men who worry about the money, I have a timer that dings every fifteen minutes to keep them aware of the time. I don't want anyone to be surprised."

"Don't they want to call you directly? You know, cut out the middleman and pay you less."

"A few have suggested it, but I wouldn't dream of cutting Velvet out. Anyway, I don't want to give out my home number."

"Yeah, I understand. How many regular customers do you have?" Alice took a large bite of her sandwich.

"I take three hours of calls a night, that's usually between four and six callers. Some are prearranged, some just random. The first-time clients take a bit longer since I have to take my time and find out what they want." Betsy poured a lake of ketchup beside the french fries on her plate.

"That sounds really scary. What if they aren't satisfied?"

"There's no guarantee, of course, and they take that risk. Most men want pretty much the same things and they make their needs quite clear from the beginning."

"Lots of four letter words and adjectives?"

Betsy chuckled and chewed her fry. "Some. Others just want someone to talk to. Some want to tell *their* exploits, some want to talk about doing things their wives don't want to do, some just want to masturbate while you *watch*."

"Wives? Are they married? That never occurred to me. I thought most of them would he horny single guys with no one to play with."

"That's what I thought when I started. Lots of them, however, are men with wives they think wouldn't understand their desires. Some want to talk about bondage, spanking, or anal sex, things they think *nice girls* like their wives wouldn't be interested in."

"I see."

Betsy raised an inquiring eyebrow. "Want to meet Velvet?"

"I think I would."

"I'll set something up and let you know."

They continued to eat, and talked about other matters. Alice felt both light and terrified, and the feelings hadn't changed by the following Saturday afternoon when she pulled into the driveway of a small house in Putnam Valley. She had considered how to dress and had changed clothes after Dr. Tannenbaum's office closed. She had finally decided on a pair of tan slacks, a brown turtleneck sweater, and an oatmeal-colored wool jacket. As she walked up the driveway, she tried not to prejudge, but she knew that she had already created a mental image of Velvet that was surprisingly like the bosomy madam of old western movies. Over made up, slightly overdressed, with eyes that knew everything about men that there was to know.

The woman who answered the door couldn't have resembled her image less. "Hello. You must be Alice." She was dressed in jeans and a pale blue sweatshirt. "Obviously, I'm Velvet. Come on in." Alice followed in a daze. Velvet was in her mid-thirties, with carefully blow-dried hair and just a hint of makeup. She was about five foot six, and weighed only about a hundred and ten pounds. She was not particularly pretty, but she had large eyes that were so deep blue as to be almost black, with long lashes. And she was almost completely flat-chested. Why had Alice expected big breasts?

"I thought we could talk in the den," Velvet said, taking Alice's jacket and leading the way through a neat, tastefully furnished, split-level house. They walked through the living room to the back of the house and stopped at the doorway of a wood-paneled room furnished with two comfortable leather lounge chairs. The den was occupied by a boy of about Brandon's age, and a girl who looked to be about five. They were stretched out on the floor, the boy working on a half-built model car and the girl carefully coloring a picture of the Little Mermaid. "Matthew and Caitlin, say hello to Ms. Waterman."

"Hello, Ms. Waterman," the two said in unison.

"I need to use this room for a little while." She opened a closet above the TV and fished out a video. "How about *Milo and Otis*? You two can watch in my room while I talk with Ms. Waterman."

"That movie's dumb. Can I work on my car?"

"Put down lots of newspaper and be careful with the glue. Okay?"

"Okay." The boy gathered the pieces of his model and the rest of the paraphernalia and started toward the door.

"Can we have ice cream?" Caitlin asked.

"It's too close to dinnertime."

"Please. Pretty please with sugar on it." Alice could tell from Matthew's expression that he usually let Caitlin do the wheedling.

"No ice cream. Daddy's in the basement. Ask him to cut up an apple for each of you and you can take that and a can of soda upstairs. But don't spill."

"Thanks, Mommy," Caitlin said.

"And after the movie, can I play Nintendo?" Matthew added.

Velvet turned to Alice. "They both have great futures as negotiators." She turned back to her children. "Okay, if there's time. Now scoot."

The two bounced from the room, yelling, "Daddy, we get sodas."

Velvet grinned at the backs of her children. "They're a handful but I love them."

Alice's mind was boggled. She had just gotten used to her best friend, mother of her godchildren, being a phone-sex operator. Now this. Velvet wasn't at all what Alice had expected. "They are wonderful. I understand that Matthew is the same age as Brandon."

"They were born on the same day. Betsy and I treat ourselves to dinner the following week, just to prove we lived through the annual birthday parties the way we lived through childbirth." Alice and Velvet settled into the matched lounge chairs. "You look slightly like the deer caught in the headlights," Velvet said.

"I'm sorry. I've only known about you and everything for

about a week. It's still hard to wrap my mind around it all. You seem so . . ."

"Normal?"

"I guess. I'm sorry. I don't mean to be insulting."

"You're not, and I appreciate the honesty. Can I get you something to drink?"

"No, thanks."

"Why don't you tell me about yourself?"

For several minutes, Alice told Velvet about her life and about Ralph. She freely admitted that her marriage hadn't been a sexual revelation and that she was still somewhat naive. "I've been doing a lot of reading and my eyes are opening rather quickly."

"I'll bet. Betsy tells me you're something of a storyteller. She says you're very good at it."

"Yes. I guess so."

"I've been toying with an idea for several months and when Betsy called and told me about you, I thought you might just be the right person." Curious, Alice remained silent. "I've had several men ask me to tell them erotic stories. I've suggested that they read tales from books or from the Internet, but they said they wanted to hear really hot fantasies from the lips of a woman with a sexy voice."

"But you . . ."

"Not my thing. I'm good at different things." Velvet winked. "I can talk a man to orgasm really well." Velvet took a deep breath, dropped her shoulders and her chin and said, "Sometimes I have just the sexy voice they are looking for." Her voice had changed completely. It was soft, breathy, and lower pitched. Alice knew that if she were a man, that voice would go right through her.

"How do you do that?"

"It's really not difficult. I'll show you. Do you think you could make up really hot stories? You could write them beforehand, but your client might ask for something special.

You'd have to be able to think on your feet."

"I don't know. I hadn't thought about it."

"It would make things a bit easier for you until you get the hang of this."

"I guess it would be easier." Alice had thought about having to personally interact with the men on the phone, verbally being part of the sex, and that had felt like the most difficult part. Now Velvet had thought of another way. Prewritten stories.

"It would mean that you wouldn't get too many men 'off the street.' Most would be prearranged because of your specialty and it might lower your financial expectations. I gather you need the money to help your mom."

"I need about four hundred a month to get her into the best nursing home in Westchester."

Alice could see Velvet quickly calculate. "That shouldn't be a problem. Here's what I would suggest. How about writing a few stories and letting me read them? That will give me an idea of how well you express the things that men want to hear."

"That sounds like a good way to begin," Alice said, "and it takes some of the pressure off me." That way she wouldn't have to get on the phone until she was sure she could please the client. The thought of failure terrified her.

"Then we can see where we'll go from there. How about coming over next Saturday afternoon, same time and I'll read what you've written? Or, if you write something sooner you could mail it to me. I don't want to rush you, but I gather you're under some time pressure."

Alice and her sister had found an upcoming spot in a second-tier nursing home, but were still waiting to hear from Rutlandt. The current arrangement would work for another three weeks, then they would have to make a decision. "I guess Betsy told you the whole story."

"She did, and I'm really sorry. Both of my parents and

both of Wayne's are still alive and, as they age, their future concerns me."

"I'll write what I can this week, and then be back same time next Saturday and we can talk more."

"Wonderful. Betsy's one of my favorite people and I'm glad to help."

"Don't do it just for her."

"I wouldn't dream of it. This is my business and the source of all our savings. I wouldn't jeopardize it for anyone. If I don't think you'll work out, I'll tell you."

"Thanks. I just need for you to be honest."

The two women stood and Velvet handed Alice her jacket. They walked to the front door and, as she stepped into the clear late-afternoon sunshine, Velvet quickly kissed her on the cheek. "Write up a storm."

"I will, and thanks for the chance."

Chapter 5

As she drove home, Alice thought about everything Velvet had said, and realized that, as naive as she might be in her personal life, she was creative enough to give this a real try. It wasn't going to be easy, but they didn't pay big bucks because what she was trying to do was easy. It was late in the afternoon and the sun was low in the sky. Although it was late March, there was no real hint of spring yet, so as she drove, Alice turned the heater up a notch.

Heat. That was what she needed to create in any story she wrote. She'd always been good in English composition and had gotten lots of *A*'s on her writing in high school, but this wasn't high school. Not by a long shot. Oh well. She had nothing to lose.

When she arrived home, she turned on her computer and browsed the Net. She was becoming familiar with a few of the picture sites and she gazed with a clinical eye at the photos. Most of them didn't excite her, but she found that a few, involving people being tied up, made her uneasy in a not unpleasant way. She tried to think like a researcher and assumed that most of the sites were aimed at males. She gleaned lots of pointers from what the webmasters thought would appeal to men and read lots of text that was supposed to be arousing.

How could she be sure what would turn a guy on? She hadn't a clue but, she reasoned, if it made her feel sexy, then it just might work. After several hours on the Net, she finally logged off.

What to write about? *Can I do a story about straight sex? Would anyone be interested in just a man and a woman making love? There has to be lots of hands and oral sex at least,* she thought. *Lots of sucking and stroking. Can I write about oral sex even though I've never done it?* Well, she reasoned, many people write about things they've never done.

She booted up the word processor she used for occasional letters and stared at the blank screen. She typed a few sentences, then deleted them. She got as far as the first paragraph, then stared, shook her head, and again blanked her screen. After half an hour of fruitless staring, she called Betsy and filled her in on her visit with Velvet. "She's such a nice person it's hard to believe she does what she does," Alice said.

"I know. It's sometimes hard for me to believe I do what I do."

"I didn't mean to sound insulting."

"You didn't. Are you going to write tonight?"

She turned so her back was to the computer. "I'm going to try. I've been trying."

"I know you can do it, so I won't hold you up. Get cracking. See you Monday morning."

Alice hung up and her eyes returned to the blank word-processing screen in front of her. She thought for several minutes, then got up, went into the kitchen, and made herself a bite of dinner. With a cup of soup, an American-cheese sandwich and a Coke on a tray, she returned to the desk in her bedroom. She ate and stared at the screen. When she was finished eating, she took the tray back into the kitchen and washed her plate and cup and the dirty dishes left over from the day before. Then she sponged off every surface and scoured the sink.

Roger jumped onto the counter and chirruped at her. "Okay. I know, Roger," she said, carrying the cat back into the bedroom. "I'm stalling." When he again chirruped, she continued, "Don't yell at me. I just don't know whether I can do this. It's so embarrassing." Why was it embarrassing? She was alone in the apartment. No one would read anything she wrote unless she chose to show it to them. Whatever she created was hers. Private.

Alice began to write, using several stories from the Internet as models and adding her own reactions and feelings. She wrote for more than two hours, reread, and edited what she had written, then turned to Roger, now curled in a ball on the bed. "This is really weird. It embarrasses me just to read what I wrote but I think it's not too bad. Not great, but maybe not too bad." She ran her spell-checking program, then printed out the six pages. The next step was to find out whether she could actually say the words out loud. She sat on the bed beside the cat. "Okay. Here goes."

The Beige Trench Coat

Jenny loved to read and whenever she had a moment to pick up a book, she did. One evening she had a few minutes while her husband and her three children tried to fix their broken dishwasher, so she sat in the lounge chair in the living room and read several pages of a novel. The part she read involved the heroine showing up at a guy's office wearing only her mink coat. There followed a delightfully graphic description of the interlude during which the heroine and her latest conquest made love on the desk, his secretary just a few feet and one closed door away.

"Man, oh man," Jenny whispered as she read the scene for a second time. "I wish I could be like that, aggressive and sexy."

"Hey, Mom," her daughter yelled, "I think we found the problem. Remember those toothpick critters we made? Well, it looks like Robbie dumped a few in the dishwasher. They jammed this hoodingy here. Come check this out." Reluctantly, Jenny put her book down and "checked out" the dishwasher.

A few hours later Jenny was in bed, watching the eleven o'clock news when her husband, Len, came upstairs. "Hon," he said, "you left this in the living room." He entered the bedroom holding the novel open to the page Jenny had been reading. "This is really hot stuff."

"Damn. I forgot it. I'm glad you found it not one of the kids."

"Me too. This is really explicit."

"That is quite a scene, isn't it."

"Sure is. That's some lucky guy."

"He is?"

"Sure. Sexy broad comes to his office hot to trot. What do you think?"

Jenny arched her back and looked down at her moderate-size bosom, filling out the top of her lacy nightgown. "It would have to be someone really sexy for a guy to take chances like that. I mean with his secretary right there in the next room."

"Nah. Just the idea of something like that," he paused and looked down at the bulge in the front of his sweatpants, "you know, dangerous, would make any guy hot." Len came around to Jenny's side of the bed, pulled off his clothes, and made quick, hungry love to his wife.

Later, as she lay listening to her husband's breathing return to normal, Jenny thought again about the scene that had made Len so excited. *I wonder,* she thought.

By the end of the following week, Jenny had made all her plans. She had taken the afternoon off and selected her wardrobe. Around 3:00 P.M., she arrived at her husband's office, dressed in a beige trench coat. "Paula," she said to Len's secretary who was busily typing into a word processor, "I've got to talk to Len about something in private. Will you hold all his calls until we let you know otherwise? And don't let anyone interrupt."

"Sure thing, Jenny," Paula said. "Nothing wrong, I hope."

"Nothing at all, Paula," Jenny said. "We just need a little time for some private business."

"Will do," Paula said.

Jenny entered Len's small private office, quietly closed the door behind her and turned the lock. Len was fiddling with some files in his credenza so his back was to her. For a moment, Jenny almost changed her mind. Would he really find this exciting? Would she make a fool of herself? She rubbed her sweaty palms on her coat and crossed to the desk.

"Hi, Len," she said, making her voice low and throaty.

"Hi, hon," Len said, turning in his swivel chair, a folder in his hand. "What are you doing here?"

"Well, I, ah . . ."

"I am glad to see you but I'm really busy. And why aren't you at work? Is something wrong?"

"No, nothing's wrong. It's just . . ." Again Jenny ran her shaking hands down her coat.

"Honey, what's wrong?"

Slowly, before what little courage she had deserted her completely, she unbuttoned her coat and pulled the sides open. Beneath she wore only a black satin bra and panties, a garter belt, black stockings with lace tops and black high-heeled shoes. Silent, she stared at her husband. She watched surprise and shock flash across his face, then a slow smile spread over his mouth.

He cleared his throat. "It's that scene from that book," he said hoarsely.

"Yes," she said softly, "it is."

"Oh," he said, he breathing increasing. "Wow."

Encouraged by the look on her husband's face, Jenny slowly let the trench coat slide from her arms. "I hope you like what you see," she said, echoing the heroine's line from the book.

"Oh, baby, I certainly do. Come over here."

Mimicking the scene from the book seemed to make it easier for Jenny to climb out of herself. "Not so fast, baby," she said hoarsely. "This is my party." She pranced around the office, wiggling her hips and humming "The Stripper." "Do you like?"

Len sat and stared. "I like this very much, but I'm really waiting for a very important phone call so get over here right now." He made a grab for her but she neatly avoided his grasp. "Come on, baby," he almost whined.

"In due time."

The intercom on the phone beeped. "Baby . . ."

This part hadn't been in the scene from the book so Jenny sighed and said, "Maybe you'd better get that."

"Yes," Len said as he put the receiver to his ear.

Jenny settled herself on Len's lap and could hear Paula's voice clearly. "I'm sorry, Len, but Mr. Haverstraw is on the line and he's leaving his office soon. I know that your wife didn't want you two to be disturbed, but I thought you would want to take this call."

Jenny could hear Len's deep sigh. "I guess I have to," he said, wiggling out from under Jenny's almost-bare behind. He covered the mouthpiece with his hand. "Baby, just hold that sexy thought for about five minutes. Okay?"

"Sure," Jenny said, deflated.

Len pushed the lighted button on his phone. "Mr. Haverstraw. I'm glad to finally get to talk to you."

Jenny sat in a chair on the opposite side of Len's desk and pondered. What would the woman in the book have done? Certainly not just sit here. An idea formed in Jenny's head and for several minutes she argued with herself, then decided. *The hell with it. I'm going to go for it.*

Now paying no attention to his wife, Len was furiously making notes on a yellow pad.

Slowly, Jenny made her way around the desk and, as Len distractedly made room for her, she wiggled under the desk. With trembling hands, she quickly unzipped Len's pants and pulled out his flaccid cock. She cradled it in her hand and watched it come to life.

Len pushed his chair back and stared at Jenny sitting in the kneehole. With his hand against the mouthpiece, he whispered, "Baby, please . . ." He pushed the chair back against the desk and Jenny could hear his pen scratching on the pad. She leaned forward and took Len's now semierect cock between her lips and sucked it into her warm mouth.

She heard Len gasp, then hiss, "Stop that!" Then he said, "No Mr. Haverstraw, not you. No, there's nothing wrong."

Smiling, Jenny sucked. This was extra delicious, she realized. Since Len had to continue his conversation, she would continue her ministrations as well. She fondled and sucked, then reached into his pants and squeezed his testicles.

"Mr. Haverstraw," Len said, his voice hoarse and tentative. "We're having some, er, electrical problems here. Can I call you back?" There was a pause. "Yes, I think I have enough to begin a rough estimate."

Jenny flicked her tongue over the tip of Len's cock, then pulled the thick, hard member into her mouth again.

"Yes, I'll get back to you tomorrow."

When she heard Len hang up, she slid from under the

desk. Len grabbed her and spun her around, pushing her down so she was bent over his desk, papers and pens flying in all directions. With one quick movement, he ripped off her panties and plunged his hard cock into her steaming pussy. "God, I'm so hot," she moaned.

"Me too," Len said, grasping Jenny's hips and forcing her even more tightly against his groin. "God, baby."

It took only a few thrusts for Len to shoot his load into his wife's hot cunt, making strangling sounds, trying not to yell. Then he reached around and rubbed Jenny's clit until she came, almost silently.

"Len," Paula said through the locked door, "is everything all right?"

Len cleared his throat, Jenny still bent over the desk. "Everything's just great, Paula."

Len collapsed into his desk chair and pulled his wife onto his lap, then kissed her deeply. "I can't believe you did that," he said finally.

Jenny giggled. "I can't either." She got up from Len's lap and grabbed a wad of tissues from her purse. "Was I too outrageous?"

"Oh, baby. It was difficult there for a while, and I'll have to make a few excuses to Haverstraw, but it was wonderful."

Jenny picked up the coat and put it back on. "Yeah, it was, wasn't it." After a few more kisses, she unlocked the door and walked out. "We're done, for the moment, Paula."

"That's great, Jenny," Paula said. "I hope everything worked out."

"Oh yes," Jenny and Len said, almost simultaneously, "it certainly did work out."

"God. I actually got through it," Alice said, stacking the pages of her story. "What do you think, Roger? Does that make it?" She looked at the cat, who was now fast asleep, and giggled. "I hope you're not a good judge of quality."

Initially she had strangled on the more graphic words, but she had eventually said them all, and the more often she said them, the easier they became. "I can say *clit* and *pussy* and *cock*. I've come a long way, baby." She giggled again, then laughed out loud. "If Ralph could only see me now."

The following day was Sunday, so after a quick visit to Queens, Alice spent the rest of the day either writing or surfing the Internet for ideas. She worked until almost midnight and, by the time she climbed into bed, she had written three more stories. The following morning she put them all in a large brown envelope and dropped them off at the post office on her way to work.

The week dragged. Alice visited her mother and sister on Wednesday and on the drive to Queens, she worked out exactly what she was going to tell her family. "I think I might have a really exciting new job one or two nights a week," she told her sister and brother-in-law.

"Doing what?" Sue asked.

"Phone sales," Alice answered, as she had rehearsed. "It's a bit complicated to explain, but it pays really well and I don't have to sell anything I don't believe in." She almost choked on the last phrase, but she hoped she would cover all the bases so there wouldn't be any awkward questions. "Any luck with Rutlandt?" she asked, changing the subject as quickly as she could.

"I got a letter from them. They have Mom at the top of the waiting list but they have no way of knowing when they will have an opening. I don't know whether we can afford it." Sue looked like she was coping as best she could, but it was difficult for both of them.

Alice patted her sister's hand. "I'll have a better idea by Saturday, when I find out about this new job. If it pans out, we'll be okay." If Velvet gave her the go-ahead, she'd empty her meager savings if she had to and replace the money as she got paid.

"Then I'll keep my fingers crossed for you."

Alice held up her hands, all fingers linked to others. "I've got everything crossed but my eyes."

She tried not to count on the job too much but the following Saturday afternoon she had her heart in her mouth as she drove to Velvet's house. As she had the previous week, Velvet, dressed as Alice was, in jeans and a man-tailored shirt, escorted her into the den, this week free of children. "They're at the movies with Wayne. You didn't meet Wayne the last time you were here, did you?"

"No." Alice was having difficulty focusing on Velvet's conversation.

Velvet picked up Alice's envelope and paced as she talked. "I'm sorry. Let's get to it. The stories are sensational."

Alice let out a long sigh of relief. "Do you really think so?"

"I do. You've got just the right amount of hot sex without the raunchy stuff that Velvet Whispers usually avoids. There are so many 'You phone, I'll pretend to suck you off' phone services that we try for something a bit more upscale and our clients have responded. I have a few guys who will love this stuff."

"That's wonderful."

"I know this must come as a relief to you. I've been giving this a lot of thought and I have one idea. It would sound more personal if the stories from a woman's point of view were in first person. Like 'I did this and that.' They could sound like they were personal revelations that you've never told anyone before. The ones from a man's might be stories someone told you. Personal tales, not something someone made up. I think that would go over better. What do you think?"

Alice considered Velvet's suggestion for only a moment. "You're right, of course. I'm annoyed that I didn't think of that."

"Great. Now here's my idea. We'll call you Sheherazade

and I'll tell a few guys that you're a new erotic storyteller I've found. They might want to hear something specific, like," Velvet tapped her front teeth as she thought, "like the first time you made love or something naughty you did last week. You could write them out in advance but you'd have to roll with it from time to time. You'll have to be able to think fast and vary the story to go along with their ideas and desires." Alice could see the wheels turning as Velvet created her identity. Sheherazade's Secrets.

The more Velvet talked, the more it seemed to Alice that she might be able to make it all work. "Can you say this stuff out loud?" Velvet asked.

Alice smiled. "Well, I've read all these stories to my cat, if that counts. After listening to these tales I'll bet he's the hottest animal in town."

"Great," Velvet said with a chuckle. "This might just make us each some money. Let me make a few calls to men who I think would be interested, and I'll see what I can set up. Are you willing to get started next week?"

Next week! "I'm game." She took a deep breath. "Let's do it."

"Wonderful. I'll call you midweek and we'll nail down the specifics. What nights do you want to work, for now?"

"I thought about Mondays, Wednesdays, and Fridays. Are the weekends your busiest times? I could work Saturdays too."

"You know, it varies. Some weekends it seems the entire male population of the world calls, and others it's really silent. You get fifty percent of whatever the callers are charged, based only on actual time on the phone, of course. The usual rate is $2.99 per minute. I'd like you to get a timer that will ding every ten minutes so those who care will know how much they're paying. For the most part, however, I've found that most of these guys don't give a damn."

"How long should the calls go? I know Betsy said some of hers go more than half an hour."

"Yours will too," Velvet said. "It should take twenty minutes to half an hour to read a seven- or eight-page story, more if your tales get longer or if you talk slowly. If someone wants to limit the amount of money he spends, you can suggest that you can continue the story next week. You'll have to take notes and pick up just where you left off. Your clients will remember every detail." Velvet continued to think out loud. "To create regular customers, you might want to have some of your stories continued, like X-rated soap operas. Everyone should get off in each segment, but you can reuse the same characters. That's all up to you."

"Do you want me to start with someone who's not a paying customer to make sure that you like what I'm doing?"

"We can if you like," Velvet said, her smile warm and open, "but I'm confident that you can do this."

Suddenly unsure, Alice asked, "How can you be so sure? You don't know me at all."

"Actually, I do. I know you through these wonderful stories you wrote, and I've talked about you with Betsy several times this week. We both think it will work out wonderfully well for you. Anything else?"

"I'd like to start with only one or two people and test it all out. I don't want you to make any promises we can't keep."

"That sounds fine with me." She stood up and walked Alice to the front door. As Alice stepped out onto the porch, Velvet said, "Go get 'em, Sherry."

"Sheherazade. Sherry. I like that." With a quick motion, she kissed Velvet on the cheek. "Thanks."

"You're certainly welcome. And I'm not a charity. We're both going to make some nice bucks out of this. I'll call you."

Alice called Betsy as soon as she got home and filled

her in on the meeting with Velvet. "She's a love."

"She certainly is, and, with the women she's got working for her and very little overhead, she makes a really nice living too."

"I'll bet. I've got stories to write now. I want a few of every type that men might ask for. Give me some clues. What kind of sex do men want from their encounters?"

"Most of my clients enjoy the idea of a woman performing oral sex on them. I guess it's something that their wives won't do."

"Oh. Don't women like that sort of thing?"

"I guess not. Did you and Ralph . . ."

"No. He was just a missionary position kind of guy. Do you and Larry?"

"Of course. It's wonderful. You might think about having sex in semipublic places, too, for your stories. I have a few clients who love the idea of possibly being found out. And of course, you need lots of control stories."

"I know. I've read a lot of those, where the men almost rape the women."

"Don't overlook the men who want to be dominated too. Oh, and one more thing: Men love to think about two women making love. Lesbian sex seems to turn guys on."

Alice was taken aback. She had never considered that men might want such a thing. "Phew. I don't know about that."

"You don't have to *do* it, just talk about it. I do. Several times I've told stories about my supposed adventures with another woman."

Alice gasped. "Have you ever?"

"No. But I can invent stories and before you say it, no, it's not lying. These men know who and what you are. It's the fantasy they're after, not the reality of who you really are. They understand. It's just a way for them to get off."

After Alice hung up, she booted up her computer and began to type. For the rest of the weekend, except for her visit to her sister's, she did nothing but write, edit, and rewrite. When she temporarily ran out of ideas, she prowled the Internet, not stealing stories, just getting her mind loosened up.

On Monday evening, she got a call from Velvet. "I talked to a man named Vic. He's a really sweet guy who's always asking me to tell him about my lurid past. I told him about Sheherazade and he's really psyched. He'd like to call you on Wednesday evening at about nine. Would that work for you?"

Vic. Her first client. Alice's hands trembled and she could barely get out the words, "That would be fine."

"I know you're probably nervous, but try not to be. He's just a really nice, sort of shy guy who just enjoys getting his rocks off once a week with a dirty conversation. And he's got the money to be able to do just that."

Alice barked out a rueful laugh. "He's shy and I'm terrified. What a pair we'll make."

"You'll do fine. He usually stays on the phone for about half an hour. That's forty-five dollars for you for just a short bit of work. Think of it that way if it makes it easier."

"Is there anything special he wants in my story?"

"He likes hot, aggressive women who like a bit of danger. That's about all I can think of."

Alice thought about a story she'd just finished. "Actually that will work out nicely."

"Good. I told him to call me right after he talks to you so he can let me know how he likes you and whether he wants to call again next week. Then I'll call you. If you both think it went well, he'll become as regular as he wants. We can use him as a sort of test case. If it works out, I'll see who else I can set you up with."

"Great. It's kind of like the ultimate job interview."

Velvet's laugh was warm and comforting. "I know you'll be great. A few tips. When you talk, deliberately relax your shoulders and drop both the pitch and volume of your voice. Get just a bit of breath into it, but don't get all Mae West or Marilyn Monroe either. You might want to have a few beers before he calls, just to relax you."

After a few more minutes, the two women hung up and Alice reread the story she thought Vic might like. *This might just please him,* she thought.

All week Alice was in a tizzy. She talked with Betsy almost incessantly, looking for reassurance. The women met Wednesday for lunch and Alice asked Betsy several times whether she thought that her storytelling would work. Over coffee Betsy finally said, "I think I'm going to strangle you. If you don't want to do this, then don't. If you do, then just take your chances and do it. If it all falls apart and you're terrible, you're no worse off than you would have been if it had never happened."

"I guess that's right." Alice smiled and winked at her friend. "Thanks. I needed that."

On her way home from lunch, Alice bought a six-pack of Budweiser. She didn't particularly like beer and she hated the calories that went with it, but tonight she'd need to unwind. The afternoon dragged by and she was sorry that her first call had been planned for a Wednesday, the only day during the week that she didn't work. At least at Dr. Tannenbaum's office the day would pass more quickly. As it was, the afternoon seemed about three days long.

Alice sipped a beer with dinner, one for dessert, and yet another at about eight-thirty. Like medicine, she told herself. When the phone rang at nine o'clock, she was seated on the edge of the bed, just slightly buzzed. She listened to the first ring, then picked it up on the second. "Hello?"

"Is this Sheherazade?"

"Yes," she said, her heart pounding. "You must be Vic."

"That's me. How are you tonight?"

"I'm fine. I've been waiting for your call. I have a story for you that you might enjoy."

"That's great. First, tell me what you look like."

"Tonight, I'm twenty-five, slim, with 36D breasts and long legs."

She heard a deep breath. "That's great," Vic said. "Blond hair and blue eyes?"

"Why yes," Alice said, putting a bit of surprise in her voice. "How did you know?"

"I guess I'm just lucky. That's the way I like to picture women."

Alice made a few notes on the pad beside her. "That's really lucky. I'm glad I'm just what you wanted."

"Are you ready to tell me your story, Sheherazade?"

"Oh yes. I love telling stories about all the women inside of me."

"Okay. I'm putting my feet up and I'm ready."

Alice picked up the pages she had written. She'd use them as a guideline, and improvise when she had to.

Chapter 6

"You know, Vic, I have a secret. I love tollbooths. I know that's a ridiculous statement, but after you've heard my story, I think you'll understand. It happened a while ago, but I still remember it.

"Let me back up. Throughout college, I loved to wear tight jeans, and sweaters cut just low enough to reveal my cleavage. I enjoyed the way guys in my classes looked at me. I developed a clumsy way of dropping my books so I could bend over and watch them as they watched me.

"When I graduated, I got a job as a secretary in a large, very formal accounting firm. It was all terribly gray-flannel: women in tailored suits worn with blouses buttoned up to the neck. Each morning, I put my long hair up, using dozens of pins to keep it neat. By the end of each day, all I could think about was taking my clothes off, unpinning my hair, and relaxing. But the work was interesting and the pay was great so I put up with the minor disadvantages. You know how it can be."

"Oh yes," Vic said. "I do. I used to work in a place like that myself."

"Then you do understand. Well, after almost a year, I treated myself to a tiny red convertible. Instead of taking the commuter train, I started to drive to work every morning on the parkway, my blouse primly buttoned and my hair up. Unhappily, I had to keep the top of the car closed or the wind would have ruined my appearance.

"On the way home, however, I was under no such restrictions. I could unbutton, unpin, and unwind. After a few weeks, the weather turned warm and I decided to lower the top of my car for the drive home. The spring air was soft and warm one afternoon so I removed my jacket and unbuttoned my blouse. Then I took five minutes and pulled every pin out of my hair, until it fell in soft waves down my back. I felt free."

"Was it long and blond?"

"Of course. A soft yellow like . . ." she struggled for a phrase, "new wheat."

"Wow."

"So that afternoon I shifted into first and eased my car out of the garage and into traffic. As I drove along the parkway toward my apartment I was exhilarated by the feel of the wind in my hair and down the front of my blouse. I could feel my nipples harden under the silky fabric. I pulled into the line of traffic and, quarter in hand, I slowly inched my way toward the tollbooth just before my exit. As I reached out to put the quarter in the outstretched hand, I glanced at the toll taker. What do you look like, Vic?"

"I'm about thirty-five, with brown hair and brown eyes."

"Do you have a nice body?"

"It's not much," Vic said softly.

"Oh, I'll bet it is. I'll bet you have nice shoulders, just like the toll taker. I remember him. He had great shoulders. Do you have good hands?"

"I never thought about it. I guess I do."

"Wonderful. Just like him. So each evening, I drove home the same way. About a week later, I found myself gazing at the same guy. Brown hair, brown eyes, and great shoulders and hands." She sighed. "Anyway, as he took my quarter, he looked me over and then he squeezed my hand. I smiled at him and pulled away.

"For the next few days, I made sure to be in his lane. Each day, I gave him a better view of my body. I began to deliberately hike up my skirt and pull my blouse open so he could see my low-cut bra."

"You did?"

"Oh yes. I loved it that he liked looking at me. By the end of the third week, I realized that I was wet just thinking about my drive home. I said hello to him each night and he stared down my blouse and said hello too.

"One evening I casually asked him when his shift was over. 'Midnight,' he told me. That was just what I wanted to hear.

"Well, Vic. You'll never guess what I did. The following evening, I had dinner near my office and returned to work. I had a desk full of things that needed my attention so I had no trouble finding enough work to keep me busy until almost eleven. When I could concentrate no longer, I stretched, rubbed the back of my neck, and smiled. I was going to be so bad.

"When I got to my car, the garage was almost empty and the corner I had parked in was not well lit. I glanced around and saw no one so I quickly pulled off my skirt and my half-slip. I glanced down at my sheer black stockings and black garter belt topped by tiny black bikini panties. Can you picture it, Vic?"

"Oh yes. I'll bet you looked sexy."

"I think I did. As I slid into the car I enjoyed the feel of the leather upholstery on the backs of my thighs and the slithery feeling of my soaking cunt. I had put a large silk scarf in the car that morning and now I pulled it across my lap, covering me up to the bottom of my blouse. My show was for only one man.

"It was almost 11:45 when I lowered the top of the car and drove through the warm spring air toward the toll plaza. As I drove up to the booth I could see the familiar face as he stretched to take money from a car in front of me. I unbuttoned my blouse all the way and pulled it open to reveal my black lace half-bra that barely covered my nipples. I moved the scarf over onto the passenger seat and pulled up next to him.

"Distractedly he leaned out to take my toll, but when he saw me, he just stared. It was the most beautiful look I've ever received. His eyes caressed every inch of my skin until I couldn't sit still any longer. Fortunately there were no other cars around so, as he watched, I slipped my hand between my legs and stroked my wet pussy through the thin crotch of my tiny panties. It took only a moment until I came, waves of orgasm engulfing my body. When I calmed and looked at him, I could tell that he wanted to touch me, but his fingers couldn't quite reach."

"Oh, wow. That's fantastic," Vic said.

"That's what he thought too. 'I get off at midnight,' he said. 'Why not save some of that for me?'

"'Where?' I asked.

"Quickly he wrote an address on a piece of paper and handed it to me. I'll wait for you in front of my building at about twelve-fifteen.' "

"Did you go?" Vic asked, his voice hoarse.

"I hadn't decided yet, I guess. Without saying yes or no, I drove away, my quarter and his address in my hand. As soon as I got to an exit, I turned off of the parkway, pulled my car to a stop, and considered. I was still high and hungry. I rubbed my soaked crotch until I came again, but the orgasm was unsatisfying. I needed a cock inside of me, preferably his. I guess I had made the decision before I even left work that night.

"So I buttoned my blouse, wriggled into my skirt as best I could and drove to the address the man had written down. I didn't even know his name, Vic, but I guess I didn't care."

"You actually did it? Met him?"

"I did. He drove up at exactly twelve-fifteen and I got out of my car. 'I don't even know your name,' we said simultaneously.

"I didn't want to tell him my real name so I made one up. 'Mine's Christine,' I said.

"You know," Alice said to Vic. " I just remembered. His name was Vic too."

"Really?" Vic said.

"Oh yes. 'I'm Vic,' he said. 'Come on. I'll let us in.' "

"I know his name wasn't Vic, but I like it this way," the phone voice said. "Go on."

"The apartment was small and inexpensively furnished but I barely got a chance to look around. We got inside and, without waiting, Vic wrapped his arms around me and his lips engulfed my mouth. He tangled his hands in my hair and held my head while his tongue invaded and explored. He pressed his body against mine and I could feel his huge dick pressing against my belly. I wrapped my arms around his neck and surrendered to his kiss.

"His hands roamed my back, pressing my full breasts harder against his chest. It was as though he wanted to pull me inside of his skin.

"I slowly pulled away and looked into Vic's eyes. 'You enjoyed watching me before so let's not change things just yet,' I said."

Alice switched the phone to her other ear. "Vic. Would you like to hear about how I stripped in the story?"

"Oh yes. Very much," he said.

"Well. I unbuttoned his shirt and pressed my toll taker into an easy chair. I ran my hands over his chest, loosened his belt, and unsnapped his jeans. Then I backed away.

"One button at a time, I unfastened my black silk blouse. I watched his eyes. They never left my fingers as I played with my buttons.

"He reached out and tried to rush me but I pushed his hands away. 'This is my show,' I told him. 'Just be patient.'"

It was obvious to Alice that Vic was getting into the tale. "Can you be patient, Vic?"

"I'll be patient," he said into the phone.

"I'm sure you will. My toll taker sat, looked into my eyes and smiled. 'Just don't take too long,' he said. 'I may be able to wait, but I'm not sure about my cock.' "

Alice could hear Vic's warm laugh. "I opened the side button on my skirt and let it fall to the ground. I hadn't put my slip back on, so I could watch him stare at my nylon-encased legs and tiny panties. I slipped my blouse off, dropped it next to my skirt, and watched his eyes as they roamed my body.

"I began to run my hands over my belly and breasts. I stroked my nipples through the satin and lace of my bra. I ran my fingers over the soaked crotch of my panties. I closed my eyes and let my fingertips drift over my skin.

"After a few moments, I pulled my long hair forward, over my shoulders and breasts, then I unhooked my bra and pulled it off. The strands of hair parted only slightly, just enough to allow my erect nipples to protrude."

Alice heard a long-drawn-out sigh and a whispered, "Yes."

"I swayed slightly, enjoying the feel of my hair as it brushed back and forth across my breasts. Suddenly, showing Vic my body wasn't enough. I needed his hands and mouth on me.

"I knelt down in front of Vic's chair, looked up at him and smiled. He reached down, pulled my hair out of the way and took my breasts in his hands.

"His fingers found my hard nipples and he squeezed, tiny pinches that sent shivers up my spine. He pulled me up so my tits were level with his mouth and he licked the hard buds with the tip of his tongue. He swirled his tongue around and flicked it back and forth, wetting and teasing me. He leaned back slightly and blew on my wet skin. The sensation almost made me climax, but I held it back. This wasn't how I wanted to come.

"When I just couldn't wait any longer," Alice said, "I pulled him to his feet and almost ripped off his jeans. He was magnificent naked, with his hard cock beckoning me. I needed him inside me.

"'Take off those panties,' Vic said, 'but leave the rest on. I like you that way.'

"I pulled my panties off as he sat back down in the chair and grabbed my arms. I half dropped, half fell onto his lap, facing him. He lifted me slightly and then drove my body down, impaled on his huge cock."

Alice could hear the rasping sound of Vic's breathing through the phone. She trembled, feeling like the woman in the story. Brazen and able to ask for what she wanted. Able to do anything. "'Yes, fuck me,' I screamed as he penetrated me. 'Fuck me hard.'

"He wrapped his hands around my waist and rhythmically lifted and dropped me. My knees were buried in the deep chair cushions, my hands held his hair. He pounded inside of me until we both came, screaming."

Suddenly there was a loud gasp through the phone, then an, "Oh, shit."

"Is anything wrong, Vic?" Alice said.

"No. Not really. I just don't like to come so fast."

There was a long pause during which Alice couldn't stop grinning. She had done it. She had made a man come just from her words. *I really am hot stuff.*

"Did you ever see him again?"

"We met at his place occasionally for a night of hot sex but eventually he moved to the west coast."

"That was wonderful. Sheherazade, can I call you again next week? Please. Can you tell me more about your history?" He paused. "I know they're just stories, but I want to hear more."

"Of course. I'd love to tell you lots of tales about my past. Is there any kind of story you'd particularly like to hear?"

"Oh, no. I'll let you pick. And thanks."

"I'm glad you called and I'll look forward to hearing from you next week, at the same time."

She heard Vic hang up, and Alice dropped on the bed, pounded her fists, and kicked her heels. "Yes!" she yelled. "Yes!"

A half an hour later, the phone rang again. "Vic was delighted," Velvet said without preamble. "He said you were just the right kind of a slut for him." When Alice gasped, Velvet continued, "He meant it as a compliment. He loved hearing about your supposed lurid past." She chuckled. "I gather you took my advice and moved into first person."

"Did he really believe I had done what I told him in the story?"

"Probably not, but who knows, and who cares. He loved what you said and wants to call you again next week, and that's the only testimonial I care about. I've got a few more men I can recommend. How about Monday evening? I think I can set up two or three, starting at about eight. Would that work?"

"Would it? That would be terrific."

Velvet took a few minutes to tell Alice about the men she had in mind. "I'll call you over the weekend and make it official. Welcome to the family."

"Thanks."

After she hung up with Velvet, Alice called Sue. After a few pleasantries and the news that her mother was essentially unchanged, Alice said, "If Rutlandt calls, tell them yes."

"You got the job?" Sue shrieked. "That's great. I hope you aren't taking on too much."

"Not at all," Alice said, hating to deceive her sister. "I'm really going to enjoy what I'll be doing."

"That's fantastic. I'll call Rutlandt tomorrow and tell them that we're a go whenever they have a room. They said last Friday that they thought there'd be something this week."

The following Monday evening, a man named Scott called for a story. Velvet had told Alice that he would probably like a story about a man being educated by older women. Alice had decided that he'd want it told from the boy's point of view so over the weekend she had given a lot of thought to how to pull it off. Finally, Sunday evening she had had an idea, so after she and Scott had chatted for a few minutes, Alice said, "You know, Velvet said you might like to hear about my brother. He had an experience, well, he was very naughty. He told me in confidence but I don't think he'd mind if I told you."

"Really? Tell me."

"I have to tell you that Carter, that's my brother, wasn't very knowledgeable at all. My family was extremely protective and he had been more sheltered than most boys. He was also rather unattractive and painfully shy. He was just eighteen years old and a senior in high school when his first time happened, and it happened on a snowy winter weekend. He used to shovel driveways to earn extra money.

"He had already done two that afternoon so he was really exhausted. His last driveway was owned by a female customer who was unmarried and quite well to do. Let's call her Mrs. Jones. This particular afternoon, she invited him in and asked him to sit down and have something to eat. 'Lord knows your parents don't seem to feed you, so someone should,' she said.

"He was wet and shivering as he sat down at the table in her kitchen. 'They feed me, but I'm always hungry,' he said.

"'Carter, your clothes are wet and you're chilled straight through. Why don't you take off those wet things? I'll put them in the dryer and you can wrap yourself in this big towel.' She handed him a tremendous bath towel and hustled him into the bathroom."

Alice dropped her voice to a slight whisper. "We know he shouldn't have taken off all his clothes, but he was so naive."

"Maybe he wasn't," Scott said. "Maybe he knew exactly what was going to happen."

"You know, maybe he did," Alice said. "So anyway, when he returned to the kitchen wrapped in the towel, Mrs. Jones said, 'Now isn't that better? I've made you a sandwich and some hot cocoa. It will help to warm you up while I put your things in the dryer.'

"Carter told me that after a few minutes he became really sleepy so Mrs. Jones suggested that he lie down for a bit. She said she'd wake him in a little while when his clothes were dry. He agreed, knowing that he would still have enough daylight to finish shoveling the driveway." Alice paused. "At least that was what he told me."

"I think he was fibbing just a bit."

"I think so too. Mrs. Jones led him to a bedroom and tucked him in under soft blankets. She shut the door and he fell asleep quickly."

Alice grinned. "Carter told me that he really fell asleep. Maybe he was just playing possum. Is that what you would have done, Scott?"

"I might have. Don't stop now, Sheherazade."

"He told me that he had no idea how long he had been asleep when the bed moved beneath him and he woke up. He turned and saw Mrs. Jones laying beside him. He started to get up but she gently pushed him back down and giggled. 'Is this the first time you've been in bed with a woman?' she asked. When he just blushed, she continued, 'You're a virgin? I never suspected.' She smiled at him. 'That's all right,' she said. 'I'm glad that you are.' Her hands parted his towel and slid down his smooth chest." Alice took a deep breath. "Can you picture all this, Scott?"

"Oh yes. I certainly can. Did your brother tell you more?"

"He told me that he started to breathe like he'd been running a race. 'Good,' Mrs. Jones said as she noticed the blankets sticking up below his waist. 'Very good. You won't be a stranger to sex much longer.'

"She parted the sides of her robe and said, 'Now look at me and touch me. Touch me anywhere you want.' He placed his hands on her face and started to caress her. When he tried to touch her large breasts, however, he became scared and froze. She took his hand, pressed it to one breast and said, softly, 'It's okay, Carter. It's really okay.'"

"Oh yes," Scott sighed. "I can see it all."

Alice smiled. "Her breasts were soft and smooth. Then she reached under the towel and gently held his dick in her hand as she started to slowly stroke it. My brother told me that he almost came right then, but he was afraid to.

"Mrs. Jones uncovered herself and removed her robe, all the while stroking his dick first with one hand, then the other. Carter stared at her and felt the heat rise in his face. 'You've never seen a naked woman or a pussy before, have you?'

"'No,' he said, 'I haven't.'

"'Well, just like my breasts, my pussy is soft and warm, but it can also get wet, Carter. All you have to do is touch and stroke it. Touch my pussy. It's okay, really it is.'

"So he touched it. Isn't that what you would have done, Scott?"

"I would have touched her all over."

"I'll bet you would have," Alice said. "My brother touched her pussy and it was soft just like she'd said it would be. 'Now,' Mrs. Jones said, 'take your finger and follow mine.' He watched as she put her finger inside her. Then she removed hers and nudged him, so he slid his finger into her. 'Now, Carter, move your finger back and forth.' He did and then she said, 'Yes. That's right. Keep it going until your finger and my cunt are sopping wet. Then comes the fun part.'

"'Fun part?' he whispered.

"'Yes, Carter. You're going to put your dick into my soft, warm pussy and gently move it back and forth.'

"Carter didn't think a woman like Mrs. Jones would actually let him but when he pulled his wet finger from her pussy, she was so wet. 'Why me?' he asked, puzzled and so excited.

"'I chose you because you're not like the other boys. You're sensitive and quiet. You keep to yourself.' She held his hot, hard dick then touched her pussy with the tip of it. He leaned toward her, dick throbbing so much it almost hurt. He closed his eyes so he could better feel what was happening. 'That's okay, Carter,' she said. 'Just feel.'

"Carter told me that Mrs. Jones's pussy was so warm and wet."

"I'll bet it was," Scott said.

"Mrs. Jones said, 'Your dick feels so good, all firm and warm and young.' She rubbed it over her wet pussy, then said, 'Now, Carter, push it all the way in.' He pushed gently but she said, 'Push harder. *Yesss.*'

"She pulled him so he was lying on top of her, his dick pushed into her cunt. My brother told me that he wanted to move but he didn't know whether he should. Should he, Scott?"

"Oh God, yes. Fuck her senseless, kid."

"Mrs. Jones said, 'Yes, Carter, move. Rock back and forth.'

"'Can I go faster?' he asked."

Scott's voice was hoarse as he said, "Go faster, kid. Fuck her hard."

"'You can,' she said, 'but since this is your first time, try to go slowly. See how nice it feels when you go slowly. We've got a long time.'

"'But your driveway . . .' "

"To hell with the driveway, Carter," Scott said, panting. "Do it."

"'It doesn't matter,' Mrs. Jones said. 'We can stay here as long as you like. Now move gently, slowly in and out.'

"'I gotta . . .' He didn't know what.

"'I know,' Mrs. Jones said. 'That's good, Carter. It means you're going to shoot. You'll lose your cherry and be a real man.' "

"'I'm gonna . . .' He did, didn't he, Scott?"

Alice heard rhythmic rustling noises through the phone. "Is he still fucking her," Scott gasped. "Young studs can come over and over. Tell me he's still fucking her."

"Oh, he is," Alice said. "His ass is pushing, driving his dick into her. He spurted, but he was hard again almost immediately. He just kept fucking her until he spurted again.

"'That was wonderful, Carter,' Mrs. Jones said, 'but now you've got to help me. I can come like that if you lick me.'"

"Oh God, do it, kid. Lick her pussy," Scott said.

"'I don't know how,' he said. He was so tired, but he wanted to do all the things that Mrs. Jones would let him do.

"'Of course you don't,' she said. 'I'll teach you. Now kneel between my legs.' He looked at her pussy, the hair all wet from his come. She smelled sweet and salty. He didn't know what to do but she put her fingers on her pussy. 'Lick here like I'm a piece of candy. Lick everywhere. You'll get the hang of it quickly. I just know you will.'

"He licked until he thought his dick would burst again. 'Can I put it in again?' he asked her.

"'In a minute,' she said, showing him where to lick more. 'And rub right here,' she said, putting her finger on the hard, swollen place. 'Yes,' she said. 'Like that.' And she was breathing hard. 'Yes,' she said again and he felt her body move and wet juice ran from her pussy. 'Now put it in again,' she said and he did. Didn't he, Scott?"

All Alice could hear was harsh breathing, then a shout. She just kept talking, waiting for Scott to tell her to stop.

"'Now, Carter, make me feel it,' Mrs. Jones said. This time Carter wasn't as scared so he could move and rub her at the same time. He thrust in and out, pulling it out and ramming himself in as far as he could. He came quickly but she didn't let him pull out. She held him tightly, rocking against him."

"Wow," Scott said, his breathing slower now. "That was quite a story. Did he go back another day?"

"My brother told me that it was just about dark when he left her house. 'Come back again tomorrow and you can finish all kinds of things,' she called after him. My brother went back lots of times that winter. He got quite an education."

"I'll be he did. Thanks for the story, Sheherazade," Scott said. "Can I call again next week?"

"Of course."

It was going to take a lot of writing time, but this was going to work out just fine. Just fine indeed.

Chapter 7

As the weeks passed Alice's business grew. She now had four steady clients and a few times Velvet had called and asked whether she could take a new customer. She was beginning to think of her income as real. A week earlier the Rutlandt Nursing Home had finally had a vacancy and her mother had been moved there. The older woman seemed happy, spending much of her day in a wheelchair in the sunny solarium with several other older residents.

One Thursday morning, both Alice and Betsy arrived at Dr. Tannenbaum's office early to catch up on some paperwork. As they updated files, Alice said, "Betsy, I have a strange problem that I need to talk to you about. I take these phone calls and that's great. The guys enjoy it and I can usually hear them climax, but it all leaves me a bit frustrated. With Larry away this week, weren't you . . . well, what do you do?"

"For someone who can talk a man to orgasm, you sure have a way with words. Don't you masturbate?"

Alice couldn't get the word out. She talked on the phone about all manner of sexual topics in graphic detail, but she couldn't bring herself to say the word *masturbate* when talking about herself. "No," she said softly.

"Ever?" Betsy said, her eyes wide.

"Not really," Alice whispered.

"Well, you should. The only way to learn about how a woman gets pleasure is to get pleasure yourself." Betsy smiled. "Let me ask you a very blunt question. Have you ever had an orgasm?"

Alice snapped out an answer. "Of course."

"That's what you tell all your other friends. This is me you're talking to. Now, think again. Have you ever had an orgasm?"

Alice sighed. "Okay, okay. You're right. I'm not really sure. Ralph wasn't the best lover that ever was. He was pretty much the stick-it-in-and-wiggle-it-around type."

Betsy guffawed. "You're impossible."

"I know," Alice said, smiling ruefully. "Seriously, all I've ever had was Ralph. I've never been with anyone else."

"Then it's time you found out. Think of it as research. It will make you so much better at entertaining your clients if you know what you're talking about."

"I guess you're right. I've been making up a lot of what I say, using stories and other people's experiences."

"So go home tonight, read a sexy story or make one up in your head and just do it. Touch where it feels good. You certainly know how, in graphic detail."

Alice blushed. "I guess I do."

That evening, Alice had a regular client named Marcus at eight and Vic called at nine. By quarter of ten, she had told two sexy stories, had two men climax on the phone with her, and she was very excited herself. Masturbate. There would never be a better time. *How can I do this?* she wondered. *It feels so awkward and so wrong. It's my body,* she told herself, *and I'm allowed to touch it if I want to. And I want to.*

She stripped out of her clothes, pulled on her Jets T-shirt and climbed between her cool sheets. Her nipples were erect and as she wiggled around in bed, they rubbed erotically against the front of the shirt. As she lay on her back, she placed one palm against her nipple, rubbing the nub against her hand. She pulled her hand back. "Stop being such a sissy," she said aloud. "You can make men quiver but you're embarrassed to touch your own body. It's yours after all." Hesitantly, Alice raised her hand again and rubbed her nipple. Small spikes of pleasure knifed through her body. She rubbed the other, feeling the rockets slice from her breasts to her belly.

She slid her hand beneath the shirt and touched her naked breasts. She played with the nipples, feeling the heady pleasure for the first time. Hands shaking, she reached lower and touched her pubic mound, sliding her fingers through the springy hair.

"Why am I so reluctant to do this?" she asked. She moved her fingers deeper and found the soft flesh that was now so wet. Slowly she explored, her fingers gliding through the thick lubricant. When she touched her swollen clit she felt a jolt of pleasure and, surprised by how strong it was, she touched again. She rubbed and pressed, finding places where the pleasure was greatest, but, although it felt wonderful, she found that no matter how much she stroked, she was unable to get over the precipice to what she knew would be her first real orgasm. She needed something inside of her. She looked furtively at her bedside table, then at the top of her dresser.

"What am I feeling so guilty about?" she asked, climbing out of bed. She opened her top dresser drawer and found an old lipstick. The tube was plastic and, she reasoned, should be the right shape. She grabbed a tissue and rubbed it all over the plastic, removing any dirt then, lipstick tube in hand, she returned to the bed. She rubbed her clit for a moment, then took the tube and stroked it around her wetness. Trembling, she pressed the tube against the opening of her vagina and felt the end slip inside. She held the tube tightly with one hand, and rubbed her clit with the other.

Suddenly she felt a tightening low in her belly and a sort of tickling and twitching in her pussy. It took only a moment for her inner spring to wind tighter, then explode. She gasped, colors whirling behind her closed eyes. Her entire body shook.

She gradually eased her rubbing and then she removed the tube from her cunt. "Holy shit," she said. "So that's what it's all about." Still panting, she wiped off the lipstick tube, then went into the bathroom and dried her pussy. "Holy shit."

For several more nights, after fevered storytelling, Alice touched her body, experimenting and quickly discovering what felt the best.

About a week after her first orgasm, when Betsy arrived, she put a brown envelope in the drawer where Alice kept her purse. "What's that?" Alice asked.

"It's something you need to look at. Call it research."

Alice pulled out the envelope and glanced at the catalog inside. "Shop till you drop," Betsy said as Alice stared at the catalog in her hand. "You need toys to play with to add to your stories."

As Alice turned to the first page of the publication, the outer door opened. She quickly replaced the catalog in the envelope and dropped it back into the drawer. She'd definitely look at it later. She'd seen a dildo that would certainly work better than a lipstick tube. Then turning, she said, "Good morning, Mrs. Grumbacher." She focused on the six-year-old trailing behind the woman. "And Tracey. How are you this morning? Are you ready to have your picture taken with Barney?"

"Only if I have no cavities," the little girl said, her chin pointed at the floor.

"Have you been brushing?"

"Oh yes," she said. "Mommy and Dr. Tannenbaum showed me how."

"Then I'm sure that your teeth will be in great shape."

The little girl smiled. "I think this one's a little loose," she said, pointing to her top tooth.

"Wow. That means you're getting older. We'll just let Dr. Tannenbaum look at it."

Mrs. Grumbacher finished hanging up her coat. "You're so good with her," she said to Alice. "She's always so nervous coming here, despite how nice the doctor is. But she cheers right up for you."

"I'm glad I can help," Alice said.

"You're such a people person."

Right. Oh, the people I deal with. Alice winked at Betsy.

That evening, Velvet called. "Alice," she said, "I have a new client and no one to give him to. You know what Fridays are like. He just wants the standard, not stories or anything. Would you like to give it a try?"

Alice thought about it. She'd been doing very well with her stories. Somehow, telling a story was different from straight phone sex. Less personal, somehow. However Velvet had been so good to her and she really wanted to help, and yet, she didn't want to disappoint anyone either. She took a deep breath. "Sure. I guess."

"Listen. Just roll with it. I've heard a lot about you from a few of your clients and I've gotten several calls from friends of theirs. You'll do fine."

Alice took a deep breath. "I certainly will. Put him through." She hung up and perched on the edge of the bed. It was like flying without a net or without a script. Of course, she often changed her prewritten stories to fit the needs of the man she was talking to and the stories seldom ended where her written material had, but she always had the safety of those pages to fall back on. Now she would be completely on her own.

Moments later the phone rang. She dropped her shoulders and lifted the receiver. "Hello?" she said, softly.

"Hi, Sherry," the voice at the other end of the phone said. "I'm Tim."

"Well, good evening, Tim. Are you feeling horny tonight?"

"That's why I called. I need you."

"Oh, baby," Alice said, "it's nice to be needed. Tell me what you need."

"I need to poke my hard cock into your sweet pussy."

"*Ohhh,*" Alice sighed. "That sounds really good. Are you in a real hurry? I usually like it slow. Would you like to touch me first?"

"Yes. I really would. Do you have big tits?"

Always big tits, Alice thought, considering her medium-size breasts. "Oh yes. I have real trouble finding bras large enough."

"What kind of bra are you wearing right now?" Tim asked.

"What would you like it to be?"

"I like the lacy ones so I can peek at your nipples. Are they big?"

"Yes, of course. Just listening to you has made them really hard. My bra is red, you know. Red satin, with small slits at the point of each cup so my hard nipples can just stick through. Can you see them? Close your eyes and see them reaching for you."

There was a long breath. "Yes. I can see them."

"I'm wearing red panties, too, small ones that barely cover my bush. I'm a redhead," she said, "so my pussy hair's deep auburn."

"Pinch your nipples for me," Tim said. "Make them really hard."

Alice was wearing a beige nylon bra, but she opened her robe and pinched her nipples, already hardening with erotic stimulation. *"Ohhh,"* she squealed. "That's nice." And it was. "Can I touch your cock too? Take off your pants so I can touch your prick."

There was a rustling and the squeak of bedsprings. "Okay. You can touch me."

"I'll touch it, but I'll have to use your hand. Wrap your fingers around it so I can feel how very hard it is."

There was another long sigh. "Are you wearing just your red bra and panties?"

"Well, I have red stockings with lacy tops that come up almost to my pussy, and red high-heeled shoes too."

"Rub the stockings and tell me how it feels."

Alice rubbed the inside of her thigh. "It feels smooth and cool to the touch. I can feel the heat pouring from my pussy too. Are we touching your cock?"

"Yes. I'm going to get some baby oil."

"Oh yes. Do that."

"Will you rub your pussy for me, through those red panties?"

"Will you be peeking? I don't know whether I can touch my pussy with anyone looking."

Tim laughed. "I won't peek, I promise. But I want you to really touch your pussy. Will you really do it for me?"

Alice reached down and touched the crotch of her beige nylon panties, lightly brushing the tip of her clit through the fabric. "Yes, I'm doing it."

"I love the feel of wet pussy," Tim said, "and the smell and the taste."

"How does your cock feel? Is it very hard?"

"It is, but I don't want to spurt until you do. Are you rubbing your pussy?"

"Yes," Alice said, finding to her surprise that she was very aroused. The muffled sensation of her fingers on her flesh, through the nylon, was delicious. "It feels really good and I'm getting really horny."

"Tell me exactly what you're doing and how it feels."

"I'm rubbing my clit through my bright-red panties. It feels hot and really good."

"Slide your fingers under the panties and feel your naked pussy. I want to see you doing that while I rub my cock."

Alice slipped her fingers beneath the waistband of her panties, down through her pubic hair to her sopping cunt. She was so wet. From her few sessions, she knew where to touch so it felt best. "You know, this makes me so hungry for a cock inside of me. What should I do?"

"Get something and fill your snatch. Stuff it full and pretend that it's my big cock."

"I've got a big dildo and I'm putting it into my pussy." Alice propped the phone against her ear, reached for the lipstick tube and pressed in into her pussy. It wasn't enough. She wanted something bigger, something that would really fill her up. Something she could fuck herself with without being afraid of it slipping all the way inside. She flashed on the catalog Betsy had given her, then Tim said, "Is your snatch full?"

"Oh, I wish it were your cock that was filling me up. I'd wrap my legs around your waist and jam that cock deep into my pussy."

"Oh, Sherry," Tim groaned. "I'd drive into you so hard that you'd scream. I'd pound harder and harder."

Alice rubbed her clit through her panties while the lipstick tube rubbed the walls of her pussy. She felt her orgasm building. "You're going to make me come, Tim," she said. "Does your big cock feel good inside of me?"

"I'm fucking you so hard." She heard his rasping breaths and his moans.

"Yes, baby," she said as the orgasm flowed from her pussy to her thighs and her belly. She curled her toes and her breath caught in her throat. "I'm coming. Yes," she gasped.

"Oh, Sherry. I came all over the bed."

"I came too," she said, surprise obvious in her voice.

"That makes it so much better somehow. Thanks, Sherry."

"You're welcome, I'm sure. I hope you'll call again."

"Maybe. My wife's away and I just needed something."

"I hope to hear from you the next time your wife's away."

"Yeah," Tim said, and she heard the click as he hung up the phone. Alice grinned and slowly stood up, pulled off her clothes and climbed between the sheets, naked tonight. As Roger curled up against her side, Alice looked at the blue denim drapes she had made for the bedroom when she and Ralph had first moved into the apartment. "You know, Roger, I think I'll get some new drapes. And maybe a matching bedspread." She reached over, turned off the light and was asleep instantly.

One Thursday morning a few weeks later, Betsy arrived at work. It was the second week in May and everyone was in a great mood. "I've got a plan," she said to Alice. "I called Velvet last night and she's free this evening. Larry's taking the boys to see *Friday the Thirteenth, Part Seventy-six, Jason Runs for Congress*, or something like that, so I'm off the hook too. I thought we'd all have a girls' night out, just the three of us, maybe at Patches. Silly drinks with lots of orange juice, rum, and those little umbrellas. How about it? Got any calls tonight?"

"No. I've settled on Mondays, Wednesdays, and Fridays."

"Great. We're meeting at Patches at seven."

"I really should get down to Rutlandt and see Mom. I haven't been there since the weekend."

"Come on, babe. You need some time for just you. You

work here five days a week, you take calls three nights, you visit your mom each weekend and at least once during the week. Take some time off."

Alice leaned back in her chair. "Maybe it would be all right. God it sounds nice."

"Great. I'm counting on you. Seven at Patches."

At just past seven, Alice arrived at Patches, a restaurant and watering hole at one end of a long enclosed mall. The place was crowded with couples with small children enjoying overstuffed sandwiches and fries, teens sharing secrets and stuffed potato skins, and businessmen in suits and ties downing a few drinks before going home. Servers of both sexes wandered between the tables, dressed in outrageous outfits, tight white T-shirts and black jeans, both covered with squares of brightly patterned fabric.

Alice looked around and found Betsy and Velvet sitting at a small table off to one side. As Alice approached the table, Velvet stood up and embraced her lightly, kissing her on each cheek. "I'm so glad this worked out. I've been meaning to get together with you."

"Yes," Betsy said. "I was afraid you'd changed your mind and gone to visit your mom after all."

"I decided I needed some time out," Alice said as she dropped into a chair. She looked at the tall glasses filled with orange liquid that stood in front of each woman. "What are those?"

"Those," Velvet said, "are Bahama Mamas: rum, pineapple juice, coconut liqueur, and heaven knows what else. They are delicious." She lifted her glass and took a long drink through the straw.

Their waitress arrived and Alice considered ordering a diet soda, then changed her mind. "I'll have one of those," she said, pointing to the tall golden drinks.

"One Bahama Mama," the waitress said, scribbling on her order pad. "Any munchies for you ladies? The buffalo wings are terrific tonight and so are the skins."

Betsy tipped her head to one side, then said, "Why not? One of each. We only live once and to hell with the calories."

"I'll bring them right over."

Velvet leaned toward Alice. "You are really quite something," she said. "You've taken to this so quickly. The men I talk to when I route the calls rave about you. They feel they know you personally, particularly about all your daring exploits."

Alice grinned. "Thanks. It's really gotten to be fun."

"Betsy's an old hand at this, so I don't have to tell her how terrific she is now," Velvet said, patting Betsy on the hand, "but she took several months to get into the swing of it all. You've developed quite a following in the few weeks you've been doing it."

"I like my guys," Alice said. "They are really nice people. There are a few losers, of course, but most of them are just lonely men who want a warm voice with a lurid story to tell. I fit the bill."

"The men really surprised me when I first started working the phone," Betsy said. "I expected maniacs, kinky guys who wanted bizarre stuff with lots of sweaty sex but most of them are just ordinary men who want bizarre stuff and lots of sweaty sex."

The three women laughed, all sharing the same feelings. "How did you get time off this evening?" Alice asked Velvet.

"I've got another woman working the routing tonight. She's been doing it a few nights a week and it's great for me to get some time off."

The three women talked for an hour, sipping several rounds of drinks and munching on wings and skins. "Has he got the greatest buns or what?" Betsy said, gazing at one of the waiters who walked past them in his almost obscenely tight jeans.

Alice looked at the young man and sighed. "He's got a

really great body. Remember that bulge in the front of Mr. Hollingsworth's pants?"

"Who could forget?" Betsy told Velvet about their high school social studies teacher.

"Maybe I'll use him in one of my stories," Alice said. "High school teacher and unruly student."

"How about him?" Velvet said, indicating a man sitting in the corner, watching the people and sipping a glass of red wine. "That's my style."

Alice turned and looked at the man Velvet had indicated. He was in his mid-thirties, with long black hair caught in a thin, black leather thong at the base of his neck. He wore a tight black turtleneck shirt and black trousers. "There's something both attractively compelling and dangerous about him," Velvet said. "That's the stuff of my fantasies."

"Umm. I love a little danger," Betsy said.

"I'd love a little anything," Alice said, then slammed her mouth shut.

Betsy turned to her. "What does that mean?"

"Sorry. Just my big mouth and one too many Bahama Mamas. It's nothing."

"No, it's not nothing. Don't tell me you've finally decided that it's time to get out into the world." Betsy leaned toward Velvet. "She hasn't really dated since her husband split on her."

"I have too. You've set me up with lots of guys."

"Yeah. Right. You meet them at my house, have maybe one date, then nothing."

"You're kidding," Velvet said. "I would have thought you had a rich and varied dating life, from what your fans tell me."

"My fans. Guys who have no clue who I am. They all think I'm some kind of swinger with an exotic past and a spectacular future." Alice realized that she was just a bit tipsy and willing to talk about her lack of a social life. "I'm starting to think I've missed the boat. You two are married, you've got kids. Me? I play on the phone three nights a week and otherwise, nothing."

"So why don't you do something about it?"

"Like what?" Alice sipped her drink to keep the slight buzz that was allowing her to talk about herself so freely.

"Like date," Velvet said.

"Excuse me. I don't seem to see the line of nice guys queuing up to take me out. I don't know a soul except you two and the guys on the phone, and I couldn't consider them as date material."

"Why not?" Betsy chimed in. "You just finished saying that most of them are really just nice, lonely guys. Haven't any of them asked to meet you in person?"

Alice thought about Vic, her first and steadiest client. "Sure. Remember Vic, Velvet? The first guy you put me on with? He's a decent guy, lonely and alone. At least that's what he tells me. He asks me out almost every time we talk."

"So?" the two other women said in unison. "Does he live around here?"

"He lives in the city, but get real. He thinks I'm a sexual sophisticate, with blond hair and big. . ." She looked down at the front of her green blouse. "Anyway. He has no clue what Alice is like. He likes Sheherazade." She lowered to her phone voice. "Woman of the world."

"So meet some businessman who doesn't know you from Eve," Betsy said. "Go out. Have a blast."

"Where would you suggest I meet this Mr. Business? I'm not the type to sit at a bar and wait for some guy to ask me what my sign is."

Velvet sipped her drink. "I've got several single male friends, one in particular I think you'd like. If you wouldn't object, I could introduce you. I'd give him your phone number."

Alice giggled. "You're pretty good at occupying my phone."

"So," Betsy added, "why don't you let one of your phone friends take you out. What have you got to lose?"

"A client," Alice said.

"Bullshit," Velvet said. "You could have more clients than you know what to do with. Pick one who sounds nice and go for it."

"These guys will expect Sheherazade, not Alice."

"Next time someone asks you out, take some time and tell him who you are." Velvet continued, "Call him off-line and just talk."

"I couldn't do that. He'd never believe me again."

"I'm sure that only a few of the men believe you now," Velvet said. "You don't think that these guys think you've actually done all the things you tell them about, do you? They're into the fantasy. They close their eyes and live those experiences with you. They know you're making it all up but it just doesn't matter."

"Like this Vic," Betsy said. "Let him learn who the real you is and he won't be nearly as surprised as you think."

Alice giggled. "Are you two ganging up on me?"

"Yes, we are," Betsy said. "I've been trying to get you out of your shell for years. Now that I've got the chance, I'm using all the help I can get." She reached across the table and, with an exaggerated movement, shook Velvet's hand. "This is a campaign to get Alice out into the big, wide world. Right, general?"

"Right, admiral," Velvet said. "And you, private, are taking orders. Do it. Soon."

"Private," Alice said, laughing. "I'm about the most public private that ever was."

Later that night, Alice crawled into bed beside Roger. "What do you think, cat?" she said. "Are Betsy and Velvet right? Am I still the spinster type despite Sheherazade?"

Roger rolled over and allowed Alice to scratch his belly. "Right. You agree with them. Well, if the opportunity presents itself, maybe . . . I'll think about it."

Merrow.

Chapter 8

The following Monday evening, Vic called. "Hi, Sherry," he said. "Got a story for me tonight?"

"Sure thing, sweet cheeks," Alice said in her Sheherazade voice. "It's about a night when I was very naughty."

"Tell me."

"Well, you know I was married a long time ago."

"Yes. I remember."

"Well it happened back then." She thought about the story she had written about a game of strip poker. She couldn't think of Ralph ever playing like this so she decided to rename her husband. "Ted and I had met this other couple, Barb and Andy, the day after they moved in next door to us. Nice folks and we hit it off right away. It hadn't hurt that Andy was quite a hunk. He wasn't actually gorgeous, but he had great eyes and the best pair of buns I had ever seen."

"Women always like buns, don't they?"

"Actually, what appeals to me now is a nice personality and

a good sense of humor, but back then I was really into looks."

"I think I've got good buns, but only a woman would know for sure."

"I'll bet you have great buns, Vic." Alice was amazed. She was actually flirting with Vic. Back to work.

"The four of us had found ourselves meeting often beside the pool in the center of the condo complex. Friday evenings we were all tired from work and sat in the water, talking about everything from our jobs to television to sports to religion, politics and, of course, sex. As the summer wore on, we started to bring potluck suppers out to the pool area. As fall approached and we had to give up the pool, we started to alternate Friday dinners at each other's houses, and eventually Ted and I succumbed to Barb and Andy's shared love of poker.

"It started with matchsticks, then chips, and eventually we began to play for small change. We won and lost a few dollars and we put the winnings into a kitty to take us all out to an expensive restaurant."

"I like an occasional game of poker but I'm not very good," Vic said. "I can't bluff worth a damn. You can tell exactly what I'm thinking by just looking at my face."

"Me too. I'm hopeless."

"That's good. Go on with the story."

"Well, one night Barb had lost five dollars, the maximum amount allowed by our house rules. 'Okay,' she said, as Ted raked in the pile of coins from the center of the table, 'I'm tapped.' She wiggled her eyebrows. 'What shall I wager now?'

"I just stared. Her suggestion was obvious but I thought that she must be teasing. 'I'll ante for you,' I said, pushing a nickel into the center of the table."

"You were really embarrassed?" Vic asked.

"Yeah, I was." Alice smiled. "I wasn't always the sexually sophisticated woman I am now."

Softly, Vic asked, "Are you really so sophisticated or just a good storyteller?"

Alice gasped. Did he know her that well? Without answering, she continued her story. "Barb thanked me but looked a bit disappointed.

"'Rats,' my husband said. 'I was hoping for something better.' I playfully slapped him on the back of the hand. 'Not a chance, buster.'

"He laughed. 'Rats, I say again.'

"Andy, Barb's husband, dealt seven-card stud. In deference to Barb, the betting was small and we allowed her to stay in despite her continued losses. Soon she had a small pile of coins in front of her to keep track of her indebtedness. 'I'll bet a nickel. I'll win this one for sure,' she said, grinning at her cards. 'Whatever would I do if I lost?'

"'Call,' Ted said.

"'I'll call too,' I said, hoping that Barb would win and the game could continue without the double meanings that seemed to pepper the conversation now. I was really embarrassed.

"Andy called and said, 'Time to show what you've got—cards, that is.'

"'Full boat, tens over threes,' Ted said. I was sure my husband had won and confused as to what would happen then. Andy and I turned our cards face down, signaling that we couldn't beat Ted's hand. 'And you, my indebted friend?' Ted said.

"'Shit,' Barb hissed, 'I really thought I had you. I have a flush, queen high.'

"'Phew,' Andy said. 'I haven't had a hand as good as either of those all night. Ted, since you're the winner, you get to decide Barb's payment.'"

"What did he ask for?" Vic asked.

"He asked her to take off her blouse. I was shocked at my husband, but I said nothing. I was sure that Barb would be insulted and I was afraid that our wonderful Friday evenings were suddenly gone. I'll have to admit, Vic, that I was also aroused."

"I'll bet," Vic said.

"'You've got it,' Barb said, and with little hesitation, she unbuttoned her shirt and pulled it off. I kept my gaze on the coins in front of me, then slowly raised my eyes. Barb was an average-looking woman with a nice figure, shoulder-length brown hair, and green eyes covered with glasses. As I looked up, I saw her medium-size breasts, now covered only by a wispy bit of white lace. I swallowed hard, then glanced at Ted. He was looking at Barb's body, but I felt his fingers link with mine. He glanced at me and squeezed my hand.

"'I love those sexy things my wife wears,' Andy said, 'don't you?'

"'I guess,' I said. Actually Barb wasn't wearing much less than she often wore at the pool but this was so much more intimate. I could see the outline of her nipples through the sheer fabric and I was sure that the men could too.

"Andy reached over and rubbed his palm over the tips of Barb's breasts. 'God, she has great tits.' I watched Andy's hand, unable to look away.

"'Okay, that's enough,' Barb quipped. 'Let's deal.'

"It was my turn to deal and, with shaking hands, I picked up the cards and shuffled, staring at the table. 'Hey, Sherry,' Barb said, placing her hand over mine, 'I didn't mean to embarrass you. I'm really sorry. I wouldn't hurt you for the world.' She reached for her shirt and stuffed one arm into a sleeve.

"'Of course not,' the men said.

"I sighed. 'I guess I'm just a bit more of a prude than you all are.'

"'Not in bed you're not,' my husband said. 'This woman's a wildcat under the right circumstances.'

"I could feel the heat rise in my face. I loved good hot sex, but up till then I had been very private about it. Yet here my husband was, telling everyone. He was such a beast. Or was he? Was there any reason to be so afraid to let anyone know that I enjoyed good lovemaking?"

"No reason at all," Vic purred. "Do you enjoy good lovemaking now, Sherry?"

Suddenly breathless, Alice said, "Yes. I guess so."

"Do you get enough?"

"Let's get back to the story. Okay?"

"Sure," Vic said, but Alice thought she heard reluctance in his voice. "Tell me more."

"Well, I was chagrined. I wasn't a prude and I knew I had to lighten up. These were my best friends. 'Listen,' I said, 'leave the shirt off. You lost fair and square. But you'll win this hand for sure.'

"Barb did win that hand and a few more and by the end of the evening, everything was the same as it had been. After Barb and Andy were gone, I found that the thought of Barb without her shirt had me terribly turned on. Ted and I cavorted on the bed for almost an hour. Finally we lay side by side, hands clasped, our breathing slowing. 'You found that bit with Barb's blouse a turn-on, didn't you?' Ted asked.

"I thought about the answer for a minute, then said, 'I didn't think so at the time, but I guess I did. The sight of her in that bra and watching Andy's hand rubbing her made me hot.'

"'Yeah, me too,' Ted said. 'Not the sight of her tits, but watching Andy touch her. God, it made me hard as stone. It's not personal, you understand,' he continued. 'It doesn't mean I love you any less.'

"'I know that,' I said, and I did know that. I knew he loved me, but the sight of a half-naked body was a turn-on. Nothing more was said, but I lay awake for quite a while that evening.

"The following week we were at Andy and Barb's house and after dinner we moved to the card table. As the play began, Ted cleared his throat and broached the topic we were all a bit afraid of. 'I say that we cut the maximum loss to a dollar. I liked what happened last week when Barb got tapped out.'

"'I have to say that sex was great that night,' Andy said. 'Watching my wife revealed for all to see made me really hot.'

"'Dollar losses?' Ted said. He looked at me. 'Okay, babe?'

"I found my head nodding. Soon I was down my limit and then some. 'Shirt please,' Andy said."

"Could you do it?" Vic asked. "I mean just like that?"

"I didn't think about it, I just did it."

"I'll bet you have a great body."

Alice sighed. "I guess every woman wishes she had a better one."

"Every man too. Go on with your story."

"I had worn my sexiest black lace bra under my sweatshirt. I guess I had known what would happen and the whole idea really turned me on. 'God,' Andy said, 'you've got a great body.' I never thought of myself as having a good shape, but, as my face got hotter I looked at Andy. He had the most wonderful look in his eyes.

"Over the next half hour, Barb was clearly the big winner and had almost all the coins in front of her. I had almost become used to sitting at the table in only my bra. When Andy was tapped, Barb said, 'Listen, losing shirts isn't as revealing for you guys as it is for us. I demand your jeans.' I remember thinking, *God, she is a daring one.*

"I swallowed, wondering whether I would get to see those gorgeous buns covered only by a pair of shorts. Andy agreed and quickly removed his jeans. He was wearing the smallest pair of briefs I had ever seen and they barely covered the bulge caused by his obvious erection. As he sat down, he said, 'As you can obviously tell, this has gone a bit further than before. Let me be honest with you two. Barb and I have been talking. Before we moved here, we had a pair of friends and we all used to play together on occasion. No one actually did it with anyone else's husband or wife, but there was a lot of fooling around and a few times we each made love with the other couple watching. It was a great turn-on.'

"I remember how shocked I was. 'You didn't,' I said, horrified yet also soaking wet.

"'Yes, we did,' Barb said. 'We never actually swapped, but it was so hot to play and to watch. We touched one another with hands and mouth and it was incredibly exciting. We wouldn't jeopardize our friendship by asking anything you two weren't willing to do but that bra you're wearing, Sherry, says a lot.'

"'It does?' I said, trying not to sound anxious. My mouth was dry and my hands trembled.

"'I think you wore it on purpose, hoping this would happen,' Barb said.

"Ted grinned at me. 'That's what I thought when I saw you dressing, and that's why I suggested what I did.' "

"Did you 'fess up, Sherry?" Vic asked. "Had you done it on purpose?"

Alice chuckled as she looked at the story she had written. "I admitted it."

"'Have you ever played with another couple before?' Barb asked.

"'Never,' Ted said. 'We'd never even considered it until last Friday night. After you guys left we had some of the hottest sex I can remember, and I must admit that I was thinking about the sight of your body and of Andy touching you.'

"'Me too,' I whispered.

"Andy stood up and quickly slipped Barb's sweater over her head, revealing another tiny bra and her gorgeous breasts. 'Let's all get more comfortable,' he suggested, removing his sweatshirt, shoes, and socks. Barb stood, slipped out of her shoes and pulled off her jeans. She was wearing a pair of bikini panties that barely covered her mound. Ted took a deep breath, and said to me, 'Babe? Is this all right with you? If it's not we can stop now.'"

"Was it okay with you?" Vic asked, clearly excited by the picture Alice was painting.

"In answer, I stood up and pulled off my jeans. Like Barb I had worn a pair of tiny bikini panties.

"'You really are gorgeous,' Andy said. I knew better. I had a not-bad body with a little extra flesh here and there, but the look on Andy's face said that he thought I was wonderful and that made my knees turn to jelly.

"My husband was the last to strip. When he was finally down to a pair of tight briefs, I stared, then giggled. 'Those are new. I'll bet you bought those special, thinking something like this might happen.'

"'Busted,' he said. 'Last Friday made me so hot, I was just hoping.' Suddenly everyone was laughing, and moving into the living room. Standing in the middle of the room, Ted placed his lips against mine and kissed me long and deeply. His hands roamed over my back, cupped my ass, and caressed my calves. Calves? My eyes sprung open. Andy sat at my feet, his hands stroking my legs. At first I stiffened, but then I relaxed and enjoyed the feeling of someone else's hands on my body. Slowly his hands slid to the fronts of my thighs, then quieted. 'I can feel you tremble,' he said softly. 'Are you afraid? Has this gone too far?'

"'No,' I whispered. 'It all feels good.'"

"I wish I had been there," Vic said. "I'd love to touch you."

"I wish you had been too," Alice said, realizing that as she told the story, she thought about Vic. "So Barb moved behind Ted, her palms flat on his upper back. Then she turned my husband so he was facing her and she gazed into my eyes. 'If this bothers you,' she said to me, 'I'll stop.' When I didn't say anything, she slipped her arms around Ted's neck and pressed her lips against his.

"*I should make them stop,* I remember saying to myself.

Another woman's kissing my husband. But it was so sexy. As I watched, Barb rubbed her lace-covered breasts over Ted's chest. *Funny,* I said to myself, *I'm not really jealous. It's really erotic watching my husband enjoy what's happening.* And he was. His arms were around Barb and he was kissing her with the same mouth that had just been against my lips and it was all right. I knew that this wasn't going to go too far, and I could call it off at any time. But I didn't want to.

"Suddenly Andy's hands were on my naked belly, stroking, caressing, kneading. He stood up and his hands slid to my ribs. 'May I? I want so much to touch you.'"

Alice could hear Vic groan.

"I looked into his deep brown eyes, smiled, and touched his face. 'Yes,' I whispered. 'It really is all right.'

"His hands were on my breasts, cupping me, feeling the weight of my tits in his palms. His fingers found my nipples through the silky fabric and he pinched. 'Oh God,' I said as my eyes closed and my knees buckled."

"Oh God," Vic moaned.

"Quickly Andy guided me to the sofa. As I lay back on the soft material, I knew that nothing else mattered but hands and mouths and satisfying the rising tide of heat. Andy crouched between my spread thighs and his mouth found my nipples. Then his teeth. That had always been my downfall. The slight pain on my nipples drove me crazy. I held his head as he nipped and nibbled, moisture flowing between my legs, soaking the crotch of my panties. I ran my fingers through his curly hair, so unlike Ted's straight soft hair. This wasn't my husband, but it was so good.

"Suddenly there was a mouth on my other breast. My eyes flew open and I saw Ted's head bent over me. I had a mouth on each breast and Barb stood behind, stroking each man's back.

"Ted unsnapped the front hook of my bra and now

mouths engulfed naked nipples. Sharp teeth. Pinching fingers. A hand stroked me between my thighs. Ted's? Andy's? I found I didn't want to know so I closed my eyes.

"Fingers rubbed through the silk of my panties. My clit swelled to press against those hands. Fingers slipped under the edge of my panties and found my wetness. Fingers slowly found my center and one penetrated just a tiny bit. Not enough, my body cried as I thrust my hips upward. Fill me.

"Hands removed my panties and still my eyes remained closed. I wanted to imagine that they were Andy's fingers, not my husband's. Then the fingers filled me, first one, then two, then three, filling my emptiness. I drove my hips upward, forcing the fingers to fill me more deeply. I had to know.

"I opened my eyes. Ted was on his hands and knees, his head bent over my breast. Barb had one hand on the small of his back, the other obviously rubbing him between his thighs. Andy was between my legs, one hand buried in my pussy, the other stroking his now-naked cock."

"I'm going to come, Sherry," Vic cried.

Alice knew that the best way for him to get off was for her to continue the story. "Then Andy's mouth found my clit, his tongue ceaseless in its exploration, his fingers still filling me. It was too much and I came. Waves and waves of molten heat washed over me and I heard myself screaming. As I climaxed, Andy straightened and I watched a stream of come arch from his cock onto my belly. As I calmed, Ted and Barb pulled off their remaining clothing and Barb lay on the carpet. Ted bent between her legs and pressed his mouth over her clit.

"I was now almost unconscious on the couch so Andy slid to the floor and sat beside me. He reached out, laid a hand on his wife's arm and spoke softly to me. 'You've never felt anything like touching your husband while he makes love like this. Touch him.'

"Hesitantly I reached out and placed my hand on my

husband's back. I could feel the movements of his body as he licked Barb's pussy. 'If you're up to it,' Andy whispered, 'come here and touch him right.' He pulled my hand and, although I was exhausted from my own climax, I moved onto the floor until I could reach between his thighs and place my hand on Ted's cock. He was hard and hot and so smooth. I squeezed and felt his entire body tighten.

"I smiled and stroked him the way I knew he liked as I watched his head bob between Barb's thighs. I rubbed and squeezed until I knew he was getting close. I kept him there, on the edge of climax until I heard Barb scream, then I took one finger and scratched the special spot between his ass and his balls. He came, his come spurting onto Barb's thigh."

"Oh God, yes," Vic cried, his voice relaxing.

"Except for the sound of heavy breathing, the room was silent for a while. Then Ted said, 'I need a shower. Do you think there's room for four?' "

"Oh, Sherry," Vic said, his breathing slowing, "that was wonderful."

"I'm glad you enjoyed my story. It happened a long time ago."

"Did it really happen?"

"Of course."

Vic's voice got serious. "Really? Sherry, tell me about you. Are you really the woman you seem to be?"

Alice hesitated. She really liked Vic. Although she hardly knew him, she sensed that he was really lonely. "Some parts of me are, some aren't."

"We've been teasing for weeks. I ask you out and you change the subject. Let me ask again. I already know that we only live about fifty miles apart. So how about meeting me for dinner some evening? I could come up from the city and we could meet somewhere in Westchester."

"I'm not the woman you think I am, you know."

"I don't know what I think you are but I'll bet you don't

look at all like the picture I have of you."

"Not at all."

"Long blond hair? Blue eyes?"

"Brown curly hair, brown eyes. About five-three."

"Are you married? Living with someone?"

"No. I'm alone." Why had she said it quite that way?

"Listen. I've been calling sex lines for a long time and somehow you and I have some things in common. You sound like a nice person and maybe a bit lonely like me. I know a nice informal restaurant in northern Westchester." He mentioned a place called Donovan's in Mount Kisco, a twenty-minute drive from her house.

"I know the place."

"What nights do you work?"

"Mondays, Wednesdays, and Fridays."

"Okay. Saturday sounds too much like a date and this isn't. Just two friends meeting for dinner. Let's make it next Tuesday. I'll be at Donovan's at seven. I'll get a table and sit with a copy of Shakespeare's sonnets. It's hokey, but who else would have such a book. I'm thirty-eight and not much to look at so you might see me and decide to run for the hills." His laugh was self-deprecating, but warm. "I'll wait until seven-thirty, then order dinner and eat slowly. Please come."

He was so sweet and thoughtful. "I don't know."

"I don't either. I'll just hope. Okay?"

"Okay, but don't expect anything. I might not be there."

"I know. Good night, Sherry. Oh. Is that your real name?"

Alice sighed. "It's Alice. Alice Waterman. And I'm thirty-two and not much to look at either."

"Nice to meet you, Alice. I'm Vic Sanderson."

The following Thursday evening the three women met again at Patches for girls' night out. Besides Betsy, Alice had never had a good female friend and the more time she spent with Velvet, the more comfortable and the closer she felt.

The three women had arrived at six-thirty and had decided to try Caribbean Romances: pineapple juice, orange juice, rum, and amaretto. After one drink and lots of small talk, Alice broached the topic that had been troubling her since her conversation with Vic.

"I've got a problem," she said without preamble. "Vic asked me out again."

"And?"

"And I don't know what to do."

"What do you want to do?" Velvet asked.

Alice chuckled. "It depends on what time of day you ask. Sometimes I tell myself that he's a lonely, sensitive man who seems to like me. The rest of the time I think he's a man who has no clue who I am and who likes to call phone-sex lines."

"Did you make a date?"

Alice filled them in on Vic's arrangement. "Sounds sensible," Velvet said, understanding that Alice didn't want a flip answer. "Each of you has a car so you have a way out if it all goes wrong. No one knows enough about the other to be troublesome. It sounds like a good plan to me."

"I guess he must have given it quite a bit of thought," Alice admitted.

"He's obviously been planning this for quite a while," Velvet added.

"Okay," Betsy said, "let's look at this seriously. What's the downside?"

Alice considered. "He's expecting Sherry, girl sexpot. Someone who's been with everyone and done everything. And what will he get? Me."

"Do you think he wants sex with you? Right there in Donovan's?"

"No, of course not."

"Right. You'll just talk, have a nice dinner, and get to know each other. I repeat, what's the downside?"

Alice smiled ruefully. "I don't know. It just so embarrassing to have to admit that I'm not what he thinks I am."

Velvet leaned forward. "You know he doesn't believe all that sexy stuff you tell him over the phone. He knows you're not Sheherazade. Maybe he wouldn't be interested if he thought you were."

"What do you mean?"

"He's a small, lonely man who's probably never actually made love to a woman like Sherry. Maybe the idea of dating her would scare him to death. It would be like making love to some porn star, a constant judge of his technique."

"She's right, you know," Betsy said. "Most of the men I talk to aren't the worldly type who would enjoy being with the woman I pretend to be. They'd probably enjoy fucking my brains out as long as they didn't have to watch my eyes or talk to me afterward." She paused. "I'm probably pretty threatening. Maybe if they could say, 'Down on your knees, bitch,' then make me disappear."

"I never thought of it that way," Alice said.

"I don't know," Velvet said. "I've never dated any of my clients, but then I've been married the entire time and I wouldn't have even considered it."

"So we're back to the question of what's the downside," Betsy said.

Alice grinned. "I don't know. Maybe there isn't one." With two Caribbean Romances making her feel a bit mellow, Alice had to admit that if she showed up at Donovan's the following Tuesday, she had very little to lose.

Chapter 9

Alice was almost useless at Dr. Tannenbaum's office on Tuesday. At unexpected moments she'd drift off into a fantasy about her dinner date with Vic. In one, she walked into the restaurant and was greeted by a hunky guy dressed in a tuxedo, and in another he was dressed in a gorilla suit. In another dream, they sat, had dinner, and then Vic asked her to climb under that table and suck his cock. None of the dreams left her feeling comfortable.

"So what are you going to wear?" Betsy said, dropping into a chair in the reception area.

"Huh?" Alice said, returning from a vision of the two of them in a heart-shaped, vibrating bed.

"Tonight. What are you wearing?"

"I've decided not to go."

"You're crazy. At least go to Donovan's and see what he looks like. If he scares the daylights out of you, turn around, and walk out. Give it a chance."

"Why? He'll just be disappointed and I'll feel terrible."

"Both Velvet and I tried to convince you that he won't be disappointed. I think he's very perceptive to be able to see the wonderful woman you are. I'm sure it comes through in your stories. You're always considerate and thoughtful and you're such a caring person."

"Thanks for that. This whole thing's making me crazy."

"Okay. Here's what you do. Go home after work, put on those new gray linen slacks and your soft mauve silk blouse, the one you bought a few weeks ago at Macy's."

"I don't know."

"I do. Wear a pair of chunky silver earrings and that silver chain with the disk at the end." Betsy stopped to think. "Let's see. I've got the rest. Your deep burgundy wool vest in case it's chilly, and your trench coat. See? Nothing more to think about."

"But . . ."

"Enough of the buts. Just do it because Betsy says so. End of thought."

"Yes, Betsy," Alice said in a little-girl voice.

"That's a good girl," Betsy said, smiling. "You only have to walk into Donovan's and look. Then I give you permission to turn around and walk out. Okay?"

"Okay. I'll do it."

"We'll meet for lunch tomorrow so I can hear everything, good or bad."

After she and Betsy arranged their lunch, Alice hurried home from work, both exhilarated and terrified. She showered and dressed as Betsy had suggested and at seven-ten she was parked in the lot at Donovan's. She got out of her car and approached the green and white striped awning. The restaurant was American-style, the entire place decorated to resemble someone's patio, with white walls, white slatted wood tables, green and white striped chairs, table cloths, and napkins. At first look, it was blinding and it felt like being inside of a lime candy cane but it was all softened by the dozens of green plants that filled white pots throughout the dining room. The restaurant was extremely popular with well-priced dishes and a list of specials that took up half of one wall.

As she wandered toward the host, a woman offered to take her coat. "No thanks. I might not be staying." She stood at the entrance to the huge dining room and looked around. She saw a few single men, but finally her eyes rested upon a middle-aged man with a copy of Shakespeare on the table in front of him. He had shaggy brown hair, deep brown eyes, and deep laugh lines around his mouth. Alice saw that his ears were oversized, which was probably why he wore his hair long. She smiled. *He looks like a basset hound,* she thought, *comfortable somehow.* She squared her shoulders and walked into the room. The host approached and asked whether she needed a table. "No thanks, I'm meeting someone."

Vic caught her eye and when she nodded, his face lit up. He stood as she neared his table and quickly the host pulled out a chair for her. Vic was several inches taller than she was, maybe five foot eight or nine. "I'm so glad you could come," Vic said. He extended his hand and she took it briefly. His palm was warm and a bit damp, his hands soft.

"I almost didn't," Alice said, releasing his hand and settling in her chair.

"If you want the truth, I almost didn't show up either."

"How come?" Alice asked, handing her coat to the host. "Could you put this in the checkroom for me?" she asked him. She'd stay for a while at least.

"Of course," the host said, bustling away.

"All day I had these visions of you," Vic admitted, "looking like one of those Baywatch women with long legs and a big bosom. You'd take one look at me and run for the hills."

Alice laughed. "I had the same thoughts. Funny. You don't look like Hulk Hogan in a suit."

The two laughed together. "My ex-wife used to say that I looked like a basset hound with big friendly eyes."

"No," Alice said, trying to hide her chuckle. "I think you look just fine. It was so nice of you to drive all the way up here."

"Actually I love driving and I do a lot of it, usually by myself to get away and think."

They ordered a house-special chicken dish with baked potatoes and broccoli and throughout dinner the two talked like they were old friends. It turned out that they were both New York Jets fans and they talked at length about the team's prospects for the coming season. They also liked folk music. Vic raved about a small fifty-seat auditorium in Greenwich Village where they had unusual groups perform each weekend. "A few weeks ago they had a really wonderful group of Andean musicians. They played some fantastic stuff on the charango, guitar, and bombo."

"I have an album of Andean music that I particularly enjoy. Isn't one of the instruments a drum sort of thing made out of the hide of an armadillo?"

"I don't believe it," Vic said, obviously nonplussed. "No one I've ever met knows anything about Andean music. Alice, I think I love you." Alice gasped. "Don't take that seriously," Vic said quickly. "I was just kidding."

"No problem," Alice said, her heartbeat returning to normal. "I know almost nothing about you. What do you do for a living?"

"I create computer games. I'm working on one now, but eventually I'd like to write an X-rated one. I haven't worked out any of the details yet, but it will probably have a superstudly hero who has to kill the bad guys who have taken over a whorehouse. Along the way he stumbles into several rooms and takes part in the fun and games or something like that."

"You're kidding."

"Actually, I'm not. If I ever get the time, I'd love to use a few of your stories as the basis for some of the adventures."

"My stories?" Alice blushed.

"You're a very talented storyteller and the fantasies we've shared live on in my mind."

To change the subject, Alice said, "You talked about an ex-wife so I gather you're divorced. Any kids?"

"I have two teenaged daughters who live with my ex. We've been divorced for almost six years. They live on Long Island and I see them every other weekend, although it's getting harder and harder."

"How come?"

"The girls are growing up and they have their own lives. Both are in high school, and dating and hate to have their social lives messed up with a father." When Alice looked saddened, Vic added quickly, "It's okay, really. They're almost grown and will be in college soon. It's just Dad who has a bit of trouble letting go. It's great that we are really close and talk on the phone often." He paused. "Although they talk to everyone on the phone often."

"Where would any of us be without the phone?" Alice said, grinning.

"Right. How about you? I know you're not married now. Let's forget about that story you told me last week. I assume that was just fiction. Have you ever been married for real?"

Alice told Vic an abbreviated story about Ralph. "He was a nice man whom I never should have married. We got together for all the wrong reasons."

"At least there were no kids to get caught in the middle."

"Amen to that," Alice said.

When the waiter arrived to take dessert orders, Alice hesitated. "Maybe I'll just have coffee."

"Come on, Alice, be brave. Have something completely frivolous. You're entitled for putting up with me all evening."

"I didn't put up with you. I'm having a delightful evening. You're right about dessert, however. I'll have the cheesecake."

Vic grinned. "Make that two."

Alice considered. "Make that one cheesecake with two forks, if that's okay with you, Vic."

"Nice compromise. And two coffees."

As the waiter disappeared, Vic asked, "How did you get connected with Velvet Whispers? Where did you work before that?"

"I work as a receptionist in a dentist's office. You know how long I've been with Velvet Whispers. You were my first call." She told Vic a short version of her connection with Betsy and the discussion that convinced Alice to give it a try.

"You're kidding," Vic said. "I knew I was your first caller at Whispers but I assumed that you had been working somewhere else before. You were so professional and so good at it."

"Thanks for the compliment." Alice beamed.

"You mentioned your mother earlier. Is she better now?"

"No, and she won't be. She's well into her seventies and in really frail health. She's happy, however, at the Rutlandt Nursing Home and my jobs make ends meet." And more, Alice thought. She was actually putting some money in the bank.

"Fortunately my parents are still going strong," Vic said. "My dad works for American Airlines. He was a pilot and my mom was a stewardess when they met."

"How great! Does that mean you get to fly free? I've always wanted to travel."

"I can fly standby, but I seldom do. I used to when my wife and I were still together. We took the kids to Europe every summer, but now it just doesn't happen anymore. I guess I'm too caught up in my work."

"That's really too bad. I always dreamed of going to Europe."

"So come with me. We can tour for a few weeks, see London, Rome, Paris."

"Sure. We can go next week. Don't I wish I could!"

"Why can't you?"

"For starters, my jobs—both of them."

"You could work it out if you wanted to, but we can let that pass for now. By the way, I think we have a little problem regarding your job."

"Oh?" Alice said.

"Well, I'd feel a little silly calling you up on business now."

Alice blushed. "You're right. I would be mortified talking like I do to someone when I've seen his face."

"You mean you couldn't talk dirty to me over the phone."

Alice's color deepened. "Only on a very personal basis, not for money."

Vic took her hand. "Thanks. That's nice." He kept hold of her hand. "Have you ever met any of the other men you talk to?"

"Nope, and if I had, I don't think I could look them in the imaginary eye while I was talking to them. When I don't know them, they're just voices."

"I feel a bit guilty not calling you anymore. Will that louse up your income? I could call and pay, but we could just talk about anything we like."

"Don't be silly. You can call me if you like, but not for money. I have all the callers I can deal with as it is."

"Will you give me your home number?"

Alice considered. In the business she was in, giving out her home phone number was a large step, but she felt completely at home with Vic. As Velvet had said, he was a thoroughly nice and very lonely man. "Sure." They exchanged home addresses and phone numbers.

The waiter arrived with their cheesecake and the conversation wandered into other areas. When they had finished their desserts and their coffee cups had run dry, the check arrived. Vic reached for it. "I'd prefer if we split that," Alice said.

"I come from the old school. The man pays for his dates."

"You said yourself that this isn't a date. Please. I'd feel better."

"Okay. You're right. It's a not-date. Your wish is my command," Vic said. When they had worked out the details and paid the check, he stood to leave. "This has been a wonderful evening," Vic said, helping pull out her chair. "I don't want to rush you, so would you meet me again next week? Same place?"

"Another not-date?"

"I would like to make it a date this time." He placed his hand against the small of Alice's back and guided her through the maze of tables.

"That would be nice. I'd like that."

As they hit the cool, late spring air, Vic leaned over and kissed Alice softly on the lips. "I've enjoyed the evening tremendously. You're nothing like what I expected, and more wonderful."

"Thanks. I've had a great time myself."

They parted without any awkward moments.

The following day, Alice met Betsy in the Italian restaurant in the mall. "Well?" Betsy said as they settled into a booth. "No, don't tell me anything. Velvet's meeting us and you can tell us both."

At that moment, Velvet walked into the darkened room and spotted them immediately. She quickly made herself comfortable in the booth beside Betsy. "Now tell," Velvet said. "Everything."

"He's very nice," Alice said. She told the two women

about the evening in great detail. "We have another date next Tuesday."

"Fan-flippin'-tastic," Betsy said.

"Great," Velvet said. "I have something to tell you, however. I know more about Mr. Sanderson than you might think."

"Yes?" Alice said, terrified that she had dated a mass murderer or a spy.

"When he first called several years ago he said something that triggered something in my brain," Velvet said. "I let it go, but when you said you were going out with him, I looked him up in *Who's Who*. He said he works on computer games." She mentioned a very popular adventure game.

"I know that one," Betsy said. "My boys have it."

"I remember playing it one evening with Phil. He beat me seven ways from Sunday." Alice made the connection. "You mean he worked on that one?"

"He didn't just work on it," Velvet said, conspiratorially. "He invented it. Or wrote it. Or whatever you do to computer games." She mentioned several more very popular games. "Those too. He sold his company last year and made buckets of money. That's how he can afford your phone calls, among other things."

Alice was taken aback. He was rich. That cast a different light on everything. *Oh, shit,* she thought, *I argued about splitting the check. I told him about my problems needing money to support my mother. I probably sounded like a jerk.*

"You said he seemed like a regular guy," Betsy said. "I'll bet he didn't want you to know about all that money. Women don't like to think that they are being courted for their money and maybe he's the same way. He just wanted to be a nice guy you were dating."

"I know," Alice said, "but we're not in the same league."

"Hey wait a minute," Velvet said. "I didn't tell you all that to intimidate you. He's asked you out and that's that."

"I know, but he's not the man he pretended to be."

"Listen," Betsy said. "You aren't Sherry either, but does that change who you really are?"

"You are who you are," Velvet said, "and that's that. So if you had fun, just enjoy and let the chips fall where they may."

Alice sighed. "I guess you're right. Gee. All that money."

"Listen," Velvet said, bringing Alice back from her reverie, "since we're talking about dating, Wayne's got a business friend in from out of town. Interested in dinner? My place, tomorrow evening?"

Alice raised an eyebrow. "A blind date?"

"I guess you could call it that. He's not rich, and since he's from the west coast he's not geographically desirable either, but he's a really nice guy, single again, sort of hunky and cute."

"Single again?"

"Yeah. He's twice divorced, but you're not marrying him, just having dinner with him at my house."

"I don't think so," Alice said.

"Please? I really like him and he seems like a lost ship right now. Just pay a little attention to him and let him feel like a man again. Think of it as a charitable contribution."

Betsy chimed in. "Once again, what have you got to lose?"

"You two are trying to convert me into a social butterfly."

"Hardly," Velvet said. "We had nothing to do with Vic asking you out and this is just a one-night stand." She giggled. "So to speak."

"Come on, Alice. Make the big plunge."

Alice sighed. "Okay you two. How can I argue with both of you?"

"The kids are staying with Wayne's folks overnight so

we'll be able to have a grown-up evening for a change. Wayne's dad will drop them at school Friday morning so I can sleep in and Karen's routing for me so I'm off duty. This is such a pleasure. Can you be at my house about six?"

"As long as the doctor's schedule accommodates. One question. Does he know about your business, about what I do?"

"No. I don't tell too many people, especially Wayne's business associates."

Instead of the jitters she had had before her date with Vic, Thursday passed quickly and easily. Alice had already decided to wear the same gray linen slacks with a white blouse with a thin gray stripe so she dashed home from work and changed quickly. It was a warm late spring evening so instead of a coat, she put on a deep green blazer. After feeding Roger, she made the short drive to Putnam Valley in record time and arrived in Velvet's driveway with two minutes to spare.

"I didn't expect you so promptly," Velvet said as she ushered Alice into the living room. She had met Velvet's husband, Wayne, briefly before and took his outstretched hand warmly. A very ordinary-looking man, he doted on his wife and family and Velvet seemed completely in love with him.

"It's good to see you again," Alice told Wayne and shifted her gaze to the other man in the room. To say he was hunky was an understatement. He looked to be in his mid-thirties, gorgeous in a Kevin Sorbo kind of way. Soft, sandy hair that he wore curling at his shoulders, straight nose, and piercing blue eyes. The tan sports jacket and brown slacks he wore only served to accent his deliciously wide shoulders and narrow hips. Alice found herself wondering what he would look like in Sorbo's Hercules outfit: leather pants and a cloth vest revealing most of his upper body.

"You're Alice," the man said, his voice sounding like hot

fudge. "It's nice to meet you. I'm Todd." He extended his hand and Alice took it. His grip was strong and he held her hand for just a fraction longer than she had expected.

Over drinks before dinner, she learned that Todd was a salesman for a California-based manufacturing firm that did business with Wayne's electronics company. "My business is really deadly dull. Tell me about you."

Alice explained about her job in Dr. Tannenbaum's office. "Do you enjoy what you do?" Todd asked.

"It's a job, and I really like the people I deal with."

"I'm sure they like you too. I know I do."

He really comes on like gangbusters. Slow down, she said, hoping he'd read her. "Thanks. Tell me more about you."

He told her briefly that he was recently out of a messy divorce. "We'd only been married for two years, but it's amazing what you can accumulate in such a short time."

"I'll bet," Alice said.

"You know what we fought about most? Cleopatra." When Alice looked puzzled, he said, "Our brown tabby Persian cat. We each wanted to keep her and it became like a custody battle. Fortunately, about a month into the arguing, we discovered that Cleo was going to have kittens, so my wife got the cat and I got two kittens."

"How wonderful," Alice said. "I don't know how I'd manage without Roger. He's a domestic short hair and my best friend."

"I know what you mean. Cocoa and Cognac are mine."

"Great names."

"Cocoa is a little girl and Cognac is a male. They're all tan and brown so the names seemed to fit."

"What do you do with them when you travel?"

"I have a neighbor who takes care of them for me. You know, cleans the litter pan and puts down new food. They are totally indoor cats so they don't require much."

Somehow, with cats in common, Alice and Todd began to

relax with each other. Over dinner, the group talked about anything and everything, the conversation never lagging, each fighting for an opening to express another opinion. After coffee, they adjourned to the living room with glasses of brandy, where the lively conversation continued until Alice glanced at her watch. "Holy cow," she said. "It's after eleven. I'm going to be useless at work unless I get some sleep." Between her date with Vic, her work Wednesday evening, and the dinner tonight she was going to have to sleep all weekend to make up for it. And she hadn't visited her mother since the previous weekend. She stood, retrieved her jacket, and thanked Velvet and Wayne.

"And Todd, this has been a wonderful evening. I really enjoyed your company."

"I'm going to take off, too, back to my motel. Let me walk you out to your car." He grabbed his jacket, which he had taken off earlier, and slipped it on.

Alice hugged Velvet and planted a quick kiss on Wayne's cheek. "Thanks for dinner. Velvet, I'll talk to you over the weekend."

"Good night," the couple said.

Todd walked Alice to her car. "I'm going to take a risk here," Todd said, and he wrapped his arms around her lightly and leaned forward. Their lips met softly and the tender kiss totally overwhelmed Alice's senses. She pulled back slightly and looked at Todd in the moonlight. It had been years since she'd been kissed and she discovered that she liked it. She leaned forward again, touched her lips to his and sighed.

Todd made a soft sound deep in his throat and gently pressed her back against her car door. The feeling of being trapped against the cool metal made Alice tremble. Todd jumped back. "I'm sorry. I got carried away."

Alice cupped his face in her hands. "Don't be sorry. It was really nice."

Todd grinned. Then he tangled his fingers in her short curls and brought her face to his. Again they kissed, this one no longer tender. Now his mouth was hungry, heating her body and moistening her. When he pulled back, he gazed into her eyes. "My God, woman. No one should be allowed to kiss like that."

Alice was puzzled. "Like what?"

"Like you're a great vortex and I'm yearning to fall in. I want to devour you and your mouth tells me that you want it too."

Was that what her mouth was saying? It had been so long. Maybe the combination of her long time away from men and her conversations over the phone had changed her from the woman Ralph divorced to something more. Todd kissed her again, and this time she melted into it, letting her tongue roam at will, testing things she had talked about but never done. She slid her hands up his back beneath his jacket, questing the warmth of his body through his shirt. He pressed his obvious erection against her lower body and she allowed her body to press back.

They broke the kiss and, panting, she let her head fall back as Todd kissed his way down her throat. His hands slid up the sides of her shirt until his palms held her ribs and his thumbs brushed the tips of her breasts. She felt her nipples harden and her thighs shake. Without the support of her car against her back, she would have fallen from the sheer eroticism of it all.

"What's going on here?" Todd asked, his voice breathy and hoarse. "This is crazy."

Obviously he felt the burst of passion too. "I know. I have to tell you that I haven't kissed anyone in a very long time."

"I'd like to do a lot more than kiss you. I'm aching for you and this isn't the way I would have this happen."

"Why?" she whispered.

"My home's three thousand miles away and I don't get

here more than once or twice a year. I'm leaving on Tuesday to other places, other people."

"Other women?"

"Yes, and I want to make that clear up front. I have other female friends and I don't deny it. But I've never had anything hit me so hard and so suddenly and after such a short time. I want to bury myself in you until we're too exhausted to move. I want to feel you beneath me. I want to make you scream and beg and cry for it, then make you climax over and over."

Alice hadn't said it any better to any of her clients. Was it a line? Maybe. He certainly knew what buttons to push and how to push them. But was that bad? Didn't she feel the same things? "So what should we do about it?"

"Ordinarily I'd ask you out a few more times, then try to convince you to join me in bed. We don't have a few more times. Can I see you tomorrow night?"

It was Friday and she had a regular caller. "I'm afraid I have something else I have to do."

He sighed and backed away. "I understand."

She shouldn't do this. Not for any reason. Except one. She wanted to. "No, you don't. I can't tomorrow, but I'm free Saturday." She didn't confuse love and lust. This was sexual, pure and simple, and from all of her phone relationships she had learned that there was nothing wrong with sexuality just for fun. And this was going to be fun, pure and hopefully simple.

In the dim light, she could see his eyes light up. "That's great. I'll call you during the day on Saturday and we'll make plans. Pick someplace nice and we can talk. Get to know each other better. That's the place to start."

Alice didn't have to ask what they were starting. It was obvious. Something really short term and really explosive.

"Yes, it is." They exchanged phone numbers and Alice got into her car. Before she closed the door, Todd kissed her again. The kiss was just as incendiary as the last, leaving Alice's hands shaking and her mind numb. Nothing even vaguely resembling this had ever happened to her before or would probably happen to her again. She didn't care.

"Until Saturday," she said.

"Until Saturday."

Chapter 10

"So tell me about Todd," Betsy said to Alice the following morning.

"He's sexy as hell and we have a date Saturday night."

"Wonderful. Tell me everything."

"Listen. I know that this is a short-time thing. No hearts and flowers, no," she made quoting marks in the air, "*relationship*, and I really want to keep it to myself for a little while."

"Are you okay?" Betsy asked, obviously a bit put out at Alice for not sharing.

"I'm great." She gave her friend a quick hug. "I just want this to be all my decision. If I talk about it, I might change my mind and I don't want to. For once in my life I don't want to be logical."

"Hey, I wouldn't ask you to change anything. Does what you're doing feel right?"

"I'm not sure, but it feels like another 'What have I got to lose' so I'm going to wing it."

Betsy hugged her friend back. "Good for you. Have a blast."

She was going to do just that. She was going to invite Todd to her apartment for dinner and let things happen whatever way they happened. She wanted it and it was about time she took something just because she wanted it. She talked to her sister Friday evening and made plans to visit her mother on Sunday. Then, after work on Saturday, she dashed to the market and bought a thick sirloin steak, a rice mix that cooked in fifteen minutes, salad makings, and a package of frozen vegetables. Then she stopped at the liquor store and picked up a bottle of nice red wine and a bottle of rather expensive brandy, the drink that Todd had had after dinner on Thursday. Then she decided on one more stop, at a local convenience store for a three-pack of condoms. If what she expected to happen happened, she would be ready.

At home she quickly made a salad and put it into the refrigerator. It was not yet five so Alice decided that she had enough time for a bath. She turned on the hot water in the tub and poured a capful of bubble liquid beneath the tap. As the bath ran, she stripped off her clothes and stared into her closet. She quickly decided on a soft cotton sweater in a becoming shade of light blue, her softest jeans, and a pair of loafers. Easy on, easy off, she thought. Then she stashed the condoms in the table beside the bed and looked around the bedroom.

The previous evening, between phone calls she had tidied up and this morning she had changed the sheets. Three weeks before she had bought new drapes and a matching quilt in a pink and green floral pattern, and had coordinated several pillows. *Well,* she thought, *that's the best I can do.*

Back in the bathroom, she turned off the water and

climbed into the tub. With a chirrup, Roger jumped onto the toilet seat. Tail swishing, he reached out a paw and batted at the mound of bubbles just within his reach. "I know," Alice said. "You're not used to this, are you."

Merrow.

"Well, I'm not either, but I'm not too old to learn, so I'm going to do just that. It's a hell of about time, don't you think?"

Roger batted at the bubbles, his paw now covered with foam. When he started to lick it off, he sneezed. "See? Something new for all of us."

Fascinated, Roger spent the next fifteen minutes trying to understand bubbles while Alice relaxed in the tub, surprised that she wasn't more nervous. "You know, Roger," she said, finally standing up and grabbing a bath towel, "I should be really upset about this. If everything goes all right I'm about to get into what several of my callers refer to as sport fucking." She wrinkled her nose and stepped out of the tub. "Ugh. That sounds terrible, but I guess that's what it is. It's not lovemaking since there's no love involved, but it's not going to be just fucking either. It's going to be two people doing things that feel wonderful."

Merrow.

"Right. He's really cute too. Wait till you see. He likes cats but you stay out of the way. Hear?"

In her bedroom, she opened her underwear drawer. She had nothing particularly sexy, nothing like the lingerie she described in such detail three nights a week, so she did the best she could. She pulled out a stretchy, beige nylon bra and matching bikini panties. "I wish I had something lacy," she said to Roger, now washing his front paws in the middle of her new quilt. "I'll have to take some time next week and shop, in case this happens again."

Roger rolled over and Alice sat on the bed and scratched his belly. Roger's purr filled the room as Alice dressed. At ten minutes to six, Alice faced herself in the mirror. She smoothed on eyeliner, redoing it twice before it looked the way she wanted it to, then added soft pink blush and lipstick. She considered mascara, but rejected the idea. Who knew when it might smear, and under what conditions? She fluffed her short curls, unable to do anything to her hair that it didn't want. She added small pearl earrings and a strand of pearls that rested between her breasts.

She started out of the bathroom, then quickly took a small bottle of Opium that Betsy had given her last Christmas, and dabbed just a touch behind each ear and in her cleavage. "Ready as ever," she said to Roger, now fast asleep on the bed. "You'd better stay out from underfoot."

As she closed the bedroom door behind her, the doorbell rang. Her heart lurched but she calmly walked to the front door. Todd stood in front of her apartment dressed in a navy-blue blazer, gray slacks, and a yellow knit shirt. His eyes were even bluer than she remembered and gazed at her in appreciation, and puzzlement. "Hi. Am I overdressed for wherever we're going?"

"Not at all," Alice said ushering him inside. "Actually I thought we could eat here. I'm not a great cook but I broil a mean steak."

Todd grinned. "Great idea. Come here." He reached for her and drew her into his arms. "I've been thinking about this for two very long days." His lips met hers and the electricity she had felt when they first kissed surged through her again. His hands alternately massaged her back and grabbed her hair. "You know," he said when they paused to catch their breath, "I've been thinking about you and about this evening." He released her and walked into the living room. "I don't want to pressure you or anything. We're both grown-ups. I want you. I want to make love to you, with you. I don't want you to think I jump on every woman I meet but this isn't true love either. I don't want any confusion."

When she didn't respond, he continued, "I don't want anything going on under false pretenses."

Alice walked up to him and smiled. "I understand everything and I don't jump every man I meet either. Can I take your jacket?"

His grin made him look about ten years younger. He slipped his jacket off his shoulders and dropped it on the sofa. "Come here." He tangled his fingers in her hair and gently pulled her head back, then buried his mouth in the hollow at the base of her throat.

This is exactly what I wanted, Alice thought in the small part of her mind that could still think. Then that section shut down beneath the onslaught of her senses. His mouth was hot, his tongue rough as he licked the tender spot where her shoulder met her neck. His hands roamed up her sides until his thumbs brushed the lower curves of her breasts. She thought about foreplay and the slow building from embers to flames, but the flames already existed and were quickly devouring both of them.

She combed her fingers through his hair, marveling at the softness. Like baby hair, she thought. His hands were beneath her sweater now, branding her bare skin everywhere he touched. One hand cupped her buttocks and pressed her lower body against the hard ridge of flesh beneath the crotch of his slacks. "God," he purred, "I can't get close enough to you."

She marveled at the core of calm and rational enjoyment that existed beneath the raging fires that consumed her conscious mind. This was what she had been talking about all these weeks. She took the lower edge of her sweater in her hands and pulled it over her head. Then she grabbed his shirt and did the same. "Better," she whispered, rubbing her hands over his chest, sliding her fingers through the light furring of blond hair.

"This too," he growled, unhooking her bra and dragging

it off. "God yes." He cupped her breasts, his thumbs flicking over her already erect nipples. "Yes. So good."

Alice's knees threatened to buckle. "In here," she said, the words difficult to get past the passion in her throat. She led him to the bedroom and, as she opened the door, Roger trotted through. He stopped to sniff Todd's slacks, then rubbed briefly against his legs and headed off toward the kitchen.

"I'm not usually this impatient," Todd said as he entered Alice's bedroom, his fingers working at the fastenings of her jeans, "but I don't seem to be rushing you."

"You're not," Alice said, smiling at his assumption that she was an old hand at all of this. She pushed the door closed.

Quickly they removed their remaining clothes and, both naked, fell onto the bed. Todd's mouth found Alice's nipple and her back arched as shards of electric pleasure knifed through her. His fingers pinched the other nipple, causing pain that was both sharp and erotic.

She had talked about women's hands on men's cocks for weeks but she had never actually held a man's penis in her hands before. Now she touched him and he felt wonderful, like velvet over rigid muscle. His skin was soft and hot as she held him, squeezing gently.

"Do that any more and I'll lose it right here," he said hoarsely, moving her hand away.

Then his fingers slipped between her legs and found her hot and wet. "Yes," she whispered. "Oh yes." He touched and explored, then slid one finger into her channel. "Oh shit," she hissed, her back arching and her hips driving his hands against her.

When he withdrew she felt bereft, but then she heard the ripping of paper and understood. Only moments later his condom-covered cock pressed at her entrance and with one thrust Todd buried himself inside of her. It was fast, hot, and hard, Todd's hips pounding and Alice's legs wrapped around his waist. They clawed at each other's backs trying to drive deeper.

"Touch me," she cried and Todd's fingers slipped between them and found her clit. With a shout he came, and then, only moments later, Alice felt the familiar bubble growing low in her belly. Todd was still driving into her, his body spasming when she exploded, her orgasm bigger than any she had created for herself.

"God, baby," Todd said later as they calmed. "You're something."

"You're not bad yourself," Alice said. "That was amazing."

"You're amazing," he said, using a tissue to clean himself up. Then he rolled over and cuddled her against his side, her head on his shoulder. "I love a woman who enjoys good sex. There's nothing coy or reticent about you. It's wonderful."

Alice thought about what had happened. She had enjoyed it. More than that, it had been one of the greatest experiences of her life. Nothing that she had had with Ralph had prepared her for the unbridled passion of what she and Todd had done. It seemed so simple.

They had dinner and, over coffee and brandy, Todd kissed her again, more slowly this time as hands and mouths discovered erotic places. For the first time Alice touched a man's cock and was delighted when she obviously excited him. She knew what she had read and talked about, and whatever she did seemed to please Todd. When Todd touched his tongue to her clit, Alice thought she would fly into space and, with his mouth lightly sucking on her flesh and his fingers inside her pussy, she came. "God, woman, you're so responsive." Then he was inside of her and she came again as he did. They pulled the quilt over them later and, with Roger on the bed beside them, they slept until the following morning.

Todd was still asleep when Alice awoke the next day. She lay quietly and thought about the previous night. It had been wonderful, fulfilling, and electric. She had no regrets about anything and that surprised her. For weeks she had been talking a good game, and now she was playing. It was sensational. She stretched, slipped from the bed, and padded to the bathroom.

Minutes later she stood in the shower under the warm spray. She lathered her body and wondered at the slick, slipperiness of her skin. She felt her hands on her flesh and tried to feel what Todd had felt. She wasn't pretty, she didn't have a sexy body, but he had seemed to really like touching her and making love to her. In her stories she was always the ideal-looking person she had always dreamed about, but now it didn't seem to matter. Todd was gorgeous and that was what had attracted her in the first place, but after the first few minutes, it was his love of cats and his sense of humor that had kept her interest.

Suddenly the shower curtain moved and Todd climbed into the tub behind her. "Good morning."

She thought she'd feel awkward after all that they had done the previous evening, but she didn't. "Good morning. I have to visit my mom today so I thought I'd get started early so maybe we could get together again later."

"A woman with a plan. I like that. But must we waste this wonderful opportunity?" He took the shower scrubby that she used with her body wash, squeezed a large amount of aromatic gel onto it, and began to lather her body. Slowly he soaped her skin, taking time to cover her breasts and mound with bubbles. She parted her legs as he slipped the plastic sponge between her thighs and caressed her pussy with it. As he rinsed her off, she took the sponge from him and moved him beneath the spray so his back was turned toward her.

With more lather on the pink sponge, she slowly stroked

it over his back, taking time to appreciate his tight buttocks. She remembered a story she had told several times about a couple who made love in a shower and she realized that she had a perfect opportunity to get to know Todd's body better. She crouched and washed down the backs of his thighs and felt him tremble as she parted his cheeks and rubbed that hidden valley between.

Water cascaded over her head as she turned him and washed his feet and the fronts of his legs. Then she stood and lathered his softly furred chest and shoulders, his arms and hands. Now she could move to the part of his body she was most interested in. She put more gel on the sponge and knelt, stroking the slightly rough surface over his semierect penis. She allowed herself to look at his body and watch his penis react to her ministrations. She lifted his cock and gently scrubbed his testicles, then rubbed the tender area behind. As she touched, she watched his cock react and twitch, making his enjoyment obvious. She slid her fingers between his thighs and touched the slippery skin behind his balls, then slipped further backward and touched his anus. His knees almost gave out.

She had touched his erection the previous evening but now she wondered whether she could take it into her mouth as the women had in her stories. Still touching his balls and asshole, she licked the falling water from the tip of his cock with the flat of her tongue. Todd grabbed her shoulders. "Don't do that, baby," he groaned. "If you do, I'll shoot right here and now."

"Is there a problem with that?"

"Oh, God."

She was going to do it. She didn't think she could deep-throat it as her characters often did in her stories, but she drew the end of Todd's cock into her mouth. She created a vacuum and pulled her head back, creating suction. Todd tangled his fingers in her hair and held her tightly, more for his own balance than to restrain her. She felt his muscles tighten and knew that he was ready to climax. "Baby," he shouted. She wrapped one hand around his erection, feeling it swell and jerk.

She wanted to taste his come, but she didn't think she could swallow it so she opened her mouth and, as jets of thick, white jism shot from Todd's cock, she allowed most of it to flow from between her lips. The fluid was thick and viscous and tasted slightly tangy. She avidly watched his cock and her hand and she instinctively pumped the last of his climax.

"Shit, baby," Todd said. "That's not fair."

"What's not fair?" Alice said, a grin splitting her face.

"You did that to me and I didn't satisfy you."

"I am satisfied. That was amazing."

Together they lathered and rinsed and, wrapped in thick towels, wandered back into the bedroom. As Alice rubbed her curls dry, she felt herself grabbed from behind. "Get over here," Todd said. He pulled her toward the bed and then pushed her down. "We're going to play a little game," he growled. "You're going to lie there and I'm going to do to you what you just did to me."

Alice giggled and tried to get up. "That's not necessary. This isn't a tit-for-tat kind of thing. I enjoyed what happened and that's that."

"Tit for tat, eh? Well I want those tits, do you understand? Now lie down," he snapped and pushed her back onto the bed.

Alice suddenly stopped laughing. "Yes, sir," she said softly. She settled back onto the bed. There was suddenly nothing soft about Todd. There was a hard edge to his voice, ordering her to follow his instructions. She felt herself tremble with excitement.

"That's more like it. Now, spread your legs and make it quick." He stood at the foot of the bed, arms crossed over his naked chest. He was beautiful, powerful.

She did as he commanded and felt herself immediately wet. "Wider," he snapped.

Alice spread her legs as wide as they would go while Todd looked down at her. "You like that, don't you?" he said, his question not requiring an answer. "I suspected that you would. I love giving orders and seeing a beautiful woman obey."

Obey. The word made her body jolt. She did like it. Very much.

Todd parted her towel and stared at her. "I want to suck your tits. Offer one to me."

What was it that made her cup her flattened breast and hold it for him? The mastery? His aura of command? The domination? It was all of those and more, she realized.

He knelt beside the bed and placed his mouth on her fully erect nipple. She felt his teeth bite down, just enough to cause her pain. When she grunted, he said, "I wanted to do that and you wanted me to. You want this and both of us know it. Is this new for you?"

"Yes," she whispered. It was all new to her and now she wanted it all.

He grabbed her hair and held her head against the mattress. Then he ravished her mouth. There was no gentleness, but rather power and hunger. When he leaned back, he said, "Since I climaxed before, I'm not feeling impatient to have you. You're mine and I can do whatever I like to you. And I'm in no hurry." He settled onto the edge of the bed. "I've played a lot of games with women," he said as Alice stared at him. "I love sex in all forms. Now it seems I've discovered something that makes you crazy." He rubbed his finger through her sopping pussy. "Oh yes," he said. "So wet. This obviously makes you hungry."

He pulled off his towel and stretched out on top of her, his feet holding hers down and his hands grasping her wrists. She could feel the length of his body against hers and her heart pounded. His mouth devoured hers while he held her so she couldn't move. Briefly Alice wondered whether she should be reacting this way, then she stopped caring. Over the weeks she had been telling stories, she realized that everyone had their pleasures and she was entitled to feel whatever she felt and enjoy whatever gave her pleasure. And this did.

Todd stood up. "You are not to move. Just lie there with your legs wide apart and let me do whatever I want."

She choked out the word, "Yes."

Todd spent long minutes playing with her breasts. He kissed, licked, sucked, and bit until it was all Alice could do not to grab him and make him satisfy the gnawing hunger he was creating. Yet she didn't move. It had become a challenge. He had told her not to move and she wouldn't.

Finally he moved between her spread legs and gazed at her pussy. "I'll bet you've never seen a pussy," he said, "but they are so beautiful. Yours is so wet I can see the moisture." He touched her inner lips with one finger. "God, you're so hot, baby." He touched the end of her clit lightly and her hips jumped. "I told you not to move," he growled.

She concentrated on keeping her body still. "That's better," he said. He looked around the bedroom and she could see him stare at the candle she had in a holder on her dresser. She had intended to light it the previous evening but things had proceeded so quickly that she had not had the chance. He stood up and grabbed the candle, a taper about eight inches long and over an inch in diameter. He hurried into the bathroom and Alice could hear the water running. Knowing what he must have in mind, Alice felt her muscles tighten.

He returned with the candle in his hand. "See this? You've figured out what I'm going to do with it, haven't you."

She nodded.

He settled back between her legs and rubbed the wax

through the folds of her pussy then over her clit. "Here's what I'm going to do. I'm going to fuck you with this dildo. I'm going to slowly force it into your beautiful pussy. It might be a bit bigger than a cock but your body will take it, and you won't move while I do it. Then I'm going to suck your clit and I'm going to feel you come. Being fucked with a candle and having me in control of your body will make you so hot that you won't be able to help it. You won't be in control of it, I will."

He placed the candle against the opening of her pussy and, ever so slowly, pushed it into her body. It was larger than any cock she had felt and it seemed to force its way into her. Alice had never had anything but fingers and cocks inside of her and she noticed with the rational part of her brain that the candle felt cool and filled her in a way that no cock had. Deeper and deeper it penetrated until it seemed to fill not only her body but her mind. She was overwhelmed with sensations and Todd now pulled, now pushed, fucking her with the candle.

She was so close, she realized. So close that when his mouth found her clit she came, screaming. Her hips bucked so hard it was difficult for him to keep his mouth on her, but he did, pulling on her clit and drawing the climax out longer and longer. She couldn't control her body as wave after wave crashed over her. For long minutes she came and came. She finally placed her hand against his forehead and gently pushed him away.

Totally limp, she lay still as Todd climbed up the bed and settled against her side. He cradled her head against him and kissed her curls. "My god, woman. I've never seen anyone come like that. You're incredible."

"That was incredible," she whispered, unable to make any louder sound. They dozed for another hour, then dressed quickly. "I don't have anything in the house for breakfast," Alice admitted.

"Then how about the diner?" he asked.

"Sure. I've got to be at my mom's nursing home at noon so we've got some time."

"Can we get together again tonight?" Todd asked.

"I was hoping to. I'll be back here about five." She had planned to do some writing for her clients, but that would have to wait. After this morning she had so much to say and there was no possibility that she would forget any of it.

Alice and Todd talked almost nonstop while they ate and Todd kissed her deeply as they parted, to meet at her place at five-thirty. As she drove south she smiled. It had been so fantastic and she had learned a lot about herself.

Her mom seemed to be doing a bit better and Sue arrived at the nursing home at about one. Together the three women sat in the sunny garden and although she said nothing, her mother seemed to be enjoying the conversation. "Are you okay with the money?" Sue asked at one point.

"Yes. My new job is fun and pays well. I can afford this without any problem. Don't worry about a thing."

"Well, I don't think I've ever seen you look better. You've got a glow. Whatever you're doing must agree with you."

If you only knew, Alice thought.

Chapter 11

Todd arrived at Alice's apartment at five-thirty that evening with a pizza in hand. They both knew that going out to dinner wasn't going to happen so they made quick work of the pie and ended up in bed again. They made love twice that evening and again at 3:00 A.M. When the alarm rang at seven, Todd reached for her again. "Sorry," she said, "but I have to be at work at eight and a shower and a bowl of cereal are a necessity."

"Oh, baby," Todd groaned. "You're such a spoilsport."

Alice kissed him thoroughly, then said, "You can stay in bed if you like, but I'm out of here." When she returned from the bathroom, Todd was already dressed.

"I have a nine o'clock meeting that I have to dress for anyway so I thought I'd go back to my motel and shower and change there." He dragged her close. "Tonight?"

"I'm sorry, I can't."

Todd's eyes widened. "I had hoped . . ."

"I wish I could, but I can't. I have a commitment I can't change." She had three regular callers who were in for a surprise that night. She had several stories whirling in her head, all based on what she had experienced all weekend.

"I'm flying out at noon on Tuesday," Todd pouted.

Alice put her arms around him. "I know and I wish there were something I could do, but there isn't. I just can't."

"I'll see whether I can arrange a trip to New York in the fall."

Alice beamed. "Wonderful. I'll look forward to that. In the meantime, we'll e-mail and call each other."

"It won't be the same. We've only known each other for a few days but . . ."

"Don't. You said you've got other female friends and I've got men I date too. Let's just leave it that it's been great and we'll do it again when we can."

"You sound like me. I'm usually the one who makes that speech."

"Well then, you're usually the wise one."

Alice could feel Todd's chuckle deep in his chest. "It feels really strange to be on the receiving end." He pulled away and slapped her lightly on the bottom. "All right, woman, let's get going."

Alice arrived at Dr. Tannenbaum's office at exactly eight o'clock to find Betsy on the phone and the doctor's first patient sitting in the waiting room reading a magazine. Betsy put her hand over the mouthpiece of the receiver. "He's going to be about fifteen minutes late."

"Oh, Mr. Fucito," Alice said to the waiting patient as she hung up her coat. "I'm sorry. I'm sure it was unavoidable."

"No problem, Alice," the man said. "I'm not due at work until ten-thirty."

As she arrived in the reception area, Alice tried unsuccessfully to wipe off the grin that had been on her face all morning. "You look like a cat who's just eaten several very fat canaries," Betsy said. "What gives?"

"I had a weekend to write stories about."

"Tell all, and quickly."

The phone rang and Alice adjusted an appointment for the following morning. As she hung up, she said, "About this weekend . . ."

The door opened and Dr. Tannenbaum arrived with a flurry of questions and instructions. "Listen," Betsy said. "We're never going to get a chance to talk here. I know you usually have errands to run at lunch but I'm meeting Velvet. Come along and you can regale us with your weekend adventures."

Alice couldn't suppress her grin. She wanted to keep it all to herself, but she also wanted to crow a bit. "Done." Betsy disappeared into the operatory and Alice returned to her computer.

At ten after one, the three women were seated in a booth at a diner and had already ordered sandwiches and drinks. "All right," Betsy said. "Enough stalling. Tell us everything."

"You had a date with Todd," Velvet said.

"You might say that." Alice burst out laughing, then filled the two women in on her adventures of the weekend.

"Wow. A one-weekend stand," Velvet said. "God, I envy you."

"Why?" Alice said, genuinely puzzled. "Isn't Wayne good? You know what I mean."

"He's great, but there's no thrill like a new man and the adventure of new and great sex."

"As good as Larry is," Betsy added, "and we're very in tune and totally compatible, first times are something totally different, the stuff fantasies are made of."

"Well this was certainly the stuff of fantasies," Alice said, sipping her soda. "It's like I've discovered a new toy. I knew creative sex existed and I've made up dozens of stories about it, but that was from the outside looking in. Now I've opened Pandora's box and I want to sample everything inside." She thought about the catalog Betsy had given her that she had never gotten around to exploring. "I want it all."

"And you should have it," Betsy said. "Good sex is the best stuff. I know from experience."

"Are you going to see Todd again before he leaves?" Velvet asked.

"Unfortunately, no. He's leaving tomorrow and I have callers tonight."

"That's really sad."

"No, it's really not," Alice said. "This was a slice out of a fantasy. It's not real and in some ways I wouldn't want it to become too real."

"Like how?" Betsy asked.

"I don't want to know what he's like when he's cranky, or sick. I don't know whether we have much in common and this way it doesn't matter. It was neat, and now it's done. Maybe we'll do it again, and maybe not but it's all okay."

"Aren't you sad that it was so short?" Betsy continued. "I mean, that might have become something more permanent. Don't you want that?"

"In some ways I do, but this wasn't it. If he were a local, we would have dated and gotten to know each other before we ended up in bed together and that's the basis of something more. Like Vic and I are doing. Since this weekend I have a bit more of an open mind about men and dating now that I've found out more about the real me."

"Who's the real you?"

"Someone who enjoys sex for the sake of sex."

"Indulging in one-night stands isn't life. It's not real," Betsy said.

"Exactly and I know that, but it's not wrong either.

Obviously if someone comes along and we hit it off, that's wonderful. For the moment, however, I want to experiment, to explore, to experience firsthand all the things I've talked about with my callers. I want to play."

"What about Vic?" Velvet asked.

"We're meeting tomorrow night for dinner."

"Which category does he fit into?" Betsy asked.

"I haven't the faintest idea." She raised her glass. "Here's to not knowing and not caring." The three women touched glasses and toasted.

That evening Sheherazade's stories took on a new dimension. They were a bit more adventurous and there was a special music in her voice. Two of her regular callers noticed and told her that they enjoyed her tales even more than usual.

The following evening, Alice met Vic for dinner. The evening passed delightfully quickly, with good conversation and lots of laughter. There were moments when Alice thought about her split personality. Although she and Vic had become acquainted through their phone calls, so far their two "dates" had been chaste with no conversation about sex in any form.

As they sipped coffee, Vic asked, "Can I see you next Saturday? Like a real Saturday night date?"

"I'd like that." Alice stared at Vic's hands that now surrounded his coffee cup. Short, blunt fingers, wide palms. Nice, functional hands. How would they feel touching her? she wondered. *Stop that,* she told herself. *Every man isn't Todd. Every evening isn't a prelude to a romp in bed.*

"I'd love to find someplace a bit more subdued. All this green and white has me wondering whether I'm growing roots."

Alice's smile widened. "I'm not too familiar with this area. How far north do you want to drive?"

Vic winked. "Your place?" Over the sound of her breath

catching in her throat, Vic continued, "I'm so sorry. I promised myself that I wouldn't mention anything like that. I don't want you to think that I'm here because of the way we met. I mean I'm not after sex. I mean . . ." Obviously frustrated, Vic ran his fingers through his shaggy hair.

"Whoa," Alice said. "Sex doesn't have to be a taboo topic between us. We met under really bizarre circumstances so maybe it's a bit awkward but we can't trip over our tongues either."

"I know, but I don't want you to get the wrong idea."

"I won't. When two people get to know each other, like we are, it's natural that the conversation will eventually turn to sexual topics. We both understand that I'm not Sheherazade. I'm just plain Alice Waterman but I'm not a prude either." *Certainly not a prude anymore,* she thought.

"You're a delightfully creative person and I think you're terrific." Alice could see Vic begin to blush. It was strange how different he was in person from the sexy man she had known over the phone. "Let's change the subject. Is next Saturday evening okay with you?"

"I'd like that. There's a great little place in Brewster that has good food and a small dance floor. Do you like to dance?"

"I love it," Vic said.

She'd been to a few dances in high school but had gotten discouraged when the only boys who asked her to dance had had octopus hands and were interested in where they could touch. She liked music and had tried to talk Ralph into going out a few times, to no avail.

"Great. Let me check on the name of the place and I'll get directions for you and call you later in the week."

As they approached her car in the parking lot, Vic became silent. "Alice, this is really bothering me."

"What is?"

"I want to kiss you good night but I'm in that same bind

I was in before. I don't want you to get the wrong idea."

Alice turned and cupped Vic's face with her palms. "This is really silly." She touched his lips, softly tasting his mouth. As they kissed, she felt his hands lightly stroke her back. She couldn't help contrast this kiss with the toe-curling ones she had shared with Todd. This was entirely different, soft, shy, questioning, hopeful.

"Phew," Vic said as they separated. "Maybe there's more of Sheherazade in you than you know." He kissed her this time and she enjoyed the undemanding feel of his mouth on hers.

"Nice," she purred. "Very nice." Unwilling to go any further yet, she turned and unlocked her car. "I'll call you."

As she settled behind the wheel, Vic leaned over and kissed her again. "I'll look forward to that."

Nice man, she thought as she started her car. Nice, uncomplicated man.

When she got home, she found that she wasn't tired. Betsy's catalog lay on her dresser waiting for her to have some time to look through it, so she picked it up and stretched out on the bed. With his usual chirrup, Roger leaped up beside her and stretched out on his back. Idly scratching the cat's stomach, Alice propped the catalog on her raised knees and looked at the model on the front cover. "I guess that's what my guys think Sheherazade looks like," she said. "What do you think, Roger? Nothing that ten years, a face-lift, twenty-five pounds, and the right makeup wouldn't fix. Right?"

Merrow.

She flipped to an inside page. "Oh my," she said, gazing at a page full of dildos, in all colors, shapes, and textures. "I never imagined that anyone would want one of those in hot pink." Actually, she'd never imagined anyone owning one until she began telling her stories. She turned the page and found vibrators in almost as many varieties. As she thumbed through the thick catalog, she found lubes, anal plugs, cock rings, and several devices she didn't quite understand. She also found that her body responded to the pictures and the ideas they fostered. "I guess it's all research," she told the cat.

For a second time, she went through the catalog and decided to order several items. She noticed that the company had a Web site so, thinking it would be easier and less personal to purchase that way, she logged on and placed an order for a three-dildo collection and a battery-operated vibrator. Now anxious to receive the objects, she clicked on the overnight delivery icon, gave her credit-card number, and logged off. "Well, Roger, I've now ordered my first sex toys. Am I a sophisticate or what?"

Friday, when she arrived home from work, the package was waiting on her doorstep. She had almost two hours before her first client, so she made herself a peanut-butter and jelly sandwich and poured herself a diet soda. Dinner and package in hand, she adjourned to the bedroom. Still chewing her first bite, she grabbed a pair of scissors and stabbed at the tape. Finally the box opened. "Well, Pandora, I know just how you must have felt."

On top of the packaging material she found lots of literature from the company with this month's specials, movies for sale, and three paper folders from affiliated companies. As she placed them on the bed beside her, she noticed that one was for an erotic book sales business, one from a company that specialized in leather items, and one from a phone-sex line. She looked more carefully at the slick paper phone-sex ad. HOT WOMEN WITH SOPPING PUSSIES ANXIOUS FOR YOUR PRICK, one headline read. "Makes what I do sound so dirty," she said. "Amazing."

Beneath the literature, she found two boxes, one with her dildos and one with the vibrator. She opened the dildo box first. Each of the objects inside resembled an erect penis, one in soft pink plastic, about one inch in diameter with thick ridges at half-inch intervals down the shaft; one blue, shorter than the first and very thick around; and a third in soft green plastic curved to, as the box indicated, "stimulate her G-spot." She placed the three on their wide bases on the bed-table and giggled. "Three blind mice," she sang. "Oh Roger, this is so silly." Roger sniffed at the now-empty box, then put his front paws on the bedside table and sniffed at the three dildos. Then he sneezed from the plastic smell and settled on the bed. "Right attitude," Alice said.

She opened the box with the vibrator and looked at each of the tips that came with it. One was flat, with little cup-like structures all over it, one a soft nob, one a long slender rod that was for insertion and one with a long shaft with a ball at the end covered with soft, inchlong flexible fingers of latex. "Looks like the Spanish inquisition to me, but I won't dismiss any of it. Some women must like it."

She munched on her sandwich and let her mind wander. Toys. They hadn't played much of a part in her stories up to now, but with this inspiration, she might just create something new for one of her callers tonight. She also understood that as strange as these items might appear when she was calm and cool, when she was aroused, they would look entirely different. She thought about the lipstick she had used many times as a dildo. Now she had the real thing and ideas flooded her mind.

Her first caller was new and she used a story she'd told several times in the past. When she was done, she was pleased, especially when he asked whether he could call again. Her second was a regular and she continued the story she had begun several weeks earlier.

Her third caller was a man named Jacques whom Alice

had spoken to a few times. Many men used assumed names and tried to change the tone of their voice when they called her so it didn't faze her that Jacques put on a thick French accent when they spoke. He also had a delightfully creative mind. Once he had even helped with a story, making suggestions about what the characters should do. Alice gazed at the three dildos still lined up on the table beside her bed. Jacques was the perfect man for a story that had been smouldering in her mind all night.

"Jacques, you sweet thing," she said when the router put him through. "I've been waiting for you."

"I've been waiting for you too, *cherie,*" Jacques said. His accent was particularly thick that evening. She had no idea what he looked like, but even though the accent was phony, he sounded sexy as hell.

"I thought I'd tell you about a date I had a few years ago."

"Ohh," Jacques said. "I wish you would date me."

"Well, if you keep sounding so sexy, I just might."

"If I'm ever where you are, maybe we can be together."

"Well, you keep asking and maybe I'll break down one of these days." She knew this was all talk since neither of them had any idea where the other was. "What if I call the man Jacques? Then we can pretend that we were there together."

"Marvelous," he said. "I don't want to think of you with other men. Me, I would please you so much you wouldn't need anyone else."

"Oh, I know you would. Anyway," Alice began, "it was summer. Jacques and I had dated about a dozen times and, since we stayed up late making love one Saturday night, we had decided that he would stay over. Now it was morning and, when I woke up I found that his side of the bed was empty. Puzzled I got up and headed for the bathroom. On the counter beside the sink I found a large box with a note that said,

Do not open until exactly 9:00 a.m. Then unwrap this and follow the instructions inside to the letter! I'll pick you up at 10:00.

"It was only seven-thirty but I couldn't wait to see what was inside the large box. As I started to untie the bright red ribbon my eyes found the note again. . . exactly 9:00 a.m. . . . *What the hell,* I thought, *I'll play along.* Thinking about what might be in the box was making my nerve endings tingle."

"That sounds like quite a date you had. Tell me about the man. Was he tall like me, with big biceps and big shoulders? I'm big all over, you know."

"I'll bet you are," Alice said, grinning. "Actually he wasn't much to look at, but he had a gleam in his eye and a very sexy mind." In many of her stories, the men were ordinary-looking, unless her caller wanted it otherwise. No need to further the myth that sexy men were gorgeous. "Anyway, I showered, carefully washing all my special places, reveling in the feel of my bath sponge rubbing my skin. I slipped on a robe and went to the kitchen to find some breakfast. On the table, beside the morning paper was another note.

I hope you've followed my instructions and haven't opened the box yet. The anticipation is making you hot. Is it?

It sure is, I thought. The note continued:

Good. Breakfast is ready for you. I'll see you at 10:00. And remember, no touching yourself.

"I found a carefully cut grapefruit half and a bowl of cereal on the counter, with hot coffee on the warmer. He was so considerate. I ate my breakfast, unable to concentrate on anything. What was in the box?

"At 8:55 I walked back into the bedroom, fetched the box from the bathroom and put it on the bed. As the digital clock clicked from 8:59 to 9:00 A.M., I opened the red ribbon and tore through the white wrapping paper. I pulled the top off the box and folded back gobs of tissue paper. Then I found a note.

> DARLING, IN HERE YOU'LL FIND A NEW TOY I BOUGHT FOR US. INSERT IT, THEN PUT ON THE CLOTHING, AND NOTHING ELSE. WAIT FOR ME IN THE LIVING ROOM. I'LL BE THERE AT TEN. AND NO PLAYING WITH YOURSELF!

"I'm quite the devil, am I not, *cherie*?"

Jacques had gotten into the story as he always did and Alice grinned. She picked up one of the dildos, thought about an item she had seen on the Internet the previous evening, then continued the tale. "I rummaged in the box and found a sizable dildo with a narrow bulge about halfway up and another at the blunt end, and a door with some batteries inside. I tried to find a switch to turn the thing on so I could find out what it did, but there was nothing. Although it was pretty thick around, I knew it would fit inside of my pussy with little coaxing, especially since I was so excited at the sight of that new toy. As I put it aside, I wondered again what the electronic gizmo was for. I reached back into the box and pulled out the clothing, a pair of jeans, a bustier, a sheer blouse, and a pair of soft black slippers. 'There're no underwear,' I said aloud. Then I smiled. 'Fine with me.' "

"Umm. Fine with me too," Jacques said. "Tell me what you looked like. What did you do?"

"I removed my robe and stared at the dildo. Then I slowly

inserted it into my hungry pussy. At that moment I wanted nothing more than to stroke my clit and get myself off, but the note specifically said that I was not to masturbate so I reluctantly removed my fingers from my crotch. As I moved around, I discovered that the dildo stayed in place, tightly inside my cunt, held securely by the bulge in the center. Very little of it stuck out, just enough of the second bulge to keep it from sliding all the way in. I wondered where Jacques found it.

"Slowly, I stood up and put on the bustier. It was a size too small so once it was hooked up the center of the front it squeezed my ribs tightly, lifting my breasts until I almost spilled out the top. I saw that if I positioned my breasts properly my nipples poked through tiny holes. The fullness in my pussy and the tight almost corset-like fit of the bustier combined to keep my heat turned up high."

Jacques sighed. "I know you have beautiful breasts, *cherie*."

"Oh yes, I do," Alice purred. "I pulled on the jeans and found that they, too, were a size too small. I knew that Jacques knew my sizes well, so this must all be calculated to make me hot. It was certainly working. As I wiggled into the jeans I suddenly became aware that the crotch of the pants wasn't sewn closed, just laced with a red ribbon. The jeans were so tight that I had to lie on my back and loosen the ribbon to get the zipper closed. Now, if I spread my thighs, I could see the ends of the ribbon and feel air on my crotch. The dildo was held firmly in place, yet my lips were exposed to the air. Oh, Jacques, you devil."

Jacques's chuckle through the phone was warm and liquid.

Alice stood and pulled down her sweatpants. She stretched out on the bed, aroused and already wet. "I looked at the clock and discovered that is was only nine-thirty. I had thirty minutes to wait and think about

Jacques's arrival home. I hoped that he would pull these clothes off and fuck me senseless, but I knew Jacques well enough to know that this was just the beginning.

"I slipped the sheer blouse on and felt the fabric brush against my fully erect nipples. It was quite an outfit but despite all of the erotic details, it was almost decent. Since my nipples were dark and the blouse was navy blue, no one could really see that I wasn't decently clothed, and, although the ribbon showed, it could have been a decoration, not a covering for my naked crotch. And, of course, no one could know about the dildo.

"I walked into the living room and realized that, as I walked, the dildo shifted slightly inside me. God, I was hot. I wanted to wiggle my hips and touch myself, rub my clit until I came, but still I hesitated. Jacques didn't want me to. So I sat on the sofa and waited.

"At exactly ten, I heard the key in the lock. The door opened and Jacques walked in. He wore jeans, a white cotton sweater, and sneakers. He looked so ordinary. 'Stand up,' he said and I stood. 'God, you're sexy,' he growled, 'and you make me hard.' He unzipped his jeans and his fully erect cock sprang forth. 'Fix this for me,' he said.

"I love sucking him, so I quickly got down on my knees and drew his hard cock into my mouth. I did all the things I know he loves, fondled his balls, tickled his anus, flicked my tongue over the tip of his cock, and it was only moments until he filled my mouth with his come."

"Would you do that for me, *cherie*, if we were together?"

"Of course, Jacques. What would you do for me?"

"I would untie that red ribbon and kiss and suck and lick you until you begged for me. I am very talented, you know."

"I'll bet you are. And the other Jacques was a very clever lover too. Just like you. When I finished with his cock, he said, 'That's better,' and zipped up his pants.

"'Not for me,' I whispered, wanting his hands, his

mouth, his cock to relieve my incredible need.

"'I know but you've got a long day in front of you.'

"I frowned, then slipped my fingers into my crotch. Jacques slapped my hand. Hard. I had known he would and I smiled, enjoying the erotic teasing. 'Bad girl,' he snapped. 'You have to wait.' He started toward the door. 'Come with me.'

"I followed. In the driveway was a small red convertible with the top down. I smiled as I realized that he had rented it for us. He opened the door on my side and I saw that the passenger seat was covered with a furry pad. As I went to slide into the car, he grabbed my wrist. 'Just a minute.' He loosened the ribbon that held the crotch of my jeans together until the sides were widely separated. 'Now sit.'

"The furry pad rubbed against my wet lips and pressed the dildo tightly into my channel. Softly, Jacques said, 'The dildo doesn't hurt, does it?'

"'Well, yes and no,' I answered. 'It makes me really hot and so hungry I would love to jump you, but hurt? Not really.'

"Jacques grinned. 'Good.' He slammed the door and leaned into the open car. 'I don't want you to touch your pussy,' he said, 'so these are for you.' First he fastened a wide leather collar around my neck, then he pulled a pair of connected leather manacles from his back pocket and cuffed my wrists together. Then he took a small padlock and locked the short chain between the cuffs to a large ring on the collar. My hands were now at breast level and I was unable to touch my cunt. He reached in and carefully fastened my seat belt, then walked around and got into the car."

"Oh, *cherie*," Jacques said into the phone. "I can just see you like that. Tell me where you are and I'll run to your house and we can play together for the rest of our lives."

"I'm so sorry, Jacques, but you know that giving out my address or phone number is against the rules."

He sighed long and loud. "I know and I'm so sad."

"I am too," Alice said with a small sigh. "Anyway, we drove into the country, the wind in my hair, the fullness in my pussy. I was in plain sight and people in other cars must have wondered at my unusual position, but for the most part the drive was uneventful and slowly, my body calmed. At about eleven-thirty, Jacques pulled the car to the side of a tree-lined lane and stopped. 'We have a bit farther to go, but I think it's time for you to find out the secret of the dildo,' he said. 'Did you notice the battery opening? Curious? Well, here's the control.' He showed me a small box with several dials. 'Let's see how it feels if I turn this.'

"Suddenly there was a whirring and the dildo began to hum, moving inside of me like something alive. Shards of pleasure shot through me, stabbing from my pussy to my nipples. I moved my hips trying to drive the dildo deeper into my cunt." Alice pulled the crotch of her panties aside and slipped the ridged pink dildo into her pussy. As she pressed, the rings of thicker plastic pushed into her like the vibrating dildo she was creating in her story. "'And this one,' Jacques said, turning another dial. The sensation was like having my pussy channel massaged from the inside. I guessed that the bulge around the girth of the dildo was moving deeper inside of me, then further toward the base of the shaft of the artificial penis. The feeling drove me higher.

"'And this,' he said, finding another dial. The bulge around the base of the dildo moved, rubbing my clit. 'Oh, God,' I cried. 'Don't stop.' My eyes closed and my back arched. I squirmed, confined in my seat belt, unable to get my hands to my crotch. 'You can reach your tits,' he purred, 'so pinch them. And move your hips to make it better.'"

Phone propped against her ear, Alice pulled the dildo out, then pushed it in again. She allowed some of her breathlessness and excitement to flow into the story. "Jacques, can you imagine how it felt? I'm playing with a real dildo now."

"You are? Wonderful. My cock is so big and hard. I wish you were playing with it instead of my hand."

"I wish it, too, Jacques. Tell me, did you make it slippery?"

"Oh, *cherie*. It feels so good. I can picture you with that machine fucking you, so hot waiting for orgasm, just like I am right now."

"Yes, I was. I wanted it, needed it. I sat in the car, parked in the open and rolled my hardened nipples between my fingers, squeezing hard as I tried to drive the dildo more tightly into my pussy. I was higher than I had ever been, hot, swirling colors filling my vision. 'Come for me. Now!' Jacques said, and he reached between my legs and touched my clit. I came, deep, hard spasms of pleasure ricocheting throughout my body, reaching my breasts, my mouth, my cunt. It was as if every muscle in my entire body joined in the pleasure. It went on and on, lasting for long minutes."

"Oh, baby," Jacques said, his accent disappearing as it always did when he came, "damn you're good. Are you fucking yourself with the dildo? Are you close?"

"Yes," Alice whispered.

"Good. Now come for me. I want to hear it."

Alice plunged the dildo into her pussy then, leaving it in place, she rubbed her clit. "Yes," she purred as she rubbed. "Yes."

"Oh, *cherie*," he said, his accent as thick as it had been, "rub your sweet pussy. Touch it and stroke it and think of my big hard cock. Think how it would be if my fingers were stroking you and my cock was filling you."

"Yes," Alice said, feeling the now-familiar pleasures swirling through her. Soon. Just another moment.

"Now I will bite your nipple and you will come, just like you did in that car. I rub, I bite, I fuck you so hard. Come for me, *cherie*."

"Yes!" she shouted as the waves of orgasm pounded through her body. "Yes!"

There were a few moments of silence, then Alice said, "You always do that for me, Jacques."

"And you always do it for me. When I call next time will you tell me about the rest of the day you spent with the dildo in your sweet cunt?"

"Of course. The day had just begun."

"I'll call again soon."

"I hope so."

"You know so."

Chapter 12

At six o'clock Saturday evening Vic picked Alice up at her apartment. "This is lovely," he commented. "So like you, organized and conservative."

Alice wasn't sure she liked that characterization. "You make me sound almost dull."

"Not at all but so unlike Sheherazade. I like you just the way you are, Alice." He looked at her outfit, black linen slacks and a white open-collar shirt with a small tan geometric design. "Yes, I definitely like you just the way you are."

Alice thought about the way Vic saw her. That's the way I was until I started working at Velvet Whispers. Now I'm so much more. I don't want to be conservative Alice Waterman anymore. "Let me get my jacket," she said, leaving Vic in the living room. In the bedroom she peered into her closet. A classic tan linen jacket lay on the bed but suddenly she didn't want to wear it. She flipped through hanger after hanger of basic slacks, blouses, jackets, and vests. How ordinary, she thought.

Then, from the very back of her closet she grabbed a bright red blazer with gold buttons. *I must go to the mall and update my wardrobe.* She found several pins and scattered them on her lapels. Finally, she took a small ladybug pin and attached it to the top of one shoulder. Better. Then she added a bit of mascara and put a coat of red lipstick over the soft coral she had been wearing. Finally she removed the combs that had been controlling her hair and fluffed out her curls. *Conservative indeed. Maybe I want to be a little more like Sheherazade.*

When she arrived back in the living room, Vic had his back to her, gazing at her music collection. "Very eclectic," he said. "Andean, Balkan, country and western, even some Chopin and Mozart. Very nice assortment."

"Thanks," Alice said. "Shall we have dinner?"

He turned and looked at her flame-colored jacket. "Well. Not so conservative after all. You look great."

As it had the previous two dinners, the meal sped by. Conversation roamed from the situation in the Middle East to several new sitcoms on TV. They talked about the unusually warm weather and the possibility of Alice's coming into the city to see Vic's latest video game. When the music began, they danced, Vic holding her at a proper distance. Slowly she moved closer, wanting to feel his body against hers but each time he realized that they were pressed against each other, he backed up. Finally, at about eleven o'clock, they left the restaurant, with Alice aroused and frustrated. She really wanted to crack Vic's uptight facade. They had taken Vic's Buick and, when they arrived back at Alice's apartment, she invited him inside for a nightcap.

"You don't usually drink," Vic said, following Alice into her living room.

"I feel like something silly tonight. Friends and I go out once a week or so and I've gotten quite fond of a concoction made with orange juice, melon liqueur, and vodka. I got the makings recently. Can I interest you in one?"

"Okay. Sure."

Vic followed Alice into the kitchen and watched as she prepared the drinks. "They're called Melon Balls. What do you think?"

Vic sipped. "Delicious," he said downing half the drink as they walked into the living room.

As nice as Vic was being, Alice was becoming impatient with his reluctance to venture into anything even remotely resembling sexuality. She knew he wasn't gay from the stories she had told him. So what was with him?

Vic settled onto the sofa and Alice sat beside him. She touched the rim of her glass to his. "Here's to good sex." *That ought to shake him up a bit,* she thought.

"You mean now?" Vic said, staring.

Alice put her drink down. "Why not?"

"But . . .well . . .I'm not really in your league. I mean . . ."

"Vic, I think there are a few things we should get out into the open. We both know how we met and that's making this really strange. I find you attractive and sexy. This is our third date and I just thought that, since we're here, together, that we might experiment a bit."

"Experiment?"

"See whether we're compatible. Of course, if you don't find me tempting, I will certainly understand."

"Oh, Alice, I find you most tempting. It's just that, well, I'm a bit intimidated."

"I frighten you?"

"No." He paused and stared into his glass. "Sheherazade does."

"I thought we had agreed that she's not real. She's just a character I put on and take off at will."

"I know that, but somehow she's always there, in the back of my mind. I'm sorry."

Alice was somehow amused. "Sheherazade scares the daylights out of you, doesn't she?"

"I'm afraid so." He turned toward her. "Oh, Alice, I've dreamed about making love to you, but in all the dreams, just when we're about to do it, you know, there's Sherry, watching, judging how creative I am. And I always fail. Although I enjoy your stories and have my fantasies, I'm not really very adventurous."

Alice stroked Vic's cheek. "This is all silly. I am who I am and you are who you are. If we're good together, that's great. If not, well nothing's lost."

"A lot is lost. That's what you don't understand. I like you very much. I don't want to sacrifice our friendship. If we go to bed and it's terrible, then what?"

Alice touched her lips to Vic's. "Why should it be terrible?"

"My wife always said that I wasn't much in the bedroom department."

Alice sat back. "There are good and bad lovers, of course. But the bad lovers are the ones with no imagination, no ability to play, to enjoy, and to communicate. We've been communicating and imagining and playing for months on the phone so that shouldn't be a problem."

"On the phone," Vic said. "Not in real life. Face to face. I don't know whether I'm good enough for you. I might disappoint you."

"I really believe, and not from a lot of personal experience, mind you, that couples are good or bad, not individuals. I find you attractive and I'm excited by the possibility of making love with you."

"You want to make love to a basset hound?"

"That's the second time you've used that term. That really bothers you, doesn't it?"

"I guess it does. My wife used that as a term of endearment early in our marriage. Then later, it became her little joke, but eventually I didn't find it funny."

"I can imagine you didn't." Alice put her hand on Vic's

thigh. "Are you going to let her get between us too? There are too many of us here already: you, me, Sheherazade, and now your ex-wife. Let's just be you and me and see what happens."

Vic gazed into Alice's eyes, then his expression softened. "You're right, of course." He put his arms around her and kissed her, putting all the longing he was feeling into the meeting of mouths. Suddenly hunger seemed to sweep over them, ending all of Vic's hesitation. Hands unbuttoned, unbuckled, and unzipped. Mouths quested and found erotic spots, hard flesh, and wetness. "Oh God, baby," he murmured as he paused to unroll a condom over his erection. Then, still on the sofa, he was inside of her. Alice's nails dug into his back while he drove into her. She wrapped her legs around his waist and pulled him closer, bucking her hips to take him more deeply inside her.

Their climaxes were fast and hard. And loud.

"Still think you're a basset hound? I don't know any basset hounds that make love like that."

"It was all right?" Vic asked.

"It was fantastic."

Later they lay on Alice's bed, naked, side by side, sipping drinks. "Do you remember the first story you ever told me?" Vic asked, mellower than she had seen him since they'd first met face to face.

Alice thought. "It was about the toll taker, wasn't it?"

"Yes, and they made love hard and fast like we did. I lived that story a thousand times in my mind, seeing me and you. Remember? Long blond hair and blue eyes?"

Alice grinned. "Not like the real me at all."

"Nor the real me either. But in my fantasies, I was young and virile and you were blond and blue-eyed. You know what? This was much better."

"This was great," Alice said.

"Can I ask you for something really strange? Would you

tell me a story, like Sheherazade used to do? I've always fantasized about being able to touch you while you were telling me one of your wonderful tales."

Alice considered it. Sheherazade was an illusion, a voice on the phone, a figment of her imagination just as surely as her stories were. The real Alice was solid and down to earth. But were they really so separate? Hadn't the gap between her two selves narrowed over the past weeks? She had always believed that she couldn't talk as freely about lovemaking when she could look someone in the eye, but now that Vic had asked, she wanted to tell him a great story. And maybe she could find out what kinds of lovemaking he liked at the same time.

She stood up and padded around the apartment, turning out all the lights. Then, before turning out the small bedside light in the bedroom, she lit several candles, the ones still left from Todd's visit.

She stretched out on the bed and pulled a quilt over the two of them, then cuddled against Vic in the flickering light. "You have to help me," she said. "Close your eyes. Set the scene. Tell me where you are, what you're seeing. Think about the most perfect encounter you can imagine. How would it begin?"

"Boy, you're really asking me to reveal my deepest secrets, aren't you?"

"No. You can create anything you like, so go wherever you want. Let's create people for our story who are gorgeous, perfect creatures who are so sexy that no one can resist us. That's what I imagine when I tell a story."

"You have those fantasies too?"

"Sure. I have long flowing hair. Sometimes it's black, sometimes blond, sometimes red but it's always long and it blows in the wind like a shampoo commercial." She'd shared so many fantasies, but had never been this personal and honest before. She wanted Vic to know that they both had the same insecurities. "I'd have blue eyes with long black lashes, a perfect small nose, and those wonderful full lips that sort of pout, the ones that men find so kissable."

Vic propped himself on one elbow and kissed her softly, nipping at her lower lip. "I think you've got a great, sexy mouth." He lay back down.

"What do you look like in your dreams?"

"I'm tall. I'm always about six foot four, with broad shoulders and lots of muscles. I have black wavy hair and black eyes. I guess you'd say I was a stud, with women panting to get dates with me."

"So you've got all the women you want in your dreams?"

"In my dreams, the one I want most doesn't want me, except on her terms."

"Oh." Alice vaguely remembered that Velvet had told her that Vic liked aggressive women. "She's forceful?"

"Very."

"How do you two meet?" She wanted to hear, and possibly play out Vic's fantasy. "How about at a party? The wine and booze are flowing freely and everyone is feeling quite mellow. Is she there?"

She heard Vic's long-drawn-out, "*Yessss.*"

"Does she excite you?"

"Oh yes. I can't take my eyes off of her. She's tall, almost five feet ten and has long red hair that hangs almost to her waist. Her body is firm and trim with small breasts. She isn't wearing the usual party uniform: the slinky dress that advertises her availability. Instead, she's wearing a black blouse buttoned up to her throat and knotted at the waist and tight, black stretch pants. She has accentuated her waist with a silver concho belt, which matches her large silver squash-blossom earrings. She has completed her outfit with knee-high black leather boots that lace up the front with silver rings at the top.

"I start toward her. As I get closer, I admire her green eyes and smooth skin. I gaze at her red lips and feel a further tightening in my pants."

Alice felt Vic take her hand beneath the quilt. As long as Vic was willing to continue the story, Alice was anxious to listen.

"'Hi, gorgeous,' I say, using my most charming voice. 'How about I get you a fresh drink and then we can get to know each other?'

"The girl looks at me. Her eyes roam my body, making me a bit self-conscious. Then she looks away.

"I want to get to know her, then take her to bed even." Vic chuckled. "Actually I don't care if I ever get to know her, I merely want to fuck her senseless, lose myself in her body."

"I'll bet it's not going to be as easy as you think," Alice said.

"No, it's not," Vic said, squeezing her hand. "You know, this storytelling isn't as easy as I thought. It's a bit scary, like I'm telling you all about me."

"I know. If anyone listens to my stories they will find out all the things that turn me on. I can't invent a really good erotic fantasy about activities that don't get me excited." She paused. "You really don't have to make it so personal if you don't want to," Alice said. "We can certainly tell this story other, less scary ways."

"I know, but it's a sort of delicious-scary. I'd like to continue as long as I can." He took a deep breath. "So I say to the woman, 'I'm sorry. Are you with someone?'

"'No,' she says with her back to me.

"'Then why not me?' I ask.

"'You're not my type,' she says.

"Well, I am surprised. 'And what is your type?' I ask.

"She turns and looks at me. 'My type always waits for me to make the first move. As a matter of fact, my type always waits for me to make every move.' "

Alice felt his grip tighten and knew he was telling her something he wanted her to hear, something he'd probably never told anyone. In his fantasy the woman is the aggressor and he is the follower. "I'll bet that gets to you, makes you hard."

"Oh yes, it does," Vic said. "My whole body shudders and I can hardly control my excitement. My pulse is hammering and I'm panting. I can hardly get the words out. 'W-w-what would your type do right now?' I stammer."

Alice leaned close to his ear and whispered, "What does she say?"

"She smiles and says, 'My type would light a cigarette and hand it to me,' so I take out a cigarette, light it, and hand it to her with shaking fingers.

"'Hmm,' she says. 'Very good,' then she just wanders off through the crowd."

Alice held his hand tightly. "I'll bet she comes back. I would, if I were her. I like men who know how to behave and you knew exactly what to do." She heard the hiss of Vic's indrawn breath. She wanted to make him hotter, make it easier for him to talk, she realized, and she'd read enough stories to understand what he would like. "You were such a good boy."

"I was? Oh yes. Well eventually she does come back, almost an hour later. I stare at her, but she says, sternly, 'Never look me in the eye. You may only look at me from the shoulders down unless I give you permission. Understand?'

"I looked at her shiny boots, staring at the sharply pointed toes, the heavy silver rings through the zippers, and the high spike heels. 'Yes, I understand.' I can hardly speak."

"What's her name?" Alice whispered. "We can call her anything you want."

"Valerie," Vic said. "She says that her name is Valerie. 'You must learn to say, *Yes, Valerie,* or *Yes, ma'am.* Now practice that.'

"'Yes, Valerie,' I say. 'Yes, ma'am.'

"'Not bad for a beginner,' she says. As she speaks, I watch her hands with those long red fingernails that are sliding up and down the hips of her tight pants. 'Now go into the bathroom,' she says. Her voice is soft but firm and seems to brook no objections. 'Take off your shorts and bring them to me. Quickly, with no dawdling.'

"God, I'm so hot." Vic hesitated, so Alice said, "I'll bet you're a good boy and do as you're told?"

"Oh yes, I do. I almost run into the bathroom, pull off my slacks and shorts and allow my huge erection to poke from the front of my crotch. I want to touch it, rub it, but I know she's waiting, so I pull my slacks back on, ball my shorts in my hand and hurry back through the crowd. I find her where I left her, standing beside the bar. I remember and gaze down at her boots, as I surreptitiously hand her my shorts. Valerie props her elbow on the bar as she dangles my shorts from her index finger for all to see. There are several snickers from other people at the party but I'm willing to risk anything. I start to reach for the shorts but Valerie glares at me. I drop my hand and blush for the first time in years, lowering my eyes to her leather boots."

"You were being such an obedient boy," Alice says, still holding his hand, using his grip as an indication of his excitement. "I like obedient boys."

"What would you say now?" Vic asked, his voice hoarse, his need evident.

Picking up the story, Alice continued, "I would be very glad that you did as you were told. I find you quite attractive and you would be a good addition to my collection. 'I see we understand each other,' I would say. 'Go and find my coat. It's long, black leather. Bring it to me and we'll get out of here.' Will you do that, Vic?"

"Yes. Of course. I go into the bedroom and root through the coats. I find hers, then I stop for a moment and wonder why I'm doing this. Has this girl cast some kind of spell over me? She has and I know it. And I don't care. I have to have her. I will do anything she wants just to get a chance to make love to her."

Alice shifted her grip to his wrist and held it tightly. She recalled Todd's commanding tone and trembled. She knew just how Vic was feeling, wanting to be controlled by an erotic fantasy woman. She wanted Vic to continue so she said, "Tell me what happens then."

"Well, later, in the cab on the way to her apartment, she says, 'Give me your wrists.' She pulls a length of soft black rope from her purse and stares at me. I know what she wants, so I offer her my wrists and she ties them together, then reaches down and lifts the heavy silver ring that's attached to one of her boots. She takes the free end of the rope and ties it to the ring.

"When we reach our destination, the rope forces me to get out of the taxi carefully and walk bent over with my head level with her breasts. Twice, I almost stumble when Valerie takes a particularly long step." Vic hesitated.

"Tell me," Alice urged.

"This is really kinky but when I regain my balance, she laughs and I'm so aroused by her laughter that I think I'll come right there. Am I perverted, Alice?"

"Not at all. I think it's really hot," Alice said. "Does she take you to her apartment?"

"Yes. We enter her apartment and she turns on the lights. All the furniture is chrome, glass, or black lacquer. The rug is dark red with deep pile and it silences our footsteps.

"Without a word she unties the end of the rope attached to her boot and reties it to a ring embedded in the wall. Then she turns and disappears into the next room. It's very warm in her apartment so, since I'm still wearing my winter jacket, I begin to sweat and feel a trickle of perspiration run down my side. I wiggle as much as I can, trying to brush my shirt against the tiny river.

"'Don't squirm!' she snaps as she reenters the room. She has changed into a black corset that reveals her full breasts and pussy and she has put on long black gloves without fingers. She has also pulled her hair back tightly and wound it into a tight knot at the back of her neck. She's still wearing her boots and is banging a short riding crop against the top of one. God, this is really hard to talk about."

"Your story is really getting me hot." Alice took Vic's hand and placed it on her mound. His fingers slipped naturally between her lips and she knew he could feel her wetness. She didn't know whether she could actually become the character in Vic's story and play the scene out with him, but the tale was making her hungry. Now she understood exactly what her callers felt when she spun one of her fantasies. "Tell me what happens then," Alice said, an air of command in her voice.

"Valerie flicks the crop against the back of my thigh," Vic continued. "The effect is muffled by my jeans but the crop still stings. 'You were looking at me,' she snaps. I immediately drop my gaze.

"Valerie reaches up, unties my hands, and unfastens the rope from the wall. As she stretches, her naked breasts brush against me. I wonder how much of this I can take before I come in my pants."

Alice placed her hand gently over Vic's extremely hard cock. "Go on," she said, squeezing. She can hear Vic's hoarse, quick breathing and feel his body shake.

"Valerie walks over to the sofa and sits down, the rope still in her hands. 'Strip,' she orders. I obey as quickly as I can with my hands shaking as hard as they are.

"I stand before her, naked. Her eyes roam over my body, my erection poking straight in front of me, aching for relief.

"'I demand stamina from my men,' she says. 'You may not come unless I give you permission. The first time is always the most difficult so I will give you some help. Crawl over here.'

"I do it, on my hands and knees. I'll do anything she wants. 'Stand up straight,' she says, 'and touch yourself.' I have never masturbated with anyone watching so I hesitate.

The crop swishes through the air again and lands on my right ass cheek. It stings but it also heightens my awareness of my body and its needs. I reach out and wrap my hand around my huge cock."

Alice took Vic's hand and placed it on his cock. "Ohh," he groaned, trying to pull his hand away, but Alice placed her hand on top of his and urged him to keep it there. "Keep it there," she said, "just like in the story."

"Yes, ma'am." He kept his hand around his cock as he was doing in the fantasy.

"'Stroke it until you come,' Valerie says. 'Then you can serve me properly.' "

"Yes," Alice whispered, "do that for me. I want to feel your hand move."

As he continued the story, Vic's hand slowly moved over his erection. "Valerie settles back and stares at my hand.

"I am very embarrassed but also very excited. I squeeze my cock and run my fingers up and down it." With Alice's hand on top of his, Vic's hand moved faster as he lost himself in his fantasy. "Oh God, Alice, oh God." It was only a moment until he spurted all over her legs. "I'm so sorry," Vic said. "I don't know what came over me."

"I do, and it pleases me very much. The power of the images you created was erotic as hell and drove you over the edge." She handed Vic several tissues and he cleaned himself up quickly.

"I've never done that with a woman," Vic said.

"Why not? It was wonderful."

"What about you? You haven't come."

Alice placed his hand on her pussy. "Fix it! Touch me!" She felt his body react to the command in her voice. His fingers worked, rubbing her clit. She grabbed the back of his neck and pushed his face against her breast. "Suck!" Quickly, his mouth and teeth drove her upward as his fingers played her pussy like a fine instrument. He seemed to know when to stroke softly and when to press hard. "Good boy, don't stop." He slipped two fingers inside of her and found a spot that made her body jerk with erotic pleasure when he pressed. "Very good. You serve me well."

He continued to fuck her with his fingers, then slid down and took her clit between his lips and sucked. She tried to hold back, wanting the wonderful sensations he was creating to last, but she was unable to prevent the waves of erotic pleasure from engulfing her. Suddenly the orgasm burst through her clenched muscles, and lasted several minutes.

Later, Vic said, "I asked you to tell me a story and I ended up telling you my deepest secrets. You must be a witch."

They dozed and, after making love once more, Vic said, "I think I'd better go home."

"You can stay if you want," Alice said, barely able to stay awake.

"I know, but I'd prefer to head home. It's almost morning and I have a lot of thinking to do. I want to take some time alone to consider what we did tonight."

"I could order you to stay," Alice said, unsure of where Vic's head was.

"Yes, you could, and that's what I have to think about. It's really unnerving to find out that you're not the basset hound you always thought you were."

"You're no basset hound. That's for sure." Alice yawned.

"I'll call you tomorrow. Actually today. Okay?"

Still a bit insecure, she thought, even after all that they had shared. "I'll look forward to hearing from you." As she heard him close the front door behind him, she burrowed beneath her covers and slept soundly.

Chapter 13

After their first sexual encounter, Alice and Vic dated almost every weekend. There were a few repeats of the dominant games they had played, but for the most part, the sex was good, hot, and traditional. In addition, through the summer Alice continued both of her jobs working at Dr. Tannenbaum's office and taking calls three evenings. She also visited her mother at least once a week and tried to join Betsy and Velvet for girls' night out. The three women became, if possible, even closer. When the doctor's office closed for two weeks in August, Alice and Vic spent a week driving around the south, enjoying sightseeing by day and playing in motel bedrooms by night. She also dated several other men, two of whom she met through Velvet Whispers and three who were introduced to her by her two best friends. Some of these dates resulted in more dates, a few ended after one evening.

In early September, Mrs. Waterman went to sleep one evening and died quietly before morning. Although it was sad, both Alice and her sister agreed that their mother's death was peaceful and she was now beyond the pain that had begun to debilitate her. Without the drain of nursing-home payments, Alice had a newfound financial freedom, and had some serious decisions to make. She knew that she was exhausted, burning the candle at more than two ends. She needed to simplify her life but she wasn't sure how. Should she give up Velvet Whispers? That seemed the most logical thing to do.

Maybe she should tell her callers that she was taking a vacation and that Velvet would be in touch when she was ready to take calls again. Yes, she should do that.

The following evening, a regular client named Hector was her first caller. "Hi, Sherry," he said. "Got a story for me tonight? Tell me a really hot one. It's been a long, tough week." She knew the kind of stories he liked and tonight she was going to tell him a doozie. One last present for him before she retired.

"Sure thing, sweetness," Alice said in her Sheherazade voice. "It's about a night when I was very naughty."

"Tell me."

"Well, several years ago I took a job waiting tables at a place called La Contessa. I was good at my job and I liked the work, not as much as I like talking to you, but that was before. Anyway, I got as many huge tippers as I got nasty customers so it was okay." Alice laughed, remembering her short stint as a waitress just after Ralph split. "I remember the man who slipped me a thirty-dollar tip for a sixty-dollar dinner check and one who yelled at me for fifteen minutes for delivering his steak too rare."

"Yeah, I'll bet," Hector said. "I always try to be nice to waitresses. My ex-wife used to wait tables and I remember the stories she used to tell."

"I don't think your ex-wife had any experiences like this one and she probably never had a customer like this guy. I know I never had. The man was not really good-looking, but he had a sensuality that was almost palpable. He wore his ebony hair long so you just wanted to run your fingers through it. His eyes were the blue of glacial ice, yet they also seemed warm and inviting. He wore a tight black turtleneck that fit his body like a second skin with long tight cuffs that almost caressed his wrists. His black jeans were, if possible, tighter than his shirt, his boots were black with silver studs and toe tips. His only jewelry was a silver hoop in one ear."

"Sounds like quite a stud."

"He was. I spotted him as he stood waiting to be seated. Although I tried not to stare, I found myself unable to move. I wondered whether he was meeting someone." Alice's breathing quickened just thinking about the man in black she was creating and she knew her excitement would add to Hector's enjoyment. "Well, the host sat him in my section. In the corner at table thirty-five. 'Good evening,' I said in my best waitress voice. 'My name is Sherry and I'll be serving you this evening. May I get you a drink?'

"His eyes met mine and our gazes locked. He stared at me, then his eyes caressed my body from my neck to my toes. You see the outfits we wore were quite revealing. Very low-cut peasant blouses and full, red-print skirts.

"He stared, then said, 'Yes, of course. I'll have a glass of sangria, Sherry.'

"I saw that the host had put only one menu on the table so I asked, 'Will you be dining alone?'

"'Alas, yes,' he said, still staring into my eyes. 'I have set my last lover free and I'm looking for another. Are you available?' "

"Whoa," Hector said. "He was really something. Set his last lover free. What did that mean?"

"I wondered about that myself, but he kept staring at me

and I found that my knees began to tremble and my brain locked up tight. I couldn't concentrate. Was he asking me out? Several customers had done that over the months, and, although there was no strict rule against dating patrons, I had always said no. 'I'm sorry,' I answered, 'but no.' "

"I'll bet he was sorry too. I know just how he must have felt," Hector said. "How often have I gotten that same answer from you?"

Alice laughed. "Lots. But don't stop trying. It's good for my ego and sometime I might just say yes." Alice knew Hector lived in the New York area and maybe, with more time on her hands, she would agree to meet him. What did she have to lose? She dragged her thoughts back to her story. "So the man in black said, 'That's a shame.'

"I cleared my throat," Alice continued, "then said, 'I'll get your sangria while you decide what to order.' As I walked toward the bar's service area, I could feel his eyes on me. My knees shook and I could feel the wetness between my legs. He was the sexiest man I'd ever seen and there was something more. Something deeply, darkly erotic.

"When I returned with the man's drink, my hands shook so much that, as I placed the glass on the table, several drops of the blood-red liquid fell on his pants. 'I'm t-t-terribly s-s-sorry,' I stammered. I grabbed a napkin from a nearby table and dabbed at the almost-invisible stain.

"The hand that snapped around my wrist was like a vise. 'That was very careless,' the man said softly. Then he smiled. 'You really should be punished for your clumsiness.' "

"He really said that?" Hector asked, his breathing a bit faster.

Alice caught Hector's reaction. He was as excited at the way the story was unfolding as she was. Interesting. "Yes, he said *punished*. I wondered why he had said that? Would he punish me? How? Oh God. I swallowed hard.

"'That excites you, doesn't it?' the man purred. 'I can feel your pulse race.' "

"Does that idea excite you, Sherry?" Hector asked, his voice filled with longing. "God, I'd love to do bad things to you."

"Let's finish the story, sweetness, then we can talk." She heard Hector's breath catch. She was definitely tempted. "So there I was, with him holding my wrist, telling me how excited I was getting. Well I couldn't speak. All my life I had had fantasies of someone controlling me, spanking me, loving me." *Did I really have such fantasies?* Alice wondered. "Although I had had a few lovers, I had never shared my dark desires with any of them. They were too kinky. Too black. Yet here he was, a man who seemed to know my deepest wishes. Or was it just an accident. 'I'm sorry, sir,' I said, taking a deep breath. 'Can I take your dinner order?' *That's good,* I thought. *Fall back on the familiar routine.* But he was still holding my wrist."

"I know these are just stories," Hector said, "but they make me so hot. Do you really have those fantasies, Sherry? Do you really want someone to take over like that? Control you?"

What could she say? She had never thought about this kind of sex play happening to her until that weekend with Todd. It had always been just a story. Now it was becoming much more. She returned to her tale. "'Your pulse is still pounding,' the man in black whispered. 'We'll continue this later.' I wondered what he meant, but I concentrated on my job.

"I took his dinner order and tried to involve myself in caring for the other diners. When his order was up, I put the plates on my tray and served him calmly and efficiently. Or at least I tried to be calm. Tried to sound calm. His expression told me he wasn't fooled.

"As I waited on other tables, I frequently looked at him, and each time I glanced in his direction, I found his eyes on me. It wasn't just a coincidence. It felt like he was seducing me with his gaze. It was almost half an hour later when I returned to his table to retrieve his empty plates.

"'That was delicious,' he said, his voice little more than a purr, 'but not totally satisfying. I need something hot for dessert. Any suggestions?'

"Me, I wanted to say. Instead I murmured, 'We have a wonderful hot apple cobbler.'

"The man looked at his watch, hidden beneath the long sleeve of his black shirt. 'It's almost nine-thirty. What time do you finish here?'

"I cleared my throat. 'I do recommend the apple cobbler.'

"'You want this. I know you understand that you deserve what I have for you, and I also know you crave it. You are telling me that with every fiber of your being. I can read you like a book and I know exactly what you want.' "

Alice could hear Hector's heavy breathing and knew her story was having the desired effect. She also knew that her body was responding too. Fortunately she had changed into an old sweat suit after work so she rubbed her aching nipples as she continued.

"Again I swallowed and tried not to let my voice squeak. 'And what, exactly, do you think I want?'

"'You want to be punished for spilling my drink. You want me to restrain you, then spank you like the naughty girl you are. You want the feeling of surrendering to me.' " The idea of spanking appealed to Alice when she had read a story the previous week. Now it just became part of the fantasy she was creating. Did she want something like this to happen?

"I wish I could be like that guy," Hector said wistfully. "I'd love to dominate a woman like that, but I'm too much of a chicken to ever do it for real."

"Are you really?" Alice asked, then didn't wait for an answer. "Well, you'll never guess what happened next. I was standing close to the man's chair and my skirt covered his movements. Suddenly his hand was between my thighs, his fingers touching my panties. 'You want this like you've never wanted anything else. You're hot and wet and you can barely keep your thighs together.'

"He knew me too well. Much too well. Then the hand was gone. 'I get off at eleven.' I had said it, committed myself to him and to whatever he wanted from me.

"'I drive a black BMW,' he said. 'It will be parked by the back door at eleven and I will wait for fifteen minutes. Be there or regret it all your life.' "

"Did you go?" Hector asked.

"Well, silently I took his credit card and returned with the charge slip. I knew I was blushing and I could barely keep my hands from shaking. He signed and as he stood to leave, he leaned close and whispered, 'For you, my love, I might wait until eleven-thirty. Please don't disappoint us both.'

"Then he was gone. I spent the remainder of my shift in a daze. I took orders, served food and alcohol, but my mind was on the man with the BMW. Could I trust him? Could he fulfill my fantasies? Yes, I admitted to myself, to both questions."

"Wow," Hector whispered.

"It's been more than fifteen minutes, Hector," Alice said glancing at the clock. "Shall I continue?"

"Hell yes," Hector said. "Tell me the rest."

"At eleven-fifteen I walked out of La Contessa, my nipples tight and aching, my pussy soaked, my body craving what was to come. I spotted the BMW immediately, opened the passenger door, and slipped inside.

"'I'm glad you came,' the man said. 'I would have been quite sad had you not appeared.'

"'I think I would have been too,' I whispered."

"Me too," Hector said with a laugh.

"'Good girl,' he said, sounding genuinely pleased. He

reached around my waist, grabbed the seat belt and pulled it across my body. Since it was a warm midsummer evening, I hadn't worn anything over my blouse. 'Now we have some rules to agree to. Can you snap your fingers?'

"Strange request, I thought, but I snapped. 'Good,' he said. 'If you snap your fingers or say the word *marshmallow*, I will stop whatever I'm doing. Do you understand and agree?'

"'Yes.'

"'You will call me Sir. Nothing more, and nothing less. Do you understand?'

"'Yes, Sir.'

"'Excellent.' With deft fingers, the man untied the string that held the top of my blouse. The tie loosened and he pulled the top down so my bra-covered breasts were exposed. He withdrew a small pair of scissors from a compartment in his door and quickly cut the straps of my bra. It took only a moment before the bra was gone, my breasts free, the strap of the shoulder harness cold against the skin between them. My nipples were already swollen, but he pinched the turgid tips until they were aching. Then he took two small suction devices and fastened them to my tits, causing almost painful pressure. Almost painful, but not quite. It was like two mouths sucking on my breasts as hard as they could."

Alice moved her hand down her belly and slid her fingers beneath the waist of her sweatpants. She found her pussy already wet from the images imprinted on her brain.

"'Put your hands on your hips,' he said, softly but firmly, 'and don't move them. Close your eyes and think about your tits. Think about the pressure, the almost-pain and the cool wind against your skin. Think that anyone who looks carefully will know what your breasts are feeling and think about how hot this makes you. I want your tits and your mind at their most sensitive when we get to our destination. It won't take long.'

"'Yes, Sir,' I said, placing my palms against my hipbones and closing my eyes.

"We drove for only about five minutes, then I felt the car slow, turn, and stop. I heard a garage door open and the car move forward and the door close again. 'We're here,' he said.

"I opened my eyes to what had obviously been a two-car garage once. Now half of the structure was walled off. I got out of the car, the sucking devices making every move pleasure and torture. My large breasts swayed as I walked propelled by his hand in the small of my back.

"We walked through a doorway into the other half of the garage and I gasped. The room was paneled in dark wood, with a thick cream-colored carpet cushioning my steps. There were mirrors on one entire wall and the ceiling. In the center of the room there was a large X-shaped wooden frame that stood about six feet tall and was about three feet wide at the ends of the arms. In the corner was an armless desk chair. 'First,' he said, 'snap your fingers.'

"I did, remembering that I was to snap if I got into trouble. 'I understand, Sir,' I said.

"He led me over to the chair, sat in it and quickly removed all of my clothes, leaving the suction devices on my breasts. Then he pulled at one wrist and I tumbled across his lap. 'You were very clumsy earlier,' he said, his voice soft and oily. 'You deserve more than this, but I will go easy for our first time.' "

"He was going to spank you?" Hector asked. "Man, oh man."

I wondered how the story had gotten to this, but it was obviously where Hector and I wanted it to go. "Oh yes," I said. "He was going to punish me for my clumsiness."

"And you let him?"

"I not only let him, I wanted it."

"Man," Hector said, "I can see it and feel it."

"I had no time to wonder as his palm slapped my ass

cheek. I felt the sting in my tender nether parts, but it was just a sting. The second slap merely stung a bit more, but by the fifth, the sting had become pain and my entire backside was tender. Then he stopped."

"Did it hurt?" Hector asked. "My cock's all hard just thinking about it."

"Oh yes. But I was surprised that the pain was also pleasure. I was so wet and hot." Alice's fingers were rubbing her clit and she knew she was close to coming.

"Tell me more," Hector said.

"'You enjoyed that. You have discovered the pleasure in a little pain.' The man caressed my ass cheeks tenderly. Then his fingers slipped into my slit. It was sopping.'Oh yes,' he said, laughing. 'You liked this a lot.' His fingers penetrated deep into my cunt and his thumb rubbed my clit. I climaxed, my entire body quaking as the spasms took me. 'Oh my God. Good. So good,' I cried.

"'My dear, you're perfect,' he said, still gently rubbing my pussy lips as I came down from the strongest orgasm I remembered. I knew from the moment I saw you that you could be a most wonderful playmate. I would like to do so many things with you, teach you so much about your own sensuality. Would you like that?'

"I could barely get the words out. 'Oh yes, Sir.'

"The man unzipped the fly of his jeans and pulled out his swollen cock. See how excited you make me?'"

"Oh, Sherry, you make me crazy too," Hector said. "I'm going to come soon."

"That's wonderful," Alice said. "Remembering that night is making me hot too." She rubbed her pussy, almost over the edge. "So I gazed at the man's cock, then into his eyes. He nodded and I knelt between his spread knees. I took the nob into my mouth, licked and sucked at the tip, then my mouth engulfed the entire staff. Deep in my throat

I worked the base of my tongue and my cheeks, trying to give him as much pleasure as he had given me. When I cupped his balls through his jeans, he climaxed and I swallowed every drop." Alice came then, but managed to keep telling the story. "When his cock was flaccid again, I sat back on my haunches and gazed at his face. He wore an expression of pure joy, an expression I had helped put there.

"'That was beautiful,' he said softly.

"I couldn't speak.

"'Do you see that frame over there?' he asked as he removed the suckers on my tits.

"'Yes, Sir,' I said.

"'If you come here after work tomorrow night, I will tie you to that, arms spread wide over your head, legs tied far apart so I can play with your pussy at my leisure.'"

Hector gasped and I knew he was coming, but I finished my tale anyway.

"I looked, first at the frame, then at the man who had awakened so much in me.

"'And we can make love in so many ways.' He lifted my face and kissed me gently on the lips. 'Please,' he said, passion and desire in his eyes. 'I want you so much. Climb into my car each night and I will show you so much, and share pleasure you have only dreamed of.'

"'I'll be there,' I said. 'Yes, I'll be there.' "

Alice heard Hector's long sigh. "That was a wonderful story. Did you meet him the next night?"

"Yes," Alice said softly, removing her hand from between her legs.

"Will you tell me about that night next time I call?" Wasn't she going to tell him that she was retiring? One more call. What would it hurt?

"Of course, Hector."

"Next week? Monday? Same time?"

"Sure. It's a date, sweetness."

"Great, then I'll talk to you then. Will you also think about going out with me sometime? We could meet and, well, explore."

"I'll think about it."

Still unsure what she was going to do, she hung up.

Chapter 14

That Saturday night, Alice and Vic spent the evening in the city at a small club in Greenwich Village, listening to jazz. Afterward, they went back to Vic's apartment and made love. She stayed over and the following morning, they went to brunch at a trendy local restaurant. "I'm thinking about leaving Velvet Whispers," she said, sipping orange juice and champagne.

"You really should. You don't need that stuff anymore. I've been telling you that you've been doing too much and I've given it a lot of thought. I think you should marry me. Then you can give up the phone business, quit your dentist job, and move in with me." As Alice watched, Vic began to talk faster and faster. "I'm very well-off, so we could travel. See the world. I've been doing more thinking about that X-rated game I talked to you about too. We could do it together. I could pay you as a consultant if you want."

When he paused for breath, Alice put her hand on his. "You sound like you've got it all planned."

"I have. It will work. We're good together, in and out of bed."

"Vic, you know I care for you, but have you listened to yourself? You're talking like a pitchman. Who are you trying to sell, me or you? You talk about all the reasons we should get married except the most important one. You haven't mentioned love once."

"Of course I love you. That goes without saying."

"No, it doesn't and you didn't say it because it's not the most important element of your thinking. Maybe it's there between us, I don't know." Alice was sorting things out as she spoke, and she found she was seeing things more clearly. "I do know that I'm not ready to settle down yet."

"Oh, Alice, I just want to make you happy."

"I love spending time with you and I don't want that to stop but I have a few other men I date and I don't want that to stop either." When Vic looked dejected, she continued, "I can't be exclusive with you. Not yet, maybe not ever, but does that really change the good times we have?"

"I guess not, but I hate the thought of sharing you."

"I know and I'm sorry that it makes you unhappy, but I've got to have time to decide what I want. I've never had that luxury before. First I had my parents making my decisions, then Ralph. I spent a lot of years after Ralph left in limbo, drifting, then I had my mother's illness. Now I'm free to do whatever I want, and I need time to figure out what that is. I hope you can accept that."

Vic took Alice's hand across the table. "As long as I can spend time with you and you're happy, it's great. You're really going to leave Velvet Whispers?"

"I think so. It's the logical thing to eliminate. It takes up my evenings and keeps me up much later than I really want.

One night last week I was up until almost one."

"Good. I hate to think of you on those sleazy phone calls."

"You didn't think they were sleazy when you were calling me."

"That's different."

Alice raised an eyebrow. "Is it?"

"I don't know, but I'm happy you're leaving."

The idea of leaving Velvet Whispers is logical, Alice thought. *Why then does it make me so sad?* Changing the subject, Alice asked, "Did you mean what you said about the video game?"

"You mean about you helping me? Absolutely. I've got dozens of ideas for it and you'd be just the person to write the scripts."

"I think that would be a gas. Between my stories and your computer skills, we'd make one hell of an adventure game." And if she left Velvet Whispers she would have her evenings, all day on Wednesdays, and the weekends to go into the city and work with Vic. It was entirely logical.

Vic squeezed her hand. "Just tell me that you'll occasionally think about marrying me. Maybe you'll change your mind."

That afternoon, after she arrived home, Alice phoned Velvet and told her of her decision to leave Velvet Whispers. "Are you sure that's what you want to do?" Velvet asked. "I know how much you enjoy your calls and we will all miss you if you leave. You have quite a group of regulars and they will be really upset."

"I know, but it's the logical thing to do. I'll stay with Dr. Tannenbaum and keep the medical coverage and all, and Vic has asked me to work with him on his computer game."

"Oh, honey, I know that you have to make your own decisions but I just don't want to lose you, as an employee or as a friend."

"Oh, Velvet. We won't lose each other. The three of us can still have girls' night out. That will be just like it always has been."

"Shall I take you out of the computer? I won't tell any of your regulars yet. Maybe you'll change your mind."

"I don't think so. Hector is calling tomorrow night and he'll be my last caller."

"I can see I'm in for lots of disappointed men."

After she hung up with Velvet, Alice called Betsy and told her the same thing and, as she had expected, she got the identical reaction. Betsy, however, was more forceful in her suggestion that leaving wasn't necessarily the best idea. "I know it's the logical thing to do," Betsy said, "but I think you're nuts."

Through the day on Monday, Alice thought about her twin conversations. Was this really the right thing? Talking with Vic the day before, it had seemed so simple. Was it really?

That evening, Hector called precisely at eight. "You're right on time, Hector," she said.

"I'm really anxious to hear what happened to you and that guy the next night."

Alice settled onto her bed, Roger beside her. Was this going to be her last call? She could take some time, of course, and taper off, but cold turkey was the best. Well, she'd go out in a blaze of glory. "His name was Daniel. I had learned that as he drove me home after our wonderful night together. Daniel. I couldn't imagine anyone calling him Dan or Danny. I couldn't imagine myself calling him Daniel. He was just Sir.

"I arrived at La Contessa at the regular time the following evening and went through the motions of setting up for the dinner crowd. Would he be here? Would he eat at the restaurant? Would he be waiting at the back door in his BMW?

"The evening crawled by. I looked at my watch and it was six o'clock. An hour later it was only six-fifteen. It took weeks for it to become eight o'clock and decades until ten-thirty. And always my eyes scanned the incoming diners. He wasn't among them. I poured coffee for a customer, brought a check to another, all in a daze. Several times the maitre d' had to remind me to give a customer the dessert menu or refill a water glass. But I was barely functioning. He would be waiting for me outside. He had to be.

"He had given me an instruction. 'Wear no underpants,' he had told me, 'so that every time your thighs brush together and rub against your pussy, you'll think of me.' As if I could think about anything else. Would he be there? Please, be there.

"When my shift was over I grabbed my purse and ran out the rear door. I looked around the back parking lot. His car wasn't there. *Oh God,* I thought. *He isn't coming.* I looked at my watch. Five minutes to eleven. It was still early. My breathing was rapid and my hands shook. I fumbled in my purse, found my car keys and opened my car door. I'd sit in my car and wait for him. He would come."

"He did come, didn't he?" Hector asked.

"Oh yes. 'Leave your purse in the car,' a voice said from behind my shoulder. 'You won't need it.'

"I closed my eyes and took a deep breath. He had come for me after all. 'Yes, Sir,' I whispered. I put my purse under the front seat and locked the car door. Still behind me, he took the keys from my trembling hand. Then he pressed his body against mine, trapping my chest against my car's closed door. He reached around my hips and his hand quickly burrowed beneath my full flowered skirt, his fingers dipping into my sopping cunt. 'Good girl,' he said. 'You did as I asked.'

"Asked, told, demanded, it was all the same. And I couldn't do anything else. I nodded.

"'Remember last night and those suckers on your tits? Well tonight I want all your concentration between your legs.' He maneuvered a harness of some kind around my hips beneath my skirt and hooked it in place. It was soft leather, held together with cold steel rings and bits of chain. 'Spread your legs wide,' he said, still pressing me against the car with his chest.

"When my legs were spread, he bit my earlobe, just hard enough to cause me pain. 'I said wide,' he growled. I widened my stance.

"'Now hold very still and don't move.' He released the pressure against my back. For a moment I considered how this would look to someone coming out of the back door of the restaurant. I was leaning against the side of my car, with a man laying his hands all over me. What would someone think? I didn't care.

"He lifted the back of my skirt and I felt cool air against the backs of my thighs. I jumped when I felt something cold against my hot pussy lips. 'I said stand still,' he hissed.

"'I'm sorry, Sir. You just surprised me.'

"'Nothing I do, nothing we do, should surprise you,' he said, chuckling."

Alice thought about the candle Todd had used to fuck her, then continued. "'True,' I whispered, as much to myself as to him. Suddenly I was filled. My pussy lips were stretched and my passage was as full as it had ever been. A huge dildo was being pushed deep inside me. Relentlessly filling, stretching, demanding. I felt him push the rod in deeper and deeper until I knew I could take no more, yet he kept filling me. Then he stopped and I felt a strip of something pulled down my belly, between my legs, and up between my cheeks to fasten to the harness in the back. As he pulled the strap tighter, the dildo pressed even more tightly inside me.

"He quickly pulled my blouse down in the front and, with a deft flip, my breasts were out of the cups of my bra. He leaned against me, forcing my engorged nipples against the cold metal of the car. 'You're so hot you'll come with almost nothing more from me, won't you?'

"'Yes, Sir,' I said, barely able to stand, barely able to breathe.

"'We can't have you this high all evening, so I'll let you come now.' His small laugh warmed my ear. 'Let's see whether you're so high that you can come without me even touching you. Feel that artificial cock fill your cunt. Feel your hot, hard nipples against the cold window. Are you close?'

"'Yes,' I groaned.

"'How close? How close to grasping that dildo with your pussy and squeezing it, coming against it.'

"'Very.'

"'Let's measure,' he said into my ear. 'If ten is climax, where are you?'

"'Nine point nine,' I said without thinking."

Hector laughed. "Sherry, I'm at about nine point five right now."

"Don't come too fast, Hector," Alice said. "This story has a long way to go, if you want it to."

"Oh, I do."

"Then the man I called Sir licked the back of my neck, then bit the nape. 'Tell me.'

"'Nine point nine nine,' I said, barely able to speak.

"He pressed his hips against my buttocks and moved so the strap shifted the dildo inside of me. Then he pressed the tip of his tongue into my ear and fucked my ear with it. 'Tell me.'

"'Oh God,' I groaned. 'Oh God.'

"He bit my earlobe hard and I climaxed. I couldn't help it. He hadn't touched me with his hands but I was coming anyway. Hard, hot, fast, my pussy spasming against the huge dildo in my cunt. 'Yessss,' I hissed.

"'God, you're wonderful,' he said, slowly releasing the pressure of his body that forced me against the cold car, turning me around so I saw him for the first time. Tears filled my eyes as I looked at his face, warm and inviting, his eyes, dark and all-seeing, brooking no resistance from me.

"He was again wearing black, this time a soft black shirt, with full sleeves and tight cuffs. His long black hair was tied back with a leather thong. He kissed my mouth, his lips soft against mine as I descended from the dizzying pinnacle of my orgasm. 'Come,' he said, 'let's go home.'

"Could I walk with this giant cock inside of me? I found that I could, and soon I was seated in his car, seat belt tightly fastened between my bared breasts. 'Close your eyes and think about your pussy,' he said as he started the engine. 'Feel how full it is and climb to the heights again.'

"I closed my eyes. My orgasm had been so hard and so complete that I wondered whether I could get excited again, but the dildo in my cunt gave me no peace. It aroused me as I pictured my swollen lips almost kissing the blunt end of it. By the time we pulled into the familiar garage, I was hungry again.

"He guided me from the car and into his special room. 'Remember last evening I showed you that frame,' he said, pointing to the X-shaped device that he was now moving to the center of the room. It was about six feet tall and each of the four arms was upholstered in black leather. There was a flat section at the center, against which my torso would be supported, I thought. As I looked more closely I saw that the frame had flat metal hinges and small metal rings at various points. He was going to fasten me to that, I knew, and control me totally. *Marshmallow,* I remembered was the magic word that would stop everything.

"'Strip,' he said. When I didn't immediately move, he glared at me. 'I told you to do something.'

"'Yes, Sir,' I said, quickly removing my clothing, my eyes still glued to the frame. As I pulled off my skirt, I saw the black leather harness wrapped around my body just above my hipbones, and fastened at the center-front with a tiny padlock. A leather panel held the dildo in place. Wasn't he going to remove it now?

"'Come here,' he said. It was a bit difficult to walk gracefully since the dildo held my legs slightly parted but I stepped forward and stood before him. 'I discovered last evening that a little pain gives you pleasure. You know it does, don't you?'

"I wanted to deny it. It was so sick. Wasn't it? But if both of us wanted it, and it gave us both pleasure . . . 'Yes, Sir.'

"'But the pain is just a symptom of what really excites you. It's the fact that I can do anything I want to you. I control you. I can hurt you or tease you and it's all pleasure for you. I can do anything, can't I?'

"'Yes, Sir.'

"'And you can always stop me. Snap your fingers or say *marshmallow* and I'll stop. So who's really in control?'

"I'd never thought of it that way before and now I couldn't keep a small smile from crossing my lips. 'We are, Sir,' I said.

"'And you trust me?'

"'Completely, Sir.'

"'Tonight there will be no pain, just a demonstration of what control means.' He enclosed me in his arms and softly kissed me. He slid his tongue into my mouth and I stroked it with mine. I wanted to feel him, hold him but I left my arms at my sides. If he wanted me to touch him, he would tell me. And he hadn't.

"He framed my face with his hands and kissed my cheeks, then walked to a chest, opened a drawer, and withdrew a handful of what looked to me like wide leather strips. He handed one to me. 'This goes around one ankle. Put it on.'

"I was going to have to do this myself. I was going to have to admit to myself that I wanted it. I took the strap and only hesitated a moment before I buckled it around my left ankle, leaving a large ring hanging from the back. I did the same with the one for my right ankle. Then my master gently buckled cuffs around my wrists. My master. Yes, that was what he was. He looked at the frame, then at me.

"Slowly I moved to the frame, pressed my back against it, raised my arms, and spread my legs. It fully supported my back but the leg sections parted at the small of my back, so there was nothing against my ass. Quickly, four small chains and padlocks fastened my arms and legs in place. 'Now,' he said, 'try to move. I want you to know how firmly you are held. I want you to know that now your body moves only when I adjust the frame.'

"I twisted and pulled, reveling in the feeling of being unable to free myself. 'Now you know how it feels. Tell me.'

"'It feels wonderful. It frees me.'

"He smiled as his hand reached between my legs. He tapped the end of the dildo and erotic pleasure knifed through my body. He twisted the plastic cock and moved it around as much as he could with the strap in place. I closed my eyes and clutched at the feeling of pleasure.

"He released the phallus inside me and moved the frame so it was now horizontal, at exactly the level of his groin. He unzipped his pants and allowed his cock to spring free. Then he moved so his hips were near my face, his engorged member near my mouth. 'Lick the tip,' he said. 'Just lick it with the tip of your tongue.' "

"God, you're good," Hector said. "I can almost feel what you were feeling."

Alice smiled and continued, her hand again snaking into the waist of her pants. "I reached out my tongue and touched the wet tip of my master's penis. Thick, sticky fluid oozed from the opening and I caught it on my tongue. While I licked, he reached over and pinched my nipples, hard. I gasped, but he said, 'Lick softly. Control your actions as I control the pleasure you feel.'

"It was difficult to lick his cock gently while he was pinching my nipples, but I managed. My mind was in two places at once, jumping from the feel of his fingers on my tight nipples to the movements of my mouth.

"Still twisting my nipples, he lifted a small handheld device and, while I watched, turned a small knob. 'Shit,' I hissed as the dildo inside my pussy began to hum. And the strap of the harness pressed against my clit so the vibrations were transferred to my engorged nub. Now my mind was in three places, my nipples, my tongue, and my pussy.

"'Control your actions,' he growled. 'Don't stop licking me.'

"'Oh,' I groaned, trying to concentrate on my tongue. I began to get used to the buzzing in my cunt, then he turned the knob and the frequency changed. Each time I became accustomed to the devilish object inside of me, he changed its method of torture, from buzzing to a slow throb, to a fast pounding and back to a low hum. And intermittently he pinched my nipples. Everything in my body was driving me closer and closer to orgasm, yet I was supposed to lick his penis in the same, soft rhythm.

"'Are you close to coming?' he asked.

"'Oh yes,' I moaned.

"'Don't! Just lick.'

"'But Sir.'

"'No buts. You will come only when I say you may. Do you understand?' He pushed his cock closer to my lips.

"'Yes, Sir.'

"'A lesson in control, yours and mine. Now,' he said, pushing his cock against my lips, 'take it.' "

"Are you close now, Sherry?" Hector asked. "I am."

Sherry's fingers rubbed her clit. "I am too," she said honestly.

"I like that. Continue with your story."

"I parted my lips and took the length of his engorged tool into my hot mouth. I ran my tongue over the sides, and created a vacuum to draw his penis more deeply into me. All the time my body sang with the sensations he was creating with his hands and with the machine in my pussy. If I can make him come, I reasoned, he will let me climax with him. I used every skill I possessed to drive him closer to orgasm.

"'You're very good at that,' he said, 'but I learned that last night. You're a good little cocksucker but I don't want to come this way.' He pulled away.

"I didn't know where the condom had come from but now he opened the small package and, as I watched, he slowly unrolled it over his cock. He walked around the frame until he was between my spread legs. 'Do you want this?' he asked.

"'Oh yes, Sir,' I said.

"He turned off the vibrating dildo, unfastened the strap that held it in place. And slowly withdrew it from my pussy. 'I control everything you feel,' he said, 'and I want you to feel everything. Have you ever taken something in your ass?'

"In my ass? He can't mean that. His cock was so big. He couldn't possibly do that. But I knew that he could. And if he wanted it that way, then he would do it. I couldn't stop him and I didn't want to. I wanted everything he could give me. 'No, Sir.'

"'Do you want your ass filled?'

"'No, Sir. I don't think so. It will hurt.'

"'It might, but it will be incredibly exciting as well. And you won't refuse me, will you. You really want anything that I think will please you. You realize that I know you better than you know yourself.'

"'Yes, Sir,' I said, and meant it.

"'So, now we understand each other. Your body is mine and I can do with it what I want.' Suddenly I felt something cold rubbing and pressing against my rear hole. 'I could drive my cock into you,' he said as the cold rubbing continued, driving me crazy with lust. 'But for now, we'll be content with this.' Something hard was pressing against my anus, slowly slipping into the tight ring of muscle. He alternately pressed and remained still so my body could become accustomed to the unfamiliar sensation.

"For moments at a time, it hurt, and I considered saying *marshmallow* but just as the pain got too much, he stopped pushing and the discomfort subsided. Finally my ass was filled and the pain had disappeared to be replaced with heat deep in my belly. He withdrew the object and pushed it in again, fucking me with it. While my mind was centered on my ass, he inserted his cock into my pussy. He quickly established a mind-blowing rhythm, inserting his cock and withdrawing the dildo, then reversing, so one of my openings was filled while the other was empty and hungry.

"'I'm stroking my cock with the dildo, through your body,' he said. 'And we are going to come together.' Harder and harder, faster and faster, he pumped both his cock and the rod until I knew he was ready to climax. Although we both knew I was close, how was he going to create the moment? I wondered with the small bit of my brain still capable of coherent thought. I was so close that I didn't think I could delay or speed my climax. Could he control the timing?

"I needn't have worried. Suddenly his finger was on my clit and I came. 'Yes,' I screamed and wave after wave of orgasmic pleasure overwhelmed my body. I couldn't move my arms or my legs but I bucked my hips as much as possible, taking his cock as deeply into my body as I could."

Alice smiled as she realized that when the character in the story came, she did too. She was even controlling her own orgasm.

"And he screamed as well, loudly proclaiming his pleasure. Over and over he pounded his cock into me, fucking my ass with the dildo as well.

"My climax was the strongest and longest as I could

ever remember. Wave upon wave of erotic joy washed over me and just as I thought I was descending, I came again. After several minutes of almost unendurable pleasure, I began to calm.

"A long time passed before our breathing returned to almost normal. Slowly he pulled the rod from my ass and then withdrew his cock from me. Then, leaving me to compose my body, he sat in a chair, his eyes closed, his body limp and trembling. 'God, lady,' he said, 'you're amazing.'

"'You too,' I said, unable to move even if I hadn't been still fastened to the frame.

"'And this is only the beginning.'

"'Yes,' I said, then added, 'Sir.'"

"Wow," Hector said.

Alice was unsure whether Hector had come. "Are you all right?"

"I'm terrific. I came about two minutes ago," he said, "but I stayed silent so I could hear you talk. You're sensational."

Alice grinned, and at that moment she knew that she couldn't do it. She couldn't leave Velvet Whispers. She enjoyed it too much. To hell with the medical coverage. To hell with security. She'd leave Dr. Tannenbaum as soon as he could find someone else and continue to do the things that she most enjoyed, and phone sex was at the top of her list. She'd stay at Velvet Whispers as long as she loved it and the men kept calling.

"I'm glad you think so. Call me next week?"

"Sure. Can you tell me what you and that guy did on a different night?"

"Of course I can. I'll talk to you next week."

She was about to call Velvet to tell her about her change of heart when the phone rang. "Alice, I'm in a jam," Velvet said quickly. Without allowing Alice to interrupt, Velvet continued, "I know Hector was your last caller but Marie just threw up. I can reroute all of her calls but I've already got a new client on the line and I promised him someone special. Everyone else is on the phone right now and I'm routing so I can't take him. Can you do me a favor, just one last time?"

"I'm not leaving. I've changed my mind."

"Thanks for taking this one last . . . You're not leaving?"

"Of course not. I was being ridiculous. I can't leave all my friends without anyone to talk to. And they are my friends even though I've never seen them. I'll give Dr. Tannenbaum my notice in the morning."

She could hear Velvet's laugh. "I knew you'd come to your senses. You love this as much as I do. Does Betsy know yet?"

"I just hung up with Hector and he made the decision for me. He said, 'Next week?' and I just said, 'Sure.' "

"Let's have lunch, the three of us, tomorrow to celebrate. I'll even buy."

"That will be great. Now, you said you had a new client?"

"His name is Zack and he's interested in telling you about his wild date last evening. He was babbling about a video camera and several mirrors. I don't know whether your story-telling talents will be needed, so just go with the flow."

"Will do." A few moments later her phone rang. "Sherry? This is Zack."

Alice lowered her voice, stretched out on the bed, and flipped off the light. "Hi, Zack. I'm glad you called."

Dear Reader,

I hope you've enjoyed the adventures of Alice, Betsy, and Velvet as much as I enjoyed writing them. Maybe I'll revisit the Velvet Whispers phone service again in a future book.

If you enjoyed the short stories that Alice read and her adventures on the phone, please read my other books, and visit my Web site at http://www.JoanELloyd.com. I know you'll love all my characters and their antics.

I'd love to hear from you anytime, so drop me a note and let me know what you particularly enjoyed and what you would like to read about in a future book. Please write me at:

Joan E. Lloyd
P.O. Box 221
Yorktown Heights, NY 10598

or at: JoanELloyd@aol.com.

The Road to Yucca Mountain

The Road to Yucca Mountain

The Development of Radioactive Waste Policy in the United States

J. Samuel Walker

UNIVERSITY OF CALIFORNIA PRESS
Berkeley · Los Angeles · London

University of California Press, one of the most distinguished university presses in the United States, enriches lives around the world by advancing scholarship in the humanities, social sciences, and natural sciences. Its activities are supported by the UC Press Foundation and by philanthropic contributions from individuals and institutions. For more information, visit www.ucpress.edu.

University of California Press
Berkeley and Los Angeles, California

University of California Press, Ltd.
London, England

Published in 2009 by University of California Press in association with the U.S. Nuclear Regulatory Commission (NRC)

Library of Congress Cataloging-in-Publication Data

Walker, J. Samuel.
The road to Yucca Mountain : the development of radioactive waste policy in the United States / J. Samuel Walker.
p. cm.
Includes bibliographical references and index.
ISBN 978-0-520-26045-0 (cloth : alk. paper)
1. Radioactive waste disposal—Government policy—United States. 2. Radioactive waste disposal in the ground—Nevada—Yucca Mountain. I. Title.
TD898.118.W35 2009
363.72'89560973—dc22 2008050739

Manufactured in the United States of America

18 17 16 15 14 13 12 11 10 09
10 9 8 7 6 5 4 3 2 1

This book is printed on Cascades Enviro 100, a 100% post consumer waste, recycled, de-inked fiber. FSC recycled certified and processed chlorine free. It is acid free, Ecologo certified, and manufactured by BioGas energy.

Contents

Illustrations

Preface

This book is the fifth in a series of volumes on the history of nuclear regulation sponsored by the U.S. Nuclear Regulatory Commission (NRC). I am the coauthor, with George T. Mazuzan, of the first volume, *Controlling the Atom: The Beginnings of Nuclear Regulation, 1946–1962* (1984), and the author of the other previous volumes: *Containing the Atom: Nuclear Regulation in a Changing Environment, 1963–1971* (1992); *Permissible Dose: A History of Radiation Protection in the Twentieth Century* (2000); and *Three Mile Island: A Nuclear Crisis in Historical Perspective* (2004). All four books were published by the University of California Press.

The disposal of radioactive waste has long been a source of scientific inquiry, programmatic deadlock, and public controversy. This book traces the efforts of policy makers to find solutions to the complex issues that radioactive waste raised. Their approaches evolved over time in response to changing conditions, research findings, and political realities. My focus here is on waste from the commercial applications of nuclear energy, principally but not exclusively from nuclear power plants. I also examine the early history of radioactive waste disposal at government installations that produced materials for nuclear weapons. The assumptions and approaches that the U.S. Atomic Energy Commission (AEC) adopted for "defense wastes" after World War II carried over to the civilian nuclear industry when it developed in the late 1950s and 1960s. Therefore, the AEC's practices at weapons production facilities in Tennessee, Idaho, Washington State, and elsewhere are an essential part of the history of managing radioactive waste from commercial uses of nuclear energy. But I have not undertaken a comprehensive study of radioactive waste programs at plants owned and operated by the AEC and its successors. There is a need for careful scholarly treatment of waste disposal and cleanup at government facilities, but this is a quite different topic from the one I have investigated.

This book does not represent in any way an official position of the Nuclear Regulatory Commission. It is a product of my own professional training, experience, and judgment, and I bear full responsibility for its contents. The NRC placed no restrictions on me in the writing of this book, and I had complete independence in deciding on its structure, approach, and conclusions. The findings that I report and the conclusions that I reach should be viewed as my own and not as a policy statement of the NRC.

I am indebted to many people who helped make this book possible. Several friends read the entire manuscript in draft form and offered exceedingly useful and well-informed comments. I extend my deep thanks, once again, to Andy Bates, Steve Crockett, Bill Lanouette, George Mazuzan, and Allan Winkler for their suggestions and encouragement.

I benefited greatly from the research assistance of Laura Adams McHale, at that time a historian with History Associates Incorporated. During the mid-1990s, she conducted wide-ranging primary research on the history of radioactive waste policies for what I thought would be my next book. My plans changed, and I did not get around to working on waste until after I completed my book on Three Mile Island. When I began this project, I had, thanks to Laura's efforts, a filing cabinet full of well-organized documents and skillfully presented synopses of their contents.

Archivists and other professionals in a number of institutions provided invaluable services. Margaret Burri of Johns Hopkins University went beyond the call of duty in offering her expertise to ease my research in the Abel Wolman Papers, including photographs and a massive oral history. Becky Schulte and the staff of the Kenneth Spencer Research Library at the University of Kansas delivered friendly and able assistance in my examination of a wealth of documentary sources in the Kansas Collection and the University Archives. Rex Buchanan of the Kansas Geological Survey was supportive and sympathetic to the difficulties of explaining complex technical issues. Jean Bischoff, then of the Robert J. Dole Institute of Politics, was enormously helpful in responding to my requests for materials in the Dole Papers, and Randy Roberts of Pittsburg State University provided much-appreciated services in my work in the Joe Skubitz Papers. Sam Rushay, then of the Nixon Presidential Materials Project at the National Archives, tracked down obscure and useful files, and Sherrie Fletcher guided me to an abundance of interesting materials at the Ronald Reagan Library. Daniel Barbiero's assistance speeded my research in the important documents on radioactive waste in the archives of the National Academy of Sciences.

I have benefited throughout my career from the friendship and support of my colleagues in the Office of the Secretary of the NRC. Even under the pressures of heavy demands and tight deadlines, my office colleagues, and indeed my colleagues throughout the NRC, have appreciated the value of knowing about the history of the agency. My own deadlines were self-imposed and usually less urgent than those that they faced, but no one complained when I sat in my office trying to figure out a historical issue while they raced around performing tasks that had to be completed immediately. The NRC has never asked me or expected me to suspend critical faculties in writing its history; it has asked only that I perform my duties in accordance with the best standards and methods of historical scholarship. And for that I am very grateful.

Stan Holwitz of the University of California Press once again provided warm friendship, wise counsel, and strong support for my project. One of his professional colleagues at another university press told me that Stan is a "legendary editor," a judgment with which I fully concur (though Stan found it amusing). When editors at many academic presses would cringe at the thought of publishing a book written by a government historian and positively melt at the thought of navigating government contract procedures, Stan demonstrated enough faith or foolhardiness to do it several times. It is an honor for me to have published five books with a press that promotes excellence in every phase of the publication process and to have worked with the many fine people who make the University of California Press such an outstanding source of scholarly production.

Rockville, Maryland
April 2009

CHAPTER 1

A Solvable Problem

During the forty-year period from the 1940s into the 1980s, the disposal of radioactive waste evolved from a problem that experts regarded as challenging but solvable to a problem that many people viewed as bewildering and perhaps insurmountable. In 1959 Abel Wolman, a professor at Johns Hopkins University and a sanitary engineer of international renown, told a congressional committee, "There was a period, perhaps 10 years ago, when the problem of radioactive waste was considered to be nonexistent." Wolman's claim was overstated, but it captured the prevailing optimism among experts in government and industry at the time he made it. They recognized that finding suitable means of disposing of radioactive waste materials from the production of nuclear weapons and the generation of nuclear power was essential, and they expressed confidence that, in time, research on and experience with the problem would provide a solution. In 1956 the staff of the U.S. Atomic Energy Commission (AEC), the agency that Congress made responsible for building nuclear weapons, encouraging the growth of commercial nuclear power, and regulating the safety of nuclear technology, declared that "practical, safe ultimate disposal systems will be developed." Glenn T. Seaborg, chairman of the AEC, echoed that view when he commented in 1967 that "handling radioactive waste in a future large scale nuclear economy . . . was not a major problem."[1]

Other observers were considerably more troubled about the difficulties of protecting public health from the dangers of radioactive waste.

Articles in popular magazines during the 1950s and early 1960s cited the hazards of "deadly atomic garbage," "death-dealing debris," and "lethal liquid waste." In March 1960 the journalist Walter Schneir described radioactive waste as "clearly . . . the most hazardous and treacherous material man has ever tried to deal with." By that time, growing public apprehension about this "treacherous material" was obvious; indeed, as early as 1949 the AEC's director of public information had worried about "possible latent hysteria" over nuclear wastes. Thus, within a short time after the nuclear attacks on Hiroshima and Nagasaki introduced the "atomic age," the disposal of radioactive waste appeared to be both a complex technical issue and an imposing political problem. This pattern became even more pronounced as the use of nuclear technology generated growing controversy. In December 1978 *Business Week* reported in an article on opposition to nuclear power that "the most politically sensitive of all nuclear energy's problems is waste disposal." The challenge of resolving both the technical and the political questions surrounding radioactive waste periodically confronted and persistently confounded policy makers during the four decades following the dawn of the atomic age.[2]

WASTE DISPOSAL DURING THE MANHATTAN PROJECT AND THE EARLY COLD WAR

Radioactive waste in large quantities was first created as a by-product of the Manhattan Project, the herculean effort to build an atomic bomb during World War II. Amid the urgency with which they worked, responsible officials did not regard establishing a permanent repository for waste materials as a pressing matter. Instead they adopted temporary expedients with the assumption that improved approaches would be developed at a later time.

The principal sources of the most dangerous forms of highly radioactive waste were the reprocessing plants at the Hanford Engineer Works, located along the Columbia River in eastern Washington. Hanford produced the plutonium that fueled the first nuclear test explosion in New Mexico and the bomb dropped on Nagasaki in 1945. The complex process of making plutonium on an industrial scale was first carried out at Hanford during the later stages of the war. The initial step was construction of a reactor that, despite still-limited theoretical knowledge, a lack of practical experience, a time-dictated inability to conduct preoperational testing, and a series of false starts, succeeded in splitting atoms in its uranium fuel. The result of nuclear fission was the creation of a variety of radioactive "fission products" and "activation products," including plutonium-239, which can be used to trigger an atomic explosion. In order to recover the plutonium, the irradiated fuel slugs were transferred under heavy shielding to a reprocessing plant. There, after the fuel pellets were dissolved in acid, plutonium was separated by chemical extraction. Along with the plutonium, reprocessing yielded large quantities of gaseous, solid, and liquid radioactive wastes. The highly radioactive liquid wastes, which also contained a sinister brew of chemicals, were pumped into hastily fabricated, single-shell, steel-lined, underground storage tanks.

The liquid waste from reprocessing at Hanford was, in terms of volume and radioactive intensity, the most hazardous by-product of the Manhattan Project's far-flung operations. But other activities at sites around the country also created abundant lower-level radioactive waste. Huge volumes of water became irradiated when used for, among other things, cooling reactors, washing contaminated clothing, and cleaning laboratories. This liquid waste, which was far less radioactive than that from reprocessing, was often pumped into ditches or holding ponds and sometimes discharged directly into nearby streams or rivers. Solid wastes, which included contaminated equipment, pipes, valves, filters, clothing, instruments, and tools, were buried in trenches and covered with soil. Gaseous waste products were released into the atmosphere; those with the highest levels of radioactivity were first filtered or precipitated. The practices adopted during the Manhattan Project continued after World War II ended and the cold war began.[3]

RADIATION PROTECTION

Despite the limited knowledge about radioactive waste and the rudimentary treatment it received, the officials in charge of radiation safety in the Manhattan Project's facilities were convinced that the methods of disposal provided adequate protection to employees and the public, at least in the short term. Professionals in the field of radiation protection, who called themselves health physicists, carefully monitored workers' exposures and radiation releases into the environment. Their goal was to prevent health disorders that radiation could cause, including cancer, bone disease, sterility, and genetic defects. In assessing the hazards of exposure to low levels of radiation, health physicists drew on the knowledge and experience gained since the discovery of x-rays in 1895 and natural radioactivity the following year. At the same time, they were acutely mindful of the many uncertainties about the health effects of radiation. In 1934 scientific groups had for the first time announced a recommended "tolerance dose" for exposure to x-rays, which can penetrate deeply into bodily tissue. Seven years later they had taken another important step by recommending tolerance doses for the "internal emitters" radium and its decay product, the radioactive gas radon. Radium and radon present serious hazards if they become deposited inside the body after being swallowed or inhaled. Radiation experts did not claim that the tolerance doses were definitive, but they believed that the recommended limits offered an ample margin of safety for the relatively small number of persons exposed to external or internal radiation in their jobs.

Radiation protection became vastly more complex with the development of the atomic bomb and the prospect of widespread use of atomic energy for other purposes. One reason was that nuclear fission created many radioactive isotopes that did not exist in nature. Instead of dealing only with x-rays and radium, health physicists had to consider the potential hazards of new radioactive substances about which they knew little. Further, the number of people exposed to radiation from military and civilian applications of atomic energy was certain to grow greatly. Radiation protection broadened from a medical and industrial issue of limited scope to a public health question of potentially major dimensions. The possible genetic consequences of increased population exposure to radiation was a matter of particular concern. Even before World War II, genetic research had indicated that reproductive cells were especially vulnerable to small amounts of radiation and that mutant genes could be inherited from a parent with no obvious radiation-induced injuries.

Soon after the war ended, health physicists revised their approach to radiation protection in light of the new conditions. The professional organization in the United States that recommended exposure limits, which had been established in 1929 and named the National Committee on Radiation Protection (NCRP) in 1946, replaced the term "tolerance dose" with "maximum permissible dose." Its members believed that the new term better conveyed the idea that no quantity of radiation was certifiably safe. The NCRP defined its recommended permissible dose as that which, "in the light of present knowledge, is not expected to cause appreciable bodily injury to a person at any time during his lifetime." It tightened its previous recommendations by reducing the permissible dose for whole-body exposure from external sources to 50 percent of the 1934 level. It measured the whole-body limit by exposure to the "most critical" tissue, in the lenses of the eyes, the gonads, and the blood-forming organs; higher limits applied for less sensitive areas of the body. The NCRP recommended a maximum permissible dose for occupational exposure of 0.3 roentgen per six-day workweek (or 15 roentgens per year). The roentgen was a unit that indicated the quantity of x-rays that would produce a specified degree of change in the atomic structure of cells in the human body under prescribed conditions. The NCRP made comparable revisions in its recommendations on exposure to internal emitters. An international organization of radiation experts, the International Commission on Radiological Protection (ICRP), followed the lead of the NCRP in the early postwar years by adopting the term and concept "maximum permissible dose" and by recommending that occupational exposure to external sources of radiation be limited to 0.3 roentgen per week.[4]

RADIATION SAFETY AND WASTE DISPOSAL

The AEC, headed by five commissioners appointed by the president and confirmed by the Senate, was created by the Atomic Energy Act of 1946. After the agency began operations in January 1947, it followed the NCRP's recommendations on radiation protection. Its goal in radioactive waste disposal, as in all its programs, was to guard against radiation exposures that exceeded the NCRP's guidelines. The NCRP and the ICRP made clear that the permissible levels they recommended did not constitute a threshold that offered absolute safety. Although they considered the risk small, they acknowledged that a person whose exposures stayed within the dose limits might still suffer injury. In practice, they believed that the recommended doses provided a serviceable and generally applicable measure of safety.[5]

In keeping with the approach of the professional organizations, officials in charge of radiation protection at nuclear weapons plants did not regard the complete avoidance of exposures to individuals or releases to the environment as either possible or necessary. Two leading authorities at Hanford articulated this view in an internal report they prepared in August 1945. Simeon T. Cantril, assistant superintendent of industrial medicine, and Herbert M. Parker, who had established and supervised the health physics program at the site, wrote, "Never before had so many people been engaged in an occupation wherein the hazard was one of radiation and radioactive substances on so large a scale. . . . It can be stated without reservation that to date no employee . . . has received an amount of radiation which would be injurious." Cantril and Parker were also confident that radioactive releases to the environment had not endangered the public. They declared that radioactive gases from Hanford's plants were "entirely innocuous" and that radioactive wastewater channeled to the Columbia River had never "been in excess of that which would cause an overtolerance radiation exposure to any living thing immersed in it." In January 1948 Karl Z. Morgan, director of the health physics department at Clinton Laboratories in Oak Ridge, Tennessee, where much of the Manhattan Project's work on the first atomic bombs had taken place, offered an equally favorable assessment. "There is considerable evidence that as long as present standards are maintained," he wrote in *Scientific American,* "the plutonium projects will remain among the safest industrial operations in the country."[6]

The conviction that radiation exposure at levels below the permissible dose was generally safe, even if not risk-free, guided waste disposal practices of the Manhattan Project during World War II and of the AEC during the early cold war. Those responsible for radiation protection adopted two approaches for dealing with radioactive waste. The method of treating the high-level liquid wastes produced by the reprocessing of reactor fuel was to concentrate them "in as small a volume . . . as possible" and store them "in a safe manner" to prevent the escape of radioactivity. The method of handling the much larger volume of lower-level wastes was to dilute their radioactivity to levels that posed "no danger to plants, animals, or humans" and often, in the cases of liquids and gases, to disperse them into the environment. The process of nuclear fission created a variety of radioactive isotopes, many of which had very short half-lives (the time it takes one-half of the atoms to decay to a different form). The isotopes that caused the most concern were those with half-lives long enough to remain intensely radioactive for an extended period. They included strontium-90, with a half-life of 29 years, and cesium-137, with a half-life of 30 years. This meant that it would take about 300 years, a span of ten half-lives, for those elements to lose most of their radioactivity. Isotopes with much longer half-lives, such as plutonium-239 (about 24,000 years) and technetium-99 (about 210,000 years), were regarded as a less critical problem because the intensity of radioactive materials is inversely proportional to their half-lives. Consequently, those long-lived elements were grouped in the broad category of low-level waste, which included everything except the high-level liquid waste from reprocessing.[7]

The operating principle that radiation exposures below permissible doses were acceptably safe enabled health physicists at Hanford to acquiesce in a large, intentional release of iodine-131 in 1949. From the time that Hanford began plutonium production, iodine-131 was among the radioactive gases routinely dispersed to the atmosphere. It is a radioactive isotope with a half-life of eight days that concentrates in the thyroid gland if ingested or inhaled. Although information about the effects of iodine-131 was sketchy, health physicists at Hanford worried about its presence on vegetation and in livestock near the site. Parker recommended a "tolerable concentration" of iodine-131 on edible plants as early as January 1946.[8]

Despite efforts to promote safety and protect the environment from hazardous levels of radiation at Hanford, Manhattan Project and AEC officials consistently subordinated those concerns to their assessment of national security demands. The discovery that the Soviet Union had exploded its first atomic bomb placed the AEC's priorities in especially sharp relief. In October 1949, a few weeks after atmospheric sampling revealed that the Soviets had conducted a nuclear test, the AEC, the General Electric Company (which ran Hanford under a government contract), and the U.S. Air Force made plans to release radioactive gases from the Hanford site as a means to gain insight into Soviet reprocessing procedures and estimating plutonium production. The operation came to be known as the "green run," because it used "green" spent fuel elements in which the cooling period was much shorter than usual. This meant that radioactive elements in the fuel had less time to decay to stable forms and that more iodine-131 than normally present in plant emissions was introduced directly into the environment. The quantities of iodine-131 were increased further when Hanford officials deliberately bypassed filters that trapped radioactive materials. As a result, the green run, conducted on December 2–3, 1949, released about 8,000 curies—a unit of measurement that indicates the decay rate (or level of activity) of radioactive substances—of iodine-131 to the area surrounding the site. Although this was a small percentage of the total amount of iodine-131 discharged from Hanford to that time, it was probably the largest release in a single day. The green run produced high offsite radiation readings; concentrations on vegetation and in animals temporarily intensified by dramatic proportions even miles away.[9]

The offsite radiation from the green run troubled Parker and other health physicists at Hanford. Parker, a leading figure among professionals in the field of radiation protection, had first built his reputation as a medical physicist. He was born in England and after earning bachelor's and master's degrees in physics, began his career at the Holt Radium Institute in Manchester in 1932. He and the director of the institute, James Ralston Kennedy Paterson, collaborated in developing uniform doses for treating cancer with radium. This achievement, as one expert commented many years later, "revolutionized radium therapy." In 1938 Parker accepted a position at the Swedish Hospital Tumor Institute in Seattle, Washington, where he worked under the radiologist Simeon Cantril. After the United States entered World War II, he joined Cantril at Clinton Laboratories in Tennessee, to establish programs to protect Manhattan Project employees from largely uncharted radiation hazards. In 1944 he moved to Hanford to perform the same services. Thus Parker was in the vanguard of the emerging field of "health physics," a term he disliked intensely. The term was adopted during the war to disguise the purpose of the Manhattan Project, and Parker thought it was not only vague but also easily confused with his original field of medical physics. He was known to his colleagues as an exceptionally able and sometimes intimidating professional who "was quick to decimate a half-baked idea or ill-prepared presentation with his pungent British prose."[10]

Parker generally took an optimistic view of the occupational and public health hazards created by Hanford operations. He was confident that "present disposal procedures may be continued . . . with the assurance of safety for a period of perhaps 50 years." In July 1948 he suggested that even if all the high-level waste stored in tanks leaked to the ground, it would not cause a "major disaster." He acknowledged, however, that a worst case accident could require "radical curtailment of the use of river water." New research findings convinced him to modify some of his earlier views about radiation hazards. In April 1949 he voiced concern that permissible dose levels recently drafted by the NCRP did not adequately account for the concentration of certain radioactive isotopes in river plankton and fish. Investigations at Hanford had shown, for example, that plankton in the Columbia River concentrated phosphorus-32 "by a factor of two hundred thousand," which raised the threat of contaminated food chains.[11]

For the same reasons, Parker was disturbed that the green run distributed iodine-131 far beyond plant boundaries. In a report he submitted in January 1950, he noted that the green run "resulted in greater contamination spread than had been anticipated." Although he concluded that it presented only a "negligible risk" to Hanford workers, he expressed misgivings about exposing the general population to more releases of similar magnitude. The green run, Parker wrote, "came close enough to significant levels, and its distribution differed enough from simple meteorological predictions," that he and his colleagues "would resist a proposed repetition of the test." The green run demonstrated the AEC's prevailing philosophy that radiation exposures within permissible levels were acceptable for operating purposes. Parker's reaction to the test also indicated that the AEC and its contractors regarded radiation safety as an important, if secondary, consideration and that they took permissible dose limits seriously. Nevertheless, in light of the many scientific uncertainties about radiation hazards, the extent to which permissible doses could be viewed as a reliable measure of safety stirred controversy among experts and raised questions about the AEC's handling of radioactive wastes.[12]

CRITICISM OF THE AEC'S WASTE PROGRAMS

Even before Parker cited his reservations about a repeat of the green run, other prominent health physicists and sanitary engineers had criticized the AEC's waste management practices at Hanford and other sites. In April 1948 members of the AEC's Safety and Industrial Health Advisory Board raised a series of questions about the adequacy of radiation protection measures in general and waste disposal in particular. Although they did not condemn the agency's approach, they expressed skepticism about the effectiveness of existing efforts to guard against excessive occupational and public exposure to radiation. The AEC had established the advisory board in September 1947 to survey fire, construction, electrical, chemical, and radiation hazards at the many installations it had inherited from the Manhattan Project. Among the experts appointed to the board was Abel Wolman, who had urged David E. Lilienthal, chairman of the AEC, to consider the sanitary engineering problems that might "arise in the continued development of nuclear fission studies and production programs." Wolman, in addition to serving on the faculty at Johns Hopkins University, was at that time chairman of the Committee on Sanitary Engineering of the National Academy of Sciences–National Research Council, a prestigious organization that prepared a wide variety of reports on scientific issues for the federal government.[13]

As his position on the National Academy of Sciences committee indicated, Wolman was a highly regarded authority in the field of sanitary engineering. After completing graduate work in engineering at Johns Hopkins, he began his career with the Maryland Department of Health in 1915. Within a short time he made his reputation by developing, in collaboration with a former classmate, the chemist Linn Enslow, a formula for eliminating bacteria in water through chlorination. He also had a major role in designing the water system for the city of Baltimore, and he later provided similar services as a consultant for many American cities, foreign countries, and international organizations. In 1922 he became the chief engineer for the Maryland Department of Health. He joined the faculty at Johns Hopkins on a full-time basis in 1937. Wolman "became a legend in his time," the *Baltimore Evening Sun* observed when he died in 1989, in large part because of his devotion to and concern about environmental and public health issues. His commitment to environmental protection was leavened with a keen sense of what was politically, economically, and technologically practical. He did not believe that attaining a risk-free society was either possible or desirable. "I can't conceive of being promised a world in which there are no problems," he once remarked. "I don't want my grandchildren to have the feeling that's what I'm trying to give them. That would be a bore."[14]

As a pioneer in the field of sanitary engineering, Wolman took a strong interest in the potential impact of atomic energy development on public health. He first became involved in the issue when the National Academy of Sciences Committee on Sanitary Engineering requested that he visit Lilienthal to convey its uncertainty that the AEC was giving "sufficient attention" to protecting workers or the public from radiation hazards. Wolman had a high opinion of the AEC chairman, whom he knew from serving as a consultant to the Tennessee Valley Authority, which Lilienthal had headed during the 1930s. When Wolman presented the committee's misgivings in July 1947, Lilienthal replied that he thought its "worry was unwarranted." Nevertheless, he asked that Wolman talk with James B. Fisk, director of the AEC's research division, and then report back to him. When Wolman met with Fisk, whom he regarded as a "superb scientist," he was not convinced by the assurances he received. After Wolman told Lilienthal about his doubts that "adequate protection was being provided," the AEC chairman invited him to join the agency's Safety and Industrial Health Advisory Board.[15]

Wolman carried out his new responsibilities with characteristic energy and dedication. Along with other members of the board, he made extended visits to the AEC's laboratories and production facilities to evaluate their safety programs. In November 1947 he collaborated with Arthur E. Gorman, a longtime friend and well-known sanitary engineer, in drafting a memorandum on "problems of environmental sanitation encountered in atomic energy operations" for inclusion in the Safety and Industrial Health Advisory Board's report to the AEC. Wolman valued Gorman's "expertise, which was superb," and "his dynamic pursuit of anything he touched, to the point—almost—of making himself obnoxious."[16]

In their memorandum on environmental protection in atomic energy installations, Wolman and Gorman expressed their views clearly and candidly. They observed that "in the haste to produce atomic bombs during the war certain risks may have been taken . . . with the understanding that subsequently more effective control measures would ameliorate those risks." They suggested many areas in which such measures were necessary. They were disturbed that "tolerance limits for radioactive and toxic materials" had been established without review by "public health officers normally concerned with and responsible for such problems in civilian life." In matters relating directly to their own field, sanitary engineering, Wolman and Gorman found much that was worrisome. They feared that water supplies at Clinton, Hanford, and elsewhere were contaminated. They commented that radioactive waste disposal practices had "been developed without full consideration of the hazards involved." And they concluded that the "control of the disposal of radioactive and toxic materials into the atmosphere . . . is subject to criticism in varying degrees. We cannot recall a single stack in any of the areas of such height or design which would meet modern requirements of industrial or laboratory operations."[17]

Wolman and Gorman's analysis appeared virtually unchanged in the final report of the Safety and Industrial Health Advisory Board, submitted to the AEC in April 1948. The panel, chaired by Sidney J. Williams, assistant to the president of the National Safety Council, concluded that safety and health hazards, including, in addition to radiation, fires, motor vehicle traffic, construction, exposure to chemicals, and industrial hygiene, demanded more attention from top managers of the AEC and its contractors. "The Atomic Energy Commission inherited from the Manhattan Project an excellent safety program and record," the board declared. "There are recent indications that these are deteriorating."

The report's criticisms of radiation protection and waste disposal programs drew not only on Wolman and Gorman's findings but also on the comments of Hymer L. Friedell, another leading authority. Friedell, director of the radiology department at the University Hospitals of Cleveland, had served as one of the chief medical officers in charge of the Manhattan Project's efforts to manage radiation hazards. He wrote in the Safety and Industrial Health Advisory Board report that the problems the AEC faced in providing adequate radiation protection for workers and the public were "arresting in their magnitude." He suggested that although the exposure "levels that have been used have been safe during wartime," they should be "reduced as low as is practicable" during peacetime. Friedell echoed Wolman and Gorman on the subject of radioactive waste. He lamented that "no concrete program exists at the present for waste disposal" and urged that "this problem . . . be tackled at the earliest opportunity." Hanford's Herbert Parker, who was also a member of the advisory board, placed the existing radiation protection programs of the AEC and its contractors in a more favorable light. He insisted that they had produced a record that was "better than that enjoyed by any other organization," and indeed, was "phenomenally good." But he agreed with his colleagues that waste disposal was "one of the Commission's most pressing safety problems." Among its many recommendations to the AEC, the Safety and Industrial Health Advisory Board called for the creation of a health unit with "top level policy responsibility" and the appointment of a "sanitary engineer of broad experience" to the agency's staff.[18]

Wolman was disappointed that the AEC did not view radioactive waste disposal with the same urgency as did members of the advisory board. He believed that "people at the highest level in the Commission . . . discounted" the perplexities of handling high-level waste. He was especially displeased with the attitude of J. Robert Oppenheimer, chairman of the AEC's General Advisory Committee, which exercised great influence on the agency's scientific and policy decisions. At a meeting of the committee in April 1948, Oppenheimer dismissed the waste problem as "unimportant"—a prevalent judgment among physicists and other scientists who held influential posts with the AEC. Some time later, after enjoying a pleasant dinner at Oppenheimer's home, Wolman bluntly voiced his opinion. He told Oppenheimer, "[I have] tremendous respect for your field of activity and your views," but added: "When you enter my field . . . your ideas as to how we shall manage this 'unimportant' problem are characterized almost completely by a total ignorance of the nature of disposal." Wolman, who had a way of disagreeing without making enemies or holding grudges, later recalled that he and Oppenheimer "parted friends."[19]

Despite Wolman's complaints about the AEC's attitude toward waste, he and his colleagues on the Safety and Industrial Health Advisory Board succeeded in convincing the agency to take initial steps to deal with the problem. Lilienthal agreed with the board's recommendation to add a

Figure 1. The AEC's Safety and Industrial Health Advisory Board. Seated at the far left is Arthur Gorman. Seated third from the left is Abel Wolman and fifth from the left, Herbert Parker. (Abel Wolman Papers, The Johns Hopkins University)

sanitary engineer to the staff of the AEC and told Wolman, "Since you push it . . . you find me the man." Wolman quickly concluded that his friend and professional colleague Arthur Gorman was the man for the job, and he then prevailed on Gorman to leave his post as the head of water operations in Chicago and join the AEC. In 1949 Gorman hired Joseph A. Lieberman, who had earned his Ph.D. in sanitary engineering at Johns Hopkins under the direction of Wolman. For many years, Gorman and Lieberman were the entire sanitary engineering staff of the AEC, and in that capacity they sought, in the face of both technological and political hurdles, satisfactory ways to deal with growing quantities of radioactive waste.[20]

THE AEC'S PUBLIC REPORT ON WASTE

In addition to creating a small sanitary engineering staff, the AEC, apparently in response to the findings of the Safety and Industrial Health

Advisory Board, prepared and eventually published a report on waste management practices at its installations. In July 1948 the commissioners requested that the staff submit a technical analysis of waste issues to provide the basis for a public report. When a draft paper, presumably written by Gorman, was presented to the commissioners three months later, Lilienthal reiterated "that this subject would be suitable for a special public report." He hoped that the AEC's review of the problem would both inform and reassure the public. A short time later, Morse Salisbury, director of the agency's public and technical information service, received a copy of the draft and found to his dismay that it was "far more pessimistic and alarming than previous statements we have seen." He suggested that it was inconsistent with the views of other experts. Salisbury was "only too well aware of the great public interest in waste disposal problems" and was concerned about the potential impact of the report.[21]

There was little evidence to support Salisbury's impression of "great public interest" in radioactive waste. He noted that the "volume of inquiries" on the subject that the AEC received, which was "stimulated every time a sanitary engineer or a medical man makes a public talk," was "growing." The problem of waste disposal had also been discussed in ominous terms in a few newspaper articles. In October 1947 an Associated Press story on disposal of "hot" atoms declared, "There has never been a problem like this. Any disposal previously known for wastes will leave these atoms to menace present and future generations." An article in the *New York Times* a few months later pointed out that scientists could not yet offer "sure protection" from the "malignant forces" of radioactive waste. Nevertheless, the issue of waste disposal was not a matter of prominent media attention or public anxiety. The AEC's concern about the public's apprehension over waste hazards was apparently rooted in a flurry of disquieting stories in the press about radiation effects in general. Roy B. Snapp, secretary to the Commission, made this connection when he urged that the agency's report on waste make clear the "universal and constant existence of radiation." He suggested that if "we can drive home the concept" that radioactivity was not something new, "tendencies toward hysteria might be alleviated."[22]

Snapp's comments reflected the AEC's dismay about increasing public fears of radiation from nuclear weapons. In the immediate aftermath of World War II, the death and destruction caused by the blasts and heat from the atomic bombs dropped on Hiroshima and Nagasaki commanded much more attention than the effects of radiation. This changed after the United States conducted highly publicized nuclear weapons tests at Bikini Atoll in the Pacific Ocean in July 1946. Following the tests, which were witnessed by 168 reporters, many articles appeared in popular publications about the dangers of radiation. *Life* magazine told its readers that "science learned at Bikini," among other things, "that radioactive elements generated by atomic bombs are . . . even more dangerous than large-scale destruction." The potential genetic consequences of radiation exposure seemed especially alarming. *Newsweek* revealed that Hermann J. Muller, who received a Nobel Prize in 1946 for his research on genetic effects of x-rays, feared that "mass exposure to high-energy radiation can doom the human race." The journalist Edward P. Morgan warned in *Collier's* that "the a-bomb's invisible offspring" could "dangerously alter human cell structure and ultimately produce freaks."[23]

A best-selling book, *No Place to Hide,* presented the message about radiation dangers to a popular audience in an especially striking manner. Its author, David Bradley, had served as a U.S. Army physician assigned to the "radiological safety section" during the Bikini tests. Published in 1948, his book offered an absorbing account of his experiences; he concluded that "if life as we know it is to continue, men must understand and deal with the menacing aspects of atomic energy." He warned that the use of nuclear weapons "may affect the land and its wealth—and therefore its people—for centuries through the persistence of radioactivity." *No Place to Hide* spent ten weeks on the *New York Times* best-seller list and sold about 250,000 copies within a few months.[24]

Bradley's book and the numerous magazine articles that appeared in the wake of the Bikini tests undoubtedly fueled public concern about radiation hazards. But attention was largely fixed on the effects of nuclear weapons, and there was little evidence of sustained or deep-seated public anxiety about the dangers of radiation from other sources. A public opinion poll taken on November 10, 1948, indicated that despite the news reports about radiation, support for, or at least optimism about, atomic energy remained strong. The survey asked, "Do you think that, in the long run, atomic energy will do more good than harm?" By a margin of 42 percent to 23 percent, the respondents believed that it would "do more good." Among college-educated participants, the favorable response was even higher; 61 percent thought that atomic energy would "do more good," and only 18 percent thought it would "do more harm." Two years later researchers who conducted a study for the AEC on public attitudes toward atomic energy were surprised to find "a general disinterest in the subject, a lack of fear or anxiety, and a thorough lack of concern about developments in the field."[25]

Nevertheless, the stories about the effects of radiation exposure caused considerable concern to professionals in the field and to ranking officials in the AEC. Without seeking to play down genuine radiation hazards, they worried that overstated popular accounts would provoke unwarranted public fear. Herbert Parker, in his contribution to the report of the AEC's Safety and Industrial Health Advisory Board, commented that the "insidious danger of radiation damage receives a spotlight in the popular and technical press . . . out of proportion to the hazard in comparison with injury risk in many other industries." In a review of Bradley's book, Austin M. Brues, a prominent health physicist and a staff member at both Argonne National Laboratory and the Institute of Radiobiology and Biophysics at the University of Chicago, agreed that there was "plenty of reason to worry" about radiation. But he disputed Bradley's suggestion that "in radioactivity we have something which is truly and completely intolerable." David Lilienthal urged his fellow citizens to recognize that "atomic energy and atomic bombs are not synonymous." He also encouraged them to "learn the essential facts about atomic energy" so that they could make informed judgments regarding the use of "this new force that may make the difference between calamity and progress."[26]

It was in this context that the AEC drafted its public report on radioactive waste disposal. Lilienthal and his colleagues wanted a document that would inform the public and at the same time reduce the potential for excessive alarm. Preparing a report that met those criteria without compromising classified data proved more difficult and time-consuming than they anticipated. While various AEC offices worked on the report, Lilienthal, Salisbury, and Carroll L. Wilson, the agency's staff director, complained about delays in its completion and deficiencies in its presentation. In the meantime, the AEC decided to hold a meeting with representatives of professional organizations and federal agencies involved in sanitary engineering and waste disposal. It hoped to collect information and to ease the "concern which technical and administrative representatives of public and private agencies have indicated in response to waste from atomic energy operations."[27]

The meeting took place on January 24–25, 1949. In opening remarks, Lilienthal expressed confidence that "we will conquer" the waste disposal problem, which he depicted as "a part of learning how to live with radiation." He made the same points during a press conference that followed the seminar. He described radioactive waste disposal as "an extremely important problem" and acknowledged that there was "no doubt" that it was "a tough one." But Lilienthal suggested that the experts at the meeting believed solutions would be found, and he hoped that radioactive waste would not become "a subject of emotion and hysteria and fear." In a front-page story, the *New York Times* reported that "the sum of the two-day study was that the hazard was being closely monitored in every way possible."[28]

The AEC finally published its report on radioactive waste in December 1949. The objective, Salisbury reminded the commissioners, was to "inform citizens generally on a subject about which public information is needed in order to dispel misconceptions and allay possible latent hysteria." The report gave a description, in lay terms, of the nature of radioactivity and the sources of radioactive wastes. It acknowledged that radioactive wastes were "potentially harmful" and explained how they posed a danger from exposure to internal radiation. Gaseous wastes, for example, could be inhaled directly or could settle on plants and, in turn, be consumed by animals or humans. Liquid wastes could be hazardous if they contaminated water supplies or if they deposited radioactive particles in algae that were eaten by fish. The report pointed out that the quantities of radioactive waste generated in the AEC's facilities were unprecedented. It noted that "an operating nuclear reactor generates radiation equivalent to several hundred tons of the naturally radioactive element, radium," while, "in contrast, only 3 pounds of pure radium have been made available in the whole world during the last 50 years." The report concluded that "the methods of safe handling used to date have successfully protected workers and the public" but also cited the need for improved methods to deal with waste and for a "more complete understanding of the permissible doses (tolerance levels) which men, animals, and plants can absorb without affecting their health, growth, and length of life."[29]

The AEC provided a comprehensible guide to the nature of radioactive waste that was a useful introduction to the subject. In keeping with the dual and in some ways conflicting goals of the report, however, it was not entirely candid. One objective was to inform the public; the other was to reduce the potential for public alarm. As a result, the report gave few details about the great uncertainties surrounding safe disposal of high-level wastes and only passing attention to the most hazardous liquids stored in tanks at Hanford. Although it briefly discussed the discharge of low-level waste products, it did not disclose the efforts to conceal releases of iodine-131 at Hanford. The green run occurred just days before publication of the report, so there was, of course, no mention of it. But neither was there any mention of other iodine-131 releases from the plant. Indeed, the commitment to secrecy sometimes reached ludicrous levels. On at least one occasion in 1946, a Hanford scientist posed as an animal husbandry expert to clandestinely check for iodine-131 levels in the thyroids of cattle without arousing the suspicion of local farmers. Such ploys were probably effective in reducing public anxiety about radiation in the short run. But the AEC's oft-repeated concern about "hysteria" was far out of proportion to existing public attitudes, and its abridged candor undermined public confidence over the long run. The AEC recognized that waste disposal was a long-term problem but used short-term palliatives to reduce the potential for a public outcry. It assumed that over time solutions would be found that would win public acceptance because it was aware that "if the [atomic] industry is to expand, better means of isolating, concentrating, immobilizing, and controlling wastes will ultimately be required."[30]

RADIOACTIVE WASTE AND COMMERCIAL NUCLEAR POWER

In the first few years of its existence, the AEC centered its consideration of waste disposal on its own facilities. The bulk of the AEC's waste was created in the production of materials for nuclear weapons. This pattern changed significantly in 1954, when Congress passed a new Atomic Energy Act that eased restrictions on access to technical information and made possible the widespread use of nuclear energy for civilian purposes. The legislation gave the AEC statutory responsibility for both encouraging the development and regulating the safety of the peaceful applications of nuclear power. Once a commercial nuclear industry was established, it would increase, perhaps drastically, the volumes of radioactive waste that required safe handling, storage, and disposal. In its approach to civilian nuclear waste, the AEC drew on the assumptions it had adopted and the experience it had acquired in dealing with the problem at its own installations.

The treatment of radioactive waste from commercial reactors and other civilian sources was not qualitatively different from that at the AEC's own plants. Experts believed that highly radioactive spent fuel rods in power reactors would be chemically reprocessed, just as they were at Hanford and other AEC sites. This would enable the recovery of uranium-235 that was not consumed and that could be used in the fabrication of new fuel rods. It would also reduce the volume of high-level wastes that had to be stored and eventually disposed of in a suitable depository. The most serious problem in dealing with waste from nuclear power plants, as in weapons plants, would be the toxic liquids that were the by-product of reprocessing. As Arthur Gorman and Joseph Lieberman, the AEC's sanitary engineers, put it in 1956, "High-level liquid wastes presently associated with chemical reprocessing are . . . the core of the waste disposal problem." Although this problem would be qualitatively the same for both government and commercial facilities, it was likely to differ quantitatively. If the AEC carried out the mandate of the 1954 Atomic Energy Act to promote nuclear industry development, the volume of waste that commercial reactors produced would far exceed the output of its own plants.[31]

Nuclear experts believed that finding satisfactory methods of radioactive waste disposal had to be accomplished if the nuclear industry was to reach its full potential. In 1955 Glenn Seaborg, a Nobel Prize recipient for his pioneering work in identifying and isolating the element plutonium and later chairman of the AEC, declared, "Probably the most difficult problem, which may well be the limiting factor in determining the extent to which nuclear energy will be used for industrial power, is that of disposal of the tremendous quantity of radioactive waste material." He added: "These problems will be solved, however, and a nuclear energy industry will probably be developed in the future because of the advantages of this form of energy." The following year, a highly publicized report by the National Academy of Sciences on the biological effects of radiation reached a similar conclusion about future quantities of waste materials. The committee that investigated the issue, which was chaired by Abel Wolman and included Gorman and Lieberman along with other leading authorities, described radioactive waste as "an unparalleled problem." It estimated that by the year 2000 the volume of high-level liquid waste, mostly from commercial reactors, could total a staggering 2.4 billion gallons. Although the committee found that research to date "indicated that a number of systems for ultimate disposal of wastes may be feasible," it cautioned that "considerably more work is required . . . before any of them is at the point of economic operating reality."[32]

In light of the new conditions created by the 1954 act and the prospective growth of nuclear power, the AEC carefully reexamined the uncertainties surrounding radioactive waste and their potential impact on commercial applications. One source of concern was the cost of handling and disposing of waste materials. By the end of 1956 the AEC had invested about $100 million in waste facilities and was spending between $3 million and $5 million annually for treatment and disposal in its own plants. Tank construction and storage alone cost from thirty cents to two dollars per gallon, depending on the nature of the wastes being contained. Those amounts appeared to be an important obstacle to commercial nuclear power development because they were significantly higher than waste disposal expenses in other industries. Nuclear experts anticipated that the price of waste management would decline proportionately as the industry grew, and they hoped that the extraction of potentially valuable isotopes would reduce costs further. Scientists were exploring the possibility of using cesium-137 in industrial radiography, strontium-90 in storage batteries, and other radioisotopes found in nuclear waste for a variety of medical, industrial, and agricultural purposes. If recovery of some portions of radioactive wastes for constructive applications proved feasible, it could help overcome the economic burdens they imposed. *Business Week,* while reporting that safety and cost problems could make it difficult to "reap the full benefits that can come from nuclear energy," also suggested that "today's waste may be tomorrow's bonanza."[33]

The AEC's primary concern about radioactive wastes was not their cost but their threat to public health. In March 1956 the AEC staff, drawing heavily on the views of Gorman and Lieberman, reviewed the existing status of and future prospects for waste disposal in a paper prepared for the commissioners. The paper stated that "disposal of radioactive wastes is under control at all AEC installations" and that the "serious problem" of gaseous emissions at Hanford and other sites had been largely resolved by the addition of high-efficiency filters and "iodine and rare gas removal units." It also pointed out the many outstanding questions that required consideration. It maintained that neither solid nor low-level liquid wastes presented major technical difficulties but cautioned that as the commercial nuclear industry grew, finding suitable locations for dispersing liquids and burying wastes would be essential.

The disposal of highly radioactive liquids from reprocessing remained by far the most formidable waste problem facing the AEC. The staff report cited several possible approaches to ultimate disposal of high-level wastes that were being investigated and that appeared promising. One was fixation of waste products in a solid, stable medium, such as clay, synthetic feldspar, or ceramic materials, to contain their radioactivity. The solid blocks might then be buried or stored in a way that would not endanger the environment. A second approach was to discharge high-level liquid wastes directly into geologic formations that would keep their radioactivity from reaching water supplies or other natural resources. Among the kinds of sites being considered were salt beds and domes, deep basins of 5,000 to 15,000 feet that were geologically isolated, and selected shale formations. A third proposal was to remove the long-lived isotopes, strontium-90 and cesium-137, from the high-level wastes. This would ease the difficulty of controlling the remaining isotopes but would not solve the problem of what to do with the strontium-90 and cesium-137. Finally, high-level wastes might conceivably be dumped in ocean waters, but this idea seemed less attractive than the others because of "lack of knowledge of pertinent oceanographic factors and complex technical problems and costs involved."

The AEC staff expressed confidence that suitable means and sites for radioactive waste disposal would eventually be found, but it offered no imminent solutions. Research on satisfactory methods to deal with high-level waste was still in preliminary stages. The AEC was sponsoring projects at its own laboratories and at several universities and also was working with the National Academy of Sciences, the U.S. Geological Survey, and other government agencies to gather and evaluate information. The agency staff reminded the commissioners that resolving technical issues was only a part of the problem; public relations was "an especially important consideration." As the atomic industry expanded and moved into populated areas, public concern about nuclear safety generally and waste disposal specifically seemed likely to increase. Therefore, it was essential to cooperate closely with state and local government officials to explain technical matters and to secure their assistance in planning, siting, and promoting the safety of waste operations.[34]

In 1955 the AEC took an initial step to determine the best method to dispose of high-level wastes by requesting that the National Academy of Sciences establish a committee on waste disposal within its Division of Earth Sciences. In a series of seminars, representatives of the AEC and the U.S. Geological Survey, industry officials, and prominent individual scientists shared knowledge and exchanged opinions. The committee's final report, published in April 1957, declared that "radioactive waste can be disposed of in a variety of ways and at a large number of sites in the United States." It cautioned, however, that much research remained to be done "before any final conclusion is reached on any type of waste disposal" and added that "the hazard related to radio-waste is so great that no element of doubt should be allowed to exist regarding safety."

In the judgment of the Committee on Waste Disposal, the most promising approach for permanent disposal of high-level liquid wastes was to place them in salt formations. The greatest advantage of this method was that large salt deposits occur in dry geologic surroundings, and the absence of water would prevent liquid wastes from migrating to other locations. Further, fissures in salt formations, unlike those in clay, shale, or granite quarries, would be "self-sealing," thus avoiding leakage. The two principal areas in the United States with large salt deposits, the north-central states and the southern states along the Gulf Coast, had low seismic activity and were level enough to facilitate underground access. The committee made clear, however, that important technical uncertainties about using salt formations for high-level wastes had to be resolved. It was concerned about the possibility that salt cavities might collapse and urged that research be done to determine the "size and shape of openings which can be relied upon to be structurally stable." Another potentially serious problem was that the large amount of heat produced by radioactive wastes as they decay would weaken the walls of salt formations. Finally, transportation of high-level wastes from the sites of their creation to a disposal facility raised challenging cost and safety issues.

The committee cited fixation of high-level wastes in stable solids as the second most promising approach to final disposal. It suggested that if means for "forming a relatively insoluble product" could be developed, the blocks could then be stored on land, in mines, or in salt cavities. Although optimistic that solutions to high-level waste disposal would be found, the committee emphasized that many complex problems first had to be addressed. It suggested that "several years of research and pilot testing" might be necessary "before the first such disposal system can be put into operation."[35]

FUROR OVER OCEAN DUMPING

While the AEC staff and scientific experts in a number of disciplines were weighing options for dealing with radioactive waste, an unexpected public furor arose over the dumping of low-level wastes in ocean waters. The uproar was largely a result of growing public fears of radiation that were not directly related to the problem of waste disposal. The source of public anxieties that became prominent during the mid- and late 1950s was radioactive fallout from atmospheric testing of nuclear weapons by the United States, the Soviet Union, and Great Britain. Scientists disagreed sharply about the severity of the risks that fallout imposed on the population. The AEC, which was responsible for conducting the U.S. tests, insisted that the levels of radioactivity were too low to significantly threaten public health and that the risks were far less dangerous than falling behind the Soviets in the arms race. Critics were not convinced; they contended that the AEC underestimated the hazards of radioactive fallout. They suggested that even low levels of continuous fallout could pollute food supplies and cause increased rates of birth defects, cancer, and other afflictions.

The fallout debate became a prominent subject in news reports, magazine stories, political campaigns, and congressional hearings. For the first time, the dangers of exposure to low levels of radiation became a bitterly contested political question and a subject of sustained public concern. A decade earlier, the AEC's worries about "latent hysteria" over radiation were overblown, or at least premature. But in the late 1950s, public fears about the effects of low-level radiation from any source became widespread and acute. A poll taken in May 1957 showed that 52 percent of those questioned believed that fallout was a "real danger," compared to 28 percent who did not think so and 20 percent who did not know. Physicians complained that their patients were so alarmed about radiation that they resisted legitimate x-ray treatment. The fallout debate also seriously damaged the AEC's standing as a guardian of public health. The agency was so deeply concerned that growing apprehension about radiation would impair its nuclear weapons testing programs that it consistently played down the potential threat to public health that fallout conceivably represented. As a result, it forfeited much of its credibility. In 1951 investigators attributed a lack of public fear of or interest in atomic energy to trust in scientific experts and the government. By the end of the decade, however, faith in the AEC's commitment to protection of the public from radiation hazards had clearly eroded.[36]

The diminished confidence in the AEC's performance on public health issues was apparent in the protests against ocean disposal of radioactive wastes. Dumping of low-level wastes into the sea had begun as early as 1946, and for more than a decade the U.S. Navy had carried drums of waste materials from AEC facilities to selected sites in the Atlantic and Pacific Oceans. In addition, as of October 1958, the AEC had licensed six private firms to dispose of low-level wastes from hospitals, laboratories, and industrial operations at sea. Although one licensee, the Crossroads Marine Disposal Corporation, had discarded wastes in relatively shallow waters near Boston under a permit granted in 1952, the AEC, in accordance with the recommendations made by the National Committee on Radiation Protection in 1954, began to require that disposal take place at sites with a depth of at least one thousand fathoms (6,000 feet). The agency was satisfied that its procedures created no public health hazard, principally because the amount of radiation that could reach the ocean environment from dumping was minuscule compared to the billions of curies of natural radiation present in the sea.[37]

For several years, the ocean dumping of radioactive wastes attracted little public attention. But once the fallout controversy made radiation hazards a hotly disputed and highly visible subject, applications for AEC licenses to dispose of waste materials in the Gulf of Mexico and in the Atlantic Ocean stirred a storm of opposition. Citizens in several locations turned out to protest at meetings or hearings. Senator Clair Engle of California complained, "Questions have been raised regarding the prevalence of . . . radioactive material in the atmosphere. Apparently now we are going to get it in the ocean as well." The well-known writer E.B. White declared, "The sea doesn't belong to the Atomic Energy Commission, it belongs to me. I am not ready to authorize dumping radioactive waste into it, and I suspect that a lot of other people to whom the sea belongs are not ready to authorize it, either." The *Nation* accused the AEC of clandestinely carrying on "reckless dumping" for years. Other observers urged that responsibility for assuring the safety of radioactive wastes be removed from the AEC and entrusted to the U.S. Public Health Service. In a story on ocean dumping in January 1962, *Time* reported that "public uneasiness continues to increase," even though "many of the arguments against waste storage and disposal are ridiculous."[38]

AEC officials were dismayed by the outcry over ocean dumping. Although they regarded the concerns as greatly exaggerated, they took the signs of public anxiety seriously. The AEC sponsored studies of three areas in which wastes had been dumped. The investigations, carried out by the U.S. Coast and Geodetic Survey and the Public Health Service, showed no "radioactivity attributable to disposal operations." Nevertheless, the AEC decided, at least for the time being, not to issue any new licenses for ocean disposal of radioactive wastes. Chairman John A. McCone suggested that "there would be little justification at the present time to press for ocean disposal sites in the face of strong public objection—despite the fact that such objections might be founded on emotional fears and not on technical facts."[39]

In response to the "strong public objection," the AEC turned to land burial of solid low-level wastes generated by its licensees, which was both less controversial and considerably cheaper than ocean disposal. By 1963 it had issued licenses for commercial operation of three low-level sites on state-owned land in Nevada, Kentucky, and New York. At that time, about 95 percent of solid low-level waste was buried on land,

and the AEC staff concluded that ocean disposal was "no longer . . . an important service."[40]

From the late 1940s to the early 1960s, the AEC regarded management of radioactive waste as an issue that required attention. It reached this conclusion after Abel Wolman and his colleagues on the Safety and Industrial Health Advisory Board convinced Lilienthal and other leading officials to recognize the significance of waste programs both for protecting public health and for promoting the peaceful applications of atomic energy. In 1962, in a report to President John F. Kennedy on the civilian nuclear power program, the AEC declared that aside from the development of safe and commercially viable power reactors, "no other phase of the entire program is more important than that of waste disposal." But this did not mean that the agency considered waste disposal an urgent problem. It was confident that radioactive waste was under control at its own installations, even as it sought a permanent method for disposal of high-level materials. It did not view low-level waste as a major threat to public health, though it acknowledged that finding satisfactory ways to deal with large quantities of commercially generated materials was essential. The nuclear power industry was still small, so determining the best method to dispose of high-level wastes from reactors was not yet a pressing matter.

The AEC sponsored research projects on a wide variety of waste questions, and it felt no pressure to rush to settle on a solution to the many outstanding issues that those projects were investigating. It preferred to explore the advantages and disadvantages of different alternatives rather than to increase the chances for errors by moving too rapidly. But it insisted that a suitable means for ultimate disposal of the most dangerous wastes would be found in the foreseeable future. "There is no reason," an AEC report to Congress declared in January 1960, "to believe that proliferation of wastes will become a limiting factor on future development of atomic energy for peaceful purposes."[41]

Within a short time, however, the AEC's position was undermined by strong criticism of its approach to waste issues. The prevailing view within the agency and the scientific community that waste disposal was a problem that could be solved reasonably soon was challenged by a series of controversies that cast doubts on the comfortable assumptions of the previous decade. And the strong expressions of public anxieties about radioactive waste, so evident in the outcry over ocean dumping, made the siting of waste facilities, even if the scientific issues were settled, even more problematic.

CHAPTER 2

A "Huge and Ever-Increasing Problem"

During the 1960s, the AEC sponsored a wide variety of research projects in its efforts to determine the best long-term methods for disposing of high-level and low-level radioactive wastes. Although it did not find definitive answers for the problems it investigated, it was encouraged by the information it acquired and satisfied that it was making steady progress toward its goals. Some authorities, however, were less confident. Experts from other federal agencies, state governments, and the National Academy of Sciences raised questions about the safety of waste treatment at the AEC's own installations, and eventually their skepticism stirred concern among members of Congress and the public. An expanding controversy largely focused on waste management at Hanford and other AEC sites, but it inevitably carried over to wastes from commercial nuclear power reactors as well. As a result, the AEC faced increasingly intense pressure to decide promptly on a permanent solution to the disposal of the high-level wastes produced in both government and commercial plants.

RESEARCH ON RADIOACTIVE WASTE

By the early 1960s, the prevailing view among experts both inside and outside the AEC was that the best approach to high-level waste disposal would be to immobilize liquids in a solid form and then place the solid wastes in an appropriate geologic site. Joseph Lieberman, who had become chief of the AEC's environmental and sanitary engineering branch, made this point in a speech to a conference of sanitary engineers in January 1960. He suggested that an "optimum solution to the problem of final disposal of highly radioactive liquid wastes would include the conversion of the waste into a solid, preferably inert, form and the long-term, essentially permanent, storage of these solids in a specially selected geologic formation such as a salt bed." Lieberman added that "one has to be very careful to distinguish between aspiration, reality and speculation in this field" and made clear that much research remained to be performed. Nevertheless, he expressed hope that "a 'foolproof' method for fixation of high-level wastes into solids" would be developed "in less than 20 to 25 years." And he voiced his confidence that the nuclear industry could grow "in a rational way without being 'hamstrung' by its own wastes."[1]

Researchers at several AEC laboratories and production sites tested different methods of stabilizing high-level wastes through the process of calcination, in which liquids were heated to make dry, granular solids. At the National Reactor Testing Station (NRTS), an AEC-funded facility located in isolated regions of Idaho, more than 500,000 gallons of liquid waste from fuel reprocessing were converted to solid form between December 1963 and October 1964. This reduced the volume of the liquid wastes by about 90 percent. The solid wastes were stored in stainless steel bins cooled by air circulation. Other AEC installations not only explored alternative means for calcination but also sought to find "relatively non-leachable media" in which the solid wastes would be deposited. Scientists at Brookhaven National Laboratory, an AEC-supported research institution on Long Island, New York, worked on developing a continuous process in which high-level liquids would be converted to solid form and placed in long-lasting phosphate glass containers. At other sites, researchers investigated the possibility of using ceramic compounds for fixation of the calcinated wastes.[2]

The results of the research conducted at AEC installations were promising but far from proven. Even if they turned out to be effective, they did not provide means for permanent disposal of highly radioactive wastes. The solidification process at the Idaho site, for example, was useful in substantially reducing the risks that radiation from wastes would reach the environment, but it did not offer a definitive solution because the projected life of the steel storage bins was less than that of the materials they contained. At the same time that the AEC was working on calcination of liquids, it was trying to determine the most appropriate geologic formation for ultimate high-level waste disposal. In accordance with the recommendations of the National Academy of Sciences Committee on Waste Disposal in 1957, the AEC focused on investigating the feasibility of using salt formations for this purpose. In the early 1960s scientists from Oak Ridge National Laboratory (as Clinton Laboratories had been renamed after World War II) conducted a series of field experiments with simulated radioactive wastes in two abandoned salt mines in Kansas. They designed the tests to learn more about the possible effects of heat on the physical properties and stability of salt deposits. In early 1965 the AEC announced that the investigations had "shown strong promise." Although the fixation of wastes in a solid medium and transfer to a permanent repository for disposal appeared to be the likeliest approach, the AEC also sponsored research on direct injection of high-level liquid wastes into deep geologic formations. For example, scientists at the Savannah River Plant in South Carolina, built in the early 1950s to produce plutonium and tritium for nuclear weapons, conducted studies on the feasibility of disposing high-level liquids in dense bedrock.[3]

While the AEC explored methods of permanent disposal of the most dangerous waste materials, high-level liquids at its own facilities remained in underground tanks. In 1961, 174 tanks at the Hanford, Savannah River, and Idaho plants contained more than 65 million gallons of highly radioactive liquids. The bulk of this liquid waste, more than 52 million gallons, was stored at Hanford in 145 single-shell tanks. The durability of the tanks was an important consideration, and the AEC made projections from available data on corrosion rates of carbon steel. In 1959 Herbert Parker, whose position at that time was manager of Hanford Laboratories, told the AEC's congressional oversight committee, the Joint Committee on Atomic Energy, that the estimated life of the tanks was "at least several decades." Walter G. Belter, a member of the AEC's environmental and sanitary engineering staff, suggested in May 1961 that "an estimated tank life-expectancy measured in decades appears to be conservative." Several years later, three experts from Oak Ridge declared that over a period of about twenty-five years, the use of tanks as an interim measure had proven "practical, economical, and safe."[4]

Despite those assurances, tank storage was hardly trouble-free even as a temporary approach to high-level waste management. The most serious problem was the unanticipated leakage from some of the tanks. In response to questions from members of the Joint Committee on Atomic Energy in 1959, Parker commented that Hanford had experienced "what might be described as suspicious occurrences" in its tanks. But he assured the committee that after thorough investigation, "we have never detected a leak from any of these tanks." The AEC made a similar assertion in its 1959 *Annual Report to Congress,* which pointed out that "stored wastes are extremely corrosive" but that "in more than a decade of tank storage at Hanford no leaks have been detected."[5]

Unfortunately, the "suspicious occurrences" turned out to have been leaks of thousands of gallons of high-level liquids. By 1963 leaks had been found in five of the Hanford tanks. The AEC insisted that the leaks did not cause a public health hazard because the tanks were two hundred feet above the water table and the dry sediments under them were capable of absorbing large volumes of liquid. Therefore, it believed that the waste materials that escaped the tanks were unlikely to reach the Columbia River. Similar problems arose at Savannah River, where four tanks released small quantities of high-level liquids between 1957 and 1959. In 1960 the leakage rate from one tank "increased drastically," which forced plant operators to lower the level of liquid waste in it. The AEC gradually took action that it hoped would prevent further leaks, including a process called "in-tank solidification" in which much of the liquid in the older tanks at Hanford was evaporated or, over time, transferred from leak-prone single-shell tanks to newer and sturdier double-shell tanks. This left behind less mobile but still highly radioactive sludge in the 149 single-shell tanks built between 1943 and 1964. The AEC did not regard the leaks as a severe threat, but their occurrence underscored the need to find better means for storing and disposing of high-level wastes. In the late 1960s it began to separate the most worrisome isotopes, strontium-90 and cesium-137, from the wastes in the tanks and to store them in a different facility.[6]

Meanwhile, the AEC was also seeking to ensure adequate treatment of low-level materials. Low-level wastes did not, if properly controlled, pose a public health hazard of great magnitude. Their radioactivity normally measured in a range of thousandths or millionths of one curie per gallon; by contrast, the same amount of high-level waste could contain thousands of curies. The number of commercial nuclear power plants was still too small to produce sizable quantities of high-level waste. But the volume of low-level wastes generated in industry, medicine, and research was so large, estimated at billions of gallons per year, that their potential dangers could not be disregarded. The AEC's Lieberman pointed out that if low-level materials were not handled and disposed of in a suitable way, "they could be a distinct nuisance and, under certain circumstances, even a hazard." As always, the agency's goal was to prevent concentrations of radioactivity from exceeding the levels recommended by the National Committee on Radiation Protection and other professional organizations. It affirmed in 1965 that "present treatment and disposal methods in use in the United States have been demonstrated to result in concentrations in the environment well below established permissible limits."[7]

The AEC conducted studies at its own installations to make certain that radiation levels met the same objective. It continued to act on the premise that some releases of radioactive wastes to the environment were unavoidable. "It will always be necessary to use the diluting power of the environment to some extent in handling low-level waste," Lieberman explained. "The cost of 'absolutely' processing or containing these large volumes would be prohibitive." The operating principle of "dilute and disperse" guided the treatment of low-level waste at AEC sites. At Hanford, this meant that large volumes of low-level liquids were discharged into the ground or into the Columbia River and solid wastes were buried in trenches or landfills. At Oak Ridge, among other disposal practices, adjoining waterways served as sinks for low-level liquids. Environmental studies found that "concentration of radioactivity in the Clinch and Tennessee Rivers below Oak Ridge is well within internationally accepted standards."[8]

The AEC acknowledged that it needed "further fundamental and applied information on the physical, chemical, and biological dynamics of a flowing fresh water system which is receiving volumes of low-level radioactive waste." Indeed, there was still a great deal about the concentration, distribution, mobility, and other characteristics of radioactive contaminants in the environment that remained obscure even to experts. Sound long-term management of radioactive wastes required greater knowledge of their properties and possible effects, and the AEC supported wide-ranging research for that purpose. It remained keenly aware that effective control of waste was essential not only for the safety of its own sites but also for the future growth of commercial nuclear power. AEC commissioner James T. Ramey told an audience at the School of Public Health at the University of North Carolina in June 1965 that "more funds have been spent, and more scientific and technological efforts concentrated on facilities, operations, and research and development, with regard to this industrial waste than to any other industrial contaminant known." He added that despite the still unanswered questions about the hazards of radioactive waste, "it is firmly believed that waste management operations will not constitute a major obstacle in development of nuclear power—from either a safety or economic standpoint."[9]

THE COLUMBIA RIVER ADVISORY GROUP'S 1961 REPORT

Most AEC officials and the contractors who operated the agency's research and production facilities were convinced that the practices they followed on waste management and disposal provided ample protection of public health. Some experts, however, both inside and outside the AEC, were less certain. The dissenters echoed, with growing intensity and visibility, the concerns that Abel Wolman had raised in the late 1940s, especially regarding the AEC's handling of waste materials and the necessarily limited knowledge on which it acted. Following the reservations cited by the AEC's Safety and Industrial Health Advisory Board in 1948, an internal controversy about the safety of waste procedures centered, not surprisingly, on Hanford, which was then run by the General Electric Company.

In July 1949 the AEC's Hanford Operations Office established the Columbia River Advisory Group, a small committee that included representatives from the states of Washington and Oregon and from the U.S. Public Health Service. Its purpose was to enable state health officials in affected regions to learn about efforts to control radioactive contamination at Hanford and to assist the AEC in its "long-range programs concerning water pollution and public health." Presumably, the AEC also hoped that the advisory group would be helpful in preventing public "hysteria" over nuclear waste, about which it was so uneasy. The committee was formed at the same time that the AEC was preparing its public report on radioactive waste. After its first meeting in November 1949, the advisory group released a statement to the press in which it announced that "so far as the Columbia River is concerned, there are no apparent water pollution hazards resulting from the [Hanford] operations at present."[10]

The advisory group's statement troubled Arthur Gorman at AEC headquarters, who was "of the impression . . . that this [press] release was made at the suggestion" of Hanford officials. He expressed grave doubts about the "wisdom of a public release based on two and one-half days [of] sanitary engineering review of one of the most complex situations in the country." He also questioned the propriety of a "situation where the A.E.C. or one of its contractors as a producer of wastes is the principal agency involved in decisions" about the storage and release of radioactive materials. Gorman's views elicited indignant rejoinders from Hanford officials. Herbert Parker, for example, commented that the "implication that the scientific forces of the General Electric Company would adjust their technical findings to 'white-wash' practices at Hanford . . . is preposterous."[11]

The differing perspectives so evident in the early days of the Columbia River Advisory Group resurfaced when it issued an assessment of the long-term impact of Hanford on the environment in 1961. Drawing on data collected by scientists from the AEC, General Electric, and the U.S. Public Health Service, it expressed serious reservations about continued use of the river as a dump for low-level wastes from the site. The report, written by two Public Health Service officials, M.W. Lammering and Ernest C. Tsivoglou, concluded that although average radiation exposure to the downstream population from Hanford releases did not exceed existing permissible levels, it was "not far removed from the recommended limits." Further, Lammering and Tsivoglou asserted that some individuals probably received "considerably more" than the average calculations indicated. "Thus, in terms of the resulting human radiation exposure," they argued, "the capacity of the Columbia River to receive further radioactive pollution appears to be nearly if not fully exhausted for practical purposes, at least in the vicinity of Hanford Works."[12]

The assessment that Lammering and Tsivoglou presented was heavily influenced by two important developments during the previous decade. The first was that three new reactors had begun operation at Hanford, which substantially increased the volume of radioactive materials released to the Columbia River. The second was that the National Committee on Radiation Protection and the International Commission on Radiological Protection had tightened the permissible levels they recommended for radiation exposure. Both organizations reduced their suggested limits to one-third of the previous values for occupational whole-body exposure to external sources of radiation, or five rems per year. The rem was a unit of measure that applied to chronic low-level exposures and indicated the "relative biological effectiveness" of different kinds of radiation in producing biological injury. The NCRP and the ICRP lowered by corresponding proportions their recommended levels of exposure to internal emitters that could cause illness if taken into the body. And, for the first time, they agreed on levels for population exposure of one-tenth of the occupational limit for individuals (0.5 rem per year) and, to curtail genetic consequences, one-thirtieth of the occupational limit as an average for large groups exposed to radiation (0.17 rem per year). They acted in part because of scientific considerations, especially the recommendations of the National Academy of Sciences in a report on radiation hazards in 1956, and in part because of increasing public anxieties about radiation. The NCRP and ICRP emphasized that they did not tighten permissible doses because of evidence that the previous levels had been dangerously high but to keep exposures to a minimum that they judged generally safe without being impractical.[13]

The Columbia River Advisory Group's 1961 report drew on the new recommendations of the radiation protection organizations to reach the conclusion that levels of radioactive materials released by Hanford approached permissible limits for population groups and in cases of an "undetermined number" of individuals, might exceed them. "What was acceptable practice a few years ago may no longer be acceptable," it declared, "even though the actual or numerical levels of radiation exposure may not have changed materially in the interim." This evaluation caused concern and some confusion among responsible officials at the AEC and Hanford. George F. Quinn, director of the AEC's production division, could not explain the "wide discrepancies" between the advisory group's calculations on radiological conditions and the much more favorable results obtained by General Electric, even after allowing for the new recommendations on permissible exposures. Nevertheless, the AEC took modest steps to reduce the volume of radioactive liquids that reached the Columbia River, and it discussed more extensive improvements with representatives of the Public Health Service and other agencies. The sometimes contentious meetings did not fully resolve the problems cited by the Columbia River Advisory Group or the differences of opinion between experts. The debates lost much of their immediacy, however, when President Lyndon B. Johnson announced major reductions in plutonium production in 1964. This decision shut down all but one of the Hanford reactors over a period of seven years and significantly curtailed the contamination of the river. But the controversy over waste disposal was far from settled.[14]

THE NATIONAL ACADEMY OF SCIENCES AND THE AEC'S WASTE PROGRAMS

By the time the debate over the Columbia River Advisory Group's report subsided, the AEC was embroiled in an even more acrimonious dispute over many of the same issues with the Committee on Waste Disposal of the National Academy of Sciences. The committee, which the National Academy had established in 1955 at the request of the AEC, had suggested in its 1957 report that, pending the outcome of research on outstanding questions, salt formations appeared to be the most promising geologic repository for high-level wastes. In the same document, it also briefly expressed reservations about the "long-term safety of waste disposal as practiced" at AEC sites. As the committee continued its work, its members became increasingly concerned about the treatment of both high-level and low-level wastes at the AEC's plants. In April 1960 M. King Hubbert, a geologist with Shell Oil Company, told the panel's chairman, H.H. Hess, a professor of geology at Princeton University, that the AEC seemed to be plagued by a "mental fixation" and that it had been "peculiarly reluctant to face up to the fact that disposal sites for the existing plants must soon be chosen."[15]

On June 21, 1960, Hess sent the AEC a letter, largely drafted by Hubbert, that made the committee's misgivings clear. He cited its concerns that AEC installations were not located at sites where disposal of their wastes was geologically appropriate and that techniques for ultimate disposal of high-level wastes had not been developed. Hess submitted that "no system of waste disposal can be considered *safe* in which the wastes are not completely isolated from all living things for the period during which they are dangerous," which was "at least 600 years." He added that the committee considered "the establishment of waste-disposal facilities at suitable geological sites" an "urgent" requirement.[16]

The AEC responded to the comments of the Committee on Waste Disposal with impatience and irritation. One commissioner, Robert E. Wilson, complained that the committee had exceeded its mandate by addressing waste problems "in general" instead of confining its opinions to the "geologic aspects of waste disposal." Another commissioner, Loren K. Olson, wondered about the advisability of "maintaining a standing advisory committee" on waste disposal and asked the AEC staff to report on this issue. The staff, presumably reflecting the views of Joseph Lieberman, concluded that despite the "problems associated with advisory groups," the AEC's continued support of the Committee on Waste Disposal through a contract with the National Academy of Sciences was advantageous. It based its judgment on the need for continuity in evaluating long-range questions surrounding radioactive waste, the conviction that the existing panel was "highly competent and representative of the earth science disciplines," and the benefits of "a highly authoritative, independent review in a field that has potentially highly sensitive public relations implications." The staff's arguments prevailed; the AEC took no action to eliminate or replace the committee.[17]

The AEC did, however, take issue with some of the points the committee made in Hess's letter of June 21, 1960. After lengthy deliberation by the staff and commissioners, A. R. Luedecke, the AEC's staff director, responded on January 4, 1961. He expressed surprise at the committee's criticisms, since the AEC had believed that "the earth sciences aspects of our program on waste disposal development had met your general approval." He recited the research projects the AEC was sponsoring in its effort to find methods for disposing of high-level wastes and to convert liquids to solid form, which, he said, had "achieved some quite promising results." Luedecke asserted that until ultimate solutions were found, underground tank storage was "safe and entirely satisfactory." He added that the AEC saw "no necessity for going to the enormous expense of relocating fuel element reprocessing facilities as implied in [the committee's] letter." The AEC was equally annoyed by what it read as a suggestion in the Hess letter that the standard for safe treatment of radioactive wastes should be zero releases to the environment. Luedecke reminded the committee that the agency followed the guidance of leading scientific organizations on radiation protection in its waste handling procedures.[18]

The exchange between the Committee on Waste Disposal and the AEC set the tone for an increasingly strained relationship. The disagreements were drawn in especially sharp relief by one committee member, King Hubbert. Hubbert was an eminent geologist who was also well known for what one colleague later described as his "exceedingly combative personality" and his "belligerence during technical arguments." In 1956 he stirred a great deal of controversy when he predicted, despite the objections of public relations executives at his company, Shell Oil, that oil production in the United States would reach its high point in the late 1960s or early 1970s and then decline. In later years this came to be called "Hubbert's peak." Hubbert argued that as reserves of oil and other fossil fuels inevitably diminished, they could be replaced by nuclear energy. By using power from nuclear fission, he suggested, "we may at last have found an energy supply adequate for our needs for at least the next few centuries."[19]

Although Hubbert supported the development of nuclear power to meet future energy demands, he was vocally disgruntled with the AEC's waste disposal practices. He complained to an official of the National Academy of Sciences in 1961 that the AEC had "not particularly liked the advice they . . . received" from the Committee on Waste Disposal and had "shown comparatively little inclination to follow such advice." He aired his opinions publicly during hearings of the Joint Committee on Atomic Energy in February 1963. Appearing before the committee to discuss world energy supplies, Hubbert declared that nuclear energy was needed to avoid "a complete decline of civilization within a few centuries." But he cautioned that the widespread use of nuclear power raised the "complementary problem" of radioactive waste. He insisted that the waste "should be isolated permanently from the biological environment so long as there is any danger from it whatever." Hubbert maintained that low-level wastes required more careful treatment than they had received; he criticized the practices of discharging them directly into the ground at Hanford and storing them in "leaky earth pits" at Oak Ridge. The AEC responded to Hubbert's remarks by reiterating that its waste disposal methods kept concentrations of radioactivity well within permissible limits. It assured the Joint Committee that it was taking steps to improve waste management at Oak Ridge and other sites and that soil conditions at Hanford prevented significant quantities of waste materials from reaching the Columbia River.[20]

As the scientific debate over radioactive wastes intensified, the National Academy of Sciences appointed two committees to investigate the issue. In June 1964 Abel Wolman suggested to Frederick Seitz, president of the National Academy, that a review of the "state of the art of disposal of radioactive wastes" be undertaken. As a result, the organization established an ad hoc committee that was chaired by Wolman and included Hubbert among its members. The committee met on July 6, 1965, and after hearing presentations from representatives of the AEC, other government agencies, and the nuclear industry, summarized its views in a brief letter that Wolman sent to Seitz. It commended the AEC for making "great progress in waste management practices and research" over the previous five years. But it also chided the agency for a "tendency to solve storage and disposal problems on an *ad hoc* basis." The committee called on the AEC to prepare a "comprehensive plan" that would deal "not only with present problems," but would also "reflect an awareness that expedient small-scale practices may be hazardous" over the long term.[21]

Seitz forwarded Wolman's comments to AEC chairman Glenn Seaborg, who responded by outlining the agency's well-rehearsed position on its approach to radioactive waste. He was "pleased to learn" that the ad hoc committee recognized that the AEC had made "great progress." He offered assurances that the AEC's waste disposal practices had not harmed public health or the environment and that the agency was carefully considering a "long-range comprehensive waste management plan." And he further suggested that the "magnitude of the future waste disposal problem" had been "significantly reduced" by technical improvements that decreased by substantial proportions the volume of wastes generated at AEC sites. Members of Wolman's committee were not entirely convinced by Seaborg's arguments. Hubbert told Wolman that although he was "favorably impressed" with progress in dealing with high-level wastes, he was "less satisfied" with treatment of low-level materials. He believed that Seaborg and the AEC showed a "persistent tendency" to slight the potential hazards of low-level waste and to "over-emphasize their 'harmlessness.' "[22]

THE GALLEY COMMITTEE REPORT

The differences between the ad hoc committee and the AEC were mild compared to those that emerged when the other National Academy committee on radioactive waste submitted a report containing even sharper criticism of the agency's programs. After the dispute over the comments in H.H. Hess's letter to the AEC in 1960, the Academy had changed the Committee on Waste Disposal's name to the Committee on the Geologic Aspects of Radioactive Waste Disposal. Perhaps in accordance with the wishes of the AEC, it limited the group's mandate to reviewing geologic issues. For a few years, the committee did very little. Finally, after Hubbert, in his capacity as chairman of the Academy's Division of Earth Sciences, complained that the committee was merely "standing around holding its hands," the AEC asked it for a report. In early 1965 the committee began work on a survey of "ground disposal research and development" for the AEC's Division of Reactor Development and Technology, which was responsible for dealing with commercial nuclear wastes. The chairman of the panel was John E. Galley, a petroleum geologist and consultant from Midland, Texas, who had also served on Wolman's ad hoc committee. The members of the "Galley committee" were all experienced professionals in the earth sciences.[23]

In April and May 1965, the committee made brief visits to AEC installations at Savannah River, Oak Ridge, Hanford, and the National Reactor Testing Station and to demonstration projects at two abandoned salt mines in Kansas to collect information for its report on geologic disposal. It met twice during the next few months to discuss its findings and proposed recommendations. The members were keenly aware that, by contract, the scope of their review was limited to the programs of the AEC's Division of Reactor Development and Technology. But they agreed that the "charge of the Committee" was "manifestly more narrow than its concern." Therefore, they unilaterally decided to extend their mandate by commenting on issues that arose from the AEC's treatment of wastes at its own sites, which was the responsibility of its production division. Galley explained that although he and his colleagues realized that this action placed the Division of Reactor Development and Technology "in an awkward intra-organizational position," they believed that "they should not remain silent when they are aware of routine practices that are contrary to their concepts of long-term safety in the disposal of radioactive wastes."[24]

In May 1966 the National Academy sent the final version of the Galley committee's report to Seaborg. It was a dispassionate, wide-ranging, ninety-two-page assessment of the AEC's practices and programs that was neither uniformly laudatory nor relentlessly critical. On the one hand, the committee found much to like during its investigation. It was "favorably impressed by the competence, dedication and sincerity of all the people in the AEC and its contractor companies who are responsible for the safe handling of radioactive-waste materials." It applauded the efforts to solidify high-level liquid wastes and to explore the use of salt deposits for ultimate disposal. In general, the committee hailed the development of "promising techniques" for disposal that "augur well for the handling of the larger amounts of radioactivity that are expected to be produced beyond the year 2000." It concluded that "at present . . . no serious hazards have been created by the current disposal operations" at AEC installations.[25]

On the other hand, the Galley committee expressed grave reservations about waste treatment practices at AEC sites. Like previous National Academy committees, it stressed its view that the location of the plants was not suitable for permanent disposal of high-level wastes. It discussed at length its concerns that none of them was isolated far enough from groundwater to be certain of the safety of waste handling procedures for high-level or low-level materials, particularly in light of the limited understanding of the "movement of water and contained materials in porous media." This conclusion ran directly counter to the AEC's argument that the soil beneath the Hanford and Idaho sites would absorb large amounts of liquid and solid radioactive wastes. Further, a majority of the Galley committee members recommended that the AEC abandon its research on disposal of high-level waste into bedrock at Savannah River because the prospects of a successful outcome were "poor."[26]

The committee took strong exception to the AEC's position that its methods for disposing of low-level wastes did not pose a serious threat to public health. It asserted that although placing low-level liquids and solids directly into the ground or waterways might be "momentarily safe," the practice would "lead in the long run to a serious fouling of man's environment." It suggested that in some cases the AEC demonstrated "over confidence in the capacity of the local environment to contain vast quantities of radionuclides for indefinite periods without danger to the biosphere." The committee concluded its evaluation by urging the AEC to conduct extensive research on the many outstanding questions about safe disposal of waste and to develop sites in which "fresh-water aquifers are separated from potential waste-disposal reservoirs by thousands of feet of layered strata." In this way, the fundamental goal of preventing radioactivity in waste materials from reaching the "earth's biosphere before they have decayed to innocuous levels" could be achieved.[27]

As it had done in responding to the Hess letter, Hubbert's congressional testimony, and Wolman's ad hoc committee, the AEC largely dismissed the Galley committee's major criticisms. Milton Shaw, director of the Division of Reactor Development and Technology, sent a bland and understated letter to Seitz in which he expressed the AEC's appreciation for the "valuable guidance" the committee had offered. Shaw noted that there were "certain differences of opinion" between the committee and the AEC, especially with regard to acceptable radiation exposures. He suggested that the committee sought an objective of zero releases to the environment, which conflicted with the agency's application of the permissible doses recommended by scientific organizations to its treatment of radioactive wastes. Shaw also rejected the committee's proposal that research on bedrock storage of high-level liquids at Savannah River be discontinued.[28]

For his part, Galley told J. Hoover Mackin, who had succeeded Hubbert as chairman of the National Academy's Division of Earth Sciences, that the AEC had misinterpreted the committee's position on radiation exposure. He declared that it was "simply not true" that the committee called for zero releases. "There is no statement in our report," he pointed out, "which expresses this philosophy." Galley remained deeply concerned about the long-term effects of undue reliance on using the environment as a receptacle for low-level wastes, despite the AEC's "commendable limitations" on such practices.[29]

Soon after the AEC responded to the Galley committee's report, it took action that was more revealing than the conciliatory tone of Shaw's letter. In May 1967 Shaw suggested to National Academy president Seitz that "because a major part of our ground disposal R&D program is reaching a successful conclusion," the contract for the Galley committee, which was nearing its expiration date, be terminated. "It would appear," he wrote, "that there is not sufficient justification for continuing the advisory services of the group at this time." Seitz, drawing on Galley's views, replied that he would have "substantial hesitation about terminating the committee without assurances that the gap left would be appropriately filled." In an attempt to resolve this issue, the National Academy and the AEC plunged into laborious internal deliberations and extended bilateral negotiations over the way in which the role of the Galley committee would be "appropriately filled."[30]

National Academy officials insisted that the AEC was mistaken in signaling that it no longer needed advice on waste disposal from outside authorities. Mackin, chairman of the Division of Earth Sciences, told Seitz that the agency was following a "familiar pattern" of ignoring most of the recommendations it had received from successive National Academy waste disposal committees. "The chairmen of those committees," he reported, "look back on much of their work as an exercise in frustration and futility." He argued that the AEC took too lightly "the possibility that long-lived radionuclides may, because of inadequate disposal practices, move in harmful quantities into public water supplies." The AEC, despite its displeasure with the Galley committee's report, recognized the value of expert review of waste management questions. Shaw did not oppose the formation of a new committee that would, among other things, assess "AEC waste management operational practices with respect to future or long-range health and safety implications." But other agency officials, Commissioner Ramey in particular, strongly objected to an Academy committee that would "get into specific problems in AEC plants." The AEC adopted Ramey's position. It believed that a new panel with a clearly defined mandate and different membership was more likely to enhance "AEC control" of the scope of studies conducted under National Academy auspices.[31]

In March 1968 the Academy and the AEC agreed to establish a new committee with a broader representation of disciplines than that of the Galley committee, including geophysics, environmental engineering, nuclear engineering, earth sciences, industrial hygiene, and health physics. It was called the Committee on Radioactive Waste Disposal, chaired by Clark Goodman, head of the physics department at the University of Houston. The members of the committee, who were appointed by the Academy in consultation with the AEC, were distinguished professionals. But as a group they were more inclined to be sympathetic to the AEC's perspectives than previous National Academy waste disposal panels. One prominent member, for example, was Hanford's Herbert Parker. The committee was charged with the "primary task" of advising the AEC on "long-range radioactive waste management plans and programs for an expanding nuclear energy industry." By design, its mandate did not extend to making recommendations on waste disposal practices at AEC sites. With the formation of the new committee, the National Academy achieved its basic goal of maintaining, through a contract with the AEC, an authoritative committee to examine a wide range of radioactive waste issues. At the same time, the AEC hoped that it had accomplished its objective of receiving expert guidance while avoiding the problems it had encountered with earlier committees.[32]

Despite the mutually satisfactory outcome of the negotiations between the Academy and the AEC, the concerns cited by the Galley committee continued to generate criticism of the agency's performance. In May 1968 the General Accounting Office (GAO), an arm of the legislative branch of the federal government, completed an investigation of waste disposal at AEC plants that it had undertaken at the request of the Joint Committee on Atomic Energy. It expressed considerable dissatisfaction with the AEC's management of waste materials, especially high-level liquids at Hanford, Savannah River, and the NRTS.

The GAO survey focused on the leaks from storage tanks and other problems that the AEC had not solved. It argued that this was a matter of importance and some urgency for two reasons: the uncertain condition of the tanks and the likelihood that high-level wastes would remain in storage for a long period and, therefore, "have some degree of permanency." The report recommended that the AEC "devote more vigorous management attention to advancing the technology required to permit long-term storage" and that it make organizational changes to give such issues higher priority. As always, the AEC maintained that it was making good progress in dealing with the problems that GAO described, and it contended that its waste storage and disposal practices had "received priority top management attention." But it formed a task force to review the adequacy of its waste programs, and in 1970 it created the Division of Waste and Scrap Management to coordinate waste treatment programs at both AEC and commercial sites.[33]

Some observers rebuked the AEC more harshly than GAO had done. The ever blunt King Hubbert, for example, complained bitterly about the AEC's approach to waste disposal in a commentary published in 1972. He recounted the history of the National Academy's reports on waste during the 1960s in a manner distinctly unflattering to the AEC. He was especially disturbed that the agency was still exploring bedrock as a repository for high-level liquids at Savannah River. "This entire project," he said, "has been an outstanding case history of the predominance of short-term expedience and limited responsibility over hazardous long-range consequences." He added that if the repository failed after seventy-five years or so, those who supported its construction "could not be held collectively or individually accountable because, after this period of time, they would all be safely dead."[34]

GROWING PUBLIC CONCERN ABOUT WASTE

The debates between the National Academy of Sciences and the AEC over waste disposal practices and programs were carried on behind the scenes. The Academy prepared its reports at the request and for the consideration of the AEC and never intended them to be public documents. The General Accounting Office did not release its findings in 1968 to the public because they contained secret data on plutonium production. Nevertheless, ample information about radioactive waste was publicly available, and there were strong indications of growing popular concern about its hazards during the 1960s. Public misgivings were fueled by several developments. One was increasing awareness of and worry about the potential dangers of low-level radiation. The fallout debate of the late 1950s received new impetus between 1961 and 1963 when, after a moratorium of about three years, the Soviet Union and the United States resumed atmospheric testing of nuclear weapons. This revived the animated controversy over the long-term effects of exposure to radioactive fallout. Although the Limited Test Ban Treaty of 1963 took the edge off the fallout issue by ending atmospheric testing by its signatories, the debate left in its wake latent fears about the public health effects of low-level radiation.[35]

Another major development was the unexpectedly rapid expansion of commercial nuclear power. Beginning in the middle years of the decade, the nuclear industry experienced a sudden surge in reactor orders, described by one utility executive as the "great bandwagon market." Between 1966 and 1968 utilities committed to purchasing sixty-eight nuclear units, compared to the twenty-two they had ordered between 1955 and 1965. In addition to the larger number of plants that power companies planned to build, the size of individual units increased dramatically. The boom in nuclear generating capacity meant that the volume of radioactive waste to be managed would accelerate by corresponding proportions.[36]

The expansion of the nuclear power industry occurred simultaneously, if coincidentally, with the rise of the environmental movement in the United States. The emergence of environmental protection as a visible and urgent public policy issue played a substantial role in spurring public concern about radioactive waste. When the number and size of reactors grew, so too did challenges to the burgeoning nuclear industry. Environmentalists recognized the advantages of nuclear power in reducing air pollution, but they became increasingly critical of it on other grounds. Well-publicized controversies over "thermal pollution" of inland waterways, the effects of routine emissions of small amounts of low-level radiation, and the risks of an accident that could cause heavy loss of life and environmental contamination underscored uncertainties about the use of nuclear technology. As the nuclear power debate became more contentious, radioactive waste disposal became another major source of dispute.[37]

The outcry over ocean dumping during the late 1950s had clearly demonstrated the public's sensitivity to radioactive waste issues. The AEC had acted promptly to mollify critics of ocean disposal, but it realized that it still had to address other public fears about waste. A staff paper commented in 1960 that "serious public relations implications of radioactive waste management will continue to prevail." As the decade wore on, the long-term treatment of radioactive waste from AEC plants and commercial reactors triggered increasing, though sporadic, public expressions of concern. *Consumer Reports* ran a story in February 1960, for example, on the "huge and ever-increasing problem of radioactive wastes." The magazine, which had published a series of articles about the hazards of radioactive fallout and suggested that the "only *really* safe dose of radiation is none," focused on tank storage and ground disposal of waste at Hanford. But it also called attention to the likelihood that nuclear power would produce "large quantities of radioactive wastes" that were "high in radioactive content [and] harmful to man and the world he lives in."[38]

Public comments on radioactive waste appeared much less frequently after the test ban treaty largely removed the fallout debate from the headlines. The expansion of nuclear power after the mid-1960s, however, brought about renewed public scrutiny. In 1966 the Subcommittee on Science, Research and Development of the U.S. House of Representatives Committee on Science and Astronautics issued a report that questioned the future of nuclear power if "a way to rid ourselves of the toxic by-products" were not found. The subcommittee hoped "to draw interest to the subject of nuclear waste disposal and to spur people into discussing the problem." It "raised a few nuclear eyebrows in Washington," according to the trade journal *Nucleonics Week,* by challenging the jurisdiction of the Joint Committee on Atomic Energy, which always jealously guarded its control of atomic energy issues. Seaborg assured the subcommittee chairman, Emilio Q. Daddario, that waste problems were effectively managed and that the AEC and the nuclear industry had "established what we believe to be an exemplary record of environmental control of . . . potential contaminants."[39]

Daddario did not aggressively pursue the questions his subcommittee raised on radioactive waste management, but other observers expressed doubts that the AEC's record on the issue was "exemplary." An article in the environmental monthly *Scientist and Citizen* in May 1967 elaborated on the subcommittee's report by describing the "problem that won't go away" for the "mushrooming reactor industry." The author, the physicist Joel A. Snow, faulted the AEC for failing to provide "clearcut and uniform safety guidelines" on waste and argued that the "complete development" of adequate means of disposal was necessary "*before* the public can be assured that the benefits of nuclear energy may not generate unacceptable risks." The more strident views of another environmental advocate, Malcolm Kildale, were touted by the syndicated columnist Ralph de Toledano. He asserted that Kildale's "findings indicate that Americans are being led down the garden path to national radioactive poisoning" by wastes with a "deadly life-span running into the hundreds of years."[40]

The problem of radioactive waste reached new heights of public visibility in June 1968 when the supermarket tabloid *National Enquirer* published a feature story. It led with the news that "eighty million gallons of highly radioactive waste" were stored in tanks around the country and some were "leaking their poison." It quoted Snow as saying that "a single gallon of waste would be sufficient to threaten the health of several million people." The *Enquirer* cited the opinion of another expert, George G. Berg, a professor of radiation biology at the University of Rochester, that existing methods of waste treatment were "criminally shortsighted." The article warned that the rapid growth of the nuclear industry not only aggravated the "accumulation of radioactive waste" but also amplified the chances of a Hiroshima-type nuclear explosion. In that way, it advanced the widespread popular misconception that a nuclear power plant could blow up like an atomic bomb.[41]

CONTROVERSY OVER IDAHO WASTES

Although the *National Enquirer* story was exaggerated and in some respects baseless, it contributed to what AEC staff members recognized as "increasing public interest and concern" about the hazards of radioactive wastes. The issue received even more attention after controversy erupted in Idaho over the AEC's handling of waste, especially when, to the agency's discomfort, government officials and local reporters learned of the National Academy of Sciences' Galley committee report of 1966. Waste disposal became big news in Idaho after contaminated materials from a fire at an AEC plutonium-handling plant in Colorado were sent to the National Reactor Testing Station. The Rocky Flats facility, located about fifteen miles from Denver, produced plutonium cores, or "pits," used to detonate nuclear weapons. On May 11, 1969, it suffered a serious fire that caused heavy damage to processing equipment and structures. As the cleanup of the plant proceeded, the AEC made plans to bury some 300,000 cubic feet of contaminated solids in steel drums at the Idaho site, which had accepted wastes from Rocky Flats for years. In 1968, for example, it shipped about 350,000 cubic feet of waste there from Colorado.[42]

At first, the arrival of radioactive debris from the Rocky Flats fire did not generate much interest in Idaho. But the situation changed after Robert A. Erkins, owner of the Snake River Trout Company, the world's largest producer of trout, sounded an alarm. Erkins learned about the burial of waste from Rocky Flats from a customer who had read about it in the *New York Times*. He promptly sent a letter to Idaho governor Don W. Samuelson voicing his concern that radioactivity from the waste would reach the Snake River Plain Aquifer and seriously contaminate the state's water supplies. "I fail to see why Idaho should become a dumping ground for any atomic waste," he wrote. Erkins's fears made headlines in Idaho newspapers and stirred questions not only about the material from Rocky Flats but also about the disposal of all the radioactive waste stored at NRTS. William L. Ginkel, manager of the AEC's Idaho Operations Office, responded by offering blanket assurances. "There's no real

Figure 2. Interim storage of plutonium and other radioactive wastes at the National Reactor Testing Station in Idaho. As sections containing the fifty-gallon drums and fiberglass-covered boxes were filled, they were "mounded over with earth." (National Archives 434-SF-18-39)

or potential basis for alarm—ever," he announced. "Our operation is conducted on a totally sound basis." Ginkel explained that solid wastes were buried six hundred feet above the aquifer and that, over a period of fifteen years, samples of the water from the aquifer had "never found evidence of contamination." He further suggested that waste-handling procedures at the site had won the approval of the National Academy of Sciences.[43]

Ginkel's efforts to defuse the issue failed. The *South Idaho Press* commented, "We cannot afford to rely on glib, off-the-cuff explanations by the AEC." As stories about waste disposal at NRTS multiplied, Samuelson and other Idaho officials sought additional information from the AEC. Senator Frank Church, who had recently learned about the Galley committee report, demanded to know why it had not been made public. At about the same time a reporter for an Idaho newspaper requested a copy of it. The inquiries about the Galley committee's findings placed the AEC in a decidedly awkward position, not only because of the study's criticism of existing disposal practices, but also because of Ginkel's intimation that the National Academy endorsed those practices.[44]

The AEC, the National Academy, and the Galley committee itself had not viewed the report as a public document. Seaborg noted in his diary that he and his colleagues did not want to provide it to the press because it was "unfavorable in an uninformed way concerning AEC waste disposal policies." Realizing that they could not withhold the report indefinitely without being accused of suppressing it, the commissioners agreed to delay its release until the staff prepared a rebuttal. They also urged that completion of the study by the committee on waste that the National Academy had established in 1968 be expedited. Seaborg anticipated that it would present a "more balanced" assessment. Meanwhile, he told Church that the AEC staff had "many criticisms" of the Galley report and that he expected the work of the new committee, "with a broader spectrum of scientific disciplines," to be of greater value.[45]

Church was not placated. The NRTS provided important economic benefits to Idaho, and he made clear that he valued the "tremendous potential that nuclear power presents for the improvement of our environment." But he also worried that nuclear wastes could "do that same environment serious harm." Therefore, on September 12, 1969, Church requested that four federal agencies—the Public Health Service, the Water Pollution Control Administration, the Bureau of Sport Fisheries and Wildlife, and the U.S. Geological Survey—evaluate the "long range implications . . . of continued storage of radioactive wastes" above the Snake River Plain Aquifer. He specified that they should proceed without the participation of the AEC. In addition, Church urged the AEC to terminate the storage of liquid wastes at the Idaho site and to remove any that were "located over the Aquifer." His actions reflected his genuine concern about conditions at NRTS and his growing personal commitment to environmental causes.[46]

Church's efforts to gain more information about the status of waste disposal at AEC sites won important support when Senator Edmund S. Muskie, perhaps the leading environmental advocate in Congress, requested a copy of the Galley committee report from the AEC. On March 6, 1970, the commissioners agreed, after what Seaborg called "some spirited discussion," to release it. At the same time, the AEC published staff comments on the Galley committee's findings and an "interim report" of the new National Academy of Sciences Committee on Radioactive Waste Management, chaired by Goodman. The AEC staff faulted the Galley committee for exceeding its mandate by criticizing waste treatment practices at AEC sites and, as earlier, for suggesting a safety standard of zero releases to the environment. The staff also argued that, contrary to the committee's presentation, wastes were stored only temporarily at AEC installations "pending development of satisfactory disposal methods." The Goodman committee's review consisted almost entirely of descriptions of the activities it had undertaken to that time. Its only conclusion was hardly momentous; it "noted the extensiveness and care in waste management at each site visited" and praised the "quality and scope of the R&D program sponsored by the AEC."[47]

As the AEC had feared, the release of the Galley committee report commanded attention in Idaho and beyond. The *Idaho Falls Post-Register* headlined its account, "Science Academy Doubts Safety of Waste Disposal at NRTS." The *New York Times* printed the entire Galley report and ran a story under the banner, "A.E.C. Scored on Storing Waste." It cited Church's allegation that the agency had "suppressed" the study. *Science News* advised readers that the National Academy had found that the AEC was "plodding along with its old waste-disposal methods" for "lethal nuclear garbage."[48]

The impact of the release of the Galley committee report was soon compounded by the publication of a critical assessment by the Federal Water Quality Administration, which was within the Department of the Interior and had formerly been called the Federal Water Pollution Control Administration. It was one of the agencies from which Church had requested an evaluation of waste management at NRTS in September 1969. Its study echoed the reservations of the Galley committee about the uncertainties of geologic conditions at the Idaho site and the possibilities that radioactive waste materials could eventually reach the Snake River Plain Aquifer. The water quality agency concluded that "present disposal practices are a potential threat to the water resources of the State of Idaho." It recommended "abandonment of the practice of burial of radioactively contaminated solid wastes" and the "removal of the existing buried wastes." After receiving the report, Church called on the AEC "to immediately embark upon a program to remove this potential threat to the safety of my State."[49]

The Water Quality Administration's report incensed AEC officials. "It might be a time for the AEC to raise a little hell with those people," John A. Harris, director of the public information division, remarked, "for doing this sort of report without giving us an opportunity to comment." The AEC's Idaho Operations Office issued a press release that insisted that the burial of solid wastes at NRTS did "not pose a hazard to the Snake River aquifer or to the public." Staff comments on the Water Quality Administration's findings backed that claim by pointing out that measurements over a period of seventeen years showed that radioactivity from burial pits had "migrated less than a foot." Nevertheless, the AEC acted promptly to alleviate the concerns of Church and the citizens of Idaho. Commissioner Theos J. Thompson and members of the AEC staff met with Church and told him that the agency would seek congressional authorization to establish a repository, probably located in the Midwest, for permanent disposal of high-level and long-lived radioactive wastes. Once the facility was operating, wastes from Idaho, including those imported from Rocky Flats, would be shipped there. Seaborg informed Church that the AEC had concluded that an abandoned salt mine "would provide effective long-term isolation" of radioactive wastes. He expressed hope that the AEC could begin to move materials from NRTS to the permanent disposal site within a decade. This plan satisfied Church and ended the well-publicized controversy over the waste issue in Idaho. The promises the AEC made depended on the availability of an unproven site, however, and heightened the pressure to deliver on its obligations in a timely manner.[50]

The AEC was keenly aware of the importance of better management of wastes at its own sites. "There is a very real need," staff director Robert E. Hollingsworth commented in January 1970, "to improve our posture on handling radioactively contaminated trash."[51] The AEC took the matter of waste treatment seriously during the 1960s and made significant progress on a number of fronts. It reduced the volume of wastes by substantial proportions and sponsored research that yielded promising results in the search for a permanent repository. It also carefully monitored levels of radioactivity from waste storage to make certain that they stayed within existing permissible limits for occupational and public exposure. Although the AEC did not claim that it had arrived at definitive solutions to the problems of radioactive waste disposal, it was convinced that it was headed in the right direction. Seaborg's pledge to Church, though short of a firm guarantee, was a strong indication of the agency's confidence in its ability to settle on a suitable site within a reasonably short time.

Most of the controversy over radioactive waste disposal in the 1960s centered on practices at AEC installations. The agency was subjected to increasing criticism by scientists who agreed that existing conditions were acceptable but worried about the long-term consequences of AEC assumptions and procedures. The AEC distorted or dismissed many of the complaints it received from the National Academy of Sciences committees on waste, in part because it found them unduly unfavorable and in part because it had no satisfactory response to offer. In this regard, it demonstrated complacency to the point of smugness. The National Academy panels were made up of distinguished professionals who pointed out the geologic uncertainties of AEC sites and the potential pitfalls of waste management practices. The failures in high-level liquid storage tanks at Hanford and Savannah River should have encouraged greater humility on the part of the AEC, especially in light of the assurances it provided that no leaks had been detected. Instead, agency officials largely disregarded the arguments of their critics, especially regarding the potential hazards of disposing of large quantities of unpackaged low-level waste. They relied on their own judgment about existing methods of handling wastes and the likelihood that means for permanent disposal would soon be developed. In his memoirs, published posthumously in 2001, Seaborg, who served as chairman of the AEC from 1961 to 1971, acknowledged that the agency "erred in dealing with nuclear waste [by leaving] behind a terrible legacy—the massive residue of contaminated wastes at Hanford and other nuclear materials production sites."[52]

The AEC's approach to its own wastes also applied in important ways to commercial wastes. It recognized that sound treatment of radioactive waste was essential for the future of nuclear power and believed that it was nearing a solution to the problem. The excessive optimism, unexamined assumptions, and underestimated uncertainties that were prominent in its own waste programs soon proved major obstacles in its quest for a permanent repository for high-level commercial wastes.

CHAPTER 3

An "Atomic Garbage Dump" for Kansas

As a result of the clamor over waste management in Idaho, the AEC made a tentative commitment to open a repository for high-level and transuranic materials by the end of the 1970s. When AEC chairman Seaborg told Senator Church that Idaho wastes would be transferred to a permanent site, he and his colleagues were counting heavily on the availability of an abandoned salt mine in Lyons, Kansas, for burial of high-level wastes from commercial nuclear plants, as well as materials from the National Reactor Testing Station. The AEC moved rapidly to carry out its pledge by investigating the suitability of the Lyons site and making preparations to develop it as the first high-level waste repository. In the process, it provoked growing opposition from scientists and politicians in Kansas, who complained that the agency failed to treat their concerns seriously and refused to fully explore vital technical issues. The AEC's efforts eventually collapsed on both political and technical grounds; it not only took actions that antagonized key leaders in Kansas but also found that the Lyons site was inappropriate for burying radioactive wastes. The outcome of the Lyons controversy was an enormous embarrassment for the AEC and a severe setback in the search for a high-level waste repository.

PROJECT SALT VAULT

In 1957 the National Academy of Sciences Committee on Waste Disposal had published a report in which it concluded that salt formations offered the most promising geologic setting for high-level liquid radioactive wastes. It based its view on the dry, impermeable, and "self-sealing" properties of salt deposits. The plasticity of salt made it likely to seal fractures that might occur and to block the penetration of liquids. The Committee on Waste Disposal also pointed out that salt formations were abundant, generally located in areas of low seismic activity, and inexpensive to mine. Its chief concern was the structural weakness of salt deposits, and it called for research that addressed this question and other technical uncertainties. Accordingly, the AEC made arrangements to conduct preliminary investigations in an unused section of a salt mine owned by the Carey Salt Company in Hutchinson, Kansas. Scientists from Oak Ridge National Laboratory, which was operated under an AEC contract by the Union Carbide Corporation, carried out the tests. The objective was to collect information on, among other things, chemical reactions that might occur and the effects of heat on salt formations.[1]

Between 1959 and 1961 researchers ran a series of experiments by injecting simulated, nonradioactive liquid wastes into cavities drilled in the floor of the mine. At that time, the direct insertion of high-level liquids into salt deposits was still under consideration as a means of permanent disposal. The results of the work in the Hutchinson mine were encouraging but not conclusive. In May 1960 Oak Ridge project director E.G. Struxness reported to the Committee on Waste Disposal that the test on heat transfer had been "outstandingly successful"; temperatures had "not risen as much as had been predicted from theoretical considerations." Other important issues, however, required further investigation. In July 1963 the AEC announced that Oak Ridge would conduct a new battery of experiments in an abandoned salt mine in Lyons that was also owned by the Carey Salt Company. Unlike the Hutchinson tests, the Lyons study, named Project Salt Vault, would use solid radioactive wastes in the form of fuel elements from the NRTS.[2]

The Salt Vault tests were performed between November 1965 and January 1968. Their purpose was to provide information on several crucial issues, including the design of equipment and methods to move nuclear waste from a nuclear plant to a permanent repository, the effects of radiation on salt, and the extent to which elevated temperatures could cause "creep and plastic flow" in salt formations. The concern was that thermal stress could increase the flow of salt in a way that could weaken a mine's structural stability. The intensely radioactive fuel assemblies that were used for the Lyons experiments were packed in canisters at

Figure 3. Project Salt Vault researchers conduct tests on fuel assemblies buried in a salt mine in Lyons. (National Archives 434-SF-21–20)

the NRTS. The canisters were loaded into thirty-ton casks cooled by forced circulation of water and then shipped by truck on a specially designed trailer. Upon arrival at the Lyons site, the canisters were lowered into steel-lined shafts that extended about twelve feet below the floor of the mine, which was about one thousand feet underground. After six months, the canisters were replaced by different ones containing fresher fuel. Over a period of nineteen months, the salt closest to the shafts received a massive (by human health standards) average radiation dose of approximately 800 million rads.[3] The rad was a unit that replaced the roentgen to indicate the amount of energy absorbed in material exposed to radiation.

The researchers who carried out Project Salt Vault found the results "most encouraging." They believed that the tests went a long way toward confirming the feasibility of placing radioactive wastes in salt formations. In early 1970 they reported that "most of the major technical problems pertinent to the disposal of highly radioactive waste in salt have been resolved." The Oak Ridge experts concluded that "the stability of salt under the effects of heat and radiation has been shown," that the problem of salt creep could be managed by a "suitable design" for the repository, and that high-level wastes could be safely handled in an “underground environment.”[4]

The Salt Vault findings came at an opportune time for the AEC, which was then under fire from Senator Church over waste at the NRTS. On March 6, 1970, the day the commissioners agreed to release the Galley committee’s 1966 report, Seaborg noted in his diary, after receiving a briefing from Oak Ridge officials, that the results of the Lyons tests were “very encouraging.” This assessment enabled the AEC to offer assurances to Church that it would transfer the Idaho wastes to a permanent repository that it hoped to open within a decade. Meanwhile, the AEC staff began working on a plan for acquiring land and constructing a salt mine facility in central Kansas for high-level and transuranic wastes. Although it described the prospective installation as a “demonstration project,” it predicted that “the facility would ultimately be designated as the initial Federal radioactive waste repository.” The probable site was the Carey mine in Lyons, both because it had “extensive existing workings” from Project Salt Vault and because it would allow the “earliest possible start” for permanent disposal. The staff had held discussions with “principal officials” in Kansas that seemed to “indicate support for locating the proposed waste facility in the Kansas salt beds.”[5]

AMBIVALENCE IN KANSAS

Despite the AEC staff’s optimistic appraisal of local opinion, the investigations of salt mines for radioactive waste disposal elicited mixed reactions in Kansas. Some Kansans had expressed concern as soon as Oak Ridge began its first field tests in Hutchinson. On June 11, 1959, U.S. Senator Andrew F. Schoeppel joined a floor debate on ocean dumping of radioactive materials by telling colleagues of an equally “alarming situation” in Kansas. He would watch the conduct of the experiments “with great interest,” he said, because he worried that they could produce “disastrous results.” Schoeppel was under the erroneous impression that the Hutchinson tests involved pouring high-level liquid radioactive wastes directly into salt mines, and he warned his constituents that they could not be “absolutely certain” about the safety of such procedures. In November 1963 an editorial in the daily newspaper of Great Bend, a town near Lyons, presented similar misgivings. It commented that announcements about Project Salt Vault “caused murmurs of discontent” because “nobody is too wild about having atomic energy bubbling under his back yard.”[6]

Other Kansans, by contrast, strongly supported the AEC's projects. In 1962 Frank C. Foley, director of the Kansas Geological Survey, told Struxness that there was "great interest" among state officials in the potential advantages of a waste disposal facility in Kansas. Foley cautioned, however, that the "psychology of informing the public" was "of great significance." He suggested that the term "atomic waste disposal" was "not good psychology" and argued that it should be replaced by "atomic by-products storage." The AEC did not take up Foley's suggestion on the alleged benefits of obscuring the purpose of its plans for a waste repository.[7]

The citizens of Lyons offered a warm reception to Project Salt Vault and, from all indications, generally favored the construction of a permanent repository if the site turned out to be suitable. In early 1970, as rumors circulated that the AEC would settle on Lyons for its demonstration project, an informal poll indicated that most residents approved development of the installation or "were little concerned one way or the other." John Sayler, editor of the *Lyons Daily News,* believed that his neighbors were "overwhelmingly for it." Lyons was a town of about 4,500 people, located in central Kansas about sixty-five miles northwest of Wichita. One reporter described it as a "placid, pleasant town . . . with tree-lined, cobblestone streets in a region where trees are not generally plentiful." Another observer called it a place "where the air is clear as Steuben glass and the water tastes like water." Lyons was primarily an agricultural community, but a large mine operated by the American Salt Corporation was also an important source of employment. The smaller Carey Salt Company mine, the site of Project Salt Vault, ran directly under the town. It had opened in 1891 and closed in 1948. The people of Lyons had been much impressed with the scientists who had run the Salt Vault tests; one citizen commented that they had proven to be "good guys." He joined a majority of his neighbors in hoping that the waste repository would provide new jobs and income for their community.[8]

The prevailing attitude in Kansas as the AEC took preliminary action on the construction of a waste repository in spring 1970 was ambivalence. The *Topeka State Journal* captured this mood by citing, on the one hand, the economic benefits of the "somewhat debatable honor of becoming an atomic garbage dump," and, on the other, the need to resolve outstanding safety issues. It affirmed that "Kansas wants to consider this with more than the proverbial grain of salt." The fate of the project depended heavily on the position of Governor Robert B. Docking, and like many of the citizens of his state, he was undecided about how the possible economic advantages should be weighed against the potential safety risks. Docking had spent most of his professional career in business, including tenure as a bank vice president in Lawrence and a bank president in Arkansas City, Kansas. After serving as a city commissioner and mayor of Arkansas City, he had been elected governor in 1966 and had won reelection two years later. He was a Democrat in a heavily Republican state, and his success depended largely on his commitment to low taxes and other traditionally Republican doctrines. Docking announced that he would seek a third term in May 1970. Because placing a radioactive waste repository in Kansas was a potentially sensitive political issue, on both technical and political grounds, he adopted a cautious wait-and-see posture on the benefits and risks of developing a disposal site.[9]

For technical advice on the still-pending Lyons proposal, Docking looked to William W. Hambleton, the state geologist and director of the Kansas Geological Survey. Hambleton held a Ph.D. in geology from the University of Kansas and had worked for the Chevron Oil Company and the U.S. Bureau of Mines before returning to Lawrence as a professor of geology. He served as associate director of the Kansas Geological Survey from 1962 to 1970 and became its director just as the Lyons issue was gaining prominence. Hambleton knew Docking on a first-name basis from their civic activities in Lawrence and regarded him as an exceptionally thoughtful and gracious individual. The AEC had discussed its preliminary plans for Lyons with Docking in March 1970, and both he and Hambleton approached the proposal with open minds while they sought more information.[10]

On April 17, 1970, Hambleton outlined for Docking the political and technical issues that, in his judgment, required careful consideration. He pointed out that "radioactive waste disposal by anyone, anywhere is today a very sensitive public, political, and environmental issue." He suspected that the AEC would press for "relatively rapid development of this facility" and prepare a "soft-sell public relations program." Hambleton suggested that such a "soft-sell" was "no longer possible because of the number of people who no longer find appeal in making Kansas a radioactive waste disposal center." He focused on the technical questions that had not been adequately addressed. Although the AEC had "done very definitive work on the properties of salt under a wide range of pressure and temperature conditions," it had not provided the "very detailed information" that was needed to build a waste repository at a specific location. For example, more data were essential on variations in salt thickness and physical properties and on "collapse structures" in the area where the wastes would be buried. This kind of information could be obtained only by a "very careful drilling program" at the site.[11]

THE AEC'S SITE SELECTION ANNOUNCEMENT

As Kansas officials considered a series of questions surrounding the proposed waste facility, the AEC moved ahead with its plans. One step it took was to request that the National Academy of Sciences Committee on Radioactive Waste Management appoint a special panel to review the "concept of long-term storage of solid radioactive wastes in salt mines." This committee, called the Panel on Disposal in Salt Mines, included Hambleton among its seven members. At its first meeting in Oak Ridge in May 1970, it heard from John A. Erlewine, coordinator and point of contact for the AEC's waste disposal programs. Erlewine had received a law degree from Columbia University and joined the AEC as a staff attorney in 1952. He had risen quickly through the ranks of the AEC and had held the post of assistant general manager for operations since 1964. In that position, he supervised the programs of nine AEC field offices and four headquarters units, including the recently established Division of Waste and Scrap Management. Within the agency, he was highly regarded as an able administrator and an effective spokesman for its policies. Erlewine told the members of the Panel on Disposal in Salt Mines that the "Commission believes that sufficient R&D has been performed and that it is now appropriate to construct a repository as soon as possible." He revealed that the AEC would soon ask for congressional funding and that it hoped "to receive approval" from the salt panel promptly.[12]

Although the AEC had not yet designated a site for its demonstration project, the Lyons mine was the focus of attention at the conference of the Panel on Disposal in Salt Mines. Hambleton made clear that he believed more information was required before a commitment was made. After the meeting, he and his staff at the Kansas Geological Survey prepared a detailed discussion of matters that in their minds needed further research. Asserting that existing studies had provided an "oversimplified view of the geology" of the Lyons region, they expressed concern about the "inadequacy of base-line data on water quality and quantity," the presence of oil and gas drill holes in the area, the prospect of "sagging and fracturing" if salt thickness was not uniform, and the possibility of structural weaknesses in geologic formations. Hambleton thought that the investigation of those questions would produce useful data within about six months. After he shared his reservations with his colleagues on the Panel on Disposal in Salt Mines, they agreed to meet in Lawrence on June 16–17, 1970, to review outstanding technical issues.[13]

While Hambleton was expressing his misgivings, the AEC pushed ahead. On June 12, 1970, the staff recommended to the commissioners that the agency designate Lyons as the site of the demonstration project and take action to acquire the property. Although it recognized that additional geologic and hydrologic studies could "seriously challenge the suitability" of the location, it believed that, based on the findings of Project Salt Vault, the Lyons mine would prove to be "well suited for construction of a long-term facility" for disposal of high-level and transuranic wastes. The staff was "reasonably confident" that the project would be favorably received in Kansas. The commissioners approved the staff's proposal on June 15. Two days later, Erlewine announced the "tentative" plan for the Lyons repository at a press conference in Topeka, Kansas. He estimated that the cost of the work at the site would be $25 million and would employ about two hundred people, mostly from the Lyons vicinity. He reported that new studies would be conducted to confirm the acceptability of the site and added, "It will be go or no-go in the next six months."[14]

A staff member of the AEC's Division of Public Information who traveled to Topeka reported that Erlewine had clearly conveyed the conditional nature of the AEC's decision. He also suggested that the agency had done a "good job of handling notifications to state and local officials." But the AEC, in fact, had offended Kansas officials who were deliberating the same day in Lawrence over the use of the Lyons site. The meeting included members of the Panel on Disposal in Salt Mines and representatives of Oak Ridge National Laboratory, the AEC, the Kansas Geological Survey, and the Kansas Department of Health. For two days, they had engaged in detailed technical discussions of the issues that troubled the Kansas experts. But without waiting for a report from the Lawrence conference, Erlewine disclosed the tentative selection of Lyons to the press in Topeka. The announcement came as an unpleasant surprise and embarrassment to Hambleton and his colleagues, who saw it as an indication that the AEC was not taking their views seriously. The AEC committed a grievous and avoidable blunder. At least some staff members—a few had been present—were certainly aware of the meeting. The AEC apparently experienced a breakdown in internal communications, perhaps because it arranged the press briefing with ill-considered haste. It also appeared to suffer from acute tone-deafness about the potential impact of its announcement. Erlewine's careful efforts to describe the decision on Lyons as tentative were not enough to ease the disenchantment and growing distrust felt by Kansas officials, whose support for the project was vital.[15]

CONGRESSMAN SKUBITZ AND THE AEC

Although the AEC seemed oblivious to the resentment that Erlewine's announcement had generated, it was keenly aware that an outspoken member of the Kansas congressional delegation, Joe Skubitz, had serious doubts about the Lyons proposal. Skubitz's district did not include Lyons; he represented the southeastern section of Kansas, some two hundred miles away. Nevertheless, he followed the developments surrounding the Lyons project with close and increasingly critical vigilance. Skubitz, whose parents had emigrated to Kansas from Slovenia, was a native of the area that he served in Congress. His father worked as a coal miner and later ran a small grocery store; his mother became fluent in several languages and often served as a translator in local court cases involving immigrants. They had little formal schooling, and they impressed the importance of education on their son. After graduating from high school, Skubitz worked as a teacher and later as a principal and at the same time earned bachelor's and master's degrees from the local teachers' college, Pittsburg State. In 1939 he moved to Washington as an aide to Kansas senator Clyde M. Reed. While working for Congress, Skubitz went to law school and received his degree from George Washington University. He later served as an administrative assistant for Senator Andrew Schoeppel.

In 1962, after Schoeppel's death, Skubitz won a seat in Congress as a Republican. He was initially reluctant to run, he once recalled, because he worried that he would be the target of ethnic slurs. Skubitz was a gregarious, down-to-earth, and hardworking politician. Like many Republicans, he was deeply suspicious of government bureaucracy and wary of federal incursions into areas traditionally reserved for the states. He held strong and sometimes uncompromising views on political issues; at one time he and a Pittsburg newspaper publisher stopping speaking to one another for several months because of conflicting political positions. Skubitz was forthright and occasionally impolitic in expressing his opinions. As the debate over the Lyons waste repository became increasingly bitter, he publicly denounced one prominent supporter of the project as

Figure 4. Congressman Joe Skubitz, shown here with President Gerald R. Ford. (Joe Skubitz Papers, Pittsburg State University)

a "stooge of the AEC." He had first become interested in the AEC's plans for Lyons because of his experience with the issue on Schoeppel's staff. Skubitz, like Schoeppel, had gained the false impression that the AEC had intended to conduct experiments in Hutchinson a decade earlier by pouring high-level liquid radioactive wastes directly into a salt mine.[16]

Skubitz's flawed memory of the Hutchinson tests made him skeptical of the AEC's plans for the Lyons repository from the outset. In a phone call on April 23, 1970, he raised a series of questions with Erlewine and received assurances that Project Salt Vault had shown that radioactive wastes in Kansas salt deposits "would be in as safe a geologic formation as can be found in the United States." In subsequent correspondence, Skubitz asked Erlewine about the size of the proposed repository, the amount of waste that would be stored, how it would be cooled, and why Kansas was under consideration rather than other states that had large salt deposits. Erlewine replied promptly and conscientiously, but he did not ease Skubitz's growing reservations. On June 18, the day after Erlewine's press conference in Topeka, Skubitz sent a letter to Docking in which he disclosed his "grave doubts about the safety of this project in view of the many differing facts and conflicting opinions." "We are being asked to assume unknown risks to make Kansas a nuclear dumping ground for all the rest of the nation," he argued. Skubitz elaborated on his concerns in a twelve-page, single-spaced letter to AEC chairman Seaborg. Citing the geologic uncertainties that Hambleton had voiced, he asked that the AEC "make known to all Kansas citizens the exact nature of the risks and dangers" of the Lyons project. He complained that although Kansas was "expected to assume the risks of storage of nuclear waste material," it had not received the "benefits provided by a nuclear power plant" that could attract industry and deliver a "real economic boost to the entire state."[17]

A PUBLIC MEETING IN LYONS

Skubitz, like Hambleton, raised questions about the safety of the Lyons site but did not categorically reject it. The Kansas chapter of the Sierra Club, the prominent national environmental organization, took a more dogmatic stance. Ronald H. Baxter, a former aide to Docking and chairman of the chapter's executive council, revealed the day after Erlewine's June 17 press conference that his group opposed the project. "We intend to see that Kansas is not used for such a dump," he declared, "and intend to be successful in halting such action." In light of the reactions to Erlewine's announcement, the AEC decided to address the doubts that had been aired and to explain its position in a public appearance in Lyons.[18]

The meeting, held on July 29, 1970, was attended by more than one hundred fifty local citizens. It also attracted about thirty media representatives, who were mostly but not exclusively from Kansas newspapers and radio and television stations. The session was moderated

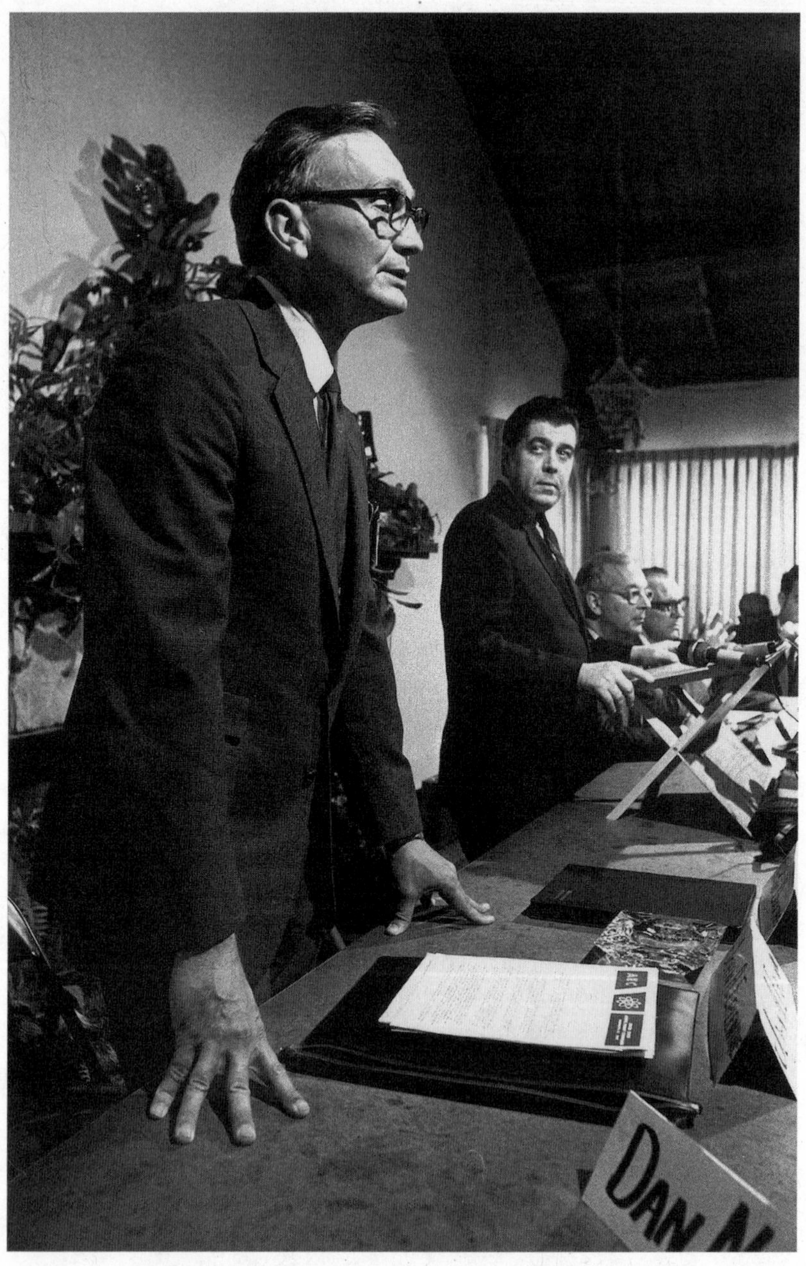

Figure 5. The AEC's John Erlewine (left) addresses a meeting in Lyons as Governor Robert B. Docking looks on, July 29, 1970. *(Topeka Capital-Journal)*

Figure 6. William W. Hambleton (left), director of the Kansas Geological Survey, talks with Howard J. Carey Jr. (center), president of the Carey Salt Co., and Dale E. Saffels, chairman of the Kansas Advisory Council on Ecology, at meeting in Lyons. *(Topeka Capital-Journal)*

by Governor Docking, who outlined his cautious approach in his first public statement on the Lyons proposal. While he hoped that the project would provide "economic gains" to the local area and the state, he emphasized, "We do not want new industry in Kansas at the expense of our citizens' health and welfare." Therefore, Docking withheld support for the Lyons repository until he received the results of the scientific investigations that were underway.

Erlewine told the audience that the AEC had the same objectives as the governor. "We sincerely believe this is a good project," he said, "but we, too, want to see the studies completed." He estimated that if the assessments were favorable, the site could open for low-level wastes in 1974 and for high-level wastes the following year. When Erlewine entertained questions from the audience, Baxter suggested that the AEC was trying to "quickly develop" the Lyons project because of its "poor prior track record" in dealing with wastes at Hanford and the National Reactor Testing Station. The Lyons meeting was informative and, inevitably, inconclusive. It made abundantly clear that the future of the Lyons proposal depended heavily on scientific evaluations of safety issues.[19]

SCIENTIFIC ASSESSMENTS OF THE LYONS PROPOSAL

The first of the studies on the Lyons site to be completed was prepared by the National Academy of Sciences Committee on Radioactive Waste Management. It drew on the findings of the Panel on Disposal in Salt Mines and submitted its report to the AEC in November 1970. The committee concluded that the "use of bedded salt for the disposal of radioactive wastes is satisfactory" and that "the site near Lyons, Kansas[,] . . . is satisfactory, subject to the development of certain additional confirmatory data and evaluation." Thus it offered a favorable but conditional endorsement of the Lyons project, and it recommended research on many of the issues that troubled the Kansas Geological Survey. Nevertheless, the AEC, while acknowledging the need to resolve outstanding issues, emphasized the support the document offered for the Lyons repository.[20]

Kansas Geological Survey scientists were less pleased with the Committee on Radioactive Waste Management's report. Hambleton thought that the committee's chair, John C. Frye of the Illinois State Geological Survey, had watered down the conclusions of the Panel on Disposal in Salt Mines. By fall 1970 Kansas geologists, in collaboration with the U.S. Army Corps of Engineers, had drilled two deep holes and about forty shallow holes in the Lyons area, and Hambleton prepared a preliminary report of their findings. The fieldwork and discussions with Oak Ridge experts alleviated some of his concerns but heightened others. One issue, which Hambleton described "as crucial to the safety of the repository site," was heat transfer from radioactive waste to salt. He regarded the heat flow equations that the AEC and Oak Ridge used as oversimplified and was dismayed that they "exhibited remarkably little interest in the heat flow problem." He feared that excessive heat could fracture rocks that sealed the salt formations and open them to the entry of water.

Hambleton expressed similar objections to the failure of Oak Ridge and the AEC to sufficiently consider radiation damage in the salt mine, which he viewed as an "extremely critical" issue. His concern was that "stored energy" in salt exposed to high levels of radiation could undergo "sudden thermal expansion" and cause small explosions that threatened the repository's integrity. In addition to the geologic questions that needed attention, provisions for transportation of waste canisters to Kansas, Hambleton and his staff believed, were "completely inadequate." Further, they complained that the AEC had developed "no contingency plans" for retrieval of the wastes in the event that the repository proved unsuitable for permanent disposal. Ernest E. Angino, deputy director of the Kansas Geological Survey, found it "confusing and disturbing" that the AEC appeared to take a "head in the sands" approach to retrieval. The findings of the Committee on Radioactive Waste Management and the preliminary report of the Kansas Geological Survey demonstrated that important technical issues remained to be addressed and suggested the difficulty of resolving them in a manner that satisfied critics of the Lyons proposal.[21]

GROWING CONTROVERSY OVER LYONS

In early 1971 the already lively debate over the Lyons repository became increasingly visible and acrimonious because of two developments. The first was the reaction to the AEC's draft environmental impact statement on its plans for the site. The other was the agency's request for an immediate $3.5 million appropriation to purchase land around Lyons and begin preliminary architectural and engineering work and for a long-term $25 million authorization for the entire project.

The AEC distributed copies of its environmental impact statement, which was required under the National Environmental Policy Act, to interested federal and state agencies in November 1970. It concluded that "no significant impact on the environment resulting from either the construction or operation of the proposed repository is anticipated." Among the evidence it cited to support its position was the report of the Committee on Radioactive Waste Management. The AEC received comments from the Department of the Interior; the Department of Health, Education, and Welfare; and the Environmental Protection Agency (EPA) that were muted in tone but clearly indicated the draft did not provide fully satisfactory answers for environmental issues the Lyons proposal raised. Kansas officials were more blunt. Hambleton dismissed "many parts" of the environmental statement as "general, meaningless, and a public relations effort design[ed] to relieve the fears of critics." Docking submitted that the "major problems not covered adequately" included "transportation, geological and site integrity, surveillance and monitoring, and retrievability."[22]

The AEC's request for an appropriation to buy land and begin work at the site, along with an authorization for future funding, stirred even harsher criticism. On February 12, 1971, Skubitz sent Docking a long, passionate letter that announced his opposition to the AEC's application for funding and to the development of the waste repository. Explaining that he had "not come lightly to this decision," he accused the AEC of ignoring both the views and the rights of Kansas. "The Federal Government cannot compel a sovereign State to do itself and its citizens possible irreparable injury if its officials refuse to be stampeded," he wrote. Skubitz complained that the AEC was "far from certain about the safety" of the site it proposed to use "as a dump for the most dangerous garbage in the knowledge of mankind." He asked that Docking, the Kansas legislature, and "cognizant State officials" offer support for his position. The letter received a great deal of attention within and beyond Kansas after the Sierra Club's Ronald Baxter released it to the press. Baxter also distributed copies of Hambleton's preliminary report of December 1970 that criticized the AEC's approach to the Lyons project.[23]

The reaction in Kansas to Skubitz's letter was mixed, reflecting the continuing ambivalence of many state officials and citizens. Some newspapers, especially in Skubitz's district, hailed his effort to stop the Lyons project. The *Parsons Sun* commented that the AEC was "tangling with a buzzsaw in Skubitz," who not only was "waging a battle for Kansas but probably for the whole nation." The *Iola Register* told its readers, "Joe Skubitz appears to be one of the few in a position of responsibility in Kansas who is looking at this question clearly." Others were less enamored with Skubitz's arguments. The *Wichita Eagle,* while calling for a careful investigation of the questions raised by the Kansas Geological Survey, remarked that "it would only hinder the search for answers if every Kansan got as hysterical as has Rep. Joe Skubitz."[24]

Docking, who had won reelection the previous fall, responded to Skubitz's appeal for support by listing the actions he had taken to investigate the safety of the Lyons site. He emphasized that if the proposed repository posed "any potential danger" to the citizens of Kansas, "*I will not hesitate to use all the powers of the governorship to halt the project*" (emphasis in original). But Docking refused to endorse Skubitz's unequivocal opposition to the project. This brought an impatient rejoinder from Skubitz, who rebuked him for a "weasling *[sic]* statement." He made his reply available to the press and told a reporter that Docking had "tried to shunt aside his responsibilities as governor."[25]

The AEC prepared its own response to Skubitz's letter of February 12. Seaborg told him that the agency had "attempted to answer forthrightly each question you have raised and to provide all information which you have requested." He reiterated that use of the Lyons site depended on the favorable outcome of scientific studies, including investigations of the issues that concerned the Kansas Geological Survey. "To date," he added, "we have no reason to believe that this important project should not proceed if authorized." Seaborg's explanations did not ease Skubitz's concerns or mollify his growing indignation. He told Seaborg in a ten-page, single-spaced letter that the key issue was the prerogative of the state to refuse to host the waste repository. He was offended by the AEC's "'big-daddy-knows-best' campaign that is at best disingenuous" and asserted that the AEC's position "won't hold water." Further, he wrote, "[it is] full of the kind of bureaucratic assurances that I have in my long experience in Washington come to mistrust." He advised the AEC to recognize that Kansans were "not country bumpkins who can be taken for granted."[26]

JOINT COMMITTEE ON ATOMIC ENERGY HEARINGS

Skubitz's correspondence with Docking and Seaborg set the stage, and the tone, for hearings conducted by the Joint Committee on Atomic Energy on the AEC's request for funding the Lyons project. The Joint Committee exercised enormous influence as the oversight committee for the AEC; both houses of Congress referred all proposed legislation relating to atomic energy to it. It also controlled the AEC's budget. The Joint Committee strongly advocated nuclear energy development and, as a rule, did not respond congenially to outside criticism of programs it supported. This pattern was clear when the committee held authorization hearings on March 16–17, 1971.[27]

Skubitz, who was not a member of the Joint Committee, led off the hearings with a lengthy statement opposing the allocation of funds for the Lyons project. "If this committee authorizes the funds and permits the AEC to purchase the ground," he declared, "it will have effectively denied Kansas people any choice in this vital issue." He denied that the AEC had demonstrated that the site would be safe. "We are talking about people's lives," he exclaimed. "The AEC is playing God." Joint Committee members, despite their efforts to observe the norms of congressional courtesy, sharply questioned Skubitz's testimony. Among other things, they quizzed Skubitz about the position of members of Congress from the area where the repository would be located. As a result, Garner E. Shriver, whose district included Lyons, and Keith Sebelius, who was likely to represent Lyons after a pending redistricting, submitted a joint statement. They called for further investigation of safety issues but, unlike Skubitz, did not oppose the AEC's request for funds.[28]

Skubitz supported his arguments about the scientific uncertainties surrounding the AEC's plans by quoting extensively from Hambleton's reports. When Hambleton took the stand, he delivered a message that distressed both the Joint Committee and the AEC. Appearing as the governor's spokesman, he announced that Docking had "reluctantly" concluded that the AEC's efforts "to minimize the problems raised by scientists in Kansas . . . support fears of many Kansans that if funds are appropriated for design and site acquisition the project cannot be stopped at a later date if it is . . . found to be unsafe." He urged that funding for the project be deferred until scientific studies were completed and the results evaluated. Docking's statement made clear that he had taken a large step closer to Skubitz's position, and it demonstrated the differing perspectives of Hambleton and representatives from Oak Ridge and the AEC. Hambleton praised the Oak Ridge experts as "cooperative, candid, and forthright" but added, "When it comes to dealing with the Atomic Energy Commission . . . we get evasive answers, and this is what causes the concern among most Kansans." He complained that the AEC had not provided reports that had been requested months earlier.[29]

Milton Shaw, director of the AEC's Division of Reactor Development and Technology, responded to Hambleton's indictment. Shaw was a strong proponent of nuclear power; the trade journal *Nucleonics Week* once described him as "probably without peer in convincing someone that nuclear power is to be embraced with little or no reservation." The AEC was convinced that the use of nuclear power could not expand unless the waste disposal issue was resolved; therefore, Shaw took an active interest in the Lyons debate. He told the Joint Committee that he was astonished by Hambleton's allegation that the AEC had withheld information. "I certainly feel we have made every reasonable attempt to keep him informed," he declared. He acknowledged, however, that bureaucratic procedures might have delayed transmission of the information that Hambleton sought. Shaw, who became so emotional during his testimony that he was "visibly shaking," disclosed that the AEC did not know of Hambleton's highly critical preliminary report of December 1970 until Erlewine received a call about it from the *New York Times*. Like Shaw, Floyd L. Culler, deputy director of Oak Ridge, said that he was perplexed by Hambleton's comments. He assured the Joint Committee that Oak Ridge was investigating the technical issues that Hambleton had raised, including heat flow and radiation damage to salt. This was welcome but surprising news to Hambleton and his deputy, Ernest Angino.[30]

The conflicting views that the hearings highlighted greatly disturbed Senator John O. Pastore, chairman of the Joint Committee. He pointed out that the AEC had not convinced key officials in Kansas that the Lyons site was suitable, and, judging from his experience as a former governor of Rhode Island, he told Shaw that the agency could not "run roughshod" over Docking or "stuff this down his throat." Pastore suggested that instead of authorizing the full $25 million the AEC had requested, the Joint Committee should approve only the $3.5 million to purchase land and draw up designs for the facility. He thought this would alleviate fears in Kansas that a $25 million authorization "would be a fait accompli." Shaw disagreed with Pastore's proposal because he preferred a "long-term commitment" to the project that would enable the AEC to attract "good people to work on it." He also contended that the smaller amount would delay if not sidetrack testing on specific conditions at the Lyons site. "We are at the point," he said, "that we must test in place." Several members of the Joint Committee took issue with Pastore and supported Shaw's arguments. When the hearings closed, the committee had not reached a decision or a consensus on funding the Lyons repository.[31]

The AEC believed that it had provided reasonable responses to the questions Kansas officials presented during the Joint Committee hearings. It affirmed that it would sponsor research on the technical issues Hambleton cited and would terminate work on the Lyons project if the mine turned out to be unsuitable. It argued that since it had transported nuclear materials safely for years, it was confident the same procedures for moving waste to Kansas were appropriate. And it pledged to design the facility in a way to allow for retrieval if it ever became necessary. Those assurances failed to satisfy Hambleton, who insisted that the essential research could and should be performed "before they actually go into this so-called demonstration site." The sometimes pointed debates during the hearings deepened the rift between state officials and the AEC over the question of authorizing funds for the repository.[32]

THE POLITICS OF WASTE

Shortly after the Joint Committee hearings, Docking commented that "AEC officials were nothing less than downright shabby" in their response to Hambleton's testimony. "They apparently thought," he added, "they could just throw their weight around and make us all play dead for them." He urged Pastore to defer funding "until safety of the project is assured" and attacked the "high-handedness of some AEC officials in their 'steam-roller' approach to moving ahead." He complained to President Richard M. Nixon about the "arrogance" and "patronizing manner" of the AEC, which, he said, had "treated as trivial the concerns of Kansans for a potentially dangerous project." Docking instructed Vern Miller, attorney general of Kansas, to explore the legal options available to the state to oppose the Lyons repository. "If the only recourse to halting the project near Lyons is a lawsuit," he told Miller, "then I would support a lawsuit."[33]

Congressman Skubitz heartily applauded the governor's more militant stance. He wired Docking, "As one who felt very alone for almost a year in this fight, . . . I commend your position in opposing the installation of a nuclear waste dump at Lyons." The governor, despite the vocal objections he expressed, sought to keep his distance from Skubitz. He still had not closed his mind to the Lyons site if the AEC agreed to delay the project until more scientific studies were completed. His staff told reporters that Docking's recent protests were not a result of "noise from Skubitz" but reflected his long-standing position that he would act to stop the project if its safety was doubtful. The Joint Committee hearings had "confirmed for him what he suspected"—that the AEC was "not inclined to pursue tests" that Hambleton thought were necessary.[34]

Hambleton felt the same way. He thanked Pastore for his "unfailing courtesy" during the hearings, which "relieved an otherwise difficult session." He summarized the differences between the AEC and the Kansas Geological Survey for the Joint Committee chairman. "The Atomic Energy Commission judges it has adequate information for proceeding with the radioactive waste disposal project . . . and that any or all problems can be engineered or designed *out* of this 'demonstration project' when and if they appear," he wrote. "The Kansas Geological Survey holds to the view that safety should be designed and engineered *into* the project before it is undertaken." Discussions with Oak Ridge scientists after the hearings had further convinced him of the need for careful investigation of heat flow, radiation damage, retrieval, and other issues. "Father knows best," Hambleton commented about the AEC at a public meeting in April 1971. "He's like a steamroller. If you don't budge, he will roll over you and treat the effect as a negligible problem."[35]

Docking and Hambleton's bitter denunciations of the AEC in the wake of the Joint Committee hearings made clear that the Lyons project faced serious if not insurmountable political difficulties. This was a source of concern for Senator Robert J. Dole and other prominent Kansas politicians who wished to mitigate the controversy. In light of the "potential energy crisis" confronting the United States, Dole maintained, nuclear power was needed to meet the nation's power demands. The future of nuclear technology required a suitable site for disposal of radioactive wastes. Dole shared many of Docking's reservations about the Lyons proposal, but he was persuaded that the basic problem was a "lack of communication" rather than AEC indifference to the concerns of Kansas. Therefore, he advised Nixon to appoint an advisory council to assess the risks of the Lyons site in a way that would satisfy both the federal government and the people of Kansas. The council would include one representative from each of four federal agencies—the Council on Environmental Quality, EPA, the White House Office of Science and Technology, and the AEC—and two representatives from Kansas.[36]

Neither the AEC nor Skubitz regarded Dole's proposal favorably. The AEC feared that it would cause unwarranted delays, and Skubitz contended that it would disregard the rights of "our own State." White House officials were also skeptical because they did not want to place the president in the middle of an increasingly polarized political controversy. Nevertheless, they realized from talking with congressional staff that Dole was "pretty committed" to establishing a council and that the AEC had lost its credibility among "environmentally-conscious Kansans."[37]

Matters came to a head after the Joint Committee voted on June 30, 1971, to approve Pastore's recommendation for a $3.5 million appropriation for the purchase of land and preliminary work at the Lyons site. It contained two conditions: the project would be canceled if it did not meet "reasonable standards" of safety, and an advisory council would be established. The Joint Committee's action brought strong protests from Docking and Skubitz. Docking informed Pastore that he would "use all the authority of the Kansas Governor's Office to prevent the AEC from forcing this potentially dangerous project on the people of Kansas." Skubitz offered an amendment on the House floor to eliminate the funds approved by the Joint Committee. After it was defeated, he appealed for support from his fellow Kansans in the Senate. He told Dole and James B. Pearson that the proposed advisory council was a "patent fraud" and that the AEC had been "ambiguous and misleading, if not dishonest, in this entire waste-project controversy."[38]

Despite their differences, Skubitz, Pearson, and Dole worked with the Joint Committee to reach a compromise on the Lyons funding. The two senators agreed on legislation that provided for a nine-member advisory council to include at least three members from Kansas. It allocated funds for the AEC to lease but not purchase land in the Lyons area. And it specified that radioactive materials could not be used for testing at the site unless they were "fully retrievable." When the Senate passed the bill with those conditions, Docking announced that he was "very encouraged." Although Skubitz complained publicly that Kansas had been "badly served" by its senators, he eventually accepted a slightly revised version of the legislation. The compromise amendment that Congress passed in August 1971 won editorial acclaim throughout Kansas.[39]

THE FAILURE OF THE LYONS PROJECT

While congressional and state leaders arrived at a compromise that resolved the political disagreements over the Lyons site more or less to their satisfaction, new and ultimately fatal technical issues arose. The problem was that information provided by the American Salt Corporation of Kansas City, Missouri, indicated that water flowing underground from previous drilling in the Lyons area could reach the Carey mine in which radioactive waste would be stored. If this occurred, the water could carry radioactivity from the repository into adjacent aquifers and contaminate water supplies. The great advantage of using salt mines for disposing of radioactive wastes was the dryness of their geologic environment, and a serious threat of penetration by moving water would clearly make the Lyons location unacceptable.

The president of the American Salt Corporation, Otto Rueschhoff, first informed Oak Ridge of his concerns about the potential vulnerability of the Carey mine on May 4, 1971. He had learned only recently that the radioactive waste vault would be an "integral part of the old Carey mine," which caused him to worry that his company's nearby mine could "act as a conduit, transporting water from the aquifer above our operations to the vicinity of the proposed repository." The entry points for the two mines were only about 1,800 feet apart. Rueschhoff also warned that oil and gas wells that had been drilled in the Lyons area could enable the movement of fluids from the "salt strata" to the aquifer. As an example of what could happen, he disclosed that while his company had been drilling on April 19, 1971, it unexpectedly hit a cavity and released "several hundred gallons of brine and muck." In a meeting with the Kansas Gelogical Survey on July 26, 1971, Rueschhoff reported that in 1965 the company had pumped about 170,000 gallons of water into an "injection well" near Lyons as a part of its "solution mining" procedures. The water, rather than circulate back to a return well, had disappeared, and the company had "no idea as to where the loss occurred or where the fluids went." This incident signaled a risk of unknown proportions that underground water could compromise the integrity of a waste repository under Lyons. Hambleton remarked that "the Lyons site is a bit like a piece of Swiss cheese, and the possibility for entrance and circulation of fluids is great."[40]

Reuschhoff's revelations provided new impetus for opponents of the Lyons project. Skubitz announced on September 30, 1971, that the "Lyons site is dead as a dodo for waste burial." The AEC, to the astonishment of Hambleton and his colleagues, denied that it had decided to abandon Lyons. Fleming M. Empson of Oak Ridge told a reporter that the AEC thought Lyons was "certainly the safest site which is available," and the agency issued a statement affirming that it was "still actively investigating the advantages of the Lyons site." Although it did not view the problems at the location as "insurmountable," it acknowledged that it would begin "looking into possible alternatives," including other salt deposits in Kansas.[41]

By that time the AEC had completely exhausted its already meager political capital in Kansas. Docking told James R. Schlesinger, who had recently replaced Seaborg as AEC chairman, that he did not believe the agency had acted "honestly and faithfully." He made a "strong recommendation" that it "extend its search for a suitable disposal area beyond the boundaries of Kansas, and beyond the boundaries of the continental United States." Schlesinger replied that the AEC had acted in a "straightforward manner" and that the state's objections "must stem from some sort of misunderstanding," which further rankled the governor. Senator Pearson, who had worked hard to achieve a compromise on the AEC's appropriation, faulted the agency for attempting to gain approval for the Lyons project "as quickly as possible" in the face of "unanswered questions about the environmental consequences."[42]

The AEC still refused to withdraw the Lyons proposal, but it eventually recognized that the site was unsalvageable, both politically and technically. By early 1972 it seemed clear to the White House Office of Science and Technology that the AEC had "all but given up" on Lyons, especially since a Kansas Geological Survey report had described the site as the "poorest choice" among seven salt formations it had surveyed. A short time later, the AEC announced that although it would continue to search for suitable salt deposits, it would shift its emphasis to storing high-level radioactive wastes in large concrete and steel structures that would be placed above ground. Skubitz remained skeptical. In response to his inquiries, he received assurances in June 1974 from Dixy Lee Ray, who followed Schlesinger as AEC chairman, that the agency did "not plan to dispose of radioactive wastes in the State of Kansas" and that it intended to "manage all high level radioactive waste in retrievable surface storage." Nevertheless, Skubitz introduced a bill in Congress three years later that would require a referendum by the citizens of a state in which a nuclear waste repository would be located. His motive, he explained, was "to prevent the Lyons, Kansas, situation from ever developing again."[43]

The AEC's first effort to identify a suitable site for disposing of high-level radioactive wastes from commercial nuclear power failed spectacularly. In its haste to fulfill its pledge to Senator Church and to build a repository for the growing quantities of commercial reactor wastes, it not only selected a location that proved unsuitable but also offended political leaders and scientists whose backing for the project was essential. The AEC was not indifferent to the safety of the Lyons site or to the welfare of the citizens of Kansas, but its ham-handed treatment of controversial issues often made it appear that way. Preliminary investigations of the Carey mine were promising enough for the agency to explore its advantages as a permanent waste repository. But the AEC became so focused on Lyons that it too easily dismissed the serious questions that the Kansas Geological Survey raised. It dealt with the reservations of Hambleton and his colleagues in much the same way that it had responded to the comments on waste hazards at AEC installations that the National Academy of Sciences had provided during the 1960s. Rather than take its time to investigate scientific uncertainties and reach strongly defensible conclusions, it offered disputable assurances and pressed ahead. The AEC knew of the presence of another salt mine and oil and gas wells close to the proposed repository, but it took no action to study the risks of previous drilling until after the American Salt Corporation expressed concerns. Its refusal to fully assess the potential pitfalls of the Lyons project was an embarrassment that could have and should have been avoided by a more deliberate approach to the inherently complex problem of disposing of radioactive wastes.

The AEC handled the political aspects of the Lyons debate in an equally inept manner. It was aware that the construction of a waste repository would not proceed without the support of the local community, and it was committed to addressing public concerns. But it did not deal adroitly with the political issues that arose in Kansas, in large part because it tended to view critics of the Lyons proposal as a monolithic whole. It failed to distinguish between the reservations that Hambleton cited and the much more strident and intractable position that Skubitz adopted. Docking and Hambleton were open-minded about the project at the outset; they eventually became disillusioned with the AEC after it dismissed or refused to aggressively investigate the questions they raised.

Long before the AEC realized that the project was technically flawed, it had lost the political support it needed. Although Kansas officials were favorably impressed with the staff members from Oak Ridge and the AEC whom they met, they were repeatedly frustrated and dumbfounded by the policy decisions of AEC headquarters. Erlewine's press conference in Topeka in June 1970 was the first in a series of political missteps the AEC took during the Lyons controversy. The agency's clumsy political performance was a result of its conviction that its procedures would assure the safety of the facility and of its unseemly rush to build a waste disposal repository. The AEC paid a heavy price for its errors. The Lyons debacle received national attention that diminished confidence in the agency and made its search for a solution to the waste problem immeasurably more difficult.

CHAPTER 4

New Directions in Radioactive Waste Management

In the wake of the Lyons embarrassment, the AEC, without abandoning the concept of salt disposal, sought new approaches to managing radioactive waste. It still faced the problem of finding a suitable site for disposing of high-level wastes generated at its own installations and at the growing number of commercial nuclear power plants. It continued to investigate the possibility of burying wastes in salt deposits or other geologic formations and also explored unconventional settings such as outer space or polar ice caps. The AEC quickly dismissed exotic locations and realized that the options it had already carefully considered would not provide prompt or certain solutions. As a result, it looked to "retrievable surface storage" as a safe, proven, and relatively long-term method of dealing with wastes until a permanent means of disposal was developed. While the agency made plans to use surface structures to store and monitor wastes, however, its progress on waste issues was encumbered by unexpected technical difficulties, new political controversies, and increasing public concern.[1]

ORGANIZATIONAL CHANGES

In July 1971, as the Lyons controversy was generating sharp criticism and revealing flaws in site evaluation procedures, the AEC took administrative action to improve its performance on waste treatment issues.

It announced the creation of the Division of Waste Management and Transportation to handle storage, disposal, and transportation of high-level and low-level commercial radioactive wastes. The AEC acted in part if not largely in response to complaints of the Joint Committee on Atomic Energy about "overlapping responsibilities" for questions relating to waste. To direct the division, the agency hired Frank K. Pittman, a nuclear energy veteran who had earned high respect from his colleagues in the field. "It is . . . encouraging to note," the professional journal *Nuclear News* commented in August 1971, "that the new division will be headed by a man of the stature of Frank Pittman."[2]

Pittman received a Ph.D. in chemistry from the Massachusetts Institute of Technology and joined the Manhattan Project in 1944. He went to work for the AEC in 1948 and ten years later became director of the Division of Reactor Development, one of the agency's most visible and demanding staff positions. From 1964 until 1971, he was an executive in the nuclear power industry, first with North American Rockwell and then with the Kerr-McGee Corporation. When appointed head of the AEC's Division of Waste Management and Transportation, he remarked that he was "glad to be back in the fold again." He returned to the fold amid the looming failure of the Lyons proposal, but he soon made a favorable impression even on critics of the project. Ronald H. Baxter of the Kansas chapter of the Sierra Club told AEC chairman James R. Schlesinger that Pittman was "a credit to federal service and a credit to the AEC" because of "his demeanor and ability to be candid and realistic."[3]

Another important change in the AEC's organization and its approach to waste issues was the arrival of Schlesinger as chairman and William O. Doub as a commissioner in August 1971. Schlesinger, who held a Ph.D. in economics from Harvard University, had earned a reputation as a skillful budget cutter and no-nonsense administrator while serving as assistant director of the Bureau of the Budget under President Nixon. Doub, described in *Nucleonics Week* as "a tough, ebullient lawyer," left his position as chairman of the Maryland Public Service Commission to join the AEC. Both Schlesinger and Doub were committed to making the agency more sensitive to the environmental impact of nuclear power and more responsive to public concerns. Although Schlesinger had annoyed Governor Docking by defending the AEC's performance on the Lyons repository, he believed that critics of the project had raised "sensible" questions and that the AEC's waste management strategies should be reevaluated.[4]

WASTE MANAGEMENT ALTERNATIVES

In January 1972 Pittman submitted a lengthy paper to the commissioners on the status of the AEC's waste disposal programs. In light of the Lyons experience, his assessment was considerably less optimistic than the prevailing agency view of the 1960s that a satisfactory solution to the problem would be found within a fairly short time. When Pittman prepared his report, the AEC had not given up on Lyons, but he suggested that the contention over the site was "already adversely affecting public acceptance of nuclear power." He expressed his concern that the waste issue "could become an unnecessarily negative factor in the Nation's ability to consider its nuclear option [for] power generation." The question of public attitudes had taken on increasing urgency for the AEC. A barrage of criticism over reactor safety, radiation protection standards, and the environmental effects of nuclear power had weakened public support for the technology and undermined confidence in the AEC. The controversy over the Lyons proposal had contributed significantly to those trends. The *Washington Post* commented in March 1971 that the "Kansas situation" reflected not only the "general fear most people have of radioactivity" but also "a basic distrust of the AEC."[5]

Pittman advised the commissioners that if the Lyons project failed, the AEC should be prepared to "move aggressively" to "develop a safe acceptable alternative approach." He made clear that no alternative to the Lyons mine was assured of technical success, public support, or timely availability. But he cited several possible methods for dealing with waste that were worth exploring. One obvious option was to search for other salt deposits that might prove more acceptable than the Lyons site. Another was to carefully investigate geologic formations other than salt, such as bedrock or basalt. A third approach was to store wastes temporarily in "carefully-engineered man-made structures." This would provide more time to locate a suitable geologic formation, develop new technology, and gain public approval. Pittman maintained that the AEC's experience at its own installations had "demonstrated that radioactive waste can be safely isolated from man's environment for many decades, even by use of relatively unsophisticated low cost tankage."

Other conceivable means of waste disposal appeared much less promising. Although wastes might be deposited in "sludges and silts of certain ocean deeps" or "in areas of perpetual ice," Pittman concluded that environmental concerns and international treaties made the chances of using such sites "remote." Sending wastes into outer space might be technologically feasible but was far from being practical in terms of cost or safety. The transmutation of radioactive isotopes in wastes into harmless forms was an appealing prospect, but it was not close to being a proven method of waste treatment. Therefore, Pittman commented, the AEC faced a sobering problem. The "currently most attractive waste management approach" of using salt deposits in Kansas was "seriously delayed and possibly excluded . . . by public disfavor." Other options required lengthy development and testing procedures and "could be subject to the same (or worse) public acceptance problems." And the need for "long-term surveillance and maintenance" made surface storage in engineered structures "undesirable as an ultimate method" of waste disposal.[6]

MONITORED RETRIEVABLE SURFACE STORAGE

After discussions with the commissioners and AEC staff experts, Pittman proposed a program for dealing with wastes on both a short-term and a long-term basis in February 1972. For the immediate future, he recommended that work begin on "conceptual design and engineering studies" for surface storage of high-level and transuranic wastes. The aboveground facility would be built with the goal of storing wastes for one hundred years in a way that allowed for their "transfer" if containers failed, for "easy complete retrieval" of waste materials, for "easy cleanup" in case of accidents or spills, and for "decontamination following final shutdown." For permanent disposal, Pittman urged that the AEC continue its search for an appropriate geologic site. Drawing on the lessons of the Lyons controversy, he further suggested that wastes placed in "pilot repositories" in geologic formations for test purposes "be completely and demonstrably retrievable." One of the chief complaints regarding the AEC's plans for Lyons was the absence of detailed provisions to remove wastes if the salt mine in which they were buried later turned out to be unsatisfactory.[7]

The commissioners approved Pittman's recommendations, and in May 1972 the AEC announced its modified approach to waste management. At hearings of a subcommittee of the House Committee on Science and Astronautics, Commissioner Doub revealed, to no one's surprise, that the agency would seek alternatives to the Lyons site. He made clear that although use of the Lyons mine seemed unlikely, the AEC would continue to sponsor research on long-term disposal in salt and other geologic formations. In the meantime, it favored the development of surface facilities in which wastes could be stored for "a minimum of 100 years." Doub predicted that over the course of a century, "the remaining questions as to geological formation storage or other management techniques should be resolved." He added that this approach would enable the AEC to "keep open all [its] options" and to "move slowly." Doub's testimony suggested, without saying so directly, that the AEC recognized it had acted too quickly in settling on Lyons before it had fully investigated the site.[8]

AEC officials elaborated on Doub's announcement in public statements on their reasons for supporting surface storage as an interim solution. Pittman asserted that tank storage at Hanford and Savannah River had shown that high-level liquid wastes could be maintained "in a manner that has not endangered the health and safety of the public." He acknowledged that the tanks had leaked on occasion but argued that the leaks were not a major concern as long as they were "quickly detected" and the liquids in the leaking tanks were "quickly transferred to other tanks." Pittman insisted that properly designed surface storage containers would offer an adequate solution to waste management for at least several decades. He emphasized that the volume of wastes from commercial nuclear power was small compared to fossil fuel plants. For example, a 1,000-megawatt coal-burning facility annually created about 200,000 tons of solid ashes and released another six million tons of gaseous wastes into the atmosphere. A nuclear plant of the same size, by contrast, generated about eight tons of solidified high-level radioactive wastes. Pittman estimated that the solid high-level waste that nuclear plants would produce by the end of the century could be safely stored on "only a few acres of land."[9]

The AEC described how surface storage would probably be carried out, subject to further research. The solidified high-level waste would be placed in steel canisters about ten feet long. The canisters would be shipped in casks that provided cooling and shielding against radiation. Once the waste arrived at the storage site, the canisters would be removed from the casks and transferred to "massive" steel and concrete modules. Since each canister would produce heat in the range of two to ten kilowatts, the wastes would be cooled by the circulation of air, water, or some other medium. The storage structures would be designed to guard against the risks of natural disasters and "all credible adverse accidental or intentional actions by man." The waste containers would be constantly monitored for leaks, overheating, deterioration, and other threats to the integrity of the storage site. The AEC was confident that this was a sound approach to relatively short-term waste treatment.

Julius H. Rubin, the AEC's assistant general manager for environment and safety, told a meeting of nuclear professionals in late 1972, "The use of man-made engineered storage facilities assures that there is a safe solution to the high-level waste problem for many tens of years and possibly several centuries."[10]

Nevertheless, the AEC realized that a series of safety and environmental questions had to be addressed before a surface storage facility was built. The first issue was siting. For a time the AEC considered the options of placing waste storage structures at one of its own installations or at commercial fuel reprocessing plants. By August 1974 the AEC had narrowed its list of potential waste storage sites to its own properties at Hanford, the NRTS in Idaho, and the nuclear weapons test site in Nevada. It had not, however, settled on a preferred location.

A second critical question for surface storage of high-level waste was design of the facility. The AEC investigated the concepts of a water basin vault in which the waste canisters would be stored in pools of circulating water and an air-cooled vault in which the canisters would be cooled by natural draft airflow. An alternative approach that the AEC found "promising" was the use of "sealed cask" storage. This was a new concept in which wastes from reprocessing, after solidification, would be placed in containers with steel walls two inches thick surrounded by an outer shell of concrete thirty-eight inches thick. The sealed casks could be stationed above ground in the open air and cooled by natural air convection. They would not require cooling vaults or emergency cooling systems. They would be built to withstand "all credible" natural and accidental threats to their structural integrity.

The AEC's support for surface storage gave increased impetus to the "glassification" of high-level wastes, in which solids would be fixed in "massive low-leachable material." In planning for the Lyons waste repository, the AEC had recognized that the steel canisters that held the solid waste would not last more than a decade or so. It did not regard this as a problem because it anticipated that salt beds would seal the waste and prevent it from reaching the environment. In surface storage, however, the AEC viewed the fixation of wastes in a solid medium as a key element in a series of barriers that would guard against dispersion of radioactivity to the environment. Research over the previous few years had produced encouraging results, and although glassification would not deliver adequate protection in itself, it would, if successfully developed on an industrial scale, reduce the risks of storing radioactive wastes by substantial proportions.[11]

One potential impediment to the AEC's plans for surface storage was transportation of highly radioactive wastes over long distances. This had emerged as a major concern during the debate over the Lyons site, and the agency carefully reviewed the public health hazards that might arise when wastes were transferred from a reprocessing plant to a storage facility. It acknowledged that casks had not yet been built specifically to ship high-level waste. But it anticipated that such containers would have shielding features similar to those it had used for years to move spent reactor fuel, which produced even more heat and radiation. Based on its experience, the AEC was confident that waste containers would be able to endure serious accidents involving "speed impact, puncture, fire, and water immersion" without "significant leakage." It dismissed as "unfounded" public fears of a heavy death toll from a worst-case "freak" accident in which a cask broke open. It insisted that transportation of wastes by truck or train under routine conditions was unlikely to cause radiation exposures to workers or the general public that even approached permissible doses.[12]

The AEC recognized that it needed more information on siting and design issues before making firm decisions on surface storage. But agency officials were optimistic that outstanding questions would be resolved soon enough to open a facility by the early 1980s. Surface storage was, Pittman told the commissioners in May 1974, the "best available solution." He suggested that the "most effective and the safest" method of storage was the "sealed cask concept." The commissioners were fully aware of the importance of waste management; they regarded it as "*the* critical issue in the nuclear power program" (emphasis in original).[13]

While the AEC focused on surface storage as the near-term solution to high-level waste treatment, it also evaluated geologic sites for permanent disposal. It still viewed salt as the likeliest receptacle and sought suitable alternatives to Lyons, both in and beyond Kansas. It also continued to weigh the feasibility of other geologic settings. Once it decided on a location, the AEC planned to build a "geologic disposal pilot plant" to "determine acceptability of a specific site." It would require that waste in the pilot plant be "readily retrievable." It also pledged that the plant would "not be converted to a full-scale repository until the public has accepted the philosophy of radioactive waste disposal in geologic formations" and until the effects of "heat-producing waste . . . have been verified." By fall 1974 AEC officials, though well aware of the uncertainties that remained, believed they were making satisfactory progress on the most critical technical issues surrounding radioactive waste from commercial nuclear power.[14]

THE REPROCESSING CONUNDRUM

In the AEC's judgment, the success of retrievable surface storage and geologic disposal depended heavily on the development of commercial reprocessing of spent fuel. Indeed, it regarded reprocessing, storage, and disposal as a closely linked triad essential to shaping a technically and politically acceptable solution to the radioactive waste problem. The AEC and the nuclear industry based their projections of the volume and radioactive hazards of commercial waste on the assumption that fuel rods would be reprocessed after use in a reactor to recover uranium and plutonium for making fresh fuel. Reprocessed uranium could be enriched to desired levels for uranium fuel; nearly all power reactors in the United States were light-water reactors that used uranium fuel enriched to about 3 percent of the fissionable isotope uranium-235. The plutonium that was recovered from reprocessing could be combined with uranium to make mixed oxide fuel. Because of uncertainties about uranium reserves and the capacity of uranium enrichment plants, nuclear experts viewed reprocessing, production of mixed oxide fuel, and development of advanced plutonium reactors as crucial steps to ensure adequate fuel supplies for the anticipated growth of nuclear power. AEC chairman Seaborg predicted in October 1970 that plutonium-fueled reactors would provide more than 50 percent of the electricity generated in the United States by the year 2000. "Plutonium, as the key to electrical energy production in the future," he declared, "is thus a vital element of the overall economic well-being of this country."[15]

Reprocessing, which had been carried out at AEC plants since the Manhattan Project, was a familiar operation, but it required careful procedures to protect workers from excessive radiation exposure. After removal from a reactor, highly radioactive spent fuel rods were chopped into small pieces and dissolved in nitric acid. Uranium and plutonium were then chemically separated from other elements and purified. The AEC estimated that reprocessing made 99.9 percent of the uranium and plutonium in spent fuel available for reuse in reactors. Although the high-level liquid waste that remained after reprocessing was a toxic mix of chemicals and fission products, it contained only traces of plutonium.[16]

In 1970 the AEC issued a series of safety requirements for commercial reprocessing plants. The regulations specified, among other things, that high-level wastes could be stored at a reprocessing site as liquids for a maximum of five years. The wastes had to be converted to a solid form approved by the AEC and then shipped to a federal repository "as soon as practicable, but in no event later than ten years following separation of fission products from the irradiated fuel." The solidified high-level wastes would be disposed of permanently on property that the federal government owned.[17]

The cost-effectiveness and safety of commercial reprocessing of nuclear fuel were far from proven in the early 1970s. At that time, one privately owned reprocessing plant was operating and two others were under construction. The first commercial facility, built by a firm called Nuclear Fuel Services on land owned by the state of New York, received an operating license from the AEC in 1966. It was located near the town of West Valley, about thirty miles from Buffalo. The plant struggled financially from the outset. Since only a few nuclear power reactors were operating, the market for reprocessed fuel was limited. The AEC provided some business for West Valley but not enough to make it profitable. The plant also caused occupational health and environmental problems that had to be addressed. Although West Valley experienced no massive failures that released large amounts of radiation to the environment or exceeded permissible limits for the surrounding area, it leaked gaseous and liquid wastes in quantities that troubled the AEC. Further, workers at the plant received exposures from design flaws and equipment malfunctions that occasionally exceeded permissible doses for individuals and consistently surpassed levels that the AEC regarded as desirable. In 1972 Nuclear Fuel Services decided to suspend operations at West Valley to make changes that it hoped would improve the plant's safety performance and financial prospects. Four years later, in response to regulatory requirements that greatly increased the cost of modifying and operating the plant, the company closed it permanently and abandoned the reprocessing business.[18]

The other two commercial reprocessing facilities also ran into severe and unanticipated problems. The General Electric Company built a technologically advanced plant near Morris, Illinois, that was designed to eliminate the need to store high-level liquids on-site by calcifying them directly. The end product would be a dry granular powder. Unfortunately, after spending $64 million and conducting tests for two years, the company announced in July 1974 that it would not open the plant because of design and equipment failures that could be fixed only at an unacceptable cost. This action was not only a setback for General Electric but also a source of "consternation" to the growing nuclear power industry, which worried about a shortage of reprocessing capacity for its spent fuel.[19]

The demise of the Morris project left the field to a plant under construction near Barnwell, South Carolina, that was owned by a consortium called Allied-General Nuclear Services. The company planned to operate Barnwell by adopting the same reprocessing methods that the AEC had used for years at Hanford, Savannah River, and other government installations. Despite long experience with the technology, building the plant to meet safety standards and competitive demands was a formidable task. It became even more difficult when the AEC imposed tighter regulations on reprocessing operations, including the requirement that high-level liquid wastes be solidified within a five-year period, a prohibition against transporting plutonium in liquid form, and a more rigorous definition of transuranic wastes that made handling and disposal of such materials more burdensome and more expensive. The greatest threat to Barnwell, however, was a controversy that erupted in the mid-1970s over the AEC's environmental impact statement for reprocessing facilities.[20]

GESMO AND SAFEGUARDS

By 1973 the AEC anticipated licensing applications for nuclear plants that would use mixed oxide fuel, and in accordance with the National Environmental Policy Act, it prepared an environmental impact statement. The document was called the "generic environmental statement on the use of mixed oxide fuel in light-water reactors," which was inevitably shortened to an acronym—GESMO. One essential step in the production of mixed oxide fuel was the separation of plutonium by reprocessing. The AEC published a draft GESMO report in August 1974. It concluded that using mixed oxide fuel in reactors would not cause greater safety problems or higher radiation exposures than the low-enriched uranium fuel "burned" in existing commercial nuclear plants. In those respects, it declared, "the differences between the two modes of operation are expected to be essentially indiscernible."[21]

In another respect, however, the use of plutonium in reactor fuel was a significant departure. It generated a great deal of controversy over the issue of "safeguards," the term applied to the protection of nuclear plants from sabotage and nuclear materials from theft. The reprocessing of spent fuel from light-water reactors and the anticipated development of "breeder" reactors that would produce bountiful quantities of plutonium stirred growing anxieties about the risk that foreign nations or terrorists could obtain the materials needed to build nuclear weapons.

Low-enriched uranium is not suitable for making a nuclear explosive, but plutonium was used to fuel the atomic bomb dropped on Nagasaki in 1945 and U.S. nuclear weapons tested after World War II. Victor Gilinsky, an analyst with the RAND Corporation, expressed the depth of concern over the future availability of plutonium from nuclear power in an article he published in 1970: "Generally speaking, the diversion of plutonium produced in civilian reactors is the chief danger associated with civilian nuclear power programs."[22]

The possibility that terrorists could acquire plutonium and build a nuclear bomb emerged as a major source of public apprehension in the early 1970s. The central figure in making nuclear terrorism a prominent public issue was Theodore B. Taylor, who had designed atomic bombs at Los Alamos Scientific Laboratory and worked on other nuclear projects in industry and government before setting up his own consulting firm in 1967. His experience had convinced him that a well-informed illicit bomb maker did not have to duplicate the Manhattan Project to build a weapon that could cause enormous destruction. Taylor pointed out that a great deal of information about how to make an atomic bomb could be gleaned from unclassified sources, and he insisted that it was not a terribly difficult task if one had the required materials. He suggested that a bomb need not be sophisticated or efficient to produce staggering death and destruction; a very crude bomb could yield enough explosive power, for example, to topple the World Trade Center in New York or destroy the Hoover Dam on the Colorado River. Taylor's views received wide attention in the scientific and popular press. An article in *Science* magazine in 1971, for example, emphasized the risks that the increasing availability of plutonium would present and asserted that "the only real obstacle now stopping anyone from building a perfectly good bomb is the present scarcity of materials and . . . tight security."[23]

Taylor's warnings were especially alarming because of the increase in terrorist activity around the world in the early 1970s. The London *Economist* observed in November 1972, "Terrorism is developing into a form of total war, the kind of war in which there is no distinction between combatants and noncombatants." The murder of Israeli athletes at the 1972 Olympics, the kidnapping of newspaper heiress Patricia Hearst in 1974, and a wave of less publicized but still distressing skyjackings, letter bombings, assassinations, and other terrorist acts heightened the impact of Taylor's arguments. He received support from other analysts who reached similar conclusions. A report commissioned by the AEC, for example, asserted in 1974 that the terrorist threat was real and growing. "Terrorist groups," it declared, "have increased their professional skills, intelligence networks, finances, and levels of armaments around the world." The AEC denied that building an atomic bomb was as easy as Taylor and others suggested. But it recognized, as one staff member told a working group of the Cabinet Committee to Combat Terrorism that President Nixon established in 1972, that the "danger of radioactive material, particularly plutonium, falling into the wrong hands, exists."[24]

Concerns about nuclear terrorism were compounded by fears that increasing quantities of plutonium would encourage international proliferation of nuclear weapons. Those forebodings were dramatically intensified when India conducted a test of what it called a "peaceful nuclear explosion" in May 1974. The Indians used materials exported for civilian purposes by Canada and almost certainly by the United States to produce plutonium for the explosion. It raised the troubling prospect of, in the words of *U.S. News and World Report,* "a 'minor league' a-bomb race." It also underscored the need to strengthen safeguards to inhibit the spread of nuclear weapons to other countries and to prevent materials that could be made into bombs from reaching the hands of terrorists or criminals.[25]

The AEC closely examined the issue of safeguards in the GESMO draft environmental impact statement. It acknowledged that reprocessing and use of mixed oxide fuel would require improved safeguards in transportation, in protection of nuclear plants from sabotage or external attacks, and in accountability procedures for keeping track of plutonium. It had already taken steps to upgrade safeguards programs, and it was considering a series of new requirements to provide better security in plutonium production and shipping. The AEC expressed a "high level of confidence" that "the safeguards problem is manageable." It saw no reason "to delay a decision to permit the use of plutonium in mixed oxide fuel for light water reactors."[26]

The AEC's conclusions drew a heavy volley of objections. Staff members of the Natural Resources Defense Council (NRDC), a leading environmental organization, charged that the AEC was "about to sow the seeds of a national crisis." They denounced the AEC's GESMO document as "a marvel of clouded reasoning and breezy optimism" that failed to adequately account for "an almost daily occurrence" of "terrorist activity and other forms of anti-social violence." They argued that the "commercialization of plutonium will bring with it a major escalation of the risks and the problems already associated with nuclear power."[27]

The NRDC's critique and similar commentaries won the attention of members of Congress and other observers. Senators Walter F. Mondale and Philip A. Hart expressed their "grave reservations" about fuel reprocessing and appealed to the AEC to defer taking action until safeguards issues received "the most searching public scrutiny." Senator Henry A. Jackson, a strong supporter of nuclear power, urged the AEC to resolve safeguards questions "on a priority basis" so that the "tremendous potential" of nuclear power could be fulfilled. Some nuclear professionals predicted that the plutonium debate that GESMO brought into sharp focus would "become the major battleground for the continuing war over nuclear power." The controversy had already increased misgivings about the wisdom of reprocessing and the use of plutonium fuel in commercial nuclear reactors. And that, in turn, added new complications and uncertainties to the problem of radioactive waste disposal.[28]

PUBLIC ATTITUDES TOWARD WASTE

The debate over reprocessing gained prominence as the public became increasingly disturbed about waste disposal in general and radioactive waste in particular. The problems presented by solid wastes from industrial, commercial, and residential applications attracted little popular or media attention before the early 1970s. The disposal of radioactive wastes in solid form was a partial exception to this pattern; it had received some notice and triggered some expressions of alarm during the 1950s and 1960s. One aspect of the growing environmental movement in the late 1960s was a greater focus on the hazards of solid waste, which joined air and water pollution in fueling public concern. Public attitudes toward radioactive wastes reflected the prevailing trends, especially after the debate over the Lyons project and the AEC's management of wastes at its own plants drew national headlines. This was clear in an opinion poll that asked, "Which of the following subjects have you heard a lot about in recent months?" In December 1969 only 16 percent of the respondents included radioactive wastes among the subjects they had "heard a lot about." By May 1971, when the Lyons controversy was reaching its peak, the number of respondents who listed radioactive wastes had risen to 29 percent. This was still much lower than many other environmental issues, but it was a telling sign of increasing public awareness.[29]

Public concern over radioactive waste management surged after a highly publicized leak of tens of thousands of gallons of high-level liquids from a storage tank at Hanford in 1973. The high-level liquid storage areas at Hanford, known as "tank farms," had continued to generate occasional frightening stories in the national media that echoed the tone and much of the content of the *National Enquirer* article of June 1968. *Parade* magazine, for example, told its readers in April 1970 that leaks from the Hanford tanks could make the Columbia River "become deadly," and added: "Potentially Hanford, Washington, is the most dangerous site in the world." Critics of the AEC argued that its waste treatment practices were far from adequate. Sheldon Novick, author of the book *The Careless Atom,* argued in early 1970 that the Hanford wastes, if released to the environment, "would constitute a hazard which could only be compared to nuclear war." He urged that the AEC devote "considerably more caution and expense" to dealing with the risks that tank storage produced. NRDC staff members complained about the "AEC's incomplete and piecemeal treatment of the general problem of radioactive waste disposal at the Hanford Reservation."[30]

The AEC reacted to such indictments in much the same way that it had addressed the concerns aired by the National Academy of Sciences waste disposal advisory committees during the 1960s. It emphasized that tank storage was a temporary approach, not a permanent means of disposal of high-level wastes. It pointed out that it had reduced the volume and mobility of liquid wastes by solidification. It contended that despite occasional leaks, the Hanford tank wastes did not threaten public health because they were separated from groundwater by at least one hundred fifty feet of absorbent soil and from the Columbia River by seven miles. The AEC denied that Novick's comparison of the dangers of Hanford wastes with nuclear war was valid on the grounds that "the destructive action of nuclear weapons is due mainly to blast or shock." It affirmed its conviction that "in-tank storage of high-level liquid radioactive wastes can be managed over a period of years so as to present no threat to the environment." Nevertheless, despite its genuinely sanguine view of waste management problems, the AEC was much more cognizant of the difficulties it faced than it had been when it had dismissed the National Academy's comments a few years earlier. One newspaper story reported that "AEC scientists worry as much as anybody about nuclear waste disposal." In June 1972 John A. Harris, director of the Office of Information Services, responded to a question from Chairman Schlesinger about a highly critical article with the handwritten comment that the "situation at Hanford is not all that clean."[31]

In the context of growing public concern over radioactive wastes, the large discharge from a tank at Hanford in 1973 was a severe setback for the AEC. The AEC first learned of the problem on June 8, 1973, when its Richland, Washington, Operations Office was informed by the contractor in charge of the tank farm, the Atlantic Richfield Hanford Company. The company reported that about 115,000 gallons of high-level liquid waste had leaked from one of the single-shell tanks built during World War II. The capacity of the tank was 533,000 gallons, and it had contained about 400,000 gallons when the leak occurred. Preliminary investigations showed that the leak had begun weeks earlier, but Atlantic Richfield had not "properly evaluated" the data it collected weekly. The AEC immediately formed a committee to review the causes and potential consequences of the release. It did not, at first, regard the leak as a matter of great concern; since 1958 Hanford had experienced fourteen known tank failures that deposited liquid wastes in amounts that ranged from "several thousand" to 70,000 gallons into the soil. "In each case," the staff told the commissioners, "the liquids released have been entrained in the soil beneath the tanks, staying well above the water table."[32]

Other observers were considerably more troubled. Consumer advocate and corporate watchdog Ralph Nader and representatives of the Union of Concerned Scientists, an influential organization that sharply criticized nuclear power, denounced the AEC's "impudence in allowing continued accumulation of radioactive wastes without prior resolution of the waste storage problem." On July 5, 1973, the *Los Angeles Times* published a front-page story under the headline, "Thousands Periled by Nuclear Waste." It charged that the AEC had mishandled wastes for three decades in a way that threatened "massive contamination." It contended further, "[The AEC] is unwilling to admit the gravity of the problem and apparently is intent on following an equally dangerous course in the future." The article discussed the recent leak at Hanford in the context of the waste management problems cited in the reports of the National Academy of Sciences and the General Accounting Office during the 1960s and the Federal Water Quality Administration in 1970.[33]

The AEC acted promptly to rebut the allegations in the *Times* story, which was widely reprinted in newspapers around the country. In a press release of July 5, it denied as "simply not true" the claim that its waste management practices endangered the "safety of thousands." It insisted that liquid wastes that had leaked from the Hanford tanks over the years had not reached the water table and suggested that they never would. In later staff comments, the AEC pointed out technical flaws in

Figure 7. Tanks for storage of high-level radioactive waste under construction at Hanford, 1964. (National Archives 434-SF-21–27)

the article, such as failing to distinguish between "storage" and "disposal" of radioactive wastes. It also complained that the account of the findings of the National Academy's Galley committee report of 1966 was distorted and misleading.[34]

Although the AEC offered a spirited defense of its waste programs in response to the *Times* story, it took the most recent leak at Hanford seriously, especially after it received the results of its investigation on July 30, 1973. The study, conducted by staff members of the Richland Operations Office, showed that the leak began on April 20. Atlantic Richfield employees monitored fluid levels in the tanks weekly, but they were not trained to interpret the information they compiled. A supervisor who was responsible for deciphering the charts was too busy to look at them, and, as a result, the leak continued unchecked and unrecognized until June 8. "The bungling attributed to Atlantic Richfield," *Science* magazine reporter Robert Gillette observed, "would be unbecoming for a municipal sewage plant, to say nothing of the nation's main repository for nuclear waste." The AEC took immediate steps to correct the weaknesses revealed by the investigation; it announced plans to install automatic leak detection equipment, improve monitoring procedures, and expedite in-tank solidification of liquid wastes.[35]

Nevertheless, the AEC was acutely aware that it had suffered a major blow, particularly since it had long cited its experience with the tanks at Hanford and Savannah River as evidence that wastes could be stored safely. Frank Pittman had argued in 1972 that leaks were not a worrisome problem if they were "quickly detected," but this obviously had not occurred in the case of the recent failure. Gillette reported in *Science* that the leak had turned into "one of the AEC's worst public relations disasters in years." AEC chairman Dixy Lee Ray, who had succeeded Schlesinger in the post, called the Hanford failures "not only regrettable, but also disgraceful" and lamented, "The fact that the Hanford leaks occurred enhances public distrust in our operations, as well it should." A public opinion poll conducted in 1974 supported her conclusion. It found that 52 percent of participants selected radioactive waste as a "serious problem" on a list of nuclear power hazards or drawbacks; less than half as many respondents, by contrast, placed "radiation discharge" or "nuclear accidents" in the same category.[36]

The problems at Hanford were not directly comparable to those surrounding the management and disposal of commercial wastes, which would not be stored in liquid form for decades before transfer to a permanent repository. But the distinction was often lost on non-experts, and the Hanford leak raised questions in many minds about the AEC's ability to deal with nuclear power wastes safely. This was clear, for example, in changing attitudes toward hosting a radioactive waste site in the state of Nevada. In May 1972, shortly after the AEC announced that it would seek alternatives to the Lyons project, Senator Howard W. Cannon urged the agency to consider Nevada as the location of a "national repository." He maintained that the Nevada Test Site, where nuclear weapons experiments had been carried out since 1951, was "probably one of the best known and understood geological areas in the country." Therefore, pending further safety evaluations, he suggested that a portion of the test site might provide an "ideal location" for reprocessing and disposing of radioactive wastes. Two years later, when the AEC identified Nevada as a possible site for a retrievable surface storage facility, officials and citizens of the state were much more skeptical. Governor Mike O'Callaghan told the AEC that Nevada could be considered only under strict conditions. These included a state role in assessing environmental impact and a "demonstrated" assurance of "adequate" radiation protection in transportation and storage. The governor insisted that the AEC "recognize the right of the State to terminate further consideration of Nevada as a specific site if such action appears to the State to be reasonable."[37]

THE END OF THE AEC

On October 11, 1974, President Gerald R. Ford signed the Energy Reorganization Act, which abolished the AEC. Its functions were assigned to two new agencies. The Energy Research and Development Administration (ERDA) took over the AEC's responsibilities for producing nuclear weapons and promoting nuclear power. The Nuclear Regulatory Commission (NRC) assumed the AEC's authority for regulating nuclear power and other commercial applications of nuclear energy. The AEC was an embattled agency when it went out of existence. It was a target of attacks from nuclear opponents on highly publicized issues that included radiation standards, reactor safety, environmental protection, and terrorist threats to nuclear plants and materials. Radioactive waste disposal was another source of criticism, especially after the demise of the Lyons project and the leaks at Hanford placed the AEC in an exceedingly unfavorable light. By the time the Energy Reorganization Act became law, both the opponents and the supporters of nuclear power had concluded that the creation of separate, independent agencies was necessary and desirable. The AEC's dual responsibilities for promoting and regulating nuclear power had undermined its credibility and fed growing public anxieties about nuclear safety.[38]

When the AEC was abolished, the three related components of its approach to commercial radioactive waste management were all floundering. The search for a site for permanent disposal, which had once seemed so promising, had started anew after the Lyons debacle, and the outcome remained uncertain. Commercial reprocessing was financially unproven and troubled by serious technical difficulties. And the separation of plutonium for use in nuclear power plants had created a great deal of political controversy. Retrievable surface storage, the AEC's short-term solution for controlling high-level commercial waste, also stirred increasing criticism. When the AEC published a draft environmental impact statement on surface storage, it received complaints from experts with divergent positions in the nuclear power debate. Terry Lash, a scientist with NRDC, commented that the AEC's plans provided "no reassurance that there will ever be a way of perpetually storing these wastes away from the environment."[39]

William D. Rowe, EPA's assistant administrator for radiation programs, made a similar point from a different perspective. He cited his agency's concern that surface storage would delay the search for a permanent repository. "While we believe that a final ultimate disposal method for high-level radioactive waste is conceptually possible," he said, "the failure to realize such a concept . . . in the reasonable future would place the nuclear energy program in a rather unfavorable light and would subject it to the criticism of many who are predisposed against nuclear energy." Rowe appealed to the AEC to increase its spending and step up its efforts to find a suitable geologic repository, a recommendation that the nuclear industry fully supported. "We think AEC and its successor organizations should pursue this venture in a timely fashion, as it is already overdue," Rowe declared in November 1974. "We consider the problem of ultimate disposal of radioactive waste to be so critical that we feel priority efforts should be exerted." Although there was wide agreement on the importance of dealing with increasing quantities of radioactive waste in a way that did not threaten public health and the environment, the AEC fell short of achieving this goal. Its legacy was a growing problem that defied easy solutions and that appeared to both critics and proponents of nuclear power to be vital to the future of the industry.[40]

CHAPTER 5

Progressing toward Stalemate

After the Energy Reorganization Act of 1974 replaced the AEC with the Energy Research and Development Administration and the Nuclear Regulatory Commission, the new agencies faced the problem of determining more precisely their respective roles and responsibilities for dealing with radioactive waste. At the same time, they inherited a series of complex and controversial waste management issues that demanded immediate attention. The most pressing, divisive, and momentous questions continued to be the advisability of reprocessing and the storage and disposal of high-level waste. ERDA, the NRC, and other federal agencies grappled with waste matters in an atmosphere of growing impatience on the part of the nuclear industry, growing criticism on the part of nuclear opponents, and growing concern on the part of the public at large. While federal agencies reviewed the problem and sought solutions, President Jimmy Carter took executive action by deciding to postpone commercial reprocessing "indefinitely" and by issuing a policy statement to introduce a "comprehensive radioactive waste program." Despite his efforts, progress on selecting a permanent disposal site remained painfully slow and, indeed, had reached a stalemate by January 1981, when he left the White House.

THE NRC AND NUCLEAR WASTE

The responsibilities that the Energy Reorganization Act assigned to ERDA and the NRC were clear in principle but sometimes less so in practice. In broad terms, the NRC assumed the licensing and regulatory authority for commercial applications of nuclear energy and ERDA took over the AEC's other functions. The NRC, which began operations on January 19, 1975, was an independent regulatory agency. This meant that its five commissioners were appointed by the president and confirmed by the Senate, but, unlike cabinet members, they could not be removed simply at the pleasure of the president. Although most of the NRC's staff had worked for the AEC's regulatory program, agency officials sought to distance themselves from their institutional legacy. Chairman William A. Anders, the only AEC commissioner to receive an appointment to the NRC, commented that the AEC's dual mandate of both promoting and regulating nuclear power had sometimes made it "hard to remember which hat you were wearing." He and his colleagues hoped to replace the perception of the AEC as a lax and conflicted regulator with public confidence in the NRC as a fair and objective regulator.[1]

The Energy Reorganization Act specifically required the NRC to license surface storage facilities and permanent disposal repositories for commercial high-level radioactive wastes. It also gave the NRC regulatory authority over sites that ERDA developed for high-level wastes from commercial uses of nuclear energy. The NRC's jurisdiction did not extend, however, to existing ERDA plants, such as Hanford and Savannah River, that stored high-level wastes from weapons production activities or to wastes that ERDA generated in research projects. Despite those limitations, the NRC clearly would play a significant and in some ways decisive role in the search for a solution to the waste problem. This forced the NRC to begin looking immediately for qualified staff, which was an administrative issue of some magnitude. The AEC's regulatory staff members brought little experience to the NRC that was directly applicable. Because the AEC had had no responsibility for licensing its own high-level waste facilities, its waste management experts had not served on the regulatory staff. They had gone to ERDA when the agency was abolished. The NRC established a waste management branch within its Office of Nuclear Materials Safety and Safeguards and gradually added staff members to it. By May 1977 the branch had hired twelve technical experts and made plans to increase to a complement of about thirty-eight. The staff was headed by William P. Bishop, who held a Ph.D. in chemistry from Ohio State University and had worked on radioactive waste programs at Sandia Laboratories, a research center in Albuquerque, New Mexico, funded by the AEC.[2]

The NRC promptly set out to evaluate the status of nuclear waste technology and to determine how best to protect public health and the environment from the hazards of radioactive waste. This process inevitably involved consideration of a series of interrelated questions that included the boundaries of the NRC's regulatory authority, the relative roles of federal agencies with statutory responsibility in the area of waste management, and the procedures and standards that the NRC would use in judging license applications.

Despite the Energy Reorganization Act's general guidance, the NRC's authority for regulating nuclear waste was, in some important respects, ambiguous. This arose in part from the existing definition of high-level radioactive waste, which, as the NRC pointed out, was "not based primarily on the degree of hazard posed by the waste, the lifetime of the waste, or the waste form." The NRC's regulations, which carried over from the AEC, defined high-level waste as the liquids that remained after the reprocessing of spent fuel rods. In light of the growing uncertainties about commercial reprocessing, the NRC faced the question of whether it had authority over disposal of spent fuel, which posed similar dangers but was not a product of reprocessing. The agency concluded that it did have jurisdiction over spent fuel sent as waste to an ERDA repository, but this judgment was not definitive.[3]

Even greater ambiguities existed about the nature and extent of the NRC's authority over transuranic wastes. They did not fall under the definition of high-level wastes, and their intensity was far lower than either liquid reprocessing wastes or spent fuel. But some transuranic elements presented serious storage and disposal problems because of the exceptional length of their half-lives. The half-life of plutonium-239, for example, is about 24,000 years. The AEC had proposed that transuranic wastes, like high-level wastes, be shipped to a federal repository but had not resolved the issue when it was abolished. The NRC had clear statutory jurisdiction over commercial storage and disposal of nonmilitary wastes contaminated with transuranic elements. But it had no explicit licensing authority over a facility operated by ERDA for handling such wastes, even if they were generated from commercial uses of nuclear power.[4]

There were other jurisdictional issues about the roles of federal agencies in waste management. The division of labor between ERDA and the NRC was a particularly urgent concern. In March 1975, two months after it began operations, ERDA published a report suggesting that outstanding waste management problems were "threatening to impede nuclear power growth." It identified a "confused and indecisive" regulatory performance as one major stumbling block to finding an appropriate solution. ERDA proposed that "it should assume an interested and active role with NRC in the pertinent regulatory activities" regarding waste and "press for early regulatory actions when these are necessary to progress toward ERDA objectives."[5]

NRC officials took a quite different position. They were determined to establish their regulatory independence and to guard against undue influence, or the appearance of influence, by ERDA. This was evident as both agencies considered preparing environmental impact statements on the potential consequences of waste management activities, including reprocessing, surface storage, and disposal. The National Environmental Policy Act of 1970 required federal agencies to analyze the environmental impact of their programs. ERDA quickly decided to withdraw the controversial document that the AEC had released in late 1974 and to draw up an expanded, improved version. It announced that it would invite the NRC to collaborate in this effort. But the NRC preferred to draft its own statement because it worried that the "appearance of collusion would erode NRC credibility" and undermine its ability to provide an independent regulatory judgment on ERDA's waste strategies.[6]

Another source of jurisdictional uncertainty and debate was the role of the U.S. Environmental Protection Agency in radioactive waste management. President Nixon had established EPA in December 1970, and within a short time, the new agency and the AEC had disagreed on their respective authority for radiation protection. The dividing line was that EPA regulated population exposure to radiation outside the boundaries of a plant, and the AEC regulated the safety programs of its licensees within the boundaries of their plants. The exercise of those responsibilities was far from clear in practice, however, and had caused considerable interagency discord before the AEC was abolished. The same kind of muted contention occurred between the AEC's successors and EPA on waste issues. EPA had, without dispute, statutory authority to prepare federal guidelines and eventually develop standards for population exposure to radiation from waste repositories. Nevertheless, important questions arose about the timing and applicability of the ambient standards that EPA would set. The NRC was concerned, for example, that EPA's guidelines might turn into inflexible requirements that would not take into proper account technological capabilities and design uncertainties.[7]

While the NRC was trying to sort out jurisdictional matters, it was also laying foundations for the major duties it would perform in the area of waste management. Marcus A. Rowden, who replaced Anders as NRC chairman in April 1976, emphasized "the need for a high-priority national effort" because "until recently, the pace and visibility . . . of our national waste management program . . . left much to be desired." The NRC took action on several fronts to carry out its regulatory responsibilities. In January 1976 it established a task force to investigate the dimensions of the problem and to recommend a series of general objectives for its waste policies. The task force, an interdisciplinary group of seven individuals from inside and outside the NRC, undertook a survey of the wide-ranging literature on radioactive waste and talked with about one hundred experts.[8]

In October 1976 the task force presented a series of broad goals to the commissioners that it viewed as essential for a successful waste management program. The objectives included explicit acknowledgment of the technical, political, organizational, and temporal uncertainties surrounding radioactive waste; full consideration of societal and institutional issues; ample allowance for meaningful public participation in waste decisions; and adequate protection of public health from the radiation hazards of nuclear waste for the present and far into the future. The task force made no claim that its findings were original or definitive, but it hoped to offer a "framework [on] which the expert architects of the waste management system can build." It emphasized above all that "waste management programs, like all human activities, involve both technical hardware and human organizations" and that "shortcomings in either will affect how well a program is implemented."[9]

While the task force was considering the general goals that the NRC should strive to achieve, the agency took preliminary steps toward preparing regulations to meet the regulatory mandate assigned to it by the Energy Reorganization Act. It recognized the need to develop performance standards in order to judge the applications for waste storage and disposal sites that it expected to receive. The NRC inherited a detailed set of radiation protection requirements from the AEC. But it still faced the long-term task of issuing regulations designed to provide "isolation of radioactive wastes from man and his environment for sufficient periods (in some cases hundreds or thousands of years)" and to reduce risks of radiation exposure from waste activities to a level that was "as low as reasonably achievable." This process promised to be complex and innately controversial. The NRC first tackled the most pressing issue—determining performance criteria for solidification and packaging of high-level wastes—by awarding contracts to Lawrence Livermore National Laboratory in California and the University of Arizona. In addition, the agency began work on a series of generic environmental impact statements on the types of waste management facilities it would be responsible for licensing.[10]

WASTE DISPOSAL AND THE LICENSING OF NUCLEAR PLANTS

In July 1976 a federal court ruling provided the NRC with further incentive to accelerate, within the boundaries of its statutory mandate, its efforts to evaluate the issues surrounding waste disposal. The decision required for the first time that the NRC's licensing procedures fully consider the possible environmental impact of waste generated by individual commercial reactors. The case originated in a petition brought by the NRDC two years earlier that had challenged the AEC's rules on the role of waste in licensing reviews. The NRDC had been founded in 1969 as a "public interest law firm" to take legal action on environmental issues. Its goal was to advance environmental protection through "responsible militancy," and it had frequently contested the policies of the AEC and its successors.[11]

In rule-making proceedings in 1973 and 1974, the AEC had examined the question of the extent to which it should include the environmental impact of the entire nuclear fuel cycle when reviewing an application for a reactor construction permit or operating license. The issue arose when it considered granting an operating license to the Vermont Yankee plant in Vernon, Vermont, in 1972. The term "fuel cycle" referred to the stages of making, using, and managing reactor fuel, from the mining of uranium to the disposal of radioactive waste. The treatment of waste after removal from a reactor was known as the "back end" of the fuel cycle. In a rule-making proceeding that followed the decision to issue a license to Vermont Yankee, the AEC determined that it should weigh the possible environmental effects of the fuel cycle in individual licensing cases only in a limited way. As a part of the rule, it included a list, labeled Table S-3, that gave numerical estimates of "environmental considerations" from the fuel cycle for a typical nuclear plant, such as land use, water consumption, and chemical and radioactive effluents. It required that the values listed on Table S-3 be factored into environmental impact statements for individual plants but otherwise determined that "no further discussion" of the fuel cycle was necessary. The AEC based its conclusion in part on the premise that it would carefully investigate the environmental impact of the back end of the fuel cycle when it received applications for waste storage and disposal facilities. And it suggested that the environmental effects from fuel cycle operations that an individual power reactor contributed were "relatively insignificant."

In a petition to the United States Court of Appeals for the District of Columbia Circuit, the NRDC contended that the AEC's rule failed to meet the requirements of the National Environmental Policy Act. It claimed that the AEC should provide broader consideration of the environmental effects of the fuel cycle in its licensing actions and that Table S-3 was inadequate for that purpose. By the time the court heard arguments on the NRDC's petition, the Nuclear Regulatory Commission had inherited the case. On July 21, 1976, the court handed down a ruling in favor of the NRDC's position. It found that there was "insufficient record to sustain a rule limiting consideration of the environmental effects of nuclear waste disposal to the numerical values in Table S-3." It added that in light of the many uncertainties about waste disposal and the vague assurances offered by the AEC during the rule-making proceedings, the restrictions placed on consideration of waste issues were "capricious and arbitrary." The court ordered that those portions of the rule be "set aside and remanded." It also remanded the issuance of an operating license to Vermont Yankee until the NRC revised the rule, though it did not require that the plant be shut down.[12]

The court's decision demanded prompt attention from the NRC because it raised crucial questions about the validity of the agency's licensing procedures. The NRC had dozens of plant applications in the pipeline, and it faced unrelenting pressure from the nuclear industry and the Joint Committee on Atomic Energy to avoid undue delays in evaluating them. The trade magazine *Nuclear Industry* told its readers that the ruling "brought frustration and uncertainty" by causing "apprehension that the licensing processes would . . . be interrupted pending the outcome of court appeals, new rulemaking, or both." The NRC, after weighing its options, took immediate steps to meet the court's directives. On August 13, 1976, it announced that it would prepare a "thorough new staff analysis" of the environmental impact of the fuel cycle operations "associated with individual nuclear power plants." The staff analysis would reconsider and perhaps revise the estimates in Table S-3 and form the basis for an extended rule-making proceeding, which could take as long as one year.

While the staff worked on its report, the NRC suspended the issuance of construction permits or operating licenses. It made clear, however, that in light of the potentially "significant impacts on the availability and costs of nuclear power facilities," it sought to avoid a lengthy moratorium. It suggested that the staff's study might provide the basis for an interim rule that would allow the resumption of licensing by December 1976.[13]

About thirty staff members, under Bishop's direction, participated in a "flat out" effort to prepare the report, and it was published in October 1976. It was a detailed study that offered a more complete analysis of the potential environmental effects of dealing with waste from individual plants than the earlier AEC estimates had delivered. Unlike the AEC survey, for example, the NRC report did not assume that spent fuel would be reprocessed, and it considered the impact of storing and disposing of fuel rods that did not undergo reprocessing. It also made some modest changes in the estimates set forth in Table S-3. Despite its revisions of the AEC's approach, the NRC report reached the same general conclusions: "environmental impacts of fuel reprocessing and waste management as they relate to individual nuclear plants continue to be small, even when impacts which were not completely accounted for in the past are considered."[14]

Drawing on the staff's report, the NRC published a proposed interim rule for public comment. This was the first step toward incorporating the study's findings into the agency's regulations and toward a prompt resumption of licensing. On November 5, 1976, the NRC announced that for applications that met other requirements, it would issue new construction permits and operating licenses on a conditional basis that depended on the adoption of the interim rule. It argued that this procedure was appropriate because of the improbability that the staff's finding about the "slight" impact of reprocessing and waste management from individual plants would "prove to be dramatically in error." The NRC's action triggered an immediate response from the NRDC. The environmental group protested that the NRC's staff report was seriously deficient and demonstrated the agency's "present inability to provide reasonable assurance that safe disposal of radioactive wastes will in fact be carried out in the future." It petitioned the NRC for a rule-making proceeding to "make a definitive finding" on whether high-level wastes could be "safely disposed of." It also requested a halt in licensing "until such time as this definitive finding of safety can be and is made."[15]

The NRDC petition went beyond the earlier question of the impact of fuel cycle operations related to individual nuclear plants. It addressed the broader issue of the safety of waste disposal practices. The commissioners and staff of the NRC deliberated over the new petition at length. They recognized that a "definitive" finding about waste could not be made, and they rejected the appeal for an indefinite moratorium on licensing. Nevertheless, they wished to make clear their commitment to resolving waste problems. In June 1977 the NRC denied the petition for rule-making but explained at some length that it believed "that the wastes can and will in due course be disposed of safely." It argued that it had no obligation to produce a "definitive" finding on waste as long as it was "reasonably confident that permanent disposal . . . can be accomplished safely when it is likely to become necessary." The agency contended that it had ample basis for such confidence, largely because of the greatly increased resources ERDA was devoting to waste issues and the progress it was making toward a solution. "The technology for disposal is reasonably available," it declared, "and the studies done to date, while not conclusive, are nevertheless promising for timely and safe implementation for the technology." The NRC's denial of the petition did not put to rest questions surrounding "waste confidence," but its position on considering waste in the licensing process received support from the United States Supreme Court. In April 1978 the Supreme Court reversed the 1976 Court of Appeals decision that the NRC's use of Table S-3 to evaluate the environmental impact of fuel cycle operations for individual nuclear plants was "insufficient." It ruled that agencies should have wide latitude to administer their own rule-making procedures.[16]

THE END OF COMMERCIAL REPROCESSING

At the same time that the NRC was examining a series of questions surrounding the prospects for safe management of radioactive waste, it was studying the protection of nuclear plants from sabotage and nuclear materials from theft, which had generated a great deal of controversy during the AEC's last few years. The safeguards issue, in turn, was directly related to the reprocessing of spent reactor fuel. The nuclear industry regarded reprocessing as essential to assure an adequate supply of fuel in the future. Nuclear critics contended that reprocessing, by isolating large quantities of plutonium, would not only expand the opportunities for terrorists to build an atomic bomb but also promote the international proliferation of nuclear weapons among nation-states. The differences over reprocessing had emerged as an increasingly visible source of debate when the AEC published its draft "generic environmental statement on the use of mixed oxide fuel in light-water reactors," or GESMO, in August 1974. The AEC's conclusion that the safeguards problem was "manageable" in the production of mixed oxide fuel had triggered strong objections from the NRDC and others. The deliberations over reprocessing and GESMO were among the complex, contentious, and unresolved issues that the NRC inherited from the AEC.

On January 20, 1975, the day after the NRC began operations, the Council on Environmental Quality (CEQ), a White House office that reported to the president, offered its views on GESMO. Chairman Russell W. Peterson told NRC chairman Anders that the AEC's draft GESMO report was a "high quality effort," but he urged the NRC to deal fully with safeguards issues before making any final decisions on reprocessing. "The potential impacts of the diversion and illicit use of . . . nuclear materials are well recognized," Peterson wrote. "This threat is so grave that it could determine the acceptability of plutonium recycle as a viable component of this Nation's nuclear electric power system." The term "recycle" referred to the reuse of fissionable material after its recovery through reprocessing. Peterson suggested that the NRC would fail to comply with the National Environmental Policy Act if it did not provide more than the AEC's "summary treatment" of safeguards in its environmental review.[17]

Peterson's comments, along with those of members of Congress and others who took a similar position on GESMO, placed the NRC in the middle of the rancorous battle over plutonium. The NRC quickly committed itself to upgrading safeguards requirements for nuclear power plants; as a first step it decided to sponsor a series of studies in which outside experts would report on the status of and possible approaches to safeguards issues. But if it agreed to Peterson's request that it delay a decision on reprocessing until it thoroughly investigated safeguards alternatives and settled on a course of action, it would arouse strong protests from the nuclear industry and government officials who focused primarily on national energy policies. The NRC staff told the commissioners in February 1975 that accepting Peterson's recommendation could postpone a final decision on reprocessing for two years or more. This, in turn, could "adversely affect the national energy supply over the next decade" by contributing to uncertainties about nuclear power economics and the availability of uranium fuel. The *Wall Street Journal* observed a short time later, "Already the industry is chafing over the delays that are likely before it can begin using plutonium."[18]

After lengthy consideration of its options, in April 1975, the commissioners decided, provisionally, to follow the recommendations of the

CEQ. The NRC issued an announcement that cited the impact of Peterson's letter to Anders and indicated that it would wait for the results of the safeguards studies then underway before making a final decision on reprocessing. It estimated that this would occur by early or mid-1978—three years away. Recognizing the impact of its action on the nuclear industry, the NRC invited public comments that it would weigh before making a firm commitment to its projected schedule. The agency's tentative decision to postpone a ruling on reprocessing, according to *Nuclear Industry,* "set the industry in a tizzy." It not only fostered short-term doubts about the timely licensing of the Barnwell reprocessing facility in South Carolina but also raised long-term concerns that "plutonium recycle might be permanently prohibited." Carl Walske, president of the Atomic Industrial Forum, which promoted the industrial applications of nuclear energy, called the NRC's statement "deplorable." His judgment was seconded by a senior official in the White House. James Cannon, assistant to the president for domestic affairs, complained to President Ford that "if the NRC decision becomes final, it will have a major, negative impact on the 'nuclear option' and on the industry."[19]

The NRC received more than two hundred comments on the proposed approach to reprocessing. A clear but not overwhelming majority, largely representing nuclear utilities and vendors, objected to the agency's plan to wait for the completion of its safeguards studies before deciding on the use of mixed oxide fuels. The NRC weighed the arguments presented by both sides and deliberated over its options with care and considerable agony. On November 11, 1975, it announced a new policy for GESMO, approved unanimously by the commissioners, that attempted to find middle ground. The NRC pledged to expedite its review of safeguards programs and set a target of mid-1976 for completion. Its findings would be published as a supplement to the AEC's draft GESMO report and followed by public hearings. The NRC hoped that those procedures would allow it to make a final decision on the use of mixed oxide fuel by early 1977. In the meantime, it would consider on a case-by-case basis the limited use of mixed oxide fuel in light-water reactors and the interim licensing of fuel reprocessing and fabrication plants. Since no commercial reprocessing plants were operating and only a small amount of mixed oxide fuel was being produced, the NRC did not anticipate that "substantial use" of mixed oxide fuel was possible until the mid-1980s, long after it reached a final decision on GESMO.[20]

The agency's announcement received a sharply divergent response along predictable lines. The industry, encouraged by the accelerated schedule the NRC proposed, expressed cautious optimism. Anders told a press conference that the primary objective of the agency's approach was to "remove the uncertainty that prevails in industry in the absence of a final decision on plutonium recycle." As a result, *Nuclear Industry* reported, "industry had good reason to applaud the way NRC is dealing with the issue." Nuclear critics, by contrast, were incensed. Gus Speth, an attorney with the NRDC, accused the NRC of reversing its previous position and added, "In brushing aside statements of concern regarding plutonium, . . . the Commission has said in effect that it is more interested in reassuring the nuclear industry than in reassuring the public. In so doing, the new agency has shown that it has no more stomach for opposing the industry than did the AEC."[21]

The NRC's projected schedule for deciding on the use of mixed oxide fuel soon proved optimistic. In December 1975 the NRDC and the state of New York sued the NRC over its approach to GESMO. They objected most stringently to the plan to allow interim licensing of reprocessing and fuel fabrication plants and limited use of mixed oxide fuel in light-water reactors. In May 1976 the United States Court of Appeals for the Second Circuit ruled that the NRC must refrain from issuing licenses for the production and use of plutonium fuel until it reached a final decision on GESMO. Although the impact of the court's ruling was uncertain, it seemed likely to delay further a final NRC determination on reprocessing and GESMO, the schedule for which was already slipping under the burden of complex safeguards issues.[22]

While the NRC was investigating safeguards, deliberating over the format for public hearings on GESMO, and deciding on a response to the Court of Appeals ruling, the question of reprocessing was receiving unprecedented national attention. One indication of the importance reprocessing had assumed was that both the *New York Times* and the *Washington Post* ran lengthy editorials supporting the judgment of the Court of Appeals. The issue gained additional prominence in the 1976 election campaigns of President Ford and his Democratic challenger, Jimmy Carter. As a candidate for his party's nomination for president, Carter emphasized his strong commitment to nonproliferation and his skepticism about nuclear power. In his campaign autobiography, *Why Not the Best?* he wrote, "The biggest waste and danger of all is the unnecessary proliferation of atomic weapons throughout the world. Our ultimate goal should be the elimination of nuclear-weapon capability among all nations." Carter also expressed reservations about nuclear power by declaring that its use should be "kept to the minimum necessary to meet our needs."[23]

Carter's thinking on the reprocessing issue followed logically from his views on proliferation and nuclear power. On May 13, 1976, he delivered a heavily publicized speech to an energy conference at the United Nations in New York. He cited the risks of nuclear power that reactor accidents, terrorist threats, and radioactive waste presented and continued: "Beyond these dangers, there is the fearsome prospect that the spread of nuclear reactors will mean the spread of nuclear weapons to many nations." He went on to explain, "The danger is not so much in the spread of nuclear reactors themselves, for nuclear reactor fuel is not suitable for use directly in the production of nuclear weapons. The far greater danger lies in the spread of facilities for the enrichment of uranium and the reprocessing of spent reactor fuel." Carter took a similar stance on domestic reprocessing. In a speech in San Diego in September 1976, he announced that, if elected, he would "seek to withhold authority for domestic reprocessing until the need for the economics, and the safety of the technology is clearly demonstrated."[24]

Carter's pronouncements prodded the Ford White House to undertake an extensive study of its options and positions on nuclear issues. Even before Carter outlined his views, Ford and his staff had attempted to sort out the problems they faced and the objectives they sought in the nation's atomic energy programs. In his State of the Union message in 1975, Ford had cited the need for two hundred nuclear power plants by 1985. But it was apparent that many uncertainties had to be resolved to achieve that goal, and the White House staff had considered how to deal with reprocessing, waste management, reactor safety, public concerns about nuclear power, and other matters. Carter's statements, especially his emphasis on the relationship between nuclear power and the threat of proliferation, gave increased urgency to Ford's determination to reach conclusions on nuclear energy policies and make his policies clear to the public.[25]

In summer 1976 the administration conducted an extensive interagency review of its positions on nuclear issues. It was coordinated by Robert Fri, deputy administrator of ERDA, who was committed to a thorough and frank assessment of policy options. The study dealt at length with international and domestic issues, including reprocessing, which could have a major impact on both. Fri told the president on August 13 that in his view "the U.S. stand on the use of plutonium recycle should rest on the policy that our purely economic interests will never dominate our nonproliferation goals." On the international front, this was, he said, "essential to our success in persuading other countries to adopt stringent controls over the proliferation of plutonium." On the domestic front, "relatively little is at stake, at least in the short run." Fri argued that the economic benefits of plutonium recycle were small and perhaps nonexistent and that a judgment on its importance for the future of the nuclear industry could wait for several years.[26]

The Fri review cited four alternatives for reprocessing. They ranged from continuing existing policies, which assumed that domestic reprocessing and plutonium recycle would be carried out, to forceful opposition to reprocessing in the United States and abroad. Although the agencies involved in the study did not all agree on a choice of policy options, none indicated support for the existing approach. A consensus favored an option that specified that "reprocessing should go ahead domestically and abroad only if safety, safeguards and economic benefits can be demonstrated clearly." Ford accepted the recommendations of his advisers. On October 28, 1976, he released a fourteen-page, single-spaced statement on nuclear policy. While affirming his strong commitment to nuclear power and pointing out that the United States alone could not control proliferation, he announced, "I have concluded that the reprocessing and recycling of plutonium should not proceed unless there is sound reason to conclude that the world community can effectively overcome the associated risks of proliferation. . . . The United States should no longer regard reprocessing of used nuclear fuel to produce plutonium as a necessary and inevitable step."[27]

By election day of 1976, both candidates had expressed deep reservations about the wisdom of and need for reprocessing spent fuel. As a result of the campaign, the relationship between reprocessing, safeguards, and proliferation took on even greater visibility and scrutiny as a public policy issue. This was not a welcome development for an embattled nuclear power industry. Industry officials insisted that recycling was essential for the growth of nuclear power and for providing adequate energy supplies in the future. Even before Ford released his statement, they made clear that they were "*very* concerned" that his views on proliferation and reprocessing "not have an adverse impact on the development of conventional nuclear power plants" (original emphasis).[28]

Carter's victory in the election left the nuclear industry uncertain about the treatment it would receive. *Nuclear News* reported on the prevailing attitude at a meeting of nuclear professionals: "Everyone had

President-elect Jimmy Carter on the brain, trying to guess what his *real* position on nuclear power would be" (original emphasis). Carter acted quickly to decide on his position. The day after he took office, national security adviser Zbigniew Brzezinski informed the heads of agencies involved in nuclear issues that the president had ordered a "thorough review" of U.S. policies regarding proliferation, including reprocessing. While the administration was conducting its study, an influential report on nuclear power, sponsored by the Ford Foundation and administered by the MITRE Corporation, was released. The report, titled *Nuclear Power: Issues and Choices,* was written by a team of experts, several of whom had since received appointments in the Carter administration. The Ford-MITRE report called for the indefinite suspension of reprocessing. Contending that proliferation was "the most serious risk associated with nuclear power," it concluded that "there is no compelling reason at this time to introduce plutonium or to anticipate its introduction in this century."[29]

On April 7, 1977, Carter issued a statement on nuclear policy that was consistent with his own views, his campaign speeches, and the conclusions of the Ford-MITRE report. He announced, "We will defer indefinitely the commercial reprocessing and recycling of the plutonium produced in the U.S. nuclear power programs." Although affirming that the "benefits of nuclear power are . . . very real and practical," he stated that "a viable and economic nuclear power program can be sustained without . . . reprocessing and recycling."[30]

While reprocessing was debated during the election campaign and considered by White House officials, the NRC carried on its deliberations over GESMO. In November 1976 it opened public hearings on the environmental and safety aspects of reprocessing. Carter's nuclear power policy statement on April 7, 1977, raised questions within the NRC about whether it should continue weighing GESMO issues in light of the president's intention to defer reprocessing. As an independent regulatory agency, it was not obligated to follow Carter's policies, but it wanted to "work constructively" with the White House. The commissioners decided to suspend GESMO proceedings and to solicit comments from the president and the public on what it should do about reprocessing. On May 5, 1977, chairman Rowden sent a letter to Carter asking for his "views on the relationship of your non-proliferation and national nuclear energy policies to the issues confronting the Commission." Stuart E. Eizenstat, assistant to the president for domestic affairs and policy, replied five months later. He advised the NRC that the "President believes that his non-proliferation initiatives would be assisted both domestically and internationally if the Commission were to terminate the GESMO proceedings."[31]

Eizenstat's letter was a clear expression of the administration's preferences, but it did not in itself settle the question of how to proceed with GESMO. It was not binding on the NRC, and the agency elected to ask for public comments on the Eizenstat letter and on the views of the NRC staff before arriving at a decision. The thirty-seven public comments it received largely reiterated previous positions on GESMO. On December 23, 1977, the commissioners, only one of whom was a Carter appointee, voted 4–0 to terminate GESMO. They did so to show respect for Carter's request and to support the goal of nonproliferation. The commissioners overruled the NRC staff's recommendation that GESMO be deferred rather than terminated.[32]

ERDA'S SEARCH FOR A WASTE DISPOSAL SITE

The end of commercial reprocessing had serious consequences for the management of radioactive waste, though those consequences were not a major consideration in the policy deliberations over the use of plutonium for generating nuclear power. While the White House weighed the potential impact of reprocessing on nonproliferation and safeguards objectives and the NRC dealt with regulatory issues, the Energy Research and Development Administration, in accordance with its mandate in the Energy Reorganization Act, actively sought suitable means for storing and disposing of nuclear wastes.

Shortly after it began operations, ERDA had moved away from the AEC's position that retrievable surface storage offered a satisfactory short-term solution for handling high-level commercial waste. The AEC had received sharp criticism of its plans from environmental groups, EPA, and others, who had suggested that building a surface storage facility would delay and perhaps terminate the search for a permanent repository. "Some people," observed Frank Pittman, who had joined ERDA when the AEC disbanded, "have said that ERDA has no intention of ever going for permanent disposal, but just plans to put it in the desert and monitor and maintain it forever." In light of those concerns, ERDA decided to completely rewrite the AEC's draft environmental impact statement on waste management. It withdrew a budget request for work on a retrievable storage site and announced that it would undertake a "comprehensive reevaluation" of its waste programs. Without abandoning surface storage, it decided to reconsider its alternatives and to place much greater emphasis on finding a permanent disposal site.[33]

ERDA staff members had no illusions that resolving outstanding waste issues would be easy. They were confident that technical solutions would be available, but they were much less certain about the outcome of the "political and societal questions" that nuclear power and waste disposal raised. They warned that the "nation's nuclear power program is now approaching a point of crisis" because of the "problems that have developed in the 'back end' of the fuel cycle." With both technical and political considerations in mind, ERDA requested an increase in funding for research and development on commercial waste programs, from about $12 million in fiscal year 1976 to almost $60 million in fiscal year 1977. It hoped to have at least one federal repository open for permanent disposal of commercial wastes by 1985.[34]

ERDA officials were keenly aware that the AEC had not treated waste disposal as a priority issue during most of its existence, and they had ample means and motivation to attack the problem aggressively. But the alternatives for deciding on the best approach to permanent disposal were the same as those the AEC had identified. A five-volume report that ERDA published in May 1976 cited three fundamental methods of "final isolation and disposal": transmutation of the elements in radioactive waste to less hazardous or long-lasting forms; "extraterrestrial ejection" by ferrying wastes into space in rockets; and placement into geologic sites. Neither of the first two options was close to proven or demonstrably practical, which left geologic disposal as the only plausible alternative. ERDA sponsored research in thirty-six states in 1976–77 to investigate the possibility of depositing radioactive waste in bedded salt, salt domes, shale, granite, quartz, and other formations. It hoped to develop six repositories in different geologic media by the mid-1990s. Based on the extensive research conducted by the AEC during the 1960s, it regarded salt beds as the likeliest setting for the first facilities to be built. "The work we've done on bedded salt to date indicates that it is not only acceptable," Pittman commented, "but, as far as we can tell, the best method of ultimate disposal."[35]

Carter's decision to suspend commercial reprocessing complicated the search for a permanent waste repository on both a short-term and a long-term basis. In the short term, it drastically modified the industry's plans to send spent fuel to a reprocessing facility. It was clear that the Barnwell reprocessing plant would not be completed in the foreseeable future, if ever. This was a critical issue for many plant owners because of a looming shortage of storage space for spent fuel rods. The NRC estimated that twenty-three reactors might be forced to shut down by 1983 because of this growing and largely unanticipated problem. Some utilities took measures to expand the capacity of spent fuel pools, but they did not regard such an approach as more than a holding action until the government developed a permanent solution to waste storage and disposal.[36]

The end of commercial reprocessing and the pending need for spent fuel storage capacity brought surface storage back to the forefront. Carter's energy adviser, James R. Schlesinger, had strongly supported building monitored retrievable surface storage vaults to hold spent fuel for decades as chairman of the AEC in the early 1970s. He pushed for this approach again as a member of the White House staff. The proposal for long-term surface storage was sharply criticized by some knowledgeable observers. Robert C. Seamans Jr., who had served as ERDA administrator under President Ford, feared that it would diminish the resources available for locating a suitable geologic site and commented that building a surface storage facility was "just temporizing." The NRC's William Bishop argued that a revitalized focus on surface storage demonstrated "a clear lack of confidence in the viability of the geologic disposal concept." He complained that it would place the NRC "in the logically awkward position of being asked to license reactors that will produce wastes without assurance that the wastes can and will be disposed of safely."[37]

Nevertheless, the Carter administration moved ahead with another form of surface storage as a way to deal with the immediate problems of handling spent fuel that would not be reprocessed. In August 1977 the president signed a law that created the cabinet-level Department of Energy (DOE), and he immediately named Schlesinger secretary of energy. ERDA was one of many agencies across the federal government whose functions were assigned to the new department. On October 18, 1977, with the approval of the president, the department announced its policy for storing spent fuel. It offered to place fuel rods in a temporary "away-from-reactor" storage facility in return for a onetime fee that utilities would pay. The department acknowledged that its proposal would require the siting and construction of both storage and permanent disposal facilities. But it suggested that the plan would mitigate the "increasing uncertainty in the utilities' economic calculations." Away-from-reactor storage differed from the AEC's earlier concept of monitored retrievable storage. The Carter administration regarded away-from-reactor storage as a short-term measure that would alleviate a pressing but temporary shortage of space for spent fuel. It would serve as a halfway shelter between a power reactor and a permanent geologic repository. Schlesinger suggested that the nearly completed Barnwell plant would be a logical site for commercial away-from-reactor storage.[38]

The indefinite deferral of reprocessing also had a significant impact on planning for a high-level waste repository. Reprocessing spent fuel would make most of the plutonium available for use in a mixed oxide form, but this would not occur in the disposal of fuel assemblies. Therefore, planning for a waste repository necessarily had to account for an increased amount of plutonium-239 and its extraordinarily long half-life of 24,000 years. If spent fuel was reprocessed, high-level wastes still included other transuranic elements with even longer half-lives, so the problem was more quantitative than qualitative. DOE did not regard the technical aspects of containing plutonium as insurmountable. Although airborne plutonium was indisputably extremely hazardous, the available evidence indicated that plutonium exposure in ways other than inhalation was much less dangerous. Uptake by plants from the soil was limited, and plutonium in food consumed by humans largely passed through the body quickly without being absorbed. Plutonium's "strong sorption" qualities in geologic media made it likely to attach to rock formations. Even if it reached groundwater, it did not dissolve in water, and it did not appear to be transported in large quantities if deposited in groundwater or surface streams. Radioactive waste experts were more concerned about the long-range risk of other transuranics, especially technetium-99. It has a half-life of about 213,000 years and can reach and be carried by groundwater more easily than plutonium. EPA estimated that over a period of 10,000 years, radioactive waste could cause between one hundred and one thousand fatal cancers. About 90 percent of those deaths would be attributable to technetium-99; less than one percent would be attributable to plutonium-239.

Government and industry officials recognized the difficulties of disposing of plutonium and other transuranics, but the political aspects of the issue seemed at least as formidable. The deferral and possible termination of reprocessing made the political situation more trying. Despite the views of experts, the public was especially fearful of plutonium. An article in *Fortune* magazine in 1979 noted that plutonium was "widely thought to be the deadliest element in reactor wastes." Robert V. Laney, deputy director of Argonne National Laboratory, told an industry group that without the removal of most plutonium through reprocessing, the ability of a waste disposal site to contain the element over thousands of years could not be convincingly demonstrated to the public. The result, he suggested, was "a stark threat to the U.S. nuclear energy system, surpassing all previous threats."[39]

A "PERSISTENT" PUBLIC CONCERN

From all indications, public concern about the feasibility and risks of nuclear waste continued to increase in the mid-1970s, in lockstep with the growing intensity and breadth of the national debate over nuclear power. Harvey Brooks, a prominent physicist at Harvard University and chairman of a National Academy of Sciences committee on nuclear power, commented, "No single aspect of nuclear power has excited so persistent a public concern as has radioactive waste management. . . . I would predict that, should nuclear energy ultimately prove to be socially unacceptable, it will be primarily because of the public perception of the waste disposal problem." Opinion polls provided support for Brooks's judgment. Harris surveys taken in 1975 and 1976, for example, showed that 63 and 67 percent of those questioned, respectively, identified radioactive wastes as a "major" problem arising from the use of nuclear power. The participants in the polls placed misgivings about waste far ahead of such matters as the release of radioactive effluents, the risk of nuclear accidents, and terrorist threats to nuclear plants and materials. Although the public did not appear to be well acquainted with radioactive waste issues, it was clearly disturbed by what it knew. In light of public attitudes toward waste of any kind, this was perhaps unavoidable. One scholar has described "waste landscapes" as "objects of cultural scorn" that arose from "their hideous, mundane nature." Combined with acute public fears of radiation in any form, it was not surprising that the public became increasingly troubled about the disposal of radioactive wastes.[40]

Antinuclear activists, whose position earned growing visibility and strength during the mid- and late 1970s, sought to capitalize on public concern about radioactive waste to advance their cause. In 1976, for example, an initiative spearheaded by nuclear opponents in California called for a phaseout of nuclear power in the state if, among other things, the waste disposal question was not resolved in a timely manner. The nuclear industry lobbied hard to defeat the measure, and voters rejected it by a margin of two to one. Nevertheless, the campaign called attention to uncertainties about how industry and the government would deal with the long-term hazards of radioactive waste. The state of California passed a law in June 1976 that prohibited the construction of new nuclear plants until a satisfactory method for dealing with the waste problem was demonstrated.[41]

Newspaper and magazine articles and television stories reported on the waste problem in tones that ranged from dispassionate to frightening. An hour-long special on NBC television in January 1977, titled *Danger! Radioactive Waste,* was a prominent example of an alarming presentation. It described nuclear waste as a "radioactive monster with no cage to keep it in" and storage sites as "cemeteries without headstones" and "colossal graves." It suggested that livestock in the area of a low-level disposal site in Kentucky had died from small releases from the facility and that twin sons of a worker at West Valley suffered severe congenital deformity from his exposure to radiation. The reaction to the program accentuated the deeply polarized nature of the nuclear power controversy. Daniel F. Ford, executive director of the Union of Concerned Scientists, told the producer, Joan Konner, that the show was "terrific." The Atomic Industrial Forum, in contrast, called it "a classic propaganda piece in the guise of news." Several pro-nuclear individuals and organizations asked the National News Council, which had been formed in 1973 to investigate complaints of media bias, to review the waste documentary. In November 1977 the council concluded that the segments of the program that linked radioactive waste to livestock deaths and genetic disorders carried "scare tactics beyond the limits of sound journalism." But it also commended NBC for "bringing this substantial controversy [over radioactive waste] to the attention of its viewers."[42]

By the time the National News Council reported on the NBC program, it was abundantly clear that waste disposal had captured the attention of sizable sectors of the population. In 1976, when ERDA had begun preliminary investigations for waste disposal sites, it encountered determined and vocal opposition. Its plan to drill on the shores of Lake Huron in Michigan to test the suitability of salt formations for a waste repository was aborted by local protests. Citizens and state officials also raised objections to ERDA's tentative proposals to search for geologic sites in Louisiana, South Dakota, and Vermont. Faced with stern resistance in potential host states, ERDA and then DOE officials increasingly placed their hopes for a technically and politically acceptable location in the three western states that had a long and congenial relationship with nuclear energy programs—New Mexico, Washington, and Nevada. DOE was making progress toward establishing a repository in salt deposits near Carlsbad, New Mexico, for transuranic wastes from weapons production plants. But local opposition to the project was growing, and DOE fretted about the possibility that no state would agree to the construction of a commercial high-level waste facility within its borders. When asked what would happen in such a situation, John M. Deutch, director of the department's Office of Energy Research, responded, "I worry about that. I don't know."[43]

While concern among the general public about radioactive waste surged, specialized segments of the population, specifically the nuclear industry and the scientific community, addressed both the technical and political aspects of the problem. Their efforts to provide perspective on and offer solutions for outstanding waste issues met with, at best, mixed results.

As the Atomic Industrial Forum's response to the NBC program demonstrated, the industry was exasperated by what it regarded as greatly inflated public fears of nuclear waste. Bertram Wolfe, vice president and general manager of General Electric's nuclear energy division, was a prominent spokesman for industry views on the subject. In late 1975, for example, he declared that he was a proponent not only of nuclear power but also of conservation, solar power, geothermal power, coal power, and any other way to meet the nation's energy demands. He was distressed by campaigns to shut down nuclear power because "it would be foolhardy to eliminate a source of energy which may be a vital part of a meaningful solution to our energy problem." He pointed out that the annual volume of solid waste from a thousand-megawatt power reactor would fill about two railroad cars and that most of it was low-level material. Waste from the same-sized coal plant, by comparison, would fill twelve thousand railroad cars.

Wolfe acknowledged that plutonium was a "hazardous material" but complained that nuclear opponents had exaggerated its dangers "to frighten people." He said that claims that a nuclear plant produced enough plutonium to kill every person on earth were no more relevant than stating that Lake Tahoe contained enough water to drown the entire world. The long half-life of plutonium sounded ominous, but Wolfe compared it to arsenic, which has no half-life because it never decays. He suggested that the United States imported enough arsenic "each year to kill five billion people." He also emphasized that the dangers posed by plutonium were not unique. The properties and biological hazards of plutonium are similar to radium-226, a radioactive element with a half-life of 1,500 years. There was so much naturally occurring radium-226 in the ocean, Wolfe argued, that "if a thousand nuclear plants operated for 100 years and all of the plutonium in the waste was deposited uniformly in the ocean it would raise the biological hazard from radioactivity by less than a hundredth of a percent compared to that of the radium 226 already there."

Wolfe made clear that his arguments were not intended to minimize the problems of dealing with radioactive waste but to offer more context than the public received from nuclear critics. "In contrast to wastes from fossil fuel energy sources," he submitted, "nuclear wastes can be practically and economically isolated from the environment." The nuclear industry contended not only that safe disposal of waste from its plants was possible but also that action was needed without delay to end the existing uncertainties and to reassure the public. An Atomic Industrial Forum study group, chaired by Wolfe, concluded in October 1978, "It is urgent from a public confidence standpoint, to have waste disposal demonstrated at the earliest possible date."[44]

SCIENTIFIC ASSESSMENTS OF WASTE DISPOSAL

As radioactive waste management took on increasing visibility and urgency, several scientific organizations sponsored careful reviews of the technical questions surrounding geologic disposal. In late 1977 the Study Group on Nuclear Fuel Cycles and Waste Management, established by the American Physical Society, a leading professional organization for physicists, released a lengthy report. The members of the study group supplied expertise in a broad range of scientific and engineering fields, and their work received financial support from the National Science Foundation. They sought to provide "an independent evaluation of the technical issues in nuclear fuel cycles and waste management." The panel reached optimistic conclusions about the technical prospects for developing satisfactory methods of disposal. "Safe and reliable management of nuclear waste," it asserted, "can be accomplished with technologies that either exist or involve straightforward extension of existing capabilities." It further suggested that there were "no important technical barriers to the development of a repository on a pilot plant scale by 1985." According to the study group, "many" suitable geologic sites were available in the United States for high-level and transuranic commercial wastes. In a departure from the prevailing view of DOE, it suggested that although salt deposits could "be a satisfactory medium," other types of formations, granite or shale in particular, "could offer even greater long-term advantages." It recommended that alternatives to salt be thoroughly investigated.[45]

Other scientific groups soon advanced similar conclusions. They offered sanguine assessments of the long-term prospects for identifying suitable geologic settings for high-level waste but expressed doubts that using salt formations was the best approach. This was a question of importance and immediacy because DOE had indicated that the first commercial waste sites it opened would probably be located in salt deposits. In June 1978 the U.S. Geological Survey published a report that underscored the uncertainties of placing high-level wastes in salt. It echoed the general concerns that the Kansas Geological Survey had aired during the Lyons controversy about the effects of heat from radioactive waste. The new study declared that thermal energy could "cause complex and mechanical changes," which could, in turn, threaten the integrity of the site. It called for research on a series of difficult matters, including the behavior of salt formations under thermal or other forms of stress, the movement of radioactive materials in groundwater, and the inherent weaknesses of predictive models for geologic repositories. A draft of a report prepared by a panel of eminent earth scientists for EPA took the same position on the need for more reliable data before making determinations on high-level waste. It cited its dismay that little information was available on alternatives to salt.

The conclusion of scientific experts that much work remained to be done before a satisfactory solution to waste management could be established increased skepticism about DOE's plans to open a repository by the mid-1980s and, more important, about the likelihood of reaching clear-cut judgments on geologic disposal within a reasonably short time. A draft paper prepared by the White House Office of Science and Technology Policy in 1978 suggested that "the knowledge and technology base available today is not yet sufficient to permit complete confidence in the safety of any particular repository design or the suitability of any particular site." Rustum Roy, director of the Materials Research Laboratory at Pennsylvania State University and chair of a National Academy of Sciences panel on solidification of high-level liquid wastes, argued that delaying a decision on the best approach to high-level waste was far preferable to acting too quickly. He regretted that "a lack of foresight and a misplacement of priorities" had prevented scientists from agreeing on a solution earlier but cautioned, "If we panic and rush into production of a waste-storage system now, before we've had a chance to explore the possibilities, we may force the American taxpayer to spend billions of dollars needlessly and find ourselves in the position, two or three years from now, of retracting our steps to find the most cost-effective solution."[46]

THE INTERAGENCY REVIEW GROUP REPORT

By early 1978 it was clear that the search for a commercial high-level waste site was mired in political controversy and technical uncertainty. Although experts were confident that a satisfactory method of disposal would be found, they were much less so about what geologic formation was most promising, where a repository would be located, or when it would be ready to receive waste. In February 1978 a DOE task force, chaired by John Deutch, submitted a detailed report on the status of existing programs and the options available for waste storage and disposal. It estimated that the target date for opening a repository would need to be pushed back at least to 1988 and perhaps to 1993. But it did not attempt to reach conclusions about the best approach to waste disposal. This caused considerable consternation among members of Congress. Senator Frank Church, who was still waiting for the removal of transuranic wastes from the National Reactor Testing Station that the AEC had promised in 1970, snapped at Deutch, "Why can't you just pick a plan and say, 'this is it?' "[47]

On March 13, 1978, in the unsettled environment of the nuclear waste debate, President Carter established an "interagency Nuclear Waste Management Task Force" to make recommendations for an "Administration policy with respect to long-term management of nuclear wastes," both military and commercial. Despite Carter's reservations about nuclear power, he viewed it as an essential component of his energy policy. He and his advisers were convinced that resolving the political and technical complexities of the waste issue was critical to the long-term prospects for the nuclear industry.

Carter directed the interagency task force to make policy recommendations to him by October 1. He appointed Secretary of Energy Schlesinger as chair, though Deutch soon assumed that post. The task force, which adopted the name Interagency Review Group on Nuclear Waste Management (IRG), included representatives of thirteen executive agencies. The NRC participated in its deliberations in a nonvoting capacity to avoid compromising its independent regulatory status.[48]

At the IRG's first meeting, Deutch announced that he expected the task force to draw up an administration position on "how nuclear waste is to be managed" and a policy statement on the "technical adequacy of geologic disposal." The IRG held a series of public meetings, member agencies submitted lengthy reports, and DOE took up the herculean task of completing a draft under a short deadline. On October 19, 1978, after early versions were reviewed by participating organizations and revised in light of sometimes harsh criticism, the IRG released a draft of its report for public comment. Despite its ambitious objectives, the new study did not advance the debate over waste much beyond previous investigations. The IRG concluded that "successful isolation of radioactive wastes from the biosphere appears feasible for thousands of years," but it acknowledged that much research was required before a specific site or geologic medium could be designated. In the meantime, it urged that the president's spent fuel surface storage plan be "aggressively implemented."

In addition to reviewing the technical aspects of waste management, the IRG carefully examined what it called "institutional issues." These issues included relationships between federal agencies, the licensing and regulatory authority of the NRC, and the role of state and local officials in dealing with the waste problem. The IRG called for a cooperative arrangement that did not require "either exclusive federal pre-emption or state veto of waste control facilities." It contended that siting should be carried out on a "regional basis" to "help reduce local concern over the use of a single location for nuclear waste from all parts of the nation." It recommended that one or more "intermediate scale facilities" be built first—to be ready as early as 1988 or as late as 1995, depending on whether they used salt or some other geologic setting—and operated on a short-term basis to test both technical and institutional approaches to waste disposal.[49]

The reaction to the IRG draft was quite favorable but clearly reflected the polarized nature of the nuclear power debate. The nuclear industry was pleased with the IRG's affirmation that the safe disposal of high-level wastes appeared feasible. The Atomic Industrial Forum's Carl Walske commented that the report showed "a significant consensus that the detailed resolution of the nuclear waste question needn't deter the future development of nuclear power." Some antinuclear groups harshly attacked the IRG's position, though the Union of Concerned Scientists and the Natural Resources Defense Council issued a joint statement that applauded the study as "an honest appraisal of some of the significant technical and institutional problems associated with long-term management of radioactive wastes." The IRG received more than 3,300 public comments on its draft, mostly from industry representatives, public interest groups, and state and local government officials. Many of the comments criticized the task force from varying perspectives, for either trying to be impartial on the question of the future of nuclear power or, conversely, for failing to achieve a neutral stance.[50]

After considering the comments it received, the IRG released the final version of its report to the president in March 1979. In light of the conflicting views among outside reviewers and within the task force, it toned down its statement that the "successful isolation of radioactive wastes from the biosphere appears feasible for thousands of years." Instead, it suggested that "if appropriate site criteria are applied," the probability of human exposure to radiation from waste materials "would be quite small." It concluded that the "most likely" way that radiation from waste could reach the environment was by "dissolution and transport by groundwater" but contended that the effects could be reduced, perhaps to "innocuous levels," if the "flow rate and "flow path" of groundwater were "very slow and long" to allow the decay of radioactive elements.

In an understated way, the IRG advised against overreliance on geologic containment. It called for establishing multiple artificial barriers to guard against the escape of radiation even if groundwater penetrated the facility. Drawing on the recent studies by the U.S. Geological Survey and EPA, the IRG cited the importance of "waste form" that would "inhibit the release of radionuclides into the water." It viewed the packaging of high-level waste as an essential means of compensating for "geologic uncertainties." Despite its generally upbeat assessment, the IRG stated clearly that the "success of the program for the management and ultimate disposal of radioactive wastes critically depends upon the choice of technical strategies." And that decision could not be made with confidence until more information was available. The IRG stressed its collective view that in searching for the best technical approaches to the waste problem, federal agencies should *"interface directly and extensively with all interested and affected parties"* (emphasis in original). It cautioned that "the resolution of institutional issues . . . is equally important as the resolution of outstanding technical issues" and could prove to "be more difficult."[51]

A PRESIDENTIAL POLICY STATEMENT

Once the IRG completed its work, it shifted responsibility for deciding on an administration policy for radioactive waste to the White House. In a twenty-five-page, single-spaced memorandum, Stuart Eizenstat and

James T. McIntyre, director of the Office of Management and Budget, told President Carter that the agencies that participated in the IRG strongly favored a presidential policy statement on nuclear waste. They suggested that his "personal and public imprint on the new waste initiatives will be beneficial to the program, help focus and orient on-going public debate and demonstrate your interest in resolving this long-standing and troublesome public policy issue." Eizenstat and McIntyre cited the "political sensitivity" of the issue and argued that the administration's "first order of business" should be "to develop a framework for Federal/State cooperation in nuclear waste matters." After outlining the status of waste programs and summarizing the findings of the IRG report, they asked Carter for a decision on procedures for site selection of the first high-level commercial waste repository. They proposed four options for exploring "different geologic environments and diverse media" to choose "qualified" sites for licensing review by the NRC. Carter picked an option that called for "site selection after 4–5 sites qualified." But he also expressed his dissatisfaction in a handwritten note with the alternatives available to him: "You all seem to want to run an experiment instead of [to] find a waste disposal site(s) and use it (them)."[52]

After Carter made his decision on site selection, his staff drafted a wide-ranging policy statement that drew heavily on the findings of the IRG. The White House released it on February 12, 1980. The president announced that he was "establishing this Nation's first comprehensive radioactive waste management program." He faulted previous efforts to deal with the problem for falling short of being "technically adequate" and for failing "to involve successfully the States, local governments, and the public." As a first step toward effective cooperation with state and local authorities, Carter created the State Planning Council. He appointed Richard Riley, governor of South Carolina, to chair the council and revealed that he planned to add fourteen other governors and state officials to work with federal agencies on waste matters. On the delicate question of a state veto over waste sites, he pledged to follow "the principle of consultation and concurrence" but cautioned that this would work only if the "States participate as partners in the program."

The president declared that technical issues would be addressed by searching for sites that could accept both high-level waste from reprocessing and spent fuel rods. He explained that after four or five locations had qualified as potentially satisfactory, "one or more" would be chosen "for further development as a licensed full-scale repository." He hoped that the first such facility would be operating by the mid-1990s.

In a departure from the recommendations of the IRG, Carter made no mention of building "intermediate scale facilities." He urged that Congress pass legislation to carry out his earlier proposal for storing spent fuel while potential disposal sites were characterized, licensed, and constructed. Carter hailed the "substantial progress" that had been made in the area of waste management and promised to "proceed steadily and with determination to resolve the remaining technical issues while ensuring full public participation."[53]

Carter's policy statement was a milestone in efforts to manage radioactive waste because of both its visibility and its thoughtful, substantive proposals to address the technical and political aspects of the problem. Since 1975 DOE, the NRC, and many other federal agencies had devoted steadily increasing attention to radioactive waste, and their budget allocations had increased greatly. They recognized the importance of finding solutions to outstanding issues for the future of the nuclear power industry and for public health. Carter's statement was a serious, and indeed a laudable, attempt to deal with a difficult issue. But it was not sufficient to arrest the growing trend toward stalemate.

Despite their optimism that geologic formations, supported by artificial barriers, would provide safe sites for radioactive waste disposal, experts made clear that critical questions remained to be answered. They called for painstaking, wide-ranging, and time-consuming research to confirm their preliminary judgments and recognized, as the newer studies of salt indicated, that the outcome was far from certain. Meanwhile, the prospects appeared dim for away-from-reactor storage as an interim approach that Carter advocated and that industry favored to the point of near-desperation. *Nuclear Industry* reported in August 1979 that as the pending lack of space for spent fuel rods was "causing nightmares for utilities," DOE's request for an authorization to proceed with away-from-reactor storage received an "indifferent, leisurely yawn" in Congress.[54]

Carter's offer to include state and local officials in waste disposal planning and to allow for full public participation in the decision-making process was both sincere and necessary to accomplish his goals. But it did not in itself remedy or even mitigate the fundamental problem—increasingly prevalent and intense public concern about radioactive waste. The public's attitudes toward waste were tied directly and unavoidably to attitudes toward nuclear power, and by the late 1970s opposition to nuclear power had expanded substantially. The growth of the technology was the source of a highly publicized and highly polarized debate that *Fortune*, on March 12, 1979, called the "bitterest environmental confrontation of the Seventies." Less than three weeks later, the contention over nuclear power took on heightened prominence and acrimony after the severe accident at the Three Mile Island nuclear plant in Pennsylvania. A Harris poll taken shortly after the crisis asked whether participants believed that "there is no satisfactory way of disposing of radioactive waste from nuclear power plants." Sixty-three percent of those questioned thought the statement was true, 19 percent regarded it as false, and 19 percent did not know. Public attitudes were not immutable; a poll taken a few months later produced quite different results. In a January 1980 survey, 62 percent of participants agreed that the "disposal of nuclear waste is a problem that can be solved in an acceptable way." Nevertheless, despite variations in poll outcomes, it was clear that radioactive waste management was a matter of increasing discomfort for the public, especially in areas that were possible locations for waste facilities. Since it was unlikely that incontestable scientific evidence about the safety of any given site would be developed, public fears were a major barrier to finding technically and politically acceptable solutions to a series of complex and inherently unresolvable waste issues.[55]

CHAPTER 6

Commercial Low-Level Waste

A "Once Low Priority Matter"

During its twenty-eight-year existence, the AEC's principal concern in dealing with radioactive waste was how to safely store and dispose of high-level liquids and spent fuel rods. It paid far less attention to the handling and disposal of low-level materials, and despite complaints about its own practices from the National Academy of Sciences and other advisory groups, the AEC did not regard low-level radioactive waste as a serious problem. By the mid-1970s, however, after the discovery of unsatisfactory conditions and mismanagement at some commercial sites, low-level waste disposal had emerged as a prominent source of public controversy. As a result, the burial of commercial low-level wastes received unprecedented scrutiny and criticism. A report published by the U.S. House of Representatives Committee on Government Operations in July 1976 concluded that low-level waste was "one of the major unresolved nuclear issues." A short time later, *Nuclear Industry* told its readers that the "once low priority matter" had proven to be "shot through with major shortcomings."[1]

LAND BURIAL OF LOW-LEVEL WASTE

The lines that divided low-level waste from high-level waste were necessarily imprecise; any radioactive waste that did not fall within the category of high-level liquids from reprocessing or spent fuel rods was regarded as low-level—far less radioactive and much less dangerous than high-level waste. The AEC recognized that the large volume of low-level wastes created a potential hazard, but it was convinced that its practices at its own sites and its requirements for licensees who handled commercial low-level materials provided ample protection of public health. The revelation of leaks and careless procedures at commercial low-level waste sites and the intensity of the controversy that followed came as unwelcome and unforeseen developments.

The primary problem with regard to low-level waste that arose in the mid-1970s was disposal of slightly contaminated solid materials. Low-level solids included an expanding volume of waste products from commercial reactor operations, such as equipment, clothing, tools, filters, and resins. Nuclear power provided a large percentage of the low-level materials sent to commercial burial sites, but medical, industrial, and research activities also contributed such items as glassware, gloves, instruments, and animal carcasses. Low-level wastes could contain small amounts of transuranic elements. In the wake of the public outcry over ocean dumping during the late 1950s and early 1960s, the AEC had issued licenses for land burial of commercially generated solid low-level wastes. It believed that land burial was both cheaper and more convenient than ocean disposal, but carrying it out depended on finding suitable sites. The AEC also was concerned about ensuring that private companies would be able to manage waste operations in a competent and responsible manner over the long periods that were necessary for radioactive wastes. Eventually, it decided that it should not infringe on the "private business rights" of firms that might want to enter into waste disposal, but it stipulated that it would only grant licenses for sites located on land owned either by a state or the federal government.[2]

In 1962 the AEC issued its first license for commercial land burial of low-level waste. The Nuclear Engineering Company of Pleasanton, California, which had provided ocean disposal services since 1957, received approval to operate a burial site near Beatty, Nevada. The state of Nevada concurred in the AEC's licensing decision and leased land it owned to Nuclear Engineering. The Beatty license required that solid waste materials be packaged in "approved containers" that would be placed in trenches twenty feet deep. The containers at the top of the piles had to be covered by at least three feet of soil.[3]

The following year, state governments that had joined the AEC's recently established "state agreements program" awarded licenses for commercial low-level waste facilities at Maxey Flats, Kentucky, and

Figure 8. Workers excavate drums containing low-level solid radioactive waste at the National Reactor Testing Station in Idaho. (National Archives 434-SF-22-25)

West Valley, New York. The agreements program enabled state governments to assume certain health and safety functions that otherwise fell within the AEC's exclusive regulatory jurisdiction. By 1971 low-level sites were also operating at Sheffield, Illinois; Barnwell, South Carolina; and the Hanford reservation in Washington. With the exception of Hanford, where the federal government leased land to the state of Washington, the low-level waste sites were located on state-owned property. Five of the burial grounds were located in "agreement states" and therefore were regulated by state agencies (Nevada joined the program after the AEC licensed Beatty). Since Illinois was not an agreement state, the AEC exercised primary regulatory responsibility over the Sheffield site. The AEC approved license applications only after determining, in collaboration with the U.S. Geological Survey, that "the geological, hydrological, and climatological characteristics of the site are adequate to assure containment of the waste materials in a manner that will not endanger public health and safety." Agreement states used the same criteria for judging the suitability of low-level waste sites.[4]

After the controversy over ocean dumping had subsided in 1960, the issue of low-level waste management largely faded from public view. There were, however, occasional flare-ups of concern in local areas. In 1969, when two companies from out of state made preliminary proposals to locate low-level radioactive waste facilities in Georgia, they set off a bitter controversy. "News media from all over Georgia are crackling with scathing charges and counter-charges," reported *Nucleonics Week*. A state senator and prospective gubernatorial candidate from Plains, Jimmy Carter, expressed his strong reservations about "this dumping." He objected to plans to transport waste to Georgia from other states and asked, "If it's so safe, why not bury the radioactive and toxic waste in their own back yards?" Local opposition soon convinced the firms to abandon their overtures.[5]

A different kind of issue generated a flurry of concern in New York after revelations that low-level waste was stored in a decidedly unauthorized manner on Long Island. The Long Island Nuclear Service Company was licensed by the state to collect low-level materials and ship them to burial sites. In 1970 the operators of the disposal facilities at Maxey Flats and West Valley refused to accept shipments from the company because it had not paid bills for previous burial services. Eventually, Oak Ridge and West Valley agreed to dispose of three truckloads of waste that Long Island Nuclear Service had shipped to their sites, and a short time later the company went bankrupt. This left one remaining truckload of material in limbo on Long Island. While questions about ownership of the trailer and the shipment of waste it contained were litigated, it sat on a construction equipment lot near Bellport for more than one year. During that time, the trailer corroded, and some of the waste containers deteriorated. The status of the trailer became the subject of television reports and newspaper stories in summer 1971 as several state agencies debated jurisdictional and financial ambiguities. Press accounts suggested that the waste posed a significant risk to public health. The *New York Times* ran a story under the headline, "Radiation from Trailer on Lot in Bellport Is Called Dangerous." The *Long Island Press* announced, "Radioactive Danger on LI," and published a photograph of "potentially deadly containers." State authorities soon made arrangements to send the waste to West Valley, quietly ending the affair. But it was at best an embarrassment that raised questions about the effectiveness of existing regulatory procedures. "The entire regulatory system ground to a halt," commented the *Long Island Press*, "because one man was going bankrupt."[6]

More serious and far-reaching problems occurred at the Maxey Flats site in northeastern Kentucky, at the top of a mesa on a 330-acre tract in a sparsely populated area. It was selected as preferable to other possible sites and judged suitable for low-level waste disposal after evaluation by several state and federal agencies. The Nuclear Engineering Company received a license from the state of Kentucky in October 1962 and began operations at Maxey Flats the following March. Waste containers shipped to the site were dumped into trenches about twenty-five feet deep. When the trenches were filled, they were covered with soil about four feet deep and topped with vegetation. Nuclear Engineering, like other low-level waste disposal firms, depended on the geologic composition of the burial grounds—in this case, layers of soil, shale, and sandstone—rather than the integrity of the waste containers, such as cardboard boxes or steel drums, to prevent radioactivity from migrating beyond the site. The containers often ruptured when dropped into the trenches or when compacted by the soil "cap" on filled trenches.

For the first few years after Nuclear Engineering received its license, periodic inspections at Maxey Flats revealed no alarming problems. Beginning in 1970, however, state officials became increasingly uneasy about conditions there. Their main concerns were the expanding volume of waste and, in an area of heavy annual rainfall, difficulties controlling water in the trenches. The materials buried at Maxey Flats included solid wastes from the growing number of nuclear power reactors and isotopes from medical and industrial activities. They also included "significant quantities" of plutonium from AEC contractors. After efforts to force Nuclear Engineering to keep water from accumulating in the trenches met with only mixed success, the state cited the company for violating the terms of its license and placed restrictions on what could be buried in the future.

The state also undertook a special study to evaluate the potential hazards of the radioactivity from the materials buried at Maxey Flats. It reported in late 1974 that some radioactive materials, including plutonium, were present in water samples collected from adjacent off-site areas. Although state officials did not regard the levels of radiation as a public health hazard, they found the results of the investigation disquieting. They consulted with the AEC, which had regularly reviewed Kentucky's performance in regulating Maxey Flats as an agreement state. The AEC supported the state's conclusion that off-site radiation measurements did not appear to present a significant threat to public health, but it urged additional studies to determine more accurately the nature and degree of the risk. A short time later, the AEC went out of existence and handed the problem off to the Nuclear Regulatory Commission.[7]

The situation at Maxey Flats fed growing misgivings about low-level waste disposal and caused dismay within the nuclear industry. The handling of low-level materials was, *Nucleonics Week* reported in April 1973, "developing into [a] new industry headache." An unnamed industry official remarked, "It's a real problem and it is going to get worse. . . . No state wants to be the nation's garbage dump." The uncertainties generated by the problems at Maxey Flats were compounded when host states for burial sites placed new restrictions on the volume, form, or packaging of low-level waste. This led to some cases in which waste shipments were rejected for burial, at least temporarily. In addition, in September 1974 the AEC published a draft rule for public comment that would prohibit burying plutonium and other transuranic elements at commercial low-level waste sites. The tighter rules for land burial that had been issued or proposed, one source commented, "would undoubtedly cause trouble for the industry."[8]

A "FUROR" OVER LOW-LEVEL WASTE

By the time the NRC began operations in January 1975, low-level waste burial at commercial sites had emerged as a high-level concern. In April 1975 Kentucky governor Julian M. Carroll wired NRC chairman William Anders to request assistance in evaluating conditions at Maxey Flats. He disclosed that he had "become increasingly concerned" about the problem since taking office four months earlier and that the safety of the facility had "been questioned" in local news coverage. The *Louisville Courier-Journal,* for example, editorialized that the operation of the "graveyard for possibly deadly nuclear materials" could only be regarded "with skepticism." NRC staff members conducted an unannounced inspection of the site in June 1975. They confirmed that radioactivity, including plutonium, had migrated beyond the boundaries of the "restricted area," but they concluded that the levels were so low that they posed "no significant public health problem." The NRC review group recommended a series of steps to improve water management at the site and found that the state was acting appropriately and effectively in carrying out its regulatory responsibilities. The state had already imposed a series of new requirements on Nuclear Engineering, including better trench construction and other methods of preventing water from reaching the buried waste. For its part, the company had hired new managers for the facility, pumped water out of the trenches, and upgraded water control measures.[9]

In addition to the efforts of the NRC, the state of Kentucky, and Nuclear Engineering, EPA conducted an investigation at Maxey Flats. The EPA study, published in February 1976, agreed with the assessments of NRC and Kentucky officials that the levels of plutonium found off-site did not present a public health hazard "at this time." But it suggested that the potential long-term dangers of the migrating radioactivity from Maxey Flats were greater than the NRC believed. It pointed out that plutonium had already moved a distance of tens or hundreds of meters from the trenches. "The burial site was expected to retain the buried Pu [plutonium] for its hazardous lifetime," the EPA report argued, "but Pu has migrated from the site in less than ten years." William D. Rowe, deputy assistant administrator for radiation programs at EPA, insisted that methods should be developed promptly to contain radiation at burial sites because the volume of low-level waste was expected to increase enormously in the future. He also announced that EPA strongly supported the proposal that the AEC had published for public comment in September 1974 to prohibit the burial of materials contaminated with transuranic elements at commercial facilities. Although action on the draft federal rule had been delayed, every state except Washington that hosted commercial sites had imposed stringent limitations on transuranic wastes by permitting the burial of only trace quantities. This meant that low-level material contaminated with plutonium and other transuranics had to be shipped to Hanford or separated and stored for eventual disposal at a federal repository.[10]

EPA's assessment focused attention on the problem of low-level waste management in a way that rivaled the earlier tumult over ocean dumping. *Nuclear Industry,* a keen observer of developments that affected nuclear power, reported that the study created a "furor" that provided "antinuclear activists . . . a hitherto disregarded weapon in their arsenal." The state of Kentucky reacted to the EPA review by adding a heavy surcharge to the costs of burying wastes at Maxey Flats. The result was that customers sent 97 percent of the volume of materials formerly shipped to Maxey Flats to Sheffield or Barnwell. This effectively shut down the Kentucky burial site, and in 1977 the state officially closed it.[11]

The impact of the EPA study was magnified by a report on low-level waste by the General Accounting Office that appeared at nearly the same time. After examining existing locations and practices, GAO concluded that greater care was needed in the selection and management of low-level burial grounds. This was essential, it argued, "because monitoring and maintenance at disposal sites will be required for many centuries." The discovery of failures not only at Maxey Flats but also at other low-level waste facilities offered strong support for GAO's findings. West Valley suffered from the same kind of water control problems that occurred at Maxey Flats. Seepage from overflowing burial trenches caused small amounts of radioactivity to spread beyond the boundaries of the site. The owner of West Valley, Nuclear Fuel Services, suspended operation of the burial grounds in March 1975 and, after fruitless negotiations with the state of New York over conditions under which it could resume accepting waste, never reopened it.[12]

At the Beatty site, the owner, Nuclear Engineering, told the state of Nevada in March 1976 about unauthorized use of a company cement mixer that solidified low-level wastes. Some employees had allowed the truck to make cement for off-site buildings, including a saloon, a municipal center, and a few private homes. The Nevada Department of Human Resources, ERDA, EPA, and the NRC conducted a survey of the local population, which extended to about two hundred fifty homes in and around Beatty. They used radiation detection equipment, a mobile laboratory, and aerial monitoring. In three homes they found traces of radioactivity that disappeared once the slightly contaminated sources were removed. As an extra precaution, the inspectors arranged for whole-body radiation counts for ten town residents "who had been in closest and most frequent proximity to contaminated items." None of those tested showed higher-than-normal levels of internal radiation.

The investigation of conditions at Beatty also revealed other violations of Nuclear Engineering's operating license. Over a period of years, company employees had transferred a wide variety of "potentially contaminated material" from the site, including hand tools, electric motors, lumber, and radio equipment. The items were so numerous that it required twenty-five truckloads to return them to the burial grounds. Although most of the items taken from the site were not contaminated and none represented a significant health risk, their removal was a serious breach of Beatty's operating license. Nuclear Engineering discharged three employees, and the state of Nevada suspended the company's operating license until it could be certain that the violations did not create a public health hazard. On May 25, 1976, the state lifted the suspension after imposing new requirements for security and control of radioactive materials at the site.[13]

THE NRC AND LOW-LEVEL WASTE

The growing uncertainties about low-level waste disposal and the problems at operating sites received critical scrutiny from Congress. Within a short time after the EPA and GAO reports were released, the Subcommittee on Conservation, Energy, and Natural Resources of the House Committee on Government Operations held hearings on the subject. Subcommittee chairman William S. Moorhead of Pennsylvania and his colleagues sharply questioned representatives of ERDA, the Nuclear Engineering Company, and the NRC. Moorhead came down especially hard on Richard E. Cunningham, acting director of the NRC's fuel cycle and material safety division of the Office of Nuclear Material Safety and Safeguards. When Cunningham offered a historical summary of the AEC's approach to regulating low-level waste, Moorhead complained that the NRC seemed to be tied to policies it had inherited. "I am disturbed that you are defending the actions of your predecessor agency," he remarked. "I don't expect you to condemn them, but I do think that the NRC should say we are a new agency, we are starting with a clean slate, and we are going to correct that which was done maybe understandably but erroneously in the past." Cunningham assured the committee that the NRC recognized that the "performance of existing sites has not been uniformly good" and that it was carefully considering the corrective measures that should be taken.

Like Cunningham, other witnesses acknowledged the need for improvements in operating and monitoring low-level waste sites. ERDA and Nuclear Engineering, however, also suggested that EPA's assessment had overstated the public health hazards of the leaks at Maxey Flats. They drew on the analyses of several scientists who disputed as unproven or unconvincing EPA's projections that plutonium would move dangerously long distances from the burial trenches. In addition, Bernard L. Cohen, a radiation expert at the University of Pittsburgh, contended that members of Congress and their staffs received annual radiation exposures "at least 100 times higher" from the marble in Capitol Hill office buildings than a member of the public might receive from Maxey Flats. Nevertheless, the committee concluded that federal agencies should act more aggressively and effectively to "establish the safest possible containment systems for all low-level radioactive wastes" and to determine "when migration has reached unacceptable . . . levels."[14]

In May 1976, shortly after the House Committee on Government Operations ended its first round of hearings, the Joint Committee on Atomic Energy conducted hearings on the management of both high-level and low-level wastes. Although the Joint Committee was less disparaging of the NRC than the Government Operations Committee had been, it made clear its concern about waste disposal practices and the availability of suitable sites. Committee chairman Pastore declared, "Unless we can control the waste, the nuclear program is dead. . . . We have to prove to the American public we can contain this waste." NRC chairman Rowden told the committee that based on a review of the status and history of dealing with nuclear wastes, "we conclude that there is every reason to believe that the technology for the handling of these wastes is either available or will soon be proven." In hearings that the Government Operations Committee reconvened in September 1976, Congressman Leo J. Ryan of California expressed greater skepticism. He suggested not only that "solutions to the problem appear as remote as ever" but also that "it is possible that there are no permanent solutions to radioactive waste disposal."[15]

The problems that had occurred at commercial low-level waste sites and the congressional interest in the subject prompted the NRC to review its programs. In response to the GAO report and questions raised in the recent congressional hearings, the agency established a task force, chaired by Richard Cunningham, to reassess federal and state roles in the regulation of commercial burial grounds. In a report completed in January 1977, it reached several major conclusions about the management of low-level waste. It found that states had performed effectively and that there was "no compelling health and safety reason" to assert exclusive federal control over low-level waste. Nevertheless, the task force cited the leakage of radiation at Maxey Flats and West Valley as vivid examples of why regulatory improvements were required. It suggested that the expectation of "zero releases" at those facilities was "not realistic" and pointed to the need for more thorough evaluations of hydrologic and geologic variables.

The task force argued that since low-level waste was a national problem rather than a local one and since the states lacked the resources or the incentive to provide "overall leadership," the NRC should assume a more active role. It also recommended that alternative methods to shallow land burial be carefully studied. The possible approaches might include the use of deep geologic formations, salt mines, or the ocean floor. "Until extensive investigation of alternatives to shallow land burial is completed," the task force commented, "the additional licensing of new shallow land burial sites should be avoided." It warned against the "undisciplined proliferation of burial sites."

Although the industry was already concerned that the effective closure of Maxey Flats and suspension of operations at West Valley could result in a shortage of space for disposing of low-level wastes, the NRC task force estimated that the capacity of existing sites would be sufficient until at least 1989. It found an "urgent need" for comprehensive standards governing commercial low-level waste management and recommended that, in cooperation with federal and state agencies, the NRC accelerate development of suitable criteria for operating, monitoring, and decommissioning burial sites. The agency began preparing regulations within a short time and published an "Advance Notice of Proposed Rulemaking" for public comment in October 1978.[16]

THE LOW-LEVEL RADIOACTIVE WASTE POLICY ACT

The NRC staff's projection that space to bury low-level wastes would be adequate until the late 1980s soon was overtaken by events. The Sheffield site in Illinois reached its capacity in April 1978, in part because of the greater volume of materials it received after Maxey Flats and West Valley closed. The Nuclear Engineering Company, which operated Sheffield, complained bitterly that the NRC had refused to rule promptly on a long-standing request to extend the boundaries of the burial grounds and then had asked for further studies. State and local officials opposed rezoning of the property to allow for expansion, at least until the NRC completed its licensing review. Rather than spend money on new evaluations, the company shut the facility. At about the same time, South Carolina reduced the amount of low-level waste that Barnwell could accept to 1977 levels. It acted in response to the sharply increased shipments to Barnwell after other installations closed.

The shuttering of three sites and the restrictions that South Carolina placed on Barnwell raised concerns about a serious nationwide shortage of capacity for low-level waste burial. By early 1978 about 60 percent of the volume of low-level commercial wastes came from nuclear power plants and other fuel cycle facilities. The threat of insufficient capacity was especially acute in the eastern and central states, where sixty of the sixty-five nuclear power reactors then operating were located. Another 30 percent of the volume of low-level wastes came from medical services and the other 10 percent from industries, laboratories, universities, and isotope suppliers. A "large portion" of those sources of low-level radioactive waste was also located in the eastern and central states.[17]

In the wake of the Three Mile Island nuclear accident in March 1979 and the heightened sensitivity to radiation hazards that it produced, the disclosure of safety lapses at the three low-level waste sites still operating elicited protests from the governors of Nevada, Washington, and South Carolina. On May 13, 1979, a truck carrying low-level waste caught fire at the Beatty site. The fire revealed that the wastes in the truck violated packing and shipping requirements of the state of Nevada and the U.S. Department of Transportation (DOT). The materials included liquids that were improperly packaged and aerosol cans that exploded during the fire to cause a "missile hazard." A short time later, Nevada governor Robert List met with NRC chairman Joseph M. Hendrie and requested that special inspections be undertaken to make certain that waste shippers complied with packaging and transportation regulations. As a result, the NRC, in collaboration with DOT and agreement states, immediately conducted a series of investigations of the practices of firms that collected and hauled low-level waste.

The special investigations disclosed leakages of waste sent to Beatty and made clear that packaging problems remained to be solved. In July 1979 Nuclear Engineering reported that it had discovered liquid wastes seeping out of a shipment from the Palisades nuclear plant in Michigan. In response, List temporarily shut down the Beatty facility. He joined with South Carolina governor Richard W. Riley and Washington governor (and former AEC chairman) Dixy Lee Ray to complain to Hendrie about "serious and repeated disregard for existing rules governing the shipments of commercially generated low level wastes, and the total lack of corrective measures by the Nuclear Regulatory Commission."

The NRC promptly took steps to improve low-level waste packaging and transportation. It required reactor and materials licensees to evaluate, and where necessary correct, their packaging and shipping practices. It met with reactor owners to press the importance of proper packaging, especially the solidification of liquid wastes before shipment. The NRC also increased inspections of low-level waste shipments at both the source and disposal sites. The closer scrutiny by federal and state agencies uncovered problems that had previously gone undetected at all three disposal facilities. Many were minor, such as broken headlights or worn brakes in trucks that carried waste packages, but others were more disturbing. The most flagrant was the discovery that some low-level materials had been buried outside the boundaries of the Beatty site.[18]

The governors of the states with low-level waste facilities reacted angrily to the new reports. In Nevada, List again shut down Beatty and state health officials suggested that it might be closed permanently. In Washington, Ray suspended operations at Hanford, citing "serious deficiencies" that included "mechanical defects, overloads, leakage, improper containerizing, and other questionable practices." In South Carolina, Riley announced that Barnwell would refuse shipments formerly destined for the closed sites and that over a two-year period it would cut in half the amount of waste it would accept. All three governors were concerned not only about conditions at the low-level sites but also about the political difficulties that publicity about radioactive waste caused. Ray, who faced a reelection campaign in 1980, was under growing political pressure from prospective opponents who were, as the *Christian Science Monitor* put it, "bent on riding a wave of antinuclear feeling in the state." Idaho governor John V. Evans told a U.S. Senate hearing in January 1980 that the low-level waste issue created "very serious political problems" for gubernatorial colleagues whose states had become the dumping grounds for the entire nation.[19]

The actions of the three governors caused consternation within the nuclear industry, the medical community, and other low-level waste producers. *Nuclear Industry* reported that the situation was "now seen as critical." Medical practitioners and researchers expressed grave concern about a shortage of low-level waste capacity. They feared that it would discourage if not prevent the vital use of radioactive materials in the diagnosis and treatment of diseases and in medical research. The American Medical Association warned that the "inability to dispose of low-level medical nuclear waste products threatens to make . . . lifesaving and diagnostic procedures unavailable to thousands of persons who desperately need these services." Political leaders rebuked states that had passed laws prohibiting radioactive waste disposal within their borders. This was, said Governor Riley, "essentially telling states like South Carolina and Washington that we must be their nuclear garbage cans forever more." In Maryland, one of the states that had banned the burial of radioactive wastes, the Department of Health and Mental Hygiene established a task force to advise the governor about options available "in the event a nuclear waste disposal crisis hits."[20]

A crisis was averted, at least in the short term, when Governors Ray and List authorized the Hanford and Beatty sites to reopen in November 1979. Ray contended that, despite the problems at Hanford, "the handling of low-level nuclear waste has . . . been more responsible, with more far-sighted planning, than the handling of any kind of waste whatever in our Nation." Once she was satisfied that the "serious deficiencies" at Hanford's commercial low-level waste facility had been corrected, she allowed it to resume operations. She explained that her decision was based primarily on public health considerations. "There is an immediate and a vital interest within the nation's medical institutions and research communities to establish storage sites for low-level radioactive residue," she said, "and there is recognition on the part of the medical fraternity that such materials must be properly packaged." List permitted Beatty to reopen after receiving assurances from the state health department that the site did not pose unacceptable risks to public health and safety.[21]

The crisis over low-level waste disposal, acute though short-lived, clearly demonstrated the importance of the long-term problem and supported the claims of the states with disposal sites that low-level waste management required a national, rather than a local, approach. President Carter made this point in the message on radioactive waste policy that he sent to Congress in February 1980. Although his policy statement focused on high-level waste, he also called on federal agencies, state governments, and private organizations to develop "national plans to establish regional disposal sites for commercial low level waste." While affirming that the "task is not inherently difficult from the standpoint of safety," he argued that "we must work together to resolve the serious near-term problem of low level waste disposal." Congress also recognized the need for timely action. When efforts to pass a comprehensive nuclear waste bill in the wake of Carter's message failed, the South Carolina congressional delegation lobbied aggressively for separate legislation on low-level waste. "It is grossly unfair, unwise, and unacceptable," Senator Strom Thurmond declared, "to expect South Carolina to assume this disproportionate burden indefinitely." Congress endorsed his position by approving the Low-Level Radioactive Waste Policy Act on December 13, 1980.[22]

The act had a text of less than three printed pages and passed with little debate. It required the individual states to take responsibility for the disposal of commercial low-level waste created within their own borders. It assigned them the task of building disposal sites, or, as an alternative, authorized and encouraged them to enter multistate compacts. The act set a deadline for states to make arrangements for disposal of their low-level waste. After January 1, 1986, states that were members of a compact could deny access to nonmember states. Thus those that did not join a compact or build their own facilities could be left without a place to send their low-level materials. As an article in the *Wall Street Journal* observed, this triggered "a lively game of musical chairs over the issue of low-level radioactive waste disposal, a subject known to cause outbreaks of yawns a few years ago."[23]

By 1985 the "game of musical chairs" had not resulted in significant progress toward the approval, licensing, or construction of new low-level waste disposal sites. After bitter complaints from the states with waste facilities, especially South Carolina, Congress passed a new act in December 1985. It averted, at least for the time being, the threat of a shutdown of the three operating sites. It also imposed a series of new conditions that were intended as incentives for large reductions in the amount of low-level waste produced, as well as for steady progress in siting new facilities. Although the first of those objectives was achieved, the second was not. Between 1986 and 2007 no new sites were established, and opposition to expanding capacity to bury low-level wastes remained strong.[24]

THE NRC'S NEW REGULATIONS ON LOW-LEVEL WASTE

While Congress and the states were addressing the low-level waste crisis, the NRC revised its regulations for issues under its jurisdiction. After publishing an Advance Notice of Proposed Rulemaking in October 1978, the staff drafted rules for licensing near-surface land disposal of low-level waste. Mindful of the deficiencies at the existing sites that had become evident over the previous few years, it sought to eliminate such problems in the future. The new regulations were intended to establish performance objectives and technical requirements for low-level sites that would minimize the migration of radioactivity and protect the public from exposure to potentially hazardous radiation levels, even after the facility closed. The proposed rule imposed much stricter licensing conditions than those that had applied to the existing facilities, such as requirements that new sites be placed in regions with good natural drainage and that they be built to prevent infiltration by surface or ground water. The draft regulations also prohibited packaging wastes in cardboard or fiberboard boxes and stipulated that liquid waste must be converted to solid form or packed in absorbent material that could soak up twice the volume of the liquid.

The NRC staff prepared new classifications of wastes that could be buried close to the surface. The categories were defined according to the intensity and the longevity of the radioactivity in the waste materials.

Class A low-level wastes, the least hazardous, made up about 60 percent of the total volume. Class B and C wastes had to meet more stringent standards for structural stability and packaging, and Class C materials had to be buried deeper than the other categories. NRC licensees would be prohibited from burying transuranic wastes at low-level sites. The proposed rule also added new requirements for tracking waste materials from the source to the disposal facility. The regulations would apply only to NRC licensees, but agreement states expressed their support and planned to impose similar requirements on low-level waste sites under their jurisdictions. After the NRC received and considered public comments, the commissioners approved the final rule by a 4–0 vote in October 1982.[25]

In addition, the NRC published a policy statement urging low-level waste generators to reduce the volume of materials they sent to disposal sites. In response to a recommendation in a 1980 GAO report, the commissioners had asked the NRC staff to prepare a policy statement on volume reduction. The staff responded that since volume reduction did not present health and safety issues and since financial pressures were driving the industry to minimize waste quantities, a policy statement was inadvisable and unnecessary. The commissioners unanimously rejected the staff's position. Consequently, on October 12, 1981, the NRC released a statement urging "all generators of low-level radioactive waste to reduce the volume of waste for disposal." It suggested that the goal could be accomplished both through administrative controls, such as better planning procedures, improved segregation of materials, and training programs, and through the installation of "advanced equipment," such as incinerators, evaporators, and compactors. It promised that the NRC would "take expeditious actions on requests for licensing volume reduction systems." Within a short time, the efforts of the nuclear industry, medical institutions, and other sources of low-level waste substantially decreased the volume of wastes shipped to burial facilities. This considerably eased but did not solve the problem of low-level waste disposal.[26]

The disposal of low-level radioactive waste was a much less complicated and dangerous task than the containment of radiation from spent fuel rods or high-level liquids from reprocessing. The shortcomings that became apparent in the early and mid-1970s arose from regulatory and operational failures that generated controversy and public concern. The problems at low-level sites commanded prompt attention from facility owners, waste generators, and state and federal agencies, all of whom took corrective actions. But the improvements they made were not sufficient to arrest public anxieties. The migration of radioactive materials, even in small amounts that did not seriously threaten public health, and the feckless management of licensed burial grounds produced public alarm that was out of proportion to the hazards that low-level wastes presented. The companies that operated low-level sites and the government agencies that regulated them were slow to recognize the intense public apprehension that potential exposure to radiation in any amount incited. The fears were fueled by press coverage that frequently if not invariably described low-level materials as "potentially deadly waste." Those who were responsible for safe handling of low-level wastes did not make certain that the sites were tightly managed, effectively operated, and closely regulated from the outset. As a result, they forfeited public confidence and created a political problem of large dimensions. The measures they took to improve the operating performance of low-level waste sites were essential, but they were not enough to overcome the growth of exaggerated public fears or the difficulty of winning public support for new sites.

CHAPTER 7

The Transportation of Nuclear Waste

As the nuclear industry's expansion created growing volumes of radioactive waste during the late 1960s and 1970s, the transportation of nuclear materials emerged as an increasingly prominent public concern. Since the 1940s the AEC had shipped various radioactive materials, including isotopes used in industry and medicine, enriched uranium, reactor fuel elements, low-level waste, and spent fuel, without causing serious accidents that endangered public health. It was confident that the experience it had gained and the precautions it had developed provided ample protection against hazardous occupational or public exposure to radiation sources in transit. Nuclear critics were not convinced, however, and the transportation of spent fuel rods became another in a series of controversial issues that surrounded the safe storage and disposal of radioactive waste.

GUARDING AGAINST TRANSPORTATION HAZARDS

The principal objective in the transportation of nuclear waste was to make certain that the containers used for shipments of intensely radioactive high-level waste or spent fuel rods did not allow the escape of harmful levels of radiation into the environment. Before President Carter announced an "indefinite deferral" of reprocessing in 1977, the focus of concern was the movement of spent fuel from nuclear power reactors to commercial reprocessing plants and solidified high-level wastes from there to yet-to-be-constructed waste repositories. Carter's decision shifted attention to the transportation of spent fuel rods directly from nuclear plants to permanent waste sites.

Before being transported, high-level waste or spent fuel was placed in steel canisters that were 6 to 24 inches in diameter and 6 to 10 feet long. The canisters, in turn, were packed in thick stainless steel casks with heavy lead or steel shielding that weighed between 15 and 100 tons. The casks, which were 10 to 16 feet long, could hold several waste canisters. Depending on their size, they could be moved by rail or by truck. By the early 1970s the AEC had made thousands of shipments of high-level waste or spent fuel from its own installations in forms it described as "chemically inert, immobile, . . . nonexplosive, [and] noncombustible" that could not turn to gases or "become easily airborne." It insisted that its practices and experiences showed that high-level waste from commercial nuclear power could be transported safely. AEC chairman Dixy Lee Ray told a Senate committee in 1974 that the performance of the nuclear industry in shipping wastes over the years had "really been phenomenally good." The agency acknowledged that the number of shipments would increase significantly as the industry continued to expand, but it argued that the total would remain a small percentage of the "30,000,000,000—30 billion—shipments of other hazardous materials every year."

The AEC was keenly aware that accidents could and probably would occur during waste shipments. It also recognized "a very real public apprehension" about the potential risks of transporting radioactive waste. It took several steps to test the safety of shipping methods and to lower the chances of serious accidents. Over the years the agency conducted hundreds of experiments to demonstrate that casks could withstand a variety of shocks without releasing radiation. They included, for example, a sequential "torture test" in which a cask was dropped thirty feet onto an "unyielding surface," then dropped four feet onto a six-inch spike, then subjected to fire that burned for thirty minutes at a constant temperature of 1,475 degrees Fahrenheit, and finally immersed in water for eight hours. The casks had to provide not only robust construction to prevent radiation leakage but also a cooling mechanism to guard against the effects of decay heat from fuel rods. The AEC approved the design of the casks used for shipping radioactive waste and carried out inspections to check on compliance with packaging requirements. It cooperated with the U.S. Department of Transportation and state regulatory agencies that exercised authority over shipments of hazardous materials, including matters such as loading procedures, weight, and

Figure 9. Cask containing spent fuel elements in transit, 1974. (National Archives 434-SF-22–18)

routing. The rules of federal and state agencies were designed to reduce the frequency and limit the consequences of accidents that could endanger public health. The AEC made no claim of "absolute safety" in the shipping of radioactive waste, but it declared "with great confidence" that the "chances of accidents seriously affecting the lives or property of people in the transportation of nuclear materials are much less than from the other hazards of everyday life."[1]

A NEW LOOK AT TRANSPORTATION SAFETY

The expanding use of nuclear power and other sources of radiation in the late 1960s and early 1970s drew unprecedented attention to transportation safety from both nuclear professionals and the general public. The rise in concern went hand in hand with the growth of the nuclear industry. "The wide spread increase in the industrial use of radioactive materials has greatly increased the number of shipments of those substances," an AEC report commented in January 1969. "The chances, therefore, of more people becoming involved in accidents in the transportation of radioactive material is much more probable now than in the past." And, as the authors of a technical paper on the subject had suggested a few years earlier, spent fuel presented "the greatest technical challenge of any radioactive material to the transportation business." During the controversy over the AEC's proposal for a waste repository in Lyons, Kansas, critics had expressed serious reservations about the adequacy of shipping procedures. The AEC had offered assurances that its experience in transporting waste for more than two decades demonstrated the safety of its practices.[2]

Nevertheless, in August 1971, as the debate over Lyons raised questions about the AEC's programs, Frank Pittman, director of the AEC's recently created Division of Waste Management and Transportation, requested a report on existing transportation requirements. He instructed his staff to examine not only the soundness of the regulations in place but also the validity of tests on various types of waste casks. The study would address, among other things, the reliability of the thirty-foot drop test and the thirty-minute fire test for judging the strength of casks under severe duress. Unnamed AEC sources told *Nucleonics Week* that the review was "especially important and timely" in light of the "rapid growth of nuclear power facilities and the greater scale of plants now being built." The report apparently was never completed, perhaps because a barrage of urgent issues arose at the time that demanded the AEC staff's immediate attention. Over a period of several years, however, the agency considered a series of problems in the shipment of radioactive waste and took actions both to improve safety and to clarify its regulatory position.[3]

One important matter that received reconsideration was the division of responsibilities between the AEC and DOT. In 1947 the Interstate Commerce Commission (ICC) had published the first regulations for shipping radioactive materials, and in later years the AEC had prepared standards for casks used to move spent fuel from its own reactors. In 1966 the two agencies reached a Memorandum of Understanding to spell out their respective roles in the safety of transportation methods that AEC licensees and contractors employed. The central feature of the agreement was that the ICC would regulate radioactive material in transit while the AEC would exercise authority over the packaging of "large sources" of radioactive material for shipment. The ICC would continue to set standards for packaging small quantities of low-level radioactive material. The two agencies further agreed that the ICC would take over the AEC's responsibilities at some point when it had the resources it needed to do so. The following year, the ICC's role in regulating the safety of radioactive shipments and the provisions of the Memorandum of Understanding with the AEC were transferred to the newly created Department of Transportation.[4]

In early 1970 DOT informed the AEC that it would not be able to assume authority over the packaging of large sources of radioactive materials in accordance with the Memorandum of Understanding of 1966. It cited a lack of funds to hire the necessary staff and the claims of safety issues it regarded as more pressing. It requested that the interagency agreement be revised to remove its obligation to regulate packaging procedures for large quantities of radioactive material in the future. As a result, DOT and the AEC negotiated new arrangements. Under a modified Memorandum of Understanding signed on March 22, 1973, the AEC accepted permanent responsibility for the "design and performance" of casks and other shipping containers, including structure, shielding, and quality control. Thus regulatory authority over the transportation of high-level waste and spent fuel was split between the AEC for packaging and DOT for hauling, including requirements for drivers' qualifications, condition of mechanical equipment, loading, and unloading.[5]

At the same time the AEC was working with DOT on the division of labor in regulating shipments of radioactive material, it was reviewing its own programs for transportation safety. It acted in part because of Pittman's request for a status report and in part because of a GAO investigation. In July 1973 GAO recommended that the AEC take several steps to improve its approach to assuring the safety of casks used for shipping "the more hazardous types of radioactive materials." In response, the AEC agreed to strengthen its quality assurance procedures, broaden requirements for reporting accidents or minor contamination incidents, and systematically assess the performance of licensees and contractors. The GAO report also expressed reservations about the reliability of older casks that were still in use and that the AEC had approved before upgrading its standards. As a result of questions from both inside and outside the agency about the ability of casks to hold up under extreme stress, the AEC decided to conduct rigorous new tests.[6]

As the AEC revised its Memorandum of Understanding with DOT, reviewed its own transportation programs, and planned tests for casks, it also drafted an environmental impact statement on shipping radioactive materials to and from nuclear power plants. The statement, published in December 1972, was intended to provide prospective owners of nuclear plants and the AEC a basis on which to judge the potential effects of transporting fresh fuel to and spent fuel from an individual power reactor. It would help to fulfill the requirement of the National Environmental Policy Act of 1969 that applicants for licenses and the AEC weigh the environmental costs and benefits of building a plant. The AEC's report concluded that for a "typical reactor," transportation of spent fuel by a truck or train that complied with regulatory standards presented only a slight risk to the environment and public health. It maintained that a severe accident that ruptured a cask was unlikely and that the consequences of such an occurrence would not be catastrophic. "When both probability of occurrence and extent of the consequences are taken into account," the survey commented, "the risk to the environment due to the radiological effects from transportation accidents is small." It noted that although three hundred mostly minor accidents in the transportation of radioactive materials had taken place in the previous twenty-five years, the millions of shipments of radioactive isotopes and 3,600 shipments of irradiated fuel had not caused "perceptible injury or death attributable to . . . radiation aspects."[7]

The AEC published its draft environmental impact statement for public comment and scheduled a rule-making hearing. The staff followed established procedures for holding a hearing on generic issues, such as emergency core cooling and radiation protection, that applied to all reactor applications. This avoided the need to consider the same matter repeatedly during licensing proceedings for individual plants. The AEC contended that "a detailed evaluation of transportation in connection with the licensing of each reactor does not appear to be warranted in view of the small environmental impact." When the agency held hearings on its draft rule on April 2, 1973, it found that some observers took a quite different position. William D. Rowe, deputy assistant administrator for radiation programs at EPA, voiced doubts about the value of using generic calculations for determining radiation exposures that were "highly dependent" on the characteristics of a specific location. He suggested that the AEC's estimated occupational and population radiation doses from transporting spent fuel were too low, though he agreed that even the higher figures he projected did not approach worrisome levels.

The sharpest criticism of the AEC's draft statement was expressed by Richard D. Sandler, an energy consultant to Ralph Nader, who had recently emerged as a highly visible opponent of nuclear power. Sandler represented several antinuclear organizations at the hearing. He complained that by analyzing the effects of transporting spent fuel from a single plant, the AEC obscured the hazards of shipments made from all operating reactors. Drawing on the AEC's prediction that about one thousand nuclear plants would be licensed by the year 2000, he claimed that transportation of spent fuel would collectively cause ten deaths and $17 million in damage annually at that time. He countered the AEC's arguments about the low risks of transportation from individual plants by asking, "Is the public still to feel at ease with such bland assurances when accident probabilities are multiplied by 1,000?"[8]

The AEC and EPA quickly reached a general resolution of their disagreement, which arose largely from differences in calculations of unavoidably speculative and imprecise potential radiation exposures. The AEC responded to Sandler by emphasizing that the rule-making proceedings on transportation were not designed "to undertake a full environmental review of transportation of fuel and waste." Rather they were intended to provide a basis for the cost-benefit assessments that were required in license applications for nuclear power plants. The AEC commented that although Sandler's arguments were "of interest," they were "beyond the scope" of the proceeding. It issued a slightly revised version of its draft statement as a final rule on the environmental impact of transporting nuclear fuel and waste in January 1975.[9]

GROWING PUBLIC CONCERN ABOUT TRANSPORTATION

The reservations that Sandler, and to a much lesser extent, EPA, expressed about the AEC's environmental impact statement on transportation in April 1973 were an indication of growing public concern about the potential hazards of spent fuel shipments. Some authorities had already taken steps to investigate the severity of the problem. In 1972 Richard B. Ogilvie, governor of Illinois, requested that his consultants on nuclear issues advise him on the risks of shipping spent fuel and high-level waste to the reprocessing plant that General Electric was building in his state. In 1973 the Oregon legislature considered a bill that would require special trains for hauling radioactive waste. The Association of American Railroads, a trade group representing the railroad industry, advanced a similar proposal. It recommended that rail shipments of spent fuel be carried only on trains with no other cargo and that their speed be restricted to no more than thirty-five miles per hour. The association contended that the AEC's drop and fire tests did not conclusively demonstrate that a damaged cask would not release radiation after a serious railroad accident.[10]

Questions about the safety of transporting nuclear waste reached new heights of visibility when the syndicated columnist Jack Anderson published an alarming report in January 1974. He cited the "frightening findings" of a "secret" study conducted by the Public Interest Research Group in Michigan (PIRGIM), an organization founded in response to Ralph Nader's appeals for student and citizen activism on public issues. Anderson called the PIRGIM account a "harrowing description" of the dangers of shipping radioactive wastes and condemned the AEC's "lax" regulatory requirements. He highlighted PIRGIM's claim that an accident involving transportation of such "deadly cargo" could not only cause thousands of fatalities but also "diseases of the skin, genitals, bones, and lungs, [and] cancer of the thyroid." In hearings of the Senate Commerce Committee on the transportation of hazardous materials in June 1974, Nader strongly endorsed the Michigan group's conclusions and warned against the "massive and unparalleled movement of poison" in spent fuel shipments.[11]

The AEC issued a strong rebuttal to PIRGIM's allegations. It complained that the report's "use of quotes out of context, selected half-truths, accusations, and unsupported judgments form a series of calculated overstatements and misstatements which are clearly designed to frighten and mislead the public." It denied the group's suggestion that a serious accident during the shipment of spent fuel would inevitably release radiation to the environment. The AEC argued that in estimating the potential dangers of transporting nuclear waste, PIRGIM relied on an analysis that "takes a series of incredible events, picks the worst of each, adds up the results, and presents them as likely conditions." It countered the study's criticism that the AEC regulatory staff did not conduct safety tests on casks by explaining that other agency divisions had "spent millions of dollars" to "verify and improve the methods used to evaluate cask integrity." The AEC insisted that its requirements for testing and building casks were sound and that it could "find no credible accidents that would kill thousands or even dozens of people anywhere."[12]

A few months after PIRGIM published its report (which Anderson had illogically described as secret), the AEC's position on transportation safety received a vote of confidence from a group of knowledgeable observers. A panel appointed by the National Academy of Sciences Committee on Radioactive Waste Management to examine transportation issues concluded that the AEC's methods for evaluating the hazards of shipping radioactive wastes were "valid" and the risks were "acceptable." The committee recommended improved quality assurance procedures and continued research on cask reliability, but it offered a general endorsement of the AEC's existing practices.[13]

Such favorable assessments about the low probability of harmful radiation releases from waste shipments did not arrest growing public concern. This was a source of perplexity and frustration for the AEC. In September 1974 William A. Brobst, chief of the agency's transportation branch, acknowledged that "one aspect of nuclear energy that strikes fear into the hearts of many is the transportation of nuclear materials." He submitted that public anxieties were "not always logical or rational" but cautioned against a tendency in the "nuclear fraternity" to "pooh-pooh the public's concern." Brobst worried that public fears placed irresistible pressures on state regulatory agencies to impose regulations on nuclear shipments that were ill considered, inconsistent, and counterproductive. Some local jurisdictions, for example, had adopted requirements that trucks could haul radioactive materials only in "the wee hours of the morning," precisely the time when most serious traffic accidents occurred. He urged closer cooperation between state and federal agencies on transportation issues. This was, he said, "vital if we are to preserve the phenomenally good safety record we have enjoyed so far."[14]

Brobst's concerns about far-reaching conflicts between the federal government on the one hand and state and local jurisdictions on the other soon proved well founded. Within a short time after the NRC took over the AEC's regulatory functions, it became involved, along with other federal agencies, in a prominent dispute with the city of New York over transportation safety. In August 1975 the New York City Health Department published a proposed amendment to its regulations that would, in effect, prohibit transporting spent fuel and other radioactive materials that exceeded a level of twenty curies of radioactivity on its streets and thoroughfares. It took this action after unsuccessfully attempting to prevent the Energy Research and Development Administration from shipping highly enriched uranium to New York's Kennedy Airport by crossing the George Washington Bridge. Despite being told by the New York Port Authority that it lacked jurisdiction over such shipments, the health department had gone ahead and drafted its proposed restrictions. If approved, the amendment would create serious difficulties for both ERDA and Brookhaven National Laboratory on Long Island, which shipped spent fuel from its experimental reactors through the city. In the long run, the health department's rule would keep the Long Island Lighting Company from using city streets and highways for moving spent fuel from its Shoreham nuclear plant, then under construction.[15]

The health department's proposal raised strong objections. An unnamed ERDA official declared that it had "put us in some consternation" and denied that the city had the legal authority to overrule federal statutes. The NRC took a similar position. It cited federal laws and a federal court ruling on the role of the states in radiation protection to argue that the federal government had "exclusive jurisdiction" over the regulation of nuclear transportation. In public hearings held on November 6, 1975, by the New York City Board of Health, which had to approve the proposed amendment, the NRC made its case largely on safety rather than legal grounds. Donald A. Nussbaumer, chief of the division that reviewed designs for waste casks, told the board that a severe accident within the New York City limits involving shipments of spent fuel and other waste materials from the Shoreham plant was highly unlikely. He also contended that the "possibility of radiological injury to anyone" from such an accident was "minimal." The Board of Health was not persuaded; on January 15, 1976, despite the opposition of the NRC, ERDA, Brookhaven, Long Island Lighting, and others, it unanimously approved the transportation restrictions.[16]

The Board of Health's decision was troubling to federal agencies and the nuclear industry because it seemed certain to create regulatory confusion and encourage other jurisdictions to take similar action. David Schweller, chief of engineering and safety at ERDA's Brookhaven office, lamented, "If the City of New York passes a ban and makes it stick, and you are the mayor of a town nearby, and you let [nuclear material] go through your town, you're not going to stay in office. . . . We can't have this if we are to have the kind of viable nuclear industry this country needs." The fear that the Board of Health's action would set a precedent was borne out when the state of Connecticut and the city of Cincinnati, Ohio, proposed measures modeled after the New York City ban. Two counties on Long Island had done so even before the Board of Health's ruling.[17]

To make matters worse from the perspective of nuclear proponents, several of the nation's railroads requested rulings from the Interstate Commerce Commission that would place severe restrictions on rail transportation of radioactive materials. If the ICC approved, railroads could stipulate that nuclear waste shipments must be carried on special trains at speeds of no greater than thirty-five miles per hour, or they could even refuse to haul radioactive materials. Nuclear industry and government officials believed that the railroads were acting out of economic self-interest. They pointed out that 35,000 coal cars were used annually to carry fuel to a 1,000-megawatt coal plant, whereas only fifteen to twenty rail shipments were needed to supply a comparable-sized nuclear reactor. The nuclear industry forcefully protested that the railroads' proposed requirements would violate federal laws and impose "staggering" costs that were far out of proportion to any projected benefits in protecting public health.[18]

After lengthy hearings in three separate cases, ICC administrative law judge Forest Gordon agreed with the nuclear industry's position. He commented that "there is no greater danger in carrying radioactive materials than there is in carrying propane gas or other hazardous materials" and that witnesses for the railroads had offered no convincing evidence that radioactive waste casks were "inadequate or unsafe." He concluded that special trains for radioactive waste would be "unnecessary and wasteful transportation" and "an uneconomic burden on shippers and the energy using public." The railroads challenged the ICC rulings in federal appeals court, but their suits were unsuccessful.[19]

The nuclear industry's arguments on transportation safety received additional support from a series of experiments on the strength of casks that ERDA performed over a period of more than two years. The tests subjected casks to stress of unprecedented magnitude. In April 1975, for example, researchers dropped a cask from a helicopter two thousand feet above hard desert ground in New Mexico. It hit with a speed of about 235 miles per hour and remained "essentially undamaged." ERDA later conducted even more dramatic tests. In March 1977 scientists at Sandia National Laboratories mounted a 22-ton cask on a tractor-trailer and used rocket propulsion to smash it into a ten-foot-thick concrete wall at a speed of 84 miles per hour. Although the impact destroyed the truck's cab and trailer, the cask survived intact. "The cask was slightly deformed as predicted," observed Robert Jefferson, manager of Sandia's Nuclear Fuel Cycle Technology Development Department, "but its basic integrity was unimpaired." Two months later, Sandia slammed a rocket-driven locomotive at a speed of 81.5 miles per hour into a trailer that held a 29-ton cask. The front part of the locomotive was "totally crushed" and the trailer twisted in a U-shape around the train. The cask was knocked into the air and bounced twice on the ground but sustained no damage beyond "minor surface dents." Sandia also ran fire resistance tests on casks. One experiment showed that a fire that burned

Figure 10. Rocket-propelled truck carrying a spent fuel cask hits a wall at 84 miles per hour. (National Archives 434-SF-79–60)

for two hours and heated a cask to about 900 degrees Fahrenheit would not have released radiation that exceeded the NRC's permissible limits for population exposure.[20]

The rulings of the ICC on rail shipments of nuclear wastes and the outcome of ERDA's cask reliability tests did not settle the controversy over transportation safety. Questions surrounding shipments by truck remained visible and divisive. They gained even greater prominence in September 1977 when a truck hauling 40,000 pounds of yellowcake, a powdery uranium concentrate that is slightly radioactive, crashed in Colorado. After the driver swerved to avoid a herd of horses crossing the road, the truck overturned in a ditch. As a result, about 15,000 pounds of yellowcake were released from the steel drums the truck carried. The accident received considerable press coverage; the *Washington Post,* for example, called it the "largest spill ever recorded" of "poisonous radioactive material." The NRC took issue with reports that in its view exaggerated the dangers. It explained that yellowcake was low-level radioactive material and maintained that the breach of the containers created no serious public health hazards. It also pointed out

Figure 11. Rocket-propelled locomotive hits a trailer carrying a spent fuel cask at 81.5 miles per hour. (National Archives 434-SF-79-57)

that the shipping drums for yellowcake were not nearly as sturdy as the casks built for spent fuel and high-level waste.[21]

Nevertheless, the accident stirred harsh criticism of the NRC and DOT. In October 1977 the Critical Mass Energy Project, a branch of Ralph Nader's organization, Public Citizen, Inc., published an analysis of the lessons of the spill. While acknowledging that yellowcake was "not as toxic as other radioactive substances," it argued that the accident "raised profound questions about the adequacy of federal standards for the shipment of radioactive materials." Critical Mass suggested that the Colorado crash presented "a rather frightening spectre of what will happen when other more difficult radiological accidents occur." It faulted both DOT and the NRC for unwarranted confidence in their safety procedures. At a press conference on Capitol Hill on October 31, Critical Mass director Richard P. Pollock was joined by Congressmen Timothy E. Wirth of Colorado and Theodore S. Weiss of New York City. Wirth complained "of a lackadaisical and dangerous attitude in the government toward the handling of hazardous materials." Weiss contended that if the accident had occurred in Denver or another large city, the "health consequences could have been disastrous." He urged support for a bill that he had introduced to prohibit the transportation of radioactive materials through any area with a population of more than twelve thousand people per square mile.[22]

DOT AND THE NEW YORK CITY BAN

The response to the Colorado accident set the stage for renewed controversy over New York City's stringent restrictions on shipments of radioactive materials. The question on which the debate centered was whether New York's regulations were "inconsistent" with federal laws. Congress assigned responsibility to DOT for determining whether state or local laws conflicted with federal statutes in the Hazardous Materials Transport Act of 1974. Under the provisions of the act, Brookhaven National Laboratory petitioned DOT to nullify New York's ban on spent fuel shipments. Since the Board of Health had approved the restrictions, Brookhaven had been forced to bypass New York by sending spent fuel by barge to Connecticut en route to its destination at ERDA's Savannah River plant in South Carolina. It had previously made shipments by truck through the city between midnight and 6:00 A.M. with a police escort. The possibility that DOT would overrule the limitations on nuclear transportation elicited angry protests from New York officials.

Leonard Solon, director of the city's Bureau for Radiation Control, suggested that a truck accident that released radiation could cause "10,000 prompt deaths and hundreds of thousands of latent cancer deaths." Congressman Weiss went even further; he declared that the toll could be "millions of lives."[23]

Representatives of the laboratory and the city presented their differing views at a public hearing that DOT held in New York on November 10–11, 1977. Solon denounced Brookhaven's petition as "deplorable." He reiterated his claim that a transportation accident could cause massive loss of life, which he based on extrapolating from worst-case estimates in an NRC report. Robert F. Barker, chief of the transportation and product standards branch of the NRC's Office of Standards Development, testified that Solon's numbers were a "gross over-estimate" and that even under "extreme conditions" the consequences of an accident would be "several orders of magnitude smaller." Peter Rathvon, attorney for Brookhaven, declared that the "risks, publicized by Dr. Solon, simply do not exist" and "are rejected by the scientific community." In light of the strength of the shipping casks, he submitted that "danger to the health and safety of any member of the public, including the truck driver, is essentially zero." Others, including four members of Congress and the assistant attorney general of New York State, expressed strong support, on legal and policy grounds, for upholding the ban. Those who spoke in favor of the city's regulations drew "sustained applause" from much of the audience.[24]

On April 5, 1978, DOT announced that it had found that existing federal law did not preempt New York City's ban. It reasoned that since the department had issued no federal regulations on routes that could be used to transport radioactive materials, the city's restrictions could remain in effect, at least for the time being. DOT disclosed that it planned to undertake rule-making proceedings to evaluate the need for a regulation on routing of radioactive shipments, a process that seemed likely to take one to two years. The ruling applied only to DOT's own regulations. DOT observed that despite its position, "the legality of New York City's health code provision . . . is still in serious doubt" because it might be preempted by the 1954 Atomic Energy Act or the interstate commerce provisions of the U.S. Constitution. DOT's decision came as an unpleasant surprise to nuclear proponents, who had anticipated a more favorable finding. William Brobst, head of DOE's transportation program, called it a "cop out" and accused DOT of "making a big fuss over something that doesn't hurt anything." *Nuclear Industry* reported that DOT's ruling was "a jolt to nuclear shippers," who feared "there would be a proliferation of similar bans in other cities and states."[25]

Those concerns soon proved justified. By January 1979 eleven states and eighteen local governments had placed restrictions on the transportation of nuclear materials. A year later, the total of states, cities, and counties that had taken such action exceeded one hundred. Many of the measures drew on the substance and language of New York City's regulation. The city council of New London, Connecticut, for example, imposed a ban similar to New York's on movement of spent fuel within its boundaries. It passed an ordinance after newspapers in the state revealed that in the wake of New York's prohibition, spent fuel from Brookhaven was carried by ferry across Long Island Sound, then unloaded in New London for shipment by truck to Savannah River. Nuclear industry representatives complained that the "growing patchwork of state and local regulations threatens to disrupt an absolutely essential transportation network." They called on the federal government to "make every effort to ensure that a comprehensive, practicable and uniform system of regulation" was established.[26]

DOT'S REGULATIONS ON SHIPPING RADIOACTIVE MATERIALS

DOT sought to achieve the nuclear industry's objective in its rule-making proceedings on routing of radioactive shipments. When the industry grumbled about the "snail's pace" of this process, DOT explained that its progress was delayed by "limited resources" and the "great care taken in developing a Federal scheme for preempting state and local regulations that states can live with." L.D. Santman, director of DOT's Materials Transportation Bureau, remarked, "I think there is a willingness on the part of most states and localities to back off if they are satisfied there is a Federal regulatory scheme" and "not just the planting of a flag." On January 31, 1980, DOT published a proposed regulation for public comment that would overrule local and state laws prohibiting or restricting nuclear shipments. *Nuclear Industry* reported, "It took the Department of Transportation four tedious years[,] . . . but nuclear shippers and carriers say the proposed rule was worth waiting for." The regulation would designate interstate highways, which had much lower accident rates than other roads, as the major avenues for shipments of large quantities of radioactive waste. It would invoke federal preemption to keep states and local jurisdictions from enacting measures that would disrupt the continuity of an interstate route, ban the use of an interstate highway without providing an alternative, or limit the hours during which nuclear materials could be transported. The DOT rule would allow for participation by state agencies in specific routing decisions, but it strongly asserted federal authority in setting overall guidelines and in disapproving local interdiction of radioactive shipments. An editorial in the *New York Times* applauded the proposal as a sign that "the Government is finally headed in the right direction—toward national regulation of a national problem."[27]

To receive comments on the proposed rule, DOT scheduled public meetings in Philadelphia, Chicago, Atlanta, Denver, Seattle, among other cities. Although some participants objected to federal preemption of state and local restrictions on nuclear traffic, the crowds were orderly and generally small. This pattern changed dramatically when DOT held a hearing in New York City on June 13, 1980. In a session that lasted for more than twelve hours, with breaks for lunch and dinner, those who packed an auditorium at police headquarters boisterously protested the proposed regulation. Fred C. Shapiro, a veteran reporter who had "covered plenty of disorderly—sometimes even chaotic—public proceedings" commented, "[This] was the only one that I thought really might end in a riot." The three DOT officials at the hearing explained the reasoning behind the proposed rule and argued that a "multiplicity of local transportation requirements" on radioactive shipments created "an entirely unworkable situation." Their position incited a torrent of abuse. One speaker compared them to the Nazi war criminal Adolf Eichmann. Another, a man who had a Ph.D. in biophysics, warned the DOT representatives that he would "watch [their] three heads being crushed like overripe watermelons"; he was followed by a professor who volunteered to help carry out the threat. The 117th and final speaker of the day exclaimed that the "Department of Transportation is a sneaky, slimy creature rising from a nest of other slimy creatures." The clearly shaken DOT staff members were escorted from the platform by police officers and sequestered in a parking lot until the crowd departed.[28]

The raucous hearing in New York testified vividly to public fears of radiation. They were fueled by the statements of public officials and antinuclear partisans who magnified the potential hazards of nuclear shipments far beyond the assessments that most experts provided. DOT and NRC staff officials acknowledged that the transportation of nuclear materials, especially spent fuel, imposed risks on the population. Spent fuel casks, like nuclear reactors, unavoidably emitted small levels of highly penetrating gamma radiation that could expose people along the routes used by shippers. The potential consequences of such releases were estimated at a small fraction of a single case of cancer in a heavily populated area annually. A severe accident or sabotage of a vehicle could conceivably rupture a cask and release dangerous amounts of radiation. The staffs of both agencies continued to consider measures to reduce the possibility of harmful exposures from serious accidents or sabotage, but they were confident that a large release of radiation even under those conditions was unlikely. They insisted that the health risks that nuclear shipments placed on the population were slight, especially when compared to the perils of hauling hazardous chemicals.[29]

On January 19, 1981, after conducting "the most burdensome rule-making in its history," including the review of more than one thousand public comments, DOT issued its final regulation. It was much the same as the proposed rule, though it made a few changes to allow state and local agencies a somewhat larger role in routing radioactive shipments. If they objected to the use of an interstate highway in their jurisdiction, they could initiate a process by which a "preferred" route could be selected. Cities or counties that wished to designate an alternative route were required to act through a state agency rather than impose their own rules. If a state sought to name a preferred route, DOT stipulated that it could not "make transportation between two points impossible by highway." The final version of the rule permitted local jurisdictions to place some limitations on the time of day when vehicles carrying large quantities of radioactive materials could use interstate highways, but it denied them authority to halt or "unnecessarily" delay a shipment. The regulation reiterated the department's view that the likelihood of serious public health effects from radioactive transportation was remote. "It is clear from the available technical information . . . that radiological risks in transporting radioactive materials resulting from both normal exposure and accidents are very low," it declared. "Even if one allows that the risk estimates developed by these technical risk studies are underestimated by an order of magnitude, the projected overall risks from the transportation of radioactive materials would still be extremely low."[30]

The city and state of New York sued DOT in federal court. On February 19, 1982, Judge Abraham Sofaer of the U.S. District Court for the Southern District of New York ruled that DOT's preemption of state and local bans on shipping large quantities of radioactive materials in heavily populated areas was "arbitrary, capricious, and an abuse of discretion." He found that the department had "failed adequately to evaluate and to address itself to the problems posed by low-probability/high consequence occurrences that are concededly 'credible.'" Sofaer later narrowed the application of his judgment to New York City, but supporters of DOT's position regarded it as an ominous precedent that would encourage other jurisdictions to take legal action to nullify the preemption provisions of the regulation. DOT appealed, and on August 10, 1983, the U.S. Court of Appeals for the Second Circuit in New York overturned Sofaer's ruling. In a 2–1 decision, it rejected Sofaer's criticism of DOT's risk assessment of the chances of a catastrophic nuclear transportation accident (which the department had defined as one that caused five deaths and as much as $9 billion in damage). "As long as the agency's choice of methodology is justifiable in light of current scientific thought, a reviewing court must accept that choice. . . . DOT considered a rule that might be expected to generate a catastrophic accident approximately once every 300 million years," the majority wrote. "After receiving advice from all sides, the Department decided that such a remote possibility, even of serious consequence, did not create a 'significant' risk for the human environment. Disquieting as it may be even to contemplate such matters, this decision cannot be said to be an abuse of discretion." The city of New York challenged the ruling, but the U.S. Supreme Court upheld DOT's regulation by refusing to review the circuit court's decision.[31]

The Supreme Court's action marked the end of the legal proceedings over DOT's transportation rules, but it did not signal the end of the debate. It provided, at best, an uneasy and temporary respite in the contention over federal authority in the routing of large quantities of radioactive materials and over the risks of nuclear shipments. The concern about the hazards of transporting the most dangerous forms of nuclear waste was still largely a hypothetical matter; nearly all the spent fuel from commercial nuclear power remained in storage at plant sites. Nevertheless, as the hearing in New York in June 1980 made abundantly clear, public anxieties were very real. Despite the extensive efforts of the responsible government agencies to reduce the risks to a minimum, nuclear transportation presented formidable problems of public acceptance that were an important part of the increasingly impassioned controversy over radioactive waste disposal.

CHAPTER 8

A Legislative "Solution"

The controversies over low-level radioactive waste burial and transportation of nuclear waste in the late 1970s and early 1980s had commanded increasing attention from local, state, and federal government agencies, from the nuclear industry, and from Congress. But the focus of concern and activity remained the storage and disposal of high-level waste. President Carter's policy statement on radioactive waste management in February 1980 elevated the question to new heights of visibility and urgency. After Ronald W. Reagan became president in January 1981, he called for the renewed growth of the nuclear power industry, and, as a corollary, he cited the importance of finding a solution to the waste issue. Both Carter and Reagan urged Congress to enact legislation that would provide suitable technical approaches and acceptable political solutions to the problem. In an effort to break the stalemate that had emerged, Congress considered various measures that reflected a wide, and sometimes bewildering, array of perspectives, priorities, and goals. Meanwhile, DOE continued its laborious efforts to investigate disposal alternatives while the NRC and EPA deliberated at length over establishing appropriate criteria for protecting public health and safety from the risks that radioactive waste presented.

THE NRC'S LICENSING PROCEDURES FOR A HIGH-LEVEL WASTE SITE

Within a short time after the NRC began to investigate the breadth of its responsibilities for protecting the public from the hazards of commercially generated radioactive waste, it took preliminary steps to develop performance standards and regulatory requirements for licensing high-level waste storage and disposal facilities. This was an essential part of carrying out the agency's regulatory mandate, but it was also an inherently imposing task because of the formidable technical, jurisdictional, and political uncertainties. Accordingly, the NRC did not publish final regulations on technical criteria for judging an application for a high-level waste site until late 1983, more than six years after it started to work on the problem.

In early 1977 the waste management staff circulated within the NRC a working paper that formed the basis for regulating high-level waste disposal in a geologic repository. When finalized, the new regulation would be published as Part 60 of Title 10 of the *Code of Federal Regulations,* and even in its initial stages, it was commonly referred to simply as "Part 60." The preparation of a draft Part 60 was, in the words of an NRC staff member, "one of the most difficult tasks we . . . ever tackled." The problems arose in part from the dearth of conclusive technical information for judging the safety of geologic disposal. At the outset, the NRC's efforts on Part 60 focused on the disposal of high-level wastes from reprocessing. The task became even more complicated after Carter announced the indefinite deferral of reprocessing. This raised a largely unexamined question: how to dispose of spent fuel rods that differed from reprocessing wastes both qualitatively and quantitatively.[1]

The NRC staff also encountered procedural perplexities when drafting Part 60. It was still unclear, for example, whether spent fuel rods qualified as high-level waste that the NRC was authorized to regulate. Further, the licensing process for a waste repository presented two troublesome issues: the NRC had never evaluated a proposal for a high-level waste site, and the applicant would be another government agency, which was sure to stir doubts about the independence of the NRC's regulatory review.[2]

After considering different approaches to the procedures it would use for licensing a high-level waste repository, the NRC published a draft policy statement for public comment in November 1978. It outlined a three-step process for reviewing a prospective facility that it hoped would conform with DOE's scheduling goals, provide flexibility on a series of pending technical issues, and, above all, afford reasonable assurance that the repository would not endanger public health and safety. The first step would be to consult informally with DOE in the selection of a site. The NRC maintained that "sound policy" required working with DOE "in an informal advisory capacity" on the "crucial" question of identifying a suitable site. A nonbinding exchange of information and concerns was consistent with the NRC's practices in judging applications for nuclear power reactors. The policy statement made clear that consultation between DOE and the NRC in the early stages of searching for a satisfactory site would not commit either agency to a specific course of action. DOE would be free to submit an application for any repository that it believed would meet the NRC's requirements, and the NRC would evaluate the application without prejudice on its merits.

The second step in the licensing process would begin when DOE made a formal application to the NRC to authorize construction of the proposed waste facility's main shaft. The NRC recognized that technical data about the site would still be incomplete at this stage, but it anticipated that enough information would be available to make a judgment about the likelihood that the repository could be built without "unreasonable risk" to the public. It would also conduct its review of the environmental impact of the project at this time. If its conclusions were favorable, it would allow DOE to start construction under the condition that unpredicted findings during "site characterization" or evidence of design flaws be reported. The final stage of the process was the NRC's approval of a license for the facility, which was necessary before DOE could place radioactive waste in it. DOE would be required to submit detailed and current technical data, results of research that addressed questions raised in previous reviews, and plans for operating the site. The NRC would then make a "definitive finding" about issuing a license. The agency would invite public comments and offer to hold public hearings as a part of its deliberations on both permitting construction and awarding a license.[3]

In October 1979, after weighing the comments it received on the policy statement and the recommendations of recent reports by the National Academy of Sciences and the Interagency Review Group on Nuclear Waste Management, the NRC staff recommended important changes in licensing procedures for a waste repository. The proposals, if accepted, would be included in Part 60. The most critical revision would substantially increase NRC requirements for exploratory construction.

Rather than authorize DOE to drill the main shaft and use the information gained to make a final licensing decision, the NRC staff argued, DOE should conduct extensive drilling, excavating, and testing "in the proposed host rock unit." This was essential "not only to determine whether serious but not readily observed defects are present, but also to determine specific properties such as homogeneity, porosity, the extent of fracturing and jointing, and the thermal response of the rock." Without such exploration and testing, the staff concluded, "neither the defects nor the key parameters can be determined with confidence." They suggested that at least three and perhaps more sites in different geologic media be characterized in this manner. They acknowledged that their proposals would cause potential delays and additional expenses in finding a suitable site but insisted that the gains in safety and public confidence would be worth the costs.[4]

DOE was not pleased with the NRC staff's proposals. When an article in *Nucleonics Week* suggested that the "lead for development of high-level waste policy appears to be shifting from DOE to NRC," an unnamed DOE official curtly responded, "DOE has the role of technology development." But it was clear that if the NRC staff's recommendations won the approval of the commissioners, they would force DOE to modify its approach to building a waste repository dramatically. DOE had planned to resolve at least some important technical issues after it received NRC's formal authorization to begin construction. But the NRC was now proposing that much more extensive research be performed before construction of the waste facility got underway. Unidentified NRC sources emphasized that the agency's role in site selection was strictly advisory. But they insisted that committing to a particular site before detailed characterization could be carried out would be a mistake. "The government cannot go out and spend all this money to get to the licensing stage and then not be able to license what we've got," said an NRC official. "What you're trading off is saving a lot of time on the front end or taking a risk and getting tied up in a long controversial hearing."[5]

The NRC published its revised rule on licensing procedures for public comment in December 1979. It also responded to congressional complaints that the proposed requirements were unnecessary for technical characterization and excessively costly. NRC chairman John F. Ahearne explained that agency experts believed that "multiple site characterization at disposal depth should be an integral part of any repository development program." He also contested DOE's claim that the price of exploring a single site in accordance with the NRC draft rule would run between $50 million and $100 million. The NRC estimated that DOE would have to spend about $20 million for each site characterization, which it viewed as a reasonable outlay for a project that DOE thought would cost $1 billion to $3 billion to build. On February 5, 1981, after considering public comments and making some minor revisions, the commissioners unanimously approved the final version of Part 60's licensing procedures.[6]

THE NRC'S TECHNICAL CRITERIA

At the same time that the NRC was working on licensing issues, it was drafting technical criteria for judging a waste repository application that would be included in Part 60. Agency staff members followed the model of the "general design criteria" for nuclear power plant applications, which listed broad requirements rather than detailed specifications. The design criteria outlined the objectives that applicants should address in their proposals without spelling out the nature and extent of the technical data that the NRC expected. They told applicants what to do but not how to do it.[7]

In November 1978 the NRC staff drew up a series of general technical criteria for a high-level waste repository in a geologic formation. The draft proposal set out guidelines for selecting a site, including the avoidance of areas with potential for seismic or volcanic activity, flooding, or hydrogeologic conditions that might allow the migration of radioactive elements to streams, lakes, or aquifers. It further specified that the chosen geologic formation should be able to tolerate temperature changes that could cause structural weakness. And it enumerated general design criteria for the construction of the facility to promote its safety. It included provisions for "multiple engineered barriers against the release of radioactivity"; the strength to withstand earthquakes, tornados, and flooding; and the ability to function even in the event of fires, explosions, or equipment breakdowns. The NRC draft placed particular emphasis on "waste form and packaging." This question had taken on increased importance after Carter decided to suspend reprocessing and authoritative studies, including the Interagency Review Group on Nuclear Waste Management's final report in 1979, concluded that geologic isolation alone was insufficient for safety. The waste packaging applied not only to the canister in which the waste (probably in the form of unreprocessed spent fuel) arrived at the repository but also to additional containers and backfill material that would provide redundant barriers to the escape of radioactivity.[8]

The NRC's draft criteria generated comments from federal and state agencies, the nuclear industry, public interest groups, individual scientists, and other interested observers. DOE, the organization that was most directly affected, took exception to some of the NRC's proposals. DOE was still focusing on geologic isolation as the primary means of safety, and *Nucleonics Week* reported that the importance the NRC attached to multiple barriers and waste packaging produced "some spirited debate between the two agencies." The NRC wanted the packaging to last without releasing radiation for at least 1,000 years. In its view, high-level waste would remain toxic for 1,000 to 10,000 years; after that time radiation levels would be "comparable to natural material deposits." It favored a requirement that the waste package should prevent the escape of any radioactivity for the first 1,000 years. It would stipulate that for the next 9,000 years or so, geologic media must keep the level of radiation releases within specified levels. Defining those levels for public exposure was the responsibility of EPA. On the packaging issue, DOE argued that although the "probability that the objective can be met" was "high," there was no sure way to demonstrate that a waste package would remain fully intact for a thousand years. Because a series of other barriers would guard against the migration of radioactive materials, it was not convinced of the need to guarantee the absolute integrity of waste packaging for such a long time. DOE and the NRC also took different positions on retrieving wastes if a licensed repository turned out to be unsuitable. DOE planned to make retrieval possible for five to ten years after the waste was placed in a repository, but the NRC supported a requirement of fifty years or more.[9]

While the NRC jousted with DOE over its proposed Part 60 design objectives, it debated with EPA, sometimes pointedly, over the draft regulation's performance requirements. The NRC complained about EPA's proposals for radiation standards for high-level waste disposal in terms similar to objections that DOE raised about the NRC. In 1976 EPA had decided that despite the many uncertainties about setting standards for population exposure to radiation from high-level waste repositories, it was obligated to offer reasonable guidelines to other federal agencies. Otherwise, "a failure on the part of EPA to provide Federal guidance could be considered a failure of EPA to perform its basic responsibility to the public." EPA officials anticipated that the criteria they issued would help to "determine the acceptability of waste disposal options," but they realized that their proposals would create "some jurisdictional differences of opinion with NRC."[10]

The requirements that EPA established were crucial to preparing the final version of the NRC's Part 60 regulations. When EPA published draft performance criteria for public comment in November 1978, the NRC's response was largely limited to requesting clarifications and changes in definitions. A few months later, however, after EPA came up with proposals on radioactive releases to the environment from a waste site, the NRC expressed strong reservations. EPA's draft standard stipulated that a high-level waste disposal site that the NRC licensed should offer "reasonable assurance" that over a period of 10,000 years, "no release" of radiation to the "accessible environment" would occur if the facility did not sustain damage from unanticipated "natural or human-induced processes or incidents." If "reasonably foreseeable" events that compromised the site's integrity took place, EPA listed the permissible amounts of several long-lived isotopes that could reach the environment over 10,000 years. The total release of plutonium-239, for example, was limited to 1,000 curies in that time. EPA further cited the acceptable probability of an event that could cause releases from the repository. The likelihood of a "reasonably foreseeable" event should not exceed "one chance in a hundred in 10,000 years." The chances of a major accident that released "more than 10 percent of the total mass of the high-level waste disposal at any location," which appeared to be "virtually impossible," should not exceed one in a million over 10,000 years.[11]

NRC officials, after meeting with their EPA counterparts, did not find the proposed requirements suitable for inclusion in Part 60. Their main objection was that there was no way to reliably predict that a licensed waste facility could meet EPA's draft standards. In a letter of June 22, 1979, NRC chairman Joseph Hendrie explained his agency's position to EPA administrator Douglas M. Costle. "We are specifically concerned about the analytical precision which may be implied by citing a probability as low as one in a million over 10,000 years," he wrote. "As it is presently drafted, the EPA standard would apparently require NRC to make a formal licensing finding in accordance with these specific probabilities. We have serious doubts that this would be possible because of the paucity of probability data in this field." EPA modified but did not remove the probability requirements from its subsequent drafts, and the NRC continued to object. John B. Martin, director of the NRC's waste management division, told EPA in May 1981 that the NRC would use numerical standards "to the extent practicable" but added that it believed "non-quantitative analyses must play a significant role in evaluating the acceptability of a waste disposal concept." He also emphasized that EPA's statutory authority applied only to setting standards, whereas the NRC's jurisdiction covered "the implementation and enforcement of such standards."[12]

As the debate with EPA proceeded, the NRC staff worked on a final version of Part 60's technical criteria. Both the staff and the commissioners carefully considered the comments on previous versions and made some changes in response. Although EPA had not yet published a final form of its standards, the NRC used "an assumed EPA standard" drawn from drafts. The NRC decided that it would use EPA's numerical requirements as an important part of its evaluation of a license application but also maintained that those standards should not be the "sole measure of performance." In light of the uncertainties in predicting the performance of engineered or geologic barriers over a long period, the NRC would also base its assessment of a proposed repository's safety on a "defense-in-depth" approach that established multiple independent barriers to the escape of radiation. It argued that "the performance of the engineered and natural barriers must each make a definite contribution in order for the Commission to be able to conclude that the EPA standard will be met."

In response to the complaints of DOE and other commenters, the NRC modified its draft rule that waste packages must not allow the escape of any radiation for a thousand years. It changed the wording to read that the packaging had to deliver "substantially complete" containment for that time. The NRC believed that this revision offered flexibility in the siting and design of a facility without sacrificing safety; DOE would still have to show that the multiple-barrier approach would meet performance standards for preventing the release of radiation to the environment. The NRC also revised its draft requirement on retrieval. It still "provisionally specified" that wastes should be retrievable for fifty years, but it allowed for changes in accordance with the findings of a "confirmation program" on the performance of a specific geologic formation. The regulation did not discuss the disposal of long-lived transuranic wastes as a separate issue, but the NRC expressed confidence that existing performance requirements would supply "adequate guidance" for transuranic materials. The NRC published its final rule on the technical criteria for licensing a high-level waste disposal site on June 21, 1983. It was keenly aware of the many uncertainties surrounding the safety of waste disposal and the applicability of its own requirements for a type of facility that had never been built and that had to perform effectively for thousands of years. But it hoped that the results of its six-year rule-making effort would provide sound, flexible, and credible guidance for constructing a functional repository without endangering public health.[13]

WASTE CONFIDENCE

While the NRC was deliberating over Part 60, it was also considering a related and even more ethereal problem: the basis for and extent of its confidence that a suitable solution for high-level waste disposal would be found. This question led to rule-making proceedings that went even longer than those for Part 60. The "waste confidence" issue had first arisen in 1977. The NRC, when denying a petition from the Natural Resources Defense Council for a "definitive finding" that high-level wastes could be "safely disposed of," had declared that it was "reasonably confident that permanent disposal . . . can be accomplished safely." It affirmed that progress was being made toward developing a waste repository and promised to review this conclusion periodically.[14]

In May 1979 the U.S. Court of Appeals for the District of Columbia Circuit gave the NRC additional incentive to examine its position on waste disposal. The court ruled on suits brought by the New England Coalition on Nuclear Pollution and the Minnesota Pollution Control Agency over the approval of license amendments for two nuclear plants, Vermont Yankee and Prairie Island. The owners of the reactors had requested NRC permission to expand their capacity for keeping spent fuel on-site while the government built a permanent repository. The court ordered the NRC to consider two questions: (1) whether there was "reasonable assurance" that a facility for storage of spent fuel from the plants would be available in 2007, when their licenses expired; and (2) if not, whether the spent fuel could be stored safely at the site beyond 2007. As a result, the agency began a rule-making proceeding to "reassess its degree of confidence that radioactive wastes produced by nuclear facilities will be safely disposed of" and to "determine when disposal will be available and . . . whether the wastes can be safely stored until safe disposal is accomplished."[15]

The NRC conducted a protracted rule-making proceeding on the question of waste confidence. It received public comments and heard oral arguments from federal agencies, state and local governments, industry, and public interest groups. It compiled an extensive record of expert opinion on waste issues and the prospects that a repository would be opened by 2007. The commissioners, despite differing views on some matters, concurred without much difficulty that there was "reasonable assurance" that high-level waste could be safely disposed of. They were less certain about how soon a repository would be built. Victor Gilinsky, who had served as a commissioner since the NRC began operations, agreed with his colleagues in July 1982 that "radioactive wastes can be stored safely at [a reactor] site beyond the expiration of a facility's license or until a permanent repository is built." But, as a keen observer of the history of radioactive waste policy, he was "not quite as confident about predicting the timely construction of the permanent repository" by 2007. Other commissioners expressed the same doubts, though they were encouraged when Congress passed the Nuclear Waste Policy Act of 1982, which set a timetable for the construction of a permanent repository for commercial high-level waste.[16]

On August 22, 1984, the NRC announced its position on waste confidence, which the commissioners approved without dissent. It disclosed that the Nuclear Waste Policy Act "had a significant bearing on the Commission's decision." Although the legislation was "intrinsically incapable of resolving technical issues," it would "establish the necessary programs, milestones, and funding mechanisms to enable their resolution in the years ahead." The commissioners found "reasonable assurance" that (1) safe disposal of high-level waste and spent fuel "in a geologic repository is technically feasible"; (2) one or more such repositories would be available by the years 2007–9; (3) high-level waste "will be managed in a safe manner until sufficient repository capacity is available"; (4) if necessary, spent fuel could be stored safely for at least thirty years after a plant's operating license expired; and (5) "safe independent onsite or offsite spent fuel storage will be made available if such storage capacity is needed." The statement added that since "unexpected events" could occur, the NRC would review its findings at least every five years until a high-level waste repository opened.[17]

DOE'S WASTE PROGRAMS

When President Carter issued his policy statement on radioactive waste in February 1980, he announced that DOE would serve as the "lead agency" in preparing a "detailed National Plan for Nuclear Waste Management." In January 1981, just before Carter left the White House, DOE published a two-volume report intended to carry out the president's directive. The department made clear that its study did not offer final answers for the many procedural and technical questions surrounding radioactive waste. But it hoped that the proposals it had developed would "provide a basis for review" of waste programs by Congress, federal, state, and local government agencies (including Indian tribes), scientific experts, industry, and the general public. In accordance with Carter's policy statement, DOE emphasized the need for broad-based public participation and the importance of cooperation with states through the State Planning Council that the president created.[18]

Although it was premature to recommend specific approaches for disposing of wastes, DOE advanced what appeared to be a realistic set of target dates for placing sites in operation. It called for the opening of a storage facility for spent fuel by 1985, a high-level waste repository by 2006 at the latest, and new commercial low-level waste burial grounds by the mid-1980s. By the time it published the report, DOE had moved away from reliance on geologic features as the primary means of containing radioactivity from waste materials. Instead, it accepted the views of the Interagency Review Group on Nuclear Waste Management, the NRC, and others that a waste disposal system must include a defense-in-depth approach with "several man-made and natural barrier components."[19]

DOE sponsored extensive research to develop a multilayered system of barriers to isolate waste. If commercial waste arrived at the disposal site in the form of spent fuel, which seemed likely, the fuel rods would be placed in a canister along with inert gas, melted glass, or liquified metal to fill unoccupied space. To guard against the penetration of water, this container would be placed in an "overpack canister" made of corrosion-resistant materials. A metal sleeve would surround the first two layers to furnish structural support and to ease retrieval if it proved necessary. Finally, a backfill material would be inserted between the sleeve and the walls of the geologic formation to absorb water and prevent migration of radioactive materials. The purpose of the multiple barriers was to meet the NRC's requirement that the packaging of radioactive waste last for 1,000 years. DOE hoped to identify backfill material that would remain effective for 10,000 years or more. This was an important consideration because spent fuel required 10,000 years to decay to a radioactive level comparable to uranium ore; high-level waste from reprocessing, by contrast, reached the same point in less than 1,000 years.

Meanwhile, DOE continued its search for sites for a high-level waste repository. Under a contract with the Battelle Memorial Institute of

Columbus, Ohio, the department spent a total of $62 million on this process in 1979 and 1980 and expected to pay out another $30 million in 1981. The objective of the program was to locate several potentially satisfactory sites in different geologic media. The suitability of each would depend on the characteristics of the geologic formation, the hydrology of the area, and evaluations of how the land had been used in the past and might be used in the future. By early 1981 DOE had turned up eight salt formations that appeared promising and had conducted exploratory work in basalt, granite, and compacted volcanic ash. Once a list of possible sites was compiled, several would be selected for detailed characterization. DOE met with state and local government officials and opinion leaders in areas of interest to explain its plans and to offer assurances that it would make no decision without allowing for ample public participation. The department hoped for but did not count on receiving state concurrence in choosing a site. It believed that, as a General Accounting Office study reported in June 1981, the "major problem associated with site selection is obtaining public and political acceptance." In the absence of state support for a siting decision, DOE was prepared to move ahead. "The waste problem is already of such paramount importance that a solution must be obtained," the GAO report commented, "even if one or more segments of the public are dissatisfied."[20]

THE REAGAN ADMINISTRATION AND NUCLEAR WASTE

When Ronald Reagan entered the White House in January 1981, the nuclear industry was suffering from a major slump. Since the mid-1970s the combined effects of inflation and economic stagnation, especially acute during the later Carter years, had reduced demand for power at the same time that they drove up the costs of building new plants. Largely as a result of "stagflation," the nuclear industry had been plagued by a sharp decline in orders and cancellations of planned projects. The industry received another crushing setback from the severe accident at the Three Mile Island nuclear plant in March 1979. The events at Three Mile Island not only substantially increased public opposition to nuclear power but also caused the NRC to impose a series of new and expensive requirements on utilities that owned nuclear plants.[21]

Reagan was committed to reviving the fortunes of commercial nuclear power. The trade journal *Nuclear Industry* reported that his election victory had generated "exhilaration in the nuclear power community" and suggested that his policies would "make a faltering nuclear industry viable and robust again." Soon after Reagan took office, cabinet members and White House staff began drafting a presidential statement on nuclear power. Its purpose was to emphasize the president's strong support for "getting nuclear power back on track." In the view of administration officials, the nuclear industry was in "deplorable condition" because of "financial uncertainties, over-regulation, and other impediments." The president's policy statement was "aimed at redressing these problems and revitalizing [the] nuclear industry."[22]

The White House released Reagan's statement on nuclear power on October 8, 1981. Because the president was busy with other obligations, Secretary of Energy James B. Edwards presented the message at a White House ceremony. The statement lamented that the growth of nuclear power had been hobbled by a "morass of regulations that do not enhance safety" and by the failure of the federal government "to work with industry to develop an acceptable system for commercial waste disposal." Accordingly, it announced, the president was taking several steps to "correct present government deficiencies." He ordered the secretary of energy to recommend improvements in licensing procedures and called on the NRC to "remove unnecessary obstacles to the deployment of the current generation of nuclear power reactors." With regard to waste issues, Reagan terminated Carter's indefinite deferral of commercial reprocessing and pledged to "pursue consistent, long-term policies concerning reprocessing of spent fuel." He directed the secretary of energy, in collaboration with industry and state governments, to "proceed swiftly" to determine a method of storing and disposing of high-level waste and to "demonstrate to the public that problems associated with management of nuclear waste can be resolved."[23]

Nuclear industry officials were pleased but not thrilled with Reagan's message. They appreciated his unequivocal endorsement of nuclear power, but they regretted that the statement was released "with little push for public attention." More important, they recognized that the actions the president announced were not enough in themselves to remedy the problems they faced. "The real issue," Herman R. Hill, executive vice president of General Electric, told a friend, "is how and whether his position will be implemented to accomplish the major, comprehensive changes required." Although the industry applauded the reversal of Carter's ban on reprocessing, it had little confidence in the commercial prospects for the technology. The owners of the Barnwell reprocessing facility in South Carolina, for example, commented that they were "convinced that nuclear fuel reprocessing is not commercially practicable."

The Atomic Industrial Forum expressed disappointment with Reagan's proposals for waste management. It complained that the policy statement did not include support for an interim spent fuel storage facility or for a reprocessing demonstration plant funded by the government.[24]

The White House was well aware of the industry's criticism of the president's statement on nuclear power. Presidential science adviser George A. Keyworth commented in a meeting of high-level staff officials in March 1982, "The words were well received but our friends are now saying that we are not implementing our own policy statement." He and his colleagues agreed that the White House should press for progress on waste management, where "our friends feel we should have taken the lead." As a result, the staff drafted a presidential message to Congress on pending nuclear waste legislation, a step that won "enthusiastic" support from Senate Republicans who were working to get a satisfactory measure passed. Reagan declared that he favored a bill that would accomplish several goals. They included provisions for "an appropriate and effective method" for state participation in waste issues, a "temporary storage facility" to ease the shortage of spent fuel storage capacity at some nuclear plants, and a permanent disposal repository "at the earliest practicable date." The president also cited his support for commercial reprocessing as a means to "provide access to significant remaining fuel value" and to "significantly reduce the volume of high-level waste." He urged Congress to act promptly on legislation that would "allow us to move ahead and deal with this issue in a timely and responsible manner."[25]

THE NUCLEAR WASTE POLICY ACT OF 1982

Well before Reagan released his appeal for waste legislation, Congress had been considering various measures. Members of Congress and their staffs weighed the technical and political complexities of waste issues partly in response to the recommendations of both Carter and Reagan. But they acted more as a result of a wide bipartisan consensus that the time had come to break the prevailing stalemate over radioactive waste storage and disposal. In an effort to deal with technical uncertainties and political sensitivities without incurring the wrath of their constituents, members of Congress advanced differing and sometimes sharply conflicting proposals. "While there seems to be general agreement on the need for legislation to establish a national waste policy," *Congressional Quarterly* reported in April 1982, "members do not relish having a waste dump in their states." In December 1982 Congress overwhelmingly passed the Nuclear Waste Policy Act. It was a compromise that inevitably failed to satisfy all interested parties but that supporters hoped would produce orderly and predictable progress toward the construction of waste disposal facilities.[26]

The waste policy act had a long gestation period. Although Congress had shown growing concern about radioactive waste during the late 1970s, the pace and intensity had picked up after Carter issued his presidential policy statement in February 1980. By the end of the year, the House and the Senate passed bills to establish a national program, but they could not agree in conference on a way to settle differences in the measures. The proposals on high-level waste expired when Congress adjourned, though sections on low-level waste were salvaged as the Low-Level Radioactive Waste Policy Act. The primary reason that high-level waste legislation failed was a conflict over the handling of military wastes, which was closely tied to questions about the authority of individual states to veto federal siting decisions and about the NRC's licensing procedures. The Senate rejected the House's support for a requirement that both military and commercial wastes would be covered by the legislation. Henry M. Jackson, chairman of the Senate Committee on Energy and Natural Resources, objected to allowing a state veto of a proposed site for disposing of military waste, even if Congress could override the state's action. He did not want to set a precedent for an expansion of state influence in national defense issues. In addition, he and his Senate colleagues opposed a law that would subject military wastes to what *Nuclear Industry* called "the Byzantine NRC licensing process." They pressed for removal of military waste from the bill, and the contention over this issue killed the chances of compromise. Nevertheless, the nuclear industry and others who favored waste legislation were encouraged that the near-success was "a good omen for passage of an acceptable bill."[27]

When the new Congress convened in January 1981, the Republicans had gained control of the Senate. A bipartisan commitment to passing a law on high-level waste remained intact, but progress on a measure that would satisfy enough members for approval remained slow and precarious. James A. McClure of Idaho, chairman of the Senate Committee on Energy and Natural Resources, took the lead by introducing legislation in September 1981. He received steadfast backing from Alan K. Simpson of Wyoming, chairman of the Subcommittee on Nuclear Regulation of the Senate Committee on Environment and Public Works. Both strongly supported nuclear power development and pushed for waste legislation as an essential step to counter the ills of the industry. "We're about to bring the nuclear industry to its knees unless we act now," Simpson declared in April 1982. In the House, waste proposals came under the jurisdiction of at least four committees that were much less favorably disposed toward nuclear power.[28]

When McClure introduced his bill, he attempted to resolve the question that had scuttled legislation in the previous session by stating that its requirements would apply strictly to high-level wastes from civilian reactors. Simpson and many of his colleagues, however, believed that Congress should not ignore the high-level wastes generated in the production of materials for nuclear weapons, which was about 90 percent of the total inventory that required disposal. The Subcommittee on Nuclear Regulation passed an amendment that finessed the issue. It placed the final decision on whether a site should be used for wastes from both nuclear power and "atomic energy defense activities" in the hands of the president. Unless the president found that separate facilities were necessary, DOE was instructed to develop a "unified system" for military and commercial wastes. This approach eventually prevailed in the Senate and served to focus attention on arrangements for storage and disposal of civilian waste.[29]

The compromise over inclusion of military wastes in the legislation settled one key dispute, but there were major differences on other issues. Although there was agreement on the need to find an appropriate geologic formation for high-level waste, the location of the facility and the role of the states in siting decisions continued to generate intense debate. Few members of Congress argued that individual states should be awarded an absolute veto over a site that detailed characterization showed to be suitable. State officials took the same position. The State Planning Council on Radioactive Waste Management, which Carter had established in 1980, commented in a report it submitted to Reagan in August 1981, "The Council believes that neither an absolute state veto nor the arbitrary preemptive imposition of Federal will is the appropriate way to resolve an impasse." Supporters of waste legislation concluded that the best method "to resolve an impasse" was to specify that Congress could override a state veto. But the questions of whether action by both the Senate and the House would be needed and where the burden would be placed for taking the initiative on sustaining a state's disapproval produced a great deal of animated discussion.[30]

Another highly divisive issue was away-from-reactor storage of spent fuel. *Nuclear Industry* reported that this was "perhaps the most contentious part" of the debate over waste legislation. The industry, worried about a pending shortage of storage capacity at operating nuclear plants, lobbied hard for temporary space for fuel rods. Carter had proposed that such a facility be built in 1977, but Congress had not taken action. The likeliest destinations for spent fuel were the three existing, though nonfunctioning, commercial reprocessing plants at West Valley, New York; Morris, Illinois; and Barnwell, South Carolina. They were equipped to receive and handle spent fuel, and DOE had sought information from their owners as a preliminary step toward purchasing them. The prospect of converting those plants to away-from-reactor storage sites triggered spirited opposition in their home states. The congressional delegations of South Carolina, Illinois, and New York feared that government-operated away-from-reactor storage installations would become permanent fixtures. "After all, when we say a 'temporary basis,'" Representative Butler Derrick of South Carolina commented, "it has been my thought and observation that this nuclear waste stays where it is first put." One reason that Reagan issued his presidential statement on radioactive waste in April 1982 was to reassure members of Congress, including pro-nuclear Republicans, that away-from-reactor storage would be limited in scope and temporary in duration.[31]

Like away-from-reactor storage, the worries of individual states that they would become that nation's radioactive waste dump heavily influenced consideration of "monitored retrievable storage." In the wake of the Lyons, Kansas, debacle, the AEC had promoted the idea of constructing concrete and steel vaults above ground to provide storage of high-level waste for a hundred years or more. This proposal had foundered after the AEC's demise, largely because of concerns that it would divert attention and resources from the search for a permanent geologic site. But retrievable storage was appealing precisely for that reason to members of Congress who feared that a permanent repository would be located in their state. The most prominent advocate of storing wastes for an extended period in structures above ground, or perhaps near the surface, was Senator J. Bennett Johnston, a Democrat from Louisiana. As an influential member of the Senate Committee on Energy and Natural Resources, he sought ways to increase energy supplies from all sources in the United States. Consequently, he favored waste legislation that would spur the growth of nuclear power. At the same time, Johnston was keenly aware that DOE was investigating salt domes in northern Louisiana as a possible site for a high-level waste repository. Therefore, he pushed for monitored retrievable storage as a long-term approach to the high-level waste problem that would not saddle his own state with the risks of permanent disposal. He argued that monitored storage vaults could be safely placed "in any State in the continental United States" and suggested that tunnels built for nuclear weapons tests in Nevada might offer an auspicious setting.[32]

Johnston's position stirred doubts from a variety perspectives. In a rare congruence, both the nuclear industry and environmental groups faulted retrievable storage as a stopgap measure. The industry was "lukewarm" because of apprehension that it would undermine away-from-reactor storage and slow progress toward a geologic repository. Environmentalists complained that it would transfer the problem of finding a solution to high-level disposal to future generations. Further, even if retrievable storage proved technically sound, it did not provide a way out of the political quandary surrounding waste. There was no reason to believe that a local population would welcome the siting of a storage vault any more warmly than a geologic repository.[33]

Both houses of Congress worked through the state veto and away-from-reactor storage and monitored retrievable storage issues slowly and at times painfully. The Senate, where key committee chairs pressed for legislation and jurisdictional lines were clear, acted first. On April 29, 1982, it approved a modified version of McClure's bill by a vote of 69–9. It set a timetable for DOE to characterize at least three geologic sites for suitability as waste repositories. By January 1, 1986, the department would recommend one of those sites to the president, who would make the final decision. By January 1, 1989, DOE would recommend a second site to the president. After the president approved a site, DOE would submit an application for a construction permit to the NRC, which was required to rule on the first application by the end of 1989 and the second by the end of 1992.

The Senate bill specified that early in the selection process, DOE would notify the state or Indian tribe on whose land the proposed repository would be located. The department would attempt to resolve questions and conflicts through "consultation and concurrence." If the state or tribe still objected, it could file a petition to Congress that would automatically be placed on the legislative calendar. The state's or tribe's veto would stand if one house of Congress passed a resolution supporting it. Otherwise, the application would proceed. The Senate defeated the efforts of members from South Carolina, New York, and Illinois to remove away-from-reactor storage from the legislation. It did, however, limit the capacity of such storage to 2,800 metric tons (the total weight of spent fuel at civilian plants at the time was about 2,500 metric tons). It also stipulated that the government could keep spent fuel in away-from-reactor storage for a maximum of twelve years. Senator Johnston was more successful than his colleagues from states with reprocessing plants in gaining support for his primary objective. The Senate bill directed DOE to provide Congress with a detailed plan within one year after enactment of the law for building at least one monitored retrievable storage facility.[34]

The bill that emerged from the Senate satisfied the White House, DOE, and the nuclear industry. Environmental critics of nuclear power, on the other hand, strongly objected to the provisions that obligated potential host states to find support in Congress for a veto and that provided for away-from-reactor storage and monitored retrievable storage. The prospects for passage of a House bill that was reasonably compatible with the Senate measure were uncertain, in part because of the influence of environmentalists and in part because of divided jurisdiction over nuclear waste issues. The chances of success were improved, however, by the positions of the chairs of three key committees and subcommittees. Morris K. Udall, chairman of the Committee on Interior and Insular Affairs, John D. Dingell, chairman of the Committee on Energy and Commerce, and Richard L. Ottinger, chairman of that committee's Subcommittee on Energy Conservation and Power, were sympathetic to environmental concerns and skeptical of nuclear power but also committed to passing radioactive waste legislation. Udall spearheaded eventual House approval of a bill after what *Congressional Quarterly* called a "long and tortuous route" to the floor.

The bill that the House passed on December 2, 1982, by a voice vote was quite different from the Senate's measure. It extended the timetable for selecting and reviewing an application for the first site by about three years. It set a considerably lower limit on the spent fuel that could be stored in an away-from-reactor facility, 1,700 metric tons instead of the 2,800 that the Senate prescribed. It also prohibited the use of the West Valley, Barnwell, or Morris plant for this purpose to placate members from their states. The House bill allowed DOE five years to conduct a study and submit a report on monitored retrievable storage. Udall argued that "MRS technology is not the best answer to our national nuclear waste problem." This judgment conflicted sharply with the views of Senator Johnston and his House colleagues from Louisiana, who regarded retrievable storage as an alternative to geologic siting and sought the results of a DOE investigation within one year. The House defeated an amendment that would have granted states and tribes an absolute veto over the location of a permanent repository, and, on this issue, it took a position consistent with the Senate by adopting the same procedures for overriding a veto.[35]

The bills passed by the House and Senate were divergent enough that agreement on a compromise measure was very much in doubt. But the proponents of legislation gradually found common ground. The timetable for selecting two sites for a geologic repository stretched the schedule in the Senate bill, but not by much. The legislation that reached the floor of each house directed DOE to conduct studies of five sites and recommend three of them to the president for detailed characterization by January 1, 1985. The president would designate one site and inform Congress by March 31, 1987, and the NRC would rule on the application for a construction permit within three years. Meanwhile, DOE would study at least five other sites and recommend three of them to the president as potential locations for a second repository by July 1, 1989. The president would decide on a second site by March 31, 1990. Utilities would be assessed a fee to pay for the costs of building a waste facility, and DOE would take possession of the spent fuel from their plants by December 31, 1998.

After tense negotiations, Udall and Johnston split the difference on the timing for DOE's planning report on monitored retrievable storage by stipulating that it should be completed within two and one-half years. The factious question of away-from-reactor storage was resolved largely along the lines that the House (and host-state senators) favored. Such a facility could be used for up to 1,900 metric tons of spent fuel, but it had to be located on existing federal property, which excluded West Valley, Barnwell, and Morris. Senator Strom Thurmond of South Carolina also won approval for an amendment that required removal of spent fuel from storage within three years after a permanent repository opened. With those and other issues settled, the prospects for enactment of a law looked promising as the congressional session neared its end.

The legislation almost failed, however, when Senator William Proxmire of Wisconsin, a potential location for a repository, threatened a filibuster unless states received greater authority to veto a site that DOE selected. In place of forcing a state to persuade one house of Congress to uphold its objection, he offered an amendment that would require both houses of Congress to override a state veto. Otherwise, the site would be eliminated. This assigned Congress the responsibility of taking action and seemed to its supporters to provide the states with more influence in a siting decision. "We believe it is extremely important that the Nuclear Waste Policy Act require action of both houses to override state disapproval," the governors of New Mexico, Nevada, Utah, and Washington argued. "The burden of proof should rest with the US Department of Energy to sustain such an override. Requiring Western states with numerically small delegations to provide the burden of proof is an overwhelming and unfair task." Proxmire's willingness to filibuster this issue would have doomed the legislation, and the Senate promptly accepted his amendment. On December 20, 1982, the Senate approved the final form of the bill by a voice vote; the House followed suit a few hours later by a vote of 256–32.[36]

The Nuclear Waste Policy Act was a milestone achievement. After years of false starts, delays, and stalemate, it made clear the government's commitment to deal with a complex and controversial issue. Industry and DOE officials expressed hope that this would reassure the public and help restore confidence in nuclear power. Loring Mills, vice president of the Edison Electric Institute, commented, "Waste legislation sets a framework that allows us to say, in fact, we know how to resolve this issue, and it's no longer an impediment to going forward with nuclear power." Robert F. Bonitati, a special assistant to President Reagan, suggested, "[The act] provides the long overdue assurance that we now have a safe and effective solution to the nuclear waste problem." Other well-informed observers were less certain that the law provided a solution to the problem it addressed. An article in *Science* magazine made a comment about the original bill the Senate passed in April 1982 that was equally applicable to the final version of the law. "A bill like this would have to be considered only a hesitant first try at solving the nuclear waste problem," wrote Eliot Marshall of the journal's staff. "It deals with none of the technical disputes and leaves the highly difficult task of site selection to the bureaucracy."[37]

THE NUCLEAR WASTE POLICY ACT AMENDMENTS OF 1987

As Marshall cautioned, formidable technical and political uncertainties surrounding high-level disposal remained even after passage of the waste policy act. It was soon clear that the law did not provide the solution that optimists had predicted. DOE, in accordance with the requirements of the law, conducted environmental evaluations of possible disposal sites and selected five leading candidates: salt deposits in Mississippi, Texas, and Utah, basalt formations at Hanford, and tuff rock in Nevada.

In May 1986 Secretary of Energy John S. Herrington disclosed that the three final choices for detailed characterization were sites in Deaf Smith County, Texas; Yucca Mountain, Nevada; and Hanford. DOE's decision stirred angry protests from the designated areas, whose representatives charged that the department's judgment was based more on political than technical considerations. Herrington also announced that the search for a second site would be suspended because the need for it was not pressing. Supporters of the waste policy act had reached an informal understanding that a second repository would be located in the eastern part of the country, and westerners denounced DOE's action. Congress responded by cutting off funds for site characterization. Congressman Udall complained in July 1987, "The program is in ruins and our goal of siting a repository seems further away than ever."[38]

Senator Bennett Johnston, who had become chairman of the Senate Committee on Energy and Natural Resources, sought to break the impasse. He and McClure introduced a bill that would effectively limit DOE's site characterization activities to a single location—Yucca Mountain. The proposal provoked bitter opposition from Nevada legislators; Senator Harry Reid labeled it the "Screw Nevada Bill" and complained that his state was targeted because it was "the small kid on the block." The protests from Nevada were to no avail. In December 1987 Congress, as a part of a budget bill, passed amendments to the waste policy act that directed DOE to conduct exploratory investigations at Yucca Mountain and to stop work at Hanford and in Deaf Smith County. If the department found Yucca Mountain unsuitable for burying high-level wastes, it was required to halt its search for a site until it received guidance from Congress. The 1987 amendments nullified the waste policy act's procedures for choosing a location for a repository. Congress removed site selection from DOE and the president and instead dictated its own decision. Johnston commented, "I think it's fair to say we've solved the nuclear waste problem with this legislation." An unnamed congressional staff member was more restrained. "It's a roll of the dice with Yucca Mountain," the aide remarked. "We have reason to believe it will work out, but if it doesn't[,] . . . man, we're in trouble."[39]

THE YUCCA MOUNTAIN CONTROVERSY

After passage of the 1987 amendments, the technical and political questions surrounding high-level waste and spent fuel disposal shifted from a broad setting to a focus on Yucca Mountain. Nevada officials adamantly opposed development of the site and undertook a series of legal, political, and public relations efforts to block it. They cited many of the same objections that critics of waste programs had raised for years, including the risks of transporting spent fuel from distant locations on interstate highways and railroads. The state mounted a formidable campaign against Yucca Mountain, but its position was always subject to being overruled by majority votes in Congress. The technical issues that arose when DOE proceeded with its detailed characterization of the site were less predictable than Nevada's dissent and fueled the controversy. By 2001 DOE had spent about $4.5 billion to build tunnels and drill bore holes a thousand feet under the surface at Yucca Mountain. Its findings greatly expanded the technical bases for making a judgment about the suitability of the site. Its research also showed that the geology of the area was more complex than originally believed and that the underground environment was not as dry as anticipated. While DOE investigated the possible effects of water flow through fractures in rock, it also sought to address concerns about the long-term reliability of new designs for waste containers that were intended to limit the release of radiation to very small amounts for 10,000 years.[40]

In February 2002 Secretary of Energy Spencer Abraham, in accordance with the procedures specified in the Nuclear Waste Policy Act of 1982, formally recommended to President George W. Bush that Yucca Mountain be constructed as the nation's first high-level waste repository. He declared that after years of research, scientists who had studied the "safety and suitability" of the site were confident that "Yucca Mountain would be safe." He argued that analyses of possible but unlikely threats from earthquakes, volcanoes, and water damage demonstrated that the site could meet EPA's standards for population exposure to radiation, which had been published in 2001. Bush immediately approved Abraham's recommendation. Kenny Guinn, governor of Nevada, protested that DOE's judgment was not based on "sound science and common sense," and he vetoed the selection of Yucca Mountain. A few weeks later, both houses of Congress, as the waste policy act allowed, gave the Yucca Mountain project a green light by voting to override Guinn's veto.[41]

The action of Congress was an important step forward for supporters of Yucca Mountain, but they acknowledged that crucial design and technical issues remained to be addressed. DOE was still investigating both the geology of the site and the performance of storage containers, and its 2010 target date for opening the repository clearly was slipping. DOE received an unexpected setback in August 2004 when the U.S.

Court of Appeals for the D.C. Circuit ruled that EPA was required by law to set radiation standards not just for 10,000 years but for one million years. The decision forced EPA to thoroughly reconsider its standards because the canisters that held the waste, the first barrier against the escape of radiation to the environment, were designed to last for 10,000 years or more but not close to one million years. In 2005 EPA published for public comment a two-tier standard that was more rigorous for the first 10,000 years (15 millirems annually). It explained that the higher permissible dose it proposed after 10,000 years (350 millirems annually) was still a low exposure, comparable to background radiation levels in many parts of the United States and considerably less than in mountainous regions. EPA's position was not convincing to Yucca Mountain opponents. Guinn called it "a ridiculous standard" that demonstrated "junk science at its worst."[42]

In June 2008 DOE submitted to the NRC an 8,600-page application for a license to build and operate the Yucca Mountain repository. Although it was still waiting for EPA to issue a final version of radiation limits, it saw no reason to delay the application. Secretary of Energy Samuel W. Bodman commented that there was "plenty of time for EPA to describe in some detail the standards they will set." Three months later, the NRC announced that the application was "sufficiently complete" to begin a comprehensive review. By law, it was required to reach a determination on licensing the facility within four years. DOE estimated that, depending on the NRC's decision and funding from Congress, the "best achievable date" for opening the Yucca Mountain repository was 2020. While owners of nuclear power plants waited for a permanent repository, they kept their spent fuel on-site in pools of water and in large dry-cask storage containers.[43]

A CONTINUING DEBATE

After more than six decades of addressing the problem of high-level radioactive waste, the related issues of storage, geologic disposal, reprocessing, and transportation continued to defy easy or certain resolution. From the late 1940s until the early 1970s, the AEC believed that it was effectively managing radioactive waste in the short term and making steady progress toward a long-term means of disposal. The Lyons fiasco finally discredited the agency's facile assumptions and forced it back to the drawing board to search for a suitable approach. Over the next decade, the AEC, its successors, and other federal agencies explored a wide range of storage and geologic disposal options that answered some questions but raised many others. The technical investigations of waste disposal procedures became more complex, more diverse, and more sophisticated. They did not provide conclusive technical solutions for the challenges of safe management of high-level commercial waste for centuries, but they offered a much stronger base of knowledge for making decisions. In that respect, the AEC's failure to build a repository was inadvertently beneficial because it would have delivered a premature and perhaps unsatisfactory solution to disposing of waste. The Lyons salt mine was the prime example, in extremis, of pushing for a site that proved glaringly and embarrassingly deficient.

Despite the uncertainties that were an unavoidable part of waste disposal programs, technical experts with a wide range of differing perspectives agreed that geologic burial was an appropriate and feasible method of safe disposal of solidified high-level waste and fuel rods. Over the years, the favored technical approach evolved from direct disposal of liquids to solidification and short-term packaging to multiple barriers and long-term packaging. By the late 1970s experts viewed a repository with a defense-in-depth design using both robust artificial packaging and natural geologic barriers as the best means of protection against radioactive hazards from waste disposal.

The safety of any waste disposal facility required the development of a satisfactory site. And this, of course, depended on winning public support for a site that experts found suitable. Shortly after it began operations, the AEC had recognized that radioactive waste was a politically sensitive issue and had sought to combat latent public "hysteria." But it made a series of blunders through the years, especially at Lyons and Hanford, that fed public anxieties and eroded confidence in its programs. In light of popular fears of radiation and the highly publicized acrimony of the nuclear power debate, strong public objections to potential waste sites were probably inevitable. But they were intensified by the AEC's grievous errors in its performance on waste issues. After the AEC was abolished, gaining public approval for a high-level waste repository was at best difficult and at worst impossible, as ERDA and DOE learned when they searched for possible sites in the late 1970s and 1980s. Congress finally tried to end political stalemate in 1987 by dictating selection of Yucca Mountain as the first, and presumably only, site to be characterized. In doing so, it short-circuited the procedures for choosing sites that the authors of the 1982 waste policy act had laboriously worked out and incited furious opposition in Nevada.

The history of the search for an acceptable location for a waste repository highlighted both technical and political complexities that responsible officials recognized but too often dealt with indifferently or incompetently between the late 1940s and the early 1970s. Progress on technical issues in the late 1970s and 1980s occurred simultaneously with setbacks on the political issues that siting triggered. The quest for a long-term solution to high-level waste disposal remained a perplexing national problem that was too important to ignore, too controversial to compromise easily, and too complicated to settle conclusively.

Notes

CHAPTER 1

1. U.S. Congress, Joint Committee on Atomic Energy, *Hearings on Industrial Radioactive Waste Disposal,* 86th Cong., 1st Sess., 1959, p. 12; *Journal of Glenn T. Seaborg,* 25 vols. (Berkeley: Lawrence Berkeley Laboratory PUB-625, 1989), vol. 14, pp. 639–40 (available in the Glenn T. Seaborg Papers, Manuscript Division, Library of Congress, Washington, DC); AEC 180/5 (March 30, 1956), Office of the Secretary, General Correspondence, Box 46 (MAT-12, Waste Processing and Disposal), Record Group 326 (Records of the Atomic Energy Commission), National Archives, College Park, MD ("AEC Papers" were prepared by the agency staff for the consideration of the commissioners in the decision-making process).

2. Robert De Roos, "What Are We Doing about Our Deadly Atomic Garbage?" *Collier's,* August 20, 1955, pp. 28–34; "Death-Dealing Debris," *Newsweek,* July 15, 1957, pp. 96–98; "The Atom: What to Do with the Waste," *Time,* January 12, 1962, p. 13; Walter Schneir, "The Atom's Poisonous Garbage," *The Reporter,* March 17, 1960, p. 18; "Nuclear Dilemma," *Business Week,* December 25, 1978, p. 60; AEC 180/1 (October 17, 1949), Office of the Secretary, General Correspondence, Box 64 (Control of Atomic Wastes), AEC Records, National Archives, College Park, MD.

3. Karl Z. Morgan, "Radiation Safety: A New Industrial Problem," *Scientific American* 178 (January 1948): 4–8; Joint Committee on Atomic Energy, *Hearings on Industrial Radioactive Waste Disposal,* pp. 171–578; Fred C. Shapiro, *Radwaste: A Reporter's Investigation of a Growing Nuclear Menace* (New York: Random House, 1981), chaps. 1, 3, 6; Michele Stenehjem Gerber, *On*

the Home Front: The Cold War Legacy of the Hanford Nuclear Site (Lincoln: University of Nebraska Press, 1992), chaps. 2–6; Kevin D. Crowley and John F. Ahearne, "Managing the Environmental Legacy of U.S. Nuclear-Weapons Production," *American Scientist* 90 (November–December 1992): 514–23; Thomas E. Marceau et al., *Hanford Site Historic District: History of the Plutonium Production Facilities, 1943–1990* (Columbus, OH: Battelle Press, 2003), chap. 6; Roy E. Gephart, *Hanford: A Conversation about Nuclear Waste and Cleanup* (Columbus, OH: Battelle Press, 2003), chaps. 1, 5; Terrence R. Fehner and F.G. Gosling, "Coming in from the Cold: Regulating U.S. Department of Energy Facilities, 1942–96," *Environmental History* 1 (April 1996): 5–33.

4. J. Samuel Walker, *Permissible Dose: A History of Radiation Protection in the Twentieth Century* (Berkeley: University of California Press, 2000), pp. 1–12; J. Samuel Walker, "The Controversy over Radiation Safety: A Historical Overview," *JAMA* 262 (August 4, 1989): 664–68.

5. Walker, *Permissible Dose,* pp. 11–15.

6. Morgan, "Radiation Safety: A New Industrial Problem," p. 8; S.T. Cantril and H.M. Parker, "The Status of Health and Protection at Hanford Engineer Works," August 24, 1945, HW-7-2136, http://www2.hanford.gov/ddrs/common/findpage.cfm?AKey = D197210637 (accessed May 26, 2005).

7. U.S. Atomic Energy Commission, *Handling Radioactive Wastes in the Atomic Energy Program* (Washington, DC: Government Printing Office, 1949); L.P. Hatch, "Ultimate Disposal of Radioactive Wastes," *American Scientist* 41 (July 1953): 410–21; Joint Committee on Atomic Energy, *Hearings on Industrial Radioactive Waste Disposal,* pp. 465–92; Gephart, *Hanford,* chap. 5.

8. H.M. Parker to W.D. Norwood, January 14, 1946, HW-7-3217, http://www2.hanford.gov/ddrs/common/findpage.cfm?AKey=D197211375 (accessed June 9, 2005).

9. Michael Joshua Silverman, "No Immediate Risk: Environmental Safety in Nuclear Weapons Production, 1942–1985" (Ph.D. diss., Carnegie Mellon University, 2000), pp. 104–66; Advisory Committee on Human Radiation Experiments, *Final Report* (Washington, DC: Government Printing Office, 1995), pp. 506–18; Gephart, *Hanford,* pp. 5.46–5.51; Gerber, *On the Home Front,* pp. 88–92.

Information about the green run and other radiation releases from Hanford remained secret for many years. When public disclosures appeared in 1986, they stirred a great deal of anger and concern among citizens in the area surrounding the plant. The Fred Hutchinson Cancer Research Center of Seattle conducted an extensive study, funded by the federal Centers for Disease Control and Prevention, to try to determine if thyroid disease "increased among persons exposed as children" to iodine-131 from Hanford between 1944 and 1957. In 2004 the investigators reported that they found "no evidence" that exposures in that period had produced "an increased cumulative incidence of thyroid cancer, benign thyroid nodules, hypothyroidism, or autoimmune thyroiditis." See Scott Davis, Kenneth J. Kopecky, Thomas E. Hamilton, Lynn Onstad, and the Hanford Thyroid Disease Study Team, "Thyroid Neoplasia, Autoimmune Thyroiditis, and Hypothyroidism in Persons Exposed to Iodine 131 From the Hanford Nuclear Site," *JAMA* 292 (December 1, 2004): 2600–13.

10. Ronald L. Kathren, Raymond W. Baalman, and William J. Bair, eds., *Herbert M. Parker: Publications and Other Contributions to Radiological and Health Physics* (Columbus, OH: Battelle Press, 1986), pp. xiii–xxiii.

11. Lauriston S. Taylor, *Organization for Radiation Protection: The Operations of the ICRP and NCRP, 1928–1974* (Washington, DC: U.S. Department of Energy, 1979), p. 7–066; Silverman, "No Immediate Risk," pp. 105–8; Gephart, *Hanford,* p. 5.40; Kathren, Baalman, and Bair, eds., *Herbert M. Parker,* pp. 710–19.

12. H.M. Parker, "Health Instrument Divisions Report for Month of December, 1949," January 6, 1950, HW-15550-E, http://www2.hanford.gov/ddrs/common/findpage.cfm?AKey = D8426122 (accessed June 10, 2005).

13. Atomic Energy Commission Press Release, September 7, 1947, Nuclear Regulatory Commission Records, NRC Public Document Room, Rockville, MD; Abel Wolman to David E. Lilienthal, July 9, 1947, Box 7.18 (U.S. Atomic Energy Commission, 1947), Abel Wolman Papers, Johns Hopkins University, Baltimore, MD.

14. *Baltimore Evening Sun,* February 23, 1989; *Baltimore Sun,* February 24, 1989; Brian Balogh, *Chain Reaction: Expert Debate and Public Participation in American Commercial Nuclear Power, 1945–1975* (Cambridge: Cambridge University Press, 1991), pp. 150–51; Walter Hollander Jr., *Abel Wolman, His Life and Philosophy: An Oral History* (Chapel Hill: Universal Printing and Publishing Co., 1981), pp. 1109–17.

15. Hollander, *Abel Wolman,* pp. 267–72; Wolman to Lilienthal, July 9, 1947, Wolman Papers.

16. Hollander, *Abel Wolman,* pp. 272–78.

17. Abel Wolman and Arthur E. Gorman, "A Memorandum on the Problems of Environmental Sanitation Encountered in Atomic Energy Operations," November 4, 1947, Box 7.18 (no folder title), Wolman Papers.

18. Safety and Industrial Health Advisory Board, "Safety and Health in AEC Operations: A Report to the Atomic Energy Commission," April 2, 1948, Box 7.17 (no folder), Wolman Papers; Barton C. Hacker, *The Dragon's Tail: Radiation Safety in the Manhattan Project, 1942–1946* (Berkeley: University of California Press, 1987), pp. 46, 50.

19. Hollander, *Abel Wolman,* pp. 290–93, 1164; Fehner and Gosling, "Coming in from the Cold," p. 9.

20. Hollander, *Abel Wolman,* pp. 275–82; A.A. Albert de la Bruheze, *Political Construction of Technology: Nuclear Waste Disposal in the United States, 1945–1972* (Enschede, The Netherlands: Universiteit Twente, 1992), p. 37; Joint Committee on Atomic Energy, *Hearings on Industrial Radioactive Waste Disposal,* p. 987.

21. Secretary to the Commission to General Manager, July 19, 1948, Minutes of 209th AEC Meeting, October 20, 1948, Morse Salisbury to Roger Warner, December 14, 1948, Office of the Secretary, General Correspondence, Box 64 (Control of Atomic Wastes), AEC Records, National Archives, College Park; de la Bruheze, *Political Construction of Technology,* pp. 52–53.

22. *Baltimore Evening Sun,* October 29, 1947; *New York Times,* April 15, 1948; Morse Salisbury to Carroll L. Wilson, January 17, 1949, Roy B. Snapp

to Salisbury, May 20, 1949, Office of the Secretary, General Correspondence, Box 64 (Control of Atomic Wastes), AEC Records, National Archives, College Park.

23. "Our Defective Race," *Newsweek,* April 14, 1947, p. 56; Edward P. Morgan, "The A-Bomb's Invisible Offspring," *Collier's,* August 9, 1947, pp. 18–19; "What Science Learned at Bikini," *Life,* August 11, 1947, pp. 74–88; Jonathan M. Weisgall, *Operation Crossroads: The Atomic Tests at Bikini Atoll* (Annapolis: Naval Institute Press, 1994), pp. 141–46. For other articles on radiation dangers following the Bikini tests, see Carl Dreher, "The Weirdest Danger in the World," *Popular Science* 149 (October 1946): 86–90; "Radiation Sickness," *Life,* January 27, 1947, pp. 81–82; David B. Parker, "Mist of Death over New York," *Reader's Digest* 50 (April 1947): 7–10; "After Hiroshima," *Newsweek,* April 7, 1947, p. 50; "Generations Yet Unborn," *Time,* April 7, 1947, pp. 57–58; H.J. Muller, "Changing Genes: Their Effects on Evolution," *Bulletin of the Atomic Scientists* 3 (September 1947): 267–71; "Radioactivity Scare," *Time,* September 1, 1947, p. 54; "Genetic Death," *Time,* September 22, 1947, pp. 44–45; "The Deadly Cloud," *Time,* April 5, 1948, p. 76. For the importance of the Bikini tests in calling attention to radiation hazards, see Ralph E. Lapp, *Must We Hide?* (Cambridge, MA: Addison-Wesley Press, 1949), p. ix; Paul Boyer, *By the Bomb's Early Light: American Thought and Culture at the Dawn of the Atomic Age* (New York: Pantheon Books, 1985), pp. 90–91, 307–8.

24. David Bradley, *No Place to Hide* (Boston: Little, Brown, 1948), pp. xiv–xvii, 165; Boyer, *By the Bomb's Early Light,* p. 91.

25. Hazel Gaudet Erskine, "The Polls: Atomic Weapons and Nuclear Energy," *Public Opinion Quarterly* 27 (Summer 1963): 155–90 (cited poll on p. 179); Charles A. Metzner and Julia B. Kessler, "What Are the People Thinking?" *Bulletin of the Atomic Scientists* 7 (November 1951): 341, 352.

26. David E. Lilienthal, "Atomic Energy Is *Your* Business," *Bulletin of the Atomic Scientists* 3 (November 1947): 335–38; Austin M. Brues, "The 'Mystery' of Biological Radiation Effects," *Bulletin of the Atomic Scientists* 4 (November 1948): 341–42; Austin M. Brues, Review of *No Place to Hide, Bulletin of the Atomic Scientists* 5 (April 1949): 128; Safety and Industrial Health Advisory Board, "Safety and Health in AEC Operations," p. 81.

27. T.G. Jones to Roger S. Warner, October 18, 1948, Morse Salisbury to Warner, December 14, 1948, Salisbury to Carroll L. Wilson, January 17, 1949, Wilson to Warner, John Z. Bowers, and Salisbury, January 17, 1949, AEC 180 (January 17, 1949), Office of the Secretary, General Correspondence, Box 64 (Control of Atomic Wastes), Frances Henderson to T.O. Jones, December 13, 1948, Office Files of David E. Lilienthal, Subject Files, Box 17 (Secretariat), AEC Records, National Archives, College Park.

28. Press Conference on Radioactive Waste Disposal, January 28, 1949, Office of the Secretary, General Correspondence, Box 64 (Control of Atomic Wastes), AEC Records, National Archives, College Park; *New York Times,* January 30, 1949.

29. AEC 180/1 (October 17, 1949), U.S. Atomic Energy Commission, *Handling Radioactive Wastes in the Atomic Energy Program* (1949), pp. v, 1, 6–7, 10–12, Office of the Secretary, General Correspondence, Box 64 (Control of

Atomic Wastes), AEC Records, National Archives, College Park; AEC Press Release, December 9, 1949, NRC Records.

30. AEC, *Handling Radioactive Wastes,* p. 10, Lawrence R. Hafstad to Those Listed Below, November 10, 1949, Office of the Secretary, General Correspondence, Box 65 (Control of Atomic Wastes), AEC Records, National Archives, College Park; J. Newell Stannard, *Radioactivity and Health: A History (DOE/RL/01830-T59)* (Washington, DC: U.S. Department of Energy, 1988), pp. 760–62.

31. AEC 180/5, AEC Records, National Archives, College Park.

32. Glenn T. Seaborg, "Peacetime Uses of Atomic Energy," July 30, 1955, Box 862 (1955–1960 Speeches), Seaborg Papers; *The Biological Effects of Atomic Radiation: A Report to the Public* (Washington, DC: National Academy of Sciences–National Research Council, 1956), pp. 30–31; *The Biological Effects of Atomic Radiation: Summary Reports* (Washington, DC: National Academy of Sciences–National Research Council, 1956), pp. 101–4.

33. AEC 180/5, AEC 180/6 (June 14, 1957), Office of the Secretary, General Correspondence, Box 46 (MAT-12, Waste Processing and Disposal), AEC Records, National Archives, College Park; Arthur E. Gorman, "Environmental Aspects of the Atomic Energy Industry," *Proceedings of the International Conference on the Peaceful Uses of Atomic Energy,* vol. 13 (New York: United Nations, 1956), pp. 298–303; "'Hot Stuff': Big Hurdle for Atomic Power," *Business Week,* July 23, 1955, pp. 72–77; Watson Davis and Helen Davis, "Reactor Ashes Precious," *Science News Letter* 68 (August 27, 1955): 131–32.

34. AEC 180/5, AEC Records, National Archives, College Park.

35. *The Disposal of Radioactive Waste on Land* (Washington, DC: National Academy of Sciences–National Research Council, 1957), pp. 2–7, 92–139.

36. Erskine, "The Polls: Atomic Weapons and Nuclear Energy," p. 188; Metzner and Kessler, "What Are the People Thinking?" p. 341; Walker, *Permissible Dose,* pp. 18–23.

37. Arnold B. Joseph, *United States' Sea Disposal Operations: A Summary to December 1956 (WASH-734)* (Washington, DC: Atomic Energy Commission, 1957); AEC-R 42/8 (April 3, 1959), AEC-R 42/9 (June 2, 1959), NRC Records, NRC Public Document Room; "Disposal of Radioactive Wastes in the Ocean," Statement of U.S. Atomic Energy Commission to State of California Senate Interim Committee on Fish and Game, October 20, 1958, Box 706 (Waste Disposal), General Correspondence, Papers of the Joint Committee on Atomic Energy, Record Group 128 (Records of the Joint Committees of Congress), National Archives, Washington, DC.

38. E.B. White, "Letter from the East," *New Yorker,* July 27, 1957, pp. 43–45; "Radioactive Graveyards," *New Republic,* February 16, 1959, pp. 4–5; "Sea Disposal of Atomic Wastes," *Bulletin of the Atomic Scientists* 16 (April 1960): 141; *Congressional Record,* 86th Cong., 1st Sess., 1959, p. 10508; "The AEC's Can of Worms," *Nation,* February 20, 1960, p. 158; "The Atom: What To Do with the Waste," *Time,* p. 14. For a detailed discussion of the controversy over ocean dumping, see George T. Mazuzan and J. Samuel Walker, *Controlling the Atom: The Beginnings of Nuclear Regulation, 1946–1962* (Berkeley: University of California Press, 1984), pp. 354–66.

39. AEC Press Releases, June 7, 1960, November 5, 1961, NRC Records, NRC Public Document Room; H.C. Brown, Memorandum for the Files, March 16, 1960, Materials-12 (Waste Processing and Disposal), AEC Records, History Division, Department of Energy, Germantown, MD; Mazuzan and Walker, *Controlling the Atom,* pp. 362–66. For a valuable account of ocean dumping, see Jacob Darwin Hamblin, *Poison in the Well: Radioactive Waste in the Oceans at the Dawn of the Nuclear Age* (New Brunswick, NJ: Rutgers University Press, 2008).

40. AEC 180/23 (May 10, 1963), NRC Records, NRC Public Document Room; Mazuzan and Walker, *Controlling the Atom,* pp. 366–68.

41. *Annual Report to Congress of the Atomic Energy Commission for 1959* (Washington, DC: Government Printing Office, 1960), p. 289; U.S. Atomic Energy Commission, *Civilian Nuclear Power: A Report to the President–1962* (Washington, DC: Government Printing Office, 1962), p. 50.

CHAPTER 2

1. Joseph A. Lieberman, "Nuclear Energy Industrial Wastes," January 27, 1960, Box 2261 (MAT-12, Radioactive Waste and Waste Disposal), Office Files of John A. McCone, Record Group 326 (Records of the Atomic Energy Commission), National Archives, College Park, MD; "Waste Solidification Gains Major Attention," *Nucleonics* 21 (February 1963): 58.

2. Walter G. Belter, "Recent Developments in the Processing and Ultimate Disposal of High-Level Radioactive Wastes," May 1961, Box 706 (Waste Disposal), General Correspondence, Papers of the Joint Committee on Atomic Energy, Record Group 128 (Records of the Joint Committees of Congress), National Archives, Washington, DC; Joint Committee on Atomic Energy, *Hearings on AEC Authorizing Legislation Fiscal Year 1966,* 89th Cong., 1st Sess., 1965, pp. 1214–20; Charles H. Fox, *Radioactive Wastes* (U.S. Atomic Energy Commission "Understanding the Atom" Booklet) (Washington, DC: Government Printing Office, 1965), pp. 29–32; Roy E. Gephart, *Hanford: A Conversation about Nuclear Waste and Cleanup* (Columbus, OH: Battelle Press, 2003), p. 8.8.

3. Belter, "Recent Developments in . . . the Disposal of High-Level Radioactive Wastes"; Joint Committee on Atomic Energy, *Hearings on AEC Authorizing Legislation,* pp. 1217–18; Fox, *Radioactive Wastes,* pp. 33–34.

4. Joint Committee on Atomic Energy, *Hearings on Industrial Radioactive Waste Disposal,* 86th Cong., 1st Sess., 1959, p. 165; R.E. Blanco, J.O. Blomeke, and J.T. Roberts, "Solving the Waste-Disposal Problem," *Nucleonics* 25 (February 1967): 58–68; Belter, "Recent Developments in . . . Disposal of High-Level Wastes"; Fox, *Radioactive Wastes,* pp. 25–27; Gephart, *Hanford,* pp. 5.6–5.10.

5. Joint Committee on Atomic Energy, *Hearings on Industrial Radioactive Waste Disposal,* p. 166; *Annual Report to Congress of the Atomic Energy Commission for 1959* (Washington, DC: Government Printing Office, 1960), p. 301.

6. "Investigation of Waste Tank Leakage, Savannah River Plant: Interim Report," April 1962, Box 14 (Engineering Dept., DPE Reports), Records of the Dupont Atomic Energy Division, Hagley Library and Museum, Wilmington, DE; Joint Committee on Atomic Energy, *Hearings on Industrial Radioactive*

Waste Disposal, p. 165; Gephart, *Hanford,* pp. 5.6–5.39; George T. Mazuzan and J. Samuel Walker, *Controlling the Atom: The Beginnings of Nuclear Regulation, 1946–1962* (Berkeley: University of California Press, 1984), pp. 368–69.

7. Lieberman, "Nuclear Energy Industrial Wastes"; Joint Committee on Atomic Energy, *Hearings on AEC Authorizing Legislation,* p. 1215; Fox, *Radioactive Wastes,* p. 36.

8. Lieberman, "Nuclear Energy Industrial Wastes"; Joint Committee on Atomic Energy, *Hearings on AEC Authorizing Legislation,* p. 1219; Gephart, *Hanford,* pp. 3.2–3.9; W.G. Belter, D.E. Ferguson, and F.L. Culler, "Waste Management: Technological Advances and Attitudes of Safety," *Nuclear News* 7 (October 1964): 94–97.

9. James T. Ramey, "Progress and Problems in Radiation Standards and Radioactive Waste Disposal," April 26, 1965, Nuclear Regulatory Commission Records, NRC Public Document Room, Rockville, MD; Joint Committee on Atomic Energy, *Hearings on AEC Authorizing Legislation,* p. 1219.

10. F.E. Adley and W.K. Crane, "Meeting of the Columbia River Advisory Group, November 21–23, 1949 (February 2, 1950), HW-15861, http://www2.hanford.gov/ddrs/common/findpage.cfm?AKey=D197308531 (accessed November 8, 2005). For an excellent extended discussion of the Columbia River Advisory Group, see Michael Joshua Silverman, "No Immediate Risk: Environmental Safety in Nuclear Weapons Production, 1942–1985" (Ph.D. diss., Carnegie Mellon University, 2000), pp. 122–61.

11. Arthur E. Gorman to L.R. Hafstad, February 3, 1950, http://www2.hanford.gov/ddrs/common/findpage.cfm?AKey=D198183662 (accessed November 8, 2005); H.M. Parker to D.G. Sturges, March 17, 1950, http://www2.hanford.gov/ddrs/common/findpage.cfm?AKey = D198183651 (accessed November 8, 2005).

12. Columbia River Advisory Group, *Evaluation of Pollutional Effects from Hanford Works* (March 1961), pp. 3, 24, Accession No. 11843, U.S. Department of Energy Public Reading Room, Richland, WA; Silverman, "No Immediate Risk," pp. 153–58; Gephart, *Hanford,* pp. 2.10–2.11.

13. J. Samuel Walker, *Permissible Dose: A History of Radiation Protection in the Twentieth Century* (Berkeley: University of California Press, 2000), pp. 23–26; Gephart, *Hanford,* p. 2.10.

14. AEC 636/4 (June 20, 1961), AEC 636/6 (July 25, 1961), AEC 636/8 (September 12, 1962), NRC Records, NRC Public Document Room; Columbia River Advisory Group, *Evaluation of Pollutional Effects from Hanford Works,* pp. 4, 24; Gephart, *Hanford,* pp. 2.11–2.12.

15. *The Disposal of Radioactive Waste on Land* (Washington, DC: National Academy of Sciences–National Research Council, 1957), p. 3; M. King Hubbert to H.H. Hess, April 19, 1960, Accession No. 79-032-2 (Committee on Geologic Aspects of Radioactive Waste Disposal, Advisory to AEC), National Academy of Sciences–National Research Council Archives, Washington, DC.

16. H.H. Hess to John A. McCone, June 21, 1960, Box 706 (Waste Disposal), General Correspondence, Joint Committee on Atomic Energy Papers.

17. Minutes of 1675th AEC Meeting, November 23, 1960, Frank K. Pittman to Commissioner Graham, December 16, 1960, AEC Records, History Division, Department of Energy, Germantown, MD.

18. A.R. Luedecke to H.H. Hess, January 4, 1961, Box 706 (Waste Disposal), General Correspondence, Joint Committee on Atomic Energy Papers.

19. M. King Hubbert, "Nuclear Energy and Fossil Fuels," March 1956, http://hubbertpeak.com/hubbert/1956/1956.pdf (accessed October 20, 2005); Transcript of Interview with Marion King Hubbert, conducted by Ronald E. Doel, January 4–February 6, 1989, pp. 267–74, Niels Bohr Library, Center for History of Physics, American Institute of Physics, College Park, MD; Kenneth S. Deffeyes, *Hubbert's Peak: The Impending World Oil Shortage* (Princeton: Princeton University Press, 2001), pp. 1–4.

20. M. King Hubbert to Linn Hoover, June 30, 1961, Accession No. 79-032-2 (Committee on Geologic Aspects of Radioactive Waste Disposal, Advisory to AEC), National Academy of Sciences–National Research Council Archives; Joint Committee on Atomic Energy, *Hearings on Development, Growth, and State of the Atomic Energy Industry,* 88th Cong., 1st Sess., 1963, pp. 168–88.

21. E.F. Cook to Philip H. Abelson, March 12, 1965, Abel Wolman to Frederick Seitz, August 11, 1965, Box 7.41 (National Academy of Sciences: NRC Ad Hoc Group on Radioactive Waste Disposal, 1965–1966), Abel Wolman Papers, Johns Hopkins University, Baltimore, MD.

22. Glenn T. Seaborg to Frederick Seitz, November 1, 1965, Accession No. 79-032-2 (Committee on Geologic Aspects of Radioactive Waste Disposal, 1965), National Academy of Sciences–National Research Council Archives; M. King Hubbert to Abel Wolman, December 29, 1965, Box 7.41 (National Academy of Sciences: NRC Ad Hoc Group on Radioactive Waste Disposal, 1965–1966), Wolman Papers; Wolman to Seitz, January 18, 1966, AEC Records, History Division, Department of Energy.

23. M. King Hubbert to Linn Hoover, June 30, 1961, Hoover to Hubbert, July 13, 1961, Walter G. Belter to John E. Galley, March 30, 1965, Accession No. 79-032-02 (Committee on Geologic Aspects of Radioactive Waste Disposal, 1965), National Academy of Sciences–National Research Council Archives; Cook to Abelson, March 12, 1965, Wolman Papers; Hubbert Oral History, p. 210; Philip Boffey, *The Brain Bank of America: An Inquiry into the Politics of Science* (New York: McGraw-Hill, 1975), pp. 94–95.

24. Joseph A. Lieberman to E.F. Cook, March 26, 1965, Walter G. Belter to John E. Galley, March 30, 1965, Belter to Cook, April 26, 1965, Galley to J. Hoover Mackin, September 10, 1965, Accession No. 79-032-2 (Committee on Geologic Aspects of Radioactive Waste Disposal, 1965), Committee on Geologic Aspects of Radioactive Waste Disposal, Minutes of Meeting of August 30–31, 1965, Accession No. 79-032-2 (Minutes—Geologic Aspects of Radioactive Waste Disposal, Advisory to AEC, 1955–1965), National Academy of Sciences–National Research Council Archives; Galley to Abel Wolman, December 11, 1965, Box 7.41 (National Academy of Sciences: NRC Ad Hoc Group on Radioactive Waste Disposal, 1965–1966), Wolman Papers.

25. John E. Galley to W.C. Belter, February 12, 1966, Galley to E.F. Cook, March 6, 1966, Committee on Geologic Aspects of Radioactive Waste Disposal of the Division of Earth Sciences, *Report to the U.S. Atomic Energy Commission,* May 1966, pp. 11, 12, 66, 69, Accession No. 79-032-2 (Committee on Geologic Aspects of Radioactive Waste Disposal, 1966–1968), National Acad-

emy of Sciences–National Research Council Archives. The Galley committee report was published in U.S. Congress, Senate, Committee on Public Works, Subcommittee on Air and Water Pollution, *Hearings on Underground Uses of Nuclear Energy,* 91st Cong., 1st Sess., 1969, pp. 462–512.

26. Committee on Geologic Aspects of Radioactive Waste Disposal, *Report to the U.S. Atomic Energy Commission,* pp. 18, 43, 64, 78.

27. Ibid., pp. 10, 18, 70, 82.

28. Milton Shaw to Frederick Seitz, November 7, 1966, Box 30 (Bedrock Waste Storage, AEC File, NAS Division of Earth Sciences), Records of the Dupont Atomic Energy Division.

29. John E. Galley to J. Hoover Mackin, May 20, 1967, Accession No. 79-032-2 (Committee on Geologic Aspects of Radioactive Waste Disposal, 1966–1968), National Academy of Sciences–National Research Council Archives.

30. Walt [Walter H. Bailey], handwritten note to Joe [Joseph W. Berg Jr.], May 16, 1967, Milton Shaw to Frederick Seitz, May 25, 1967, Seitz to Shaw, June 5, 1967, Accession No. 79-032-2 (Committee on Geologic Aspects of Radioactive Waste Disposal, 1966–1968), National Academy of Sciences–National Research Council Archives.

31. J. Hoover Mackin to Frederick Seitz, June 14, 1967, Accession No. 79-032-2 (Committee on Geologic Aspects of Radioactive Waste Disposal, 1966–1968), National Academy of Sciences–National Research Council Archives; A.F. Perge to J.A. Erlewine, November 3, 1967, Milton Shaw to Erlewine, February 26, 1968, Minutes of Information Meetings, November 30, 1967, January 19, 1968, AEC Records, History Division, Department of Energy.

32. AEC 180/29 (March 7, 1968), Glenn T. Seaborg to Frederick Seitz, March 11, 1968, AEC Press Release, August 6, 1968, NRC Records, NRC Public Document Room.

33. AEC 180/34 (April 19, 1968), AEC Records, History Division, Department of Energy; F. Costagliola to the Record, December 8, 1969, Box 706 (Waste Disposal), General Correspondence, Joint Committee on Atomic Energy Papers; Comptroller General of the United States, *Progress and Problems in Programs for Managing High-Level Radioactive Wastes (B-164052),* January 29, 1971; Joint Committee on Atomic Energy, *Hearings on AEC Authorizing Legislation Fiscal Year* 1972, 92d Cong., 1st Sess., 1971, pp. 1554–57, 2209–21.

34. M. King Hubbert, "Discussion" of Walter G. Belter, "Deep Disposal Systems for Radioactive Wastes," in *Underground Waste Management and Environmental Implications,* ed. T.D. Cook (Tulsa: American Association of Petroleum Geologists, 1972), pp. 351–54.

35. Joint Committee on Atomic Energy, *Hearings on AEC Authorizing Legislation Fiscal Year 1972,* pp. 2210–11; J. Samuel Walker, *Containing the Atom: Nuclear Power in a Changing Environment, 1963–1971* (Berkeley: University of California Press, 1992), pp. 297–99.

36. Walker, *Containing the Atom,* pp. 18–36.

37. Ibid., pp. 169–202, 267–362.

38. AEC 180/13 (September 20, 1960), NRC Records, NRC Public Document Room; "The Huge and Ever-Increasing Problem of Radioactive Wastes," *Consumer Reports* 25 (February 1960): 66–67.

39. *Nucleonics Week,* October 27, December 15, 1966; Glenn T. Seaborg to Emilio Q. Daddario, Box 706 (Waste Disposal), General Correspondence, Joint Committee on Atomic Energy Papers.

40. Joel A. Snow, "Radioactive Waste from Reactors: The Problem That Won't Go Away," *Scientist and Citizen* 9 (May 1967): 89–96; *Congressional Record,* 90th Cong., 1st Sess., 1967, p. 14176; Donald A. Ritchie, *Reporting from Washington: The History of the Washington Press Corps* (New York: Oxford University Press, 2005), p. 177; Walker, *Containing the Atom,* p. 393.

41. *National Enquirer,* June 2, 1968.

42. W.G. Belter, W. McVey, C.B. Bartlett, K.L. Mattern, and W.H. Regan, "New Developments in Radioactive Waste Management," paper delivered at the annual meeting of the American Nuclear Society, June 1969, Box 26 (AEC), Series 1, Subject Files (Salt Vault: Atomic Energy Commission), Record Group 37 (Records of the Kansas State Geological Survey), University Archives, Spencer Research Library, University of Kansas, Lawrence; *Congressional Record,* 91st Cong., 2nd Sess., 1970, pp. 6301–2; Len Ackland, *Making a Real Killing: Rocky Flats and the Nuclear West* (Albuquerque: University of New Mexico Press, 1999), pp. 146–59.

43. For newspaper coverage of the waste issue in Idaho, see *Congressional Record,* 91st Cong., 2nd Sess., 1970, pp. 6295–98. See also H. Peter Metzger, *The Atomic Establishment* (New York: Simon and Schuster, 1972), pp. 150–51.

44. *Journal of Glenn T. Seaborg,* 25 vols. (Berkeley: Lawrence Berkeley Laboratory PUB-625, 1989), vol. 20, p. 284 (available in the Glenn T. Seaborg Papers, Manuscript Division, Library of Congress, Washington, DC); *Congressional Record,* 91st Cong., 2nd Sess., 1970, pp. 6298, 13569.

45. John E. Galley to J. Hoover Mackin, March 6, 1966, Accession No. 79-032-2 (Committee on Geologic Aspects of Radioactive Waste Disposal, 1966–1968), National Academy of Sciences–National Research Council Archives; Minutes of Information Meeting, October 10, 1969, AEC Records, History Division, Department of Energy; *Journal of Glenn T. Seaborg,* vol. 20, pp. 284, 287; *Congressional Record,* 91st Cong., 2nd Sess., 1970, pp. 6298, 13569.

46. *Congressional Record,* 91st Cong., 2nd Sess., 1970, pp. 6296–97, 6310; LeRoy Ashby and Rod Gramer, *Fighting the Odds: The Life of Senator Frank Church* (Pullman: Washington State University Press, 1994), pp. 343–54.

47. *Journal of Glenn T. Seaborg,* vol. 21, p. 432; Senate Subcommittee on Air and Water Pollution, *Hearings on Underground Uses of Nuclear Energy,* pp. 461–62, 513–19.

48. *New York Times,* March 7, 1970; "Disposal of the Waste," *Science News,* March 28, 1970, p. 312; *Idaho Falls Post-Register,* May 26, 1970.

49. *Congressional Record,* 91st Cong., 2nd Sess., 1970, pp. 13877–79; Edward J. Bauser to All Members, May 1, 1970, Box 180 (National Reactor Testing Station), Craig Hosmer Papers, University of Southern California, Los Angeles.

50. [John] Harris to John [Erlewine], May 1, 1970, W.B. McCool to the File, May 7, 1970, AEC 180/84 (May 26, 1970), AEC 180/86 (June 3, 1970), AEC Records, History Division, Department of Energy; *Journal of Glenn T. Seaborg,* vol. 22, pp. 55, 239–40.

51. AEC 180/75 (January 5, 1970), AEC Records, History Division, Department of Energy.

52. Glenn T. Seaborg with Eric Seaborg, *Adventures in the Atomic Age: From Watts to Washington* (New York: Farrar, Straus and Giroux, 2001), p. 233.

CHAPTER 3

1. Joseph A. Lieberman to Frank Foley, December 22, 1958, Box 26 (AEC Oak Ridge, Salt Vault Hutchinson), Series 1, Subject Files (Salt Vault: Atomic Energy Commission), Record Group 37 (Records of the Kansas State Geological Survey), University Archives, Spencer Research Library, University of Kansas, Lawrence; Morse Salisbury to James T. Ramey, October 19, 1959, Box 705 (Waste Disposal), General Correspondence, Papers of the Joint Committee on Atomic Energy, Record Group 128 (Records of the Joint Committees of Congress), National Archives, Washington, DC; *The Disposal of Radioactive Waste on Land* (Washington, DC: National Academy of Sciences–National Research Council, 1957), pp. 4–5, 134–38; F.M. Empson, ed., *Status Report on Waste Disposal in Natural Salt Formations: III (ORNL-3053),* published by Oak Ridge National Laboratory, September 11, 1961.

2. Committee on Waste Disposal, Minutes of Meeting of May 14, 1960, Accession No. 79-032-2 (Minutes—Geologic Aspects of Radioactive Waste Disposal, Advisory to AEC), National Academy of Sciences–National Research Council Archives, Washington, DC; AEC Press Release, July 9, 1963, Box 706 (Waste Disposal), General Correspondence, Joint Committee on Atomic Energy Papers.

3. W.G. Belter, W. McVey, C.B. Bartlett, K.L. Mattern, and W.H. Regan, "The AEC's Position on Radioactive Waste Management," *Nuclear News* 12 (November 1969): 60–65; R.L. Bradshaw, F.M. Empson, W.C. McClain, and B.L. Houser, "Results of a Demonstration and Other Studies of the Disposal of High Level Solidified, Radioactive Wastes in a Salt Mine," *Health Physics* 18 (January 1970): 63–67; W.C. McClain and R.L. Bradshaw, "Status of Investigations of Salt Formations for Disposal of Highly Radioactive Power-Reactor Wastes," *Nuclear Safety* 11 (March–April 1970): 130–41; Richard Wolfson, *Nuclear Choices: A Citizen's Guide to Nuclear Technology* (Cambridge, MA: MIT Press, 1991), p. 46.

4. Bradshaw et al., "Results of a Demonstration," p. 67; McClain and Bradshaw, "Status of Investigations," p. 140.

5. *Journal of Glenn T. Seaborg,* 25 vols. (Berkeley: Lawrence Berkeley Laboratory PUB- 625, 1989), vol. 21, p. 432 (available in the Glenn T. Seaborg Papers, Manuscript Division, Library of Congress, Washington, DC); AEC 180/81 (April 23, 1970), AEC Records, History Division, Department of Energy, Germantown, MD.

6. *Congressional Record,* 86th Cong., 1st Sess., 1959, p. 10510; Joint Committee on Atomic Energy, *Hearings on AEC Authorizing Legislation Fiscal Year 1972,* 92nd Cong., 1st Sess., 1971, p. 1314; *Lyons Daily News,* October 14, 1960; *Great Bend Daily Tribune,* November 18, 1963.

7. Frank C. Foley to E.G. Struxness, February 16, 1962, Box 26 (AEC Oak Ridge, Salt Vault Hutchinson), Series 1, Subject Files (Salt Vault: Atomic Energy Commission), Kansas Geological Survey Records.

8. *Lyons Daily News,* June 5, 1970; *Kansas City Times,* June 25, 1970; *New York Times,* March 11, 1971; *Denver Post,* September 27, 1971; John Sayler, telephone interview by author, January 17, 2006.

9. *Topeka State Journal,* June 9, 1970; Joel Paddock, "Democratic Politics in a Republican State: The Gubernatorial Campaigns of Robert Docking, 1966–1972," *Kansas History* 17 (Summer 1994): 108–23; Homer E. Socolofsky, *Kansas Governors* (Lawrence: University Press of Kansas, 1990), pp. 215–18.

10. William W. Hambleton, *Selected Speeches* (Lawrence: Kansas Geological Survey, 1987), pp. iv–v; William W. Hambleton, interview by author, Lawrence, Kansas, July 13, 2005.

11. William W. Hambleton to Robert B. Docking, April 17, 1970, Box 41 (Atomic Waste Disposal 1970), Robert Docking Papers, Kansas Collection, Spencer Research Library, University of Kansas, Lawrence.

12. Cyrus Klingsberg to the Panel on Disposal in Salt Mines, June 10, 1970, Robert W. Newlin to J.A. Erlewine and D. Donoghue, July 24, 1970, AEC Records, History Division, Department of Energy; *Nucleonics Week,* November 18, 1971; E-mail message from Richard G. Hewlett to the author, March 5, 2005, in author's possession.

13. Klingberg to Panel on Disposal in Salt Mines, June 10, 1970, History Division, Department of Energy; William W. Hambleton and Gary F. Stewart to John H. Rust, June 5, 1970, Box 27 (Disposal in Salt Panel), Series 1, Subject Files (Salt Vault: Atomic Energy Commission), Kansas Geological Survey Records; Hambleton to Robert Docking, June 8, 1970, Box 41 (Atomic Waste Disposal 1970), Docking Papers.

14. AEC 180/87 (June 12, 1970), AEC Records, History Division, Department of Energy; AEC Press Release, June 17, 1970, printed in Joint Committee on Atomic Energy, *Hearings on AEC Authorizing Legislation Fiscal Year 1972,* pp. 1983–84; *Wichita Eagle,* June 18, 1970; *Washington Post,* June 18, 1970; *New York Times,* June 18, 1970.

15. Robert W. Newlin to John Harris and Joe Fouchard, June 19, 1970, Cyrus Klingsberg to the Panel on Disposal in Salt Mines, July 1, 1970, AEC Records, History Division, Department of Energy; William W. Hambleton, "Interim Report of the Kansas Geological Survey on Storage of Radioactive Waste in Salt at Lyons, Kansas," July 7, 1970, printed in Joint Committee on Atomic Energy, *Hearings on AEC Authorizing Legislation Fiscal Year 1972,* pp. 1998–2002. Hambleton and Ernest E. Angino, deputy director of the Kansas Geological Survey, vividly recalled their disaffection with the AEC over Erlewine's press conference thirty-five years after it occurred. Ernest E. Angino, interview by author, Lawrence, KS, July 13, 2005; and Hambleton, interview by author.

16. *Wichita Eagle-Beacon,* February 7, 1983; *Pittsburg Morning Sun,* February 6, 2000, September 13, 2000; *Congressional Record,* 92nd Cong., 1st Sess., 1971, p. E2426; Joe Skubitz to W.W. Chandler, June 16, 1971, Box 48 (Atomic Waste Disposal 1971), Chet Holifield Papers, University of Southern California, Los Angeles.

17. The correspondence between the AEC and Skubitz is printed in U.S. Atomic Energy Commission, *Environmental Statement: Radioactive Waste Repository, Lyons, Kansas (WASH- 1503),* June 1971, Appendix (no page numbers).

18. *Wichita Eagle,* June 19, 1970.

19. Ibid., July 30, 1970; *Topeka Daily Capital,* July 30, 1970; Robert E. Hollingsworth to Edward J. Bauser, August 26, 1970, AEC Records, History Division, Department of Energy.

20. Committee on Radioactive Waste Management, *Disposal of Solid Radioactive Wastes in Bedded Salt Deposits,* November 1970, printed in Joint Committee on Atomic Energy, *Hearings on AEC Authorizing Legislation Fiscal Year 1972,* pp. 2003–31; Panel on Disposal in Salt, Draft by William W. Hambleton, July 6, 1970, Box 26 (Salt Vault Project), Series 1, Subject Files (Salt Vault: Atomic Energy Commission), Kansas Geological Survey Records; John A. Erlewine to Robert B. Docking, November 18, 1970, Box 41 (Atomic Waste Disposal 1970), Docking Papers.

21. E.E. Angino to W.W. Hambleton, September 10, 1970, Box 27 (Salt Vault Conferences), Floyd W. Preston and John Halepaska to Hambleton, October 29, 1970, Box 27 (Correspondence: Salt Vault), Series 1, Subject Files (Salt Vault: Atomic Energy Commission), Kansas Geological Survey Records; Dale E. Saffels to Russell Train, December 1, 1970, "Preliminary Report on Studies of the Radioactive Waste Disposal Site at Lyons, Kansas by the State Geological Survey of Kansas," December 1970, Box 41 (Atomic Waste Disposal 1970), Hambleton to Patrick Burnau, August 25, 1971, Box 56 (Atomic Energy Commission, Atomic Waste Repository, Lyons), Docking Papers; Hambleton, interview by author.

22. U.S. Atomic Energy Commission, "Draft Environmental Statement, Radioactive Waste Repository, Lyons, Kansas," November 1970, Box 26 (Atomic Energy Commission), Series 1, Subject Files (Salt Vault: Atomic Energy Commission), Kansas Geological Survey Records; Comments on the Draft Environmental Statement are printed in *WASH-1503,* Appendix.

23. *Congressional Record,* 92nd Cong., 1st Sess., 1971, pp. 4342–43; *Wichita Eagle,* February 17, 1971; *New York Times,* February 17, 1971.

24. *Congressional Record,* 92nd Cong., 1st Sess., 1971, pp. 4338–40; *Wichita Eagle,* February 21, 1971.

25. *Congressional Record,* 92nd Cong., 1st Sess., 1971, pp. 4343–44; *Wichita Eagle,* February 27, 1971.

26. Glenn T. Seaborg to Joe Skubitz, February 23, 1971, and Skubitz to Seaborg, March 1, 1971, printed in U.S. Atomic Energy Commission, *Supplement to the Environmental Statement, Radioactive Waste Repository, Lyons, Kansas,* July 1971.

27. J. Samuel Walker, *Containing the Atom: Nuclear Regulation in a Changing Environment, 1963–1971* (Berkeley: University of California Press, 1992), pp. 4–7.

28. Joint Committee on Atomic Energy, *Hearings on AEC Authorizing Legislation Fiscal Year 1972,* pp. 1308–44.

29. Ibid., pp. 1350–55.

30. Ibid., pp. 1355–65, 1446; *Nucleonics Week,* June 11, 1970; "Kansas Officials Oppose AEC on Radioactive Waste Repository," *Nuclear Industry* 18 (March 1971): 24–27.

31. Joint Committee on Atomic Energy, *Hearings on AEC Authorizing Legislation Fiscal Year 1972,* pp. 1367–74, 1445–64; *Nucleonics Week,* March 25, 1971.

32. Joint Committee on Atomic Energy, *Hearings on AEC Authorizing Legislation Fiscal Year 1972,* pp. 1344–96.

33. Robert Docking to Vern Miller, March 18, 1971, Docking to John Pastore, March 19, 1971, Docking to Richard M. Nixon, Box 56 (Atomic Energy Commission, Atomic Waste Repository, Lyons), Docking Papers; Docking to Pastore, April 28, 1971, Box 48 (Atomic Waste Disposal), Holifield Papers; *Kansas City Times,* April 15, 1971.

34. Pat [Burnau], Note to the Governor, April 5, 1971, Box 56 (Atomic Energy Commission, Atomic Waste Repository, Lyons), Docking Papers; *Hutchinson News,* March 19, 1971.

35. William W. Hambleton, "Statement to the Federal and State Affairs Committee of the House of Representatives of the Kansas Legislature," March 29, 1971, Box 68 (Lyons Radioactive Storage—Kansas Legislative Hearing), Accession No. 329-89-198, Robert J. Dole Papers, University of Kansas; Joint Committee on Atomic Energy, *Hearings on AEC Authorizing Legislation Fiscal Year 1972,* pp. 2229–33; *Kansas City Times,* April 21, 1971.

36. Ward [White] to Senator Dole, n.d., Dole to Richard M. Nixon, April 26, 1971, Dole to Robert Docking, June 30, 1971, Box 68 (Lyons Radioactive Storage—Correspondence), Accession No. 329-89-198, Dole Papers; J. Frederick Weinhold to Edward E. David Jr., April 15, 1971, Subject File (Atomic Energy Commission, 1971), Record Group 359 (Records of the Office of Science and Technology Policy), National Archives, College Park, MD; Joint Committee on Atomic Energy, *Hearings on AEC Authorizing Legislation Fiscal Year 1972,* pp. 1466–68, 2228.

37. *Journal of Glenn T. Seaborg,* vol. 25, p. 137; Joe Skubitz to Robert J. Dole, April 27, 1971, John A. Erlewine to Dole, April 30, 1971, Box 68 (Lyons Radioactive Storage—Correspondence), Accession No. 329-89-198, Dole Papers; Michael Schatzlein to Peter Flanigan, June 22, 1971, White House Central Files, Subject Files: Atomic Energy, Box 2 (AT 2 Industrial), Richard M. Nixon Papers, Nixon Presidential Materials Project, National Archives, College Park.

38. Frederick C. Schuldt to the Director, July 19, 1971, White House Central Files, Staff Member and Office Files: John C. Whitaker, Box 29 (Atomic Energy Commission, 1971), Nixon Papers; Robert Docking to John Pastore, July 13, 1971, Joe Skubitz to James B. Pearson and Robert J. Dole, July 19, 1971, Box 56 (Atomic Energy Commission, Atomic Waste Repository, Lyons), Docking Papers.

39. E. J. Bauser to John O. Pastore, July 24, 1971, Box 48 (Atomic Waste Disposal 1971), Holifield Papers; Robert Cahn to Robert B. Docking, August 24, 1971, Box 56 (Atomic Energy Commission, Atomic Waste Repository, Lyons), Docking Papers; *Hutchinson News,* July 21, July 25, 1971; *Wichita Eagle,* July 24, July 28, 1971; *Manhattan Mercury,* July 21, 1971; *Kansas City Times,* July 23, 1971; *Parsons Sun,* July 23, 1971; *Emporia Gazette,* July 28, 1971.

40. Otto Rueschhoff to F.M. Empson, May 4, 1971, "Summary of Discussions with Mr. Otto Rueschhoff, Kansas City, Missouri, on July 26, 1971," Box 26 (American Salt Corp., AEC), Series 1, Subject Files (Salt Vault: Atomic Energy Commission), Kansas Geological Survey Records; Hambleton, *Selected Speeches,* pp. 140–41.

41. News Release from Congressman Joe Skubitz, September 30, 1971, Press Release Binder, Joe Skubitz Papers, Pittsburg State University, Pittsburg, KS; Robert D. O'Neill to Bob Dole, October 1, 1971, Box 68 (Lyons Radioactive Storage—Correspondence), Accession No. 329-89-198, Dole Papers; *Denver Post,* September 28, 1971; *Lyons Daily News,* September 29, 1971.

42. Robert Docking to James Schlesinger, October 27, 1971, Schlesinger to Docking, November 19, 1971, Docking to Schlesinger, November 30, 1971, Box 56 (Atomic Energy Commission, Atomic Waste Depository, Lyons), Docking Papers; *Congressional Record,* 92nd Cong., 2nd Sess., 1972, p. 4847.

43. Stephen J. Gage to Edward E. David Jr., February 18, 1972, White House Central Files, Staff Member and Office Files: Glenn R. Schleede, Box 6 (AEC–Atomic Energy Commission), Nixon Papers; AEC Press Release, January 21, 1972, Nuclear Regulatory Commission (NRC) Records, NRC Public Document Room, Rockville, MD; Joe Skubitz to Dixy Lee Ray, May 1, May 30, 1974, Ray to Skubitz, June 17, 1974, Box 113 (AEC: Waste Disposal Correspondence), Congressman Joe Skubitz News Release, March 22, 1977, Box 159, Folder 3684, Skubitz Papers; "AEC Shifts to Surface Engineered Waste Storage Facilities," *Nuclear Industry* 19 (May 1972): 25; *Nucleonics Week,* May 18, 1972.

CHAPTER 4

1. "Go with Engineered Storage, But Don't Drop Salt, AEC Advised," *Nuclear Industry* 19 (November–December 1972): 47.

2. AEC Press Release, July 1, 1971, Nuclear Regulatory Commission (NRC) Records, NRC Public Document Room, Rockville, MD; Edward J. Bauser to All Committee Members, June 29, 1971, Box 48 (Staff Memoranda 1971), Chet Holifield Papers, University of Southern California, Los Angeles; "Some Welcome News from the AEC," *Nuclear News* 14 (August 1971): 23.

3. Ronald H. Baxter to Chairman, Atomic Energy Commission, January 20, 1972, AEC Records, History Division, Department of Energy, Germantown, MD; *Nucleonics Week,* July 8, 1971; "New Division at AEC," *Nuclear News* 14 (August 1971): 35.

4. *Nucleonics Week,* July 8, 1971, August 26, 1971; Luther J. Carter, *Nuclear Imperatives and Public Trust: Dealing with Radioactive Waste* (Washington, DC: Resources for the Future, 1987), pp. 74–75; J. Samuel Walker, *Containing the Atom: Nuclear Regulation in a Changing Environment, 1963–1971* (Berkeley: University of California Press, 1992), pp. 415–25.

5. SECY-2272 (January 25, 1972), AEC Records, Department of Energy; *Washington Post,* March 19, 1971; Walker, *Containing the Atom,* pp. 387–414.

6. SECY-2272, AEC Records, Department of Energy.

7. SECY-2333 (February 24, 1972), NRC Records, NRC Public Document Room.

8. U.S. Congress, House, Committee on Science and Astronautics, Subcommittee on Science, Research, and Development, *Hearings on Energy Research and Development,* 92nd Cong., 2nd Sess., 1972, pp. 331–37, 366; *Nucleonics Week,* May 18, 1972.

9. Frank K. Pittman, "Management of Commercial High-Level Radioactive Waste," July 25, 1972, AEC Press Release, November 16, 1972, AEC Records, Department of Energy.

10. "Pittman Reports on Commercial Waste Management Status," *Nuclear Industry* 20 (August 1973): 20–23; "Go with Engineered Storage," p. 48; Pittman, "Management of Commercial High-Level Radioactive Waste," AEC Records, Department of Energy.

11. SECY-2932 (February 8, 1973), SECY-74-673 (May 21, 1974), AEC Records, Department of Energy; AEC Fact Sheet on "Commercial High-Level Radioactive Waste," June 21, 1973, Box 706 (Waste Disposal), General Correspondence, Papers of the Joint Committee on Atomic Energy, Record Group 128 (Records of the Joint Committees of Congress), National Archives, Washington, DC; U.S. Atomic Energy Commission, *Environmental Statement: Management of Commercial High Level and Transuranium-Contaminated Radioactive Waste (WASH-1539 Draft),* September 1974, pp. 2.5–1 to 2.5–34; "Status of Interim Surface Storage, Salt Mine Projects Given," *Nuclear Industry* 20 (April 1973): 46–47; "AEC Completing Statement on Solid Waste Disposal and Storage," *Nuclear Industry* 21 (August 1974): 31–32.

12. *WASH-1539 Draft,* pp. 3.3–1 to 3.3–15.

13. Minutes of Policy Session 74–48, May 1, 1974, AEC Records, Department of Energy.

14. U.S. Atomic Energy Commission, *High-Level Radioactive Waste Management Alternatives (WASH-1297),* May 1974; *WASH-1539 Draft,* pp. 2.3–19 to 2.3–25, 2.5–34 to 2.5–39.

15. Richard Wolfson, *Nuclear Choices: A Citizen's Guide to Nuclear Technology* (Cambridge, MA: MIT Press, 1991), pp. 95–118; Victor Gilinsky, "Military Potential of Civilian Nuclear Power," in *Nuclear Proliferation: Prospects for Control,* ed. Bennett Boskey and Mason Willrich (Cambridge, MA: Dunellen, 1970), pp. 41–52; Deborah Shapley, "Plutonium: Reactor Proliferation Threatens a Nuclear Black Market," *Science* 172 (April 9, 1971): 143–46; Glenn T. Seaborg and William R. Corliss, *Man and Atom: Building a New World through Nuclear Technology* (New York: E.P. Dutton, 1971), pp. 43, 51, 284–85; Glenn T. Seaborg speech, "The Plutonium Economy of the Future," October 5, 1970, NRC Records, NRC Public Document Room.

16. Wolfson, *Nuclear Choices,* pp. 236–36; AEC Fact Sheet on "Commercial High-Level Radioactive Waste," Joint Committee on Atomic Energy Papers.

17. W.G. Belter, W. McVey, C.B. Bartlett, K.L. Mattern, and W.H. Regan, "The AEC's Position on Radioactive Waste Management," *Nuclear News* 12 (November 1969): 60–65; AEC Press Release, November 11, 1970, NRC Records, NRC Public Document Room.

18. Robert Gillette, "Plutonium (I): Questions of Health in a New Industry," *Science* 185 (September 20, 1974): 1027–32; Gene I. Rochlin, Margery Held, Barbara G. Kaplan, and Lewis Kruger, "West Valley: Remnant of the AEC,"

Bulletin of the Atomic Scientists 34 (January 1978): 17–26; Carter, *Nuclear Imperatives,* pp. 98–105.

19. "Reprocessing Gap Closer," *Nuclear Industry* 21 (July 1974): 8–11; Robert Gillette, "Nuclear Fuel Reprocessing: GE's Balky Plant Poses Shortage," *Science* 185 (August 30, 1974): 770–71; Carter, *Nuclear Imperatives,* pp. 105–6.

20. Brian D. Forrow, "Spent Fuel Storage and Reprocessing," March 22, 1983, Box 26 (Nuclear Fuel Cycle—General), George Keyworth Files, Ronald Reagan Library, Simi Valley, CA; Carter, *Nuclear Imperatives,* pp. 107–12.

21. U.S. Atomic Energy Commission, *Generic Environmental Statement: Mixed Oxide Fuel (WASH-1327 Draft),* August 1974, pp. S-1–S-4; *Nucleonics Week,* September 27, 1973.

22. Gilinsky, "Military Potential of Civilian Nuclear Power," p. 46. For detailed discussions of safeguards issues, see J. Samuel Walker, "Regulating against Nuclear Terrorism: The Domestic Safeguards Issue, 1970–1979," *Technology and Culture* 42 (January 2001): 107–32; and J. Samuel Walker, "Nuclear Power and Nonproliferation: The Controversy over Nuclear Exports, 1974–1980," *Diplomatic History* 25 (Spring 2001): 215–49.

23. John McPhee, *The Curve of Binding Energy: A Journey into the Awesome and Alarming World of Theodore B. Taylor* (New York: Farrar, Straus and Giroux, 1973); "Black-Market A-Bombs?" *Newsweek,* April 26, 1971, p. 59; *New York Times,* December 21, 1971; Shapley, "Plutonium," p. 144.

24. Armin H. Meyer to Members of the Working Group, Cabinet Committee to Combat Terrorism, February 23, 1973, White House Central Files, Staff Member and Office Files: Richard Tufaro, Subject Files, Box 1 (CCCT Working Group), Richard M. Nixon Papers, Nixon Presidential Materials Project, National Archives, College Park, MD; David M. Rosenbaum, John N. Googin, Robert M. Jefferson, Daniel J. Kleitman, and William C. Sullivan, "Special Safeguards Study," April 1974, NRC Records, NRC Public Document Room; U.S. Congress, Joint Committee on Atomic Energy, *Hearings on Nuclear Reactor Safety,* 93rd Cong., 2nd Sess., 1974, pp. 518–33; "Under Skull and Crossbones," *Economist,* November 18, 1972, pp. 11–13.

25. "India: Joining the Club," *Newsweek,* May 27, 1974, p. 50; "Fresh Fears of a 'Minor League' A-Bomb Race," *U.S. News and World Report,* June 3, 1974, pp. 45–46; Robert Gillette, "India: Into the Nuclear Club on Canada's Shoulders," *Science* 184 (June 7, 1974): 1053–55; Robert Bothwell, *Nucleus: The History of Atomic Energy of Canada Limited* (Toronto: University of Toronto Press, 1988), pp. 428–30.

26. *WASH-1327 Draft,* pp. S-4–S-8; Walker, "Regulating against Nuclear Terrorism," pp. 114–22.

27. J. Gustave Speth, Arthur R. Tamplin, and Thomas B. Cochran, "Plutonium Recycle: The Fateful Step," *Bulletin of the Atomic Scientists* 30 (November 1974): 15–22.

28. Walter F. Mondale and Philip A. Hart to Dixy Lee Ray, September 26, 1974, Henry A. Jackson to Ray, November 18, 1974, NRC Records, NRC Public Document Room; Robert Gillette, "Senators Seek Delay in Plutonium Recycling," *Science* 186 (October 11, 1974): 128; "Crystal-Balling," *Nuclear News* 17 (November 1974): 54.

29. Travis Wagner, "Hazardous Waste: Evolution of a National Environmental Problem," *Journal of Policy History* 16 (2004): 306–31; John C. Whitaker, *Striking a Balance: Environment and Natural Resources in the Nixon-Ford Years* (Washington, DC: American Enterprise Institute for Public Policy Research, 1976), p. 10; Martin V. Melosi, *The Sanitary City: Urban Infrastructure in America from Colonial Times to the Present* (Baltimore: Johns Hopkins University Press, 2000), pp. 338–54.

30. Sheldon Novick, "Earthquake at Giza," *Environment* 12 (January–February 1970): 3–13; "Buried Radioactivity," *Parade,* April 26, 1970; Terry R. Lash and John E. Bryson to Julius H. Rubin, March 28, 1973, AEC Records, Department of Energy.

31. Frank K. Pittman to J.G. Speth, draft, November 11, 1971, Box 30 (Bedrock Waste Storage, AEC File), Records of the Dupont Atomic Energy Division, Hagley Library and Museum, Wilmington, DE; Donald C. Kull to Floyd V. Hicks, June 15, 1970, John Harris, note to JRS [James R. Schlesinger], June 28, 1972, AEC Records, Department of Energy; *Washington Evening Star,* July 24, 1970.

32. F.P. Baranowski to the Commission, June 15, 1973, AEC Records, Department of Energy; "Hanford Radioactive Waste Leak," *Nuclear Industry* 20 (June 1973): 26; Robert Gillette, "Radiation Spill at Hanford: The Anatomy of an Accident," *Science* 181 (August 24, 1973): 728–30.

33. Ralph Nader, Daniel F. Ford, Thomas C. Hollocher, and Henry W. Kendall to Atomic Energy Commission, June 23, 1973, AEC Records, Department of Energy; *Nucleonics Week,* June 28, 1973; *Los Angeles Times,* July 5, 1973.

34. Henry M. Jackson to Lee Dye, August 16, 1973, Box 26 (General Correspondence, Departmental—US Atomic Energy Commission 1973), Henry M. Jackson Papers, University of Washington, Seattle; "WMT Comments on Lee Dye *Los Angeles Times* Article," n.d., Box 11 (US National Academy of Sciences Radioactive Waste Management Committee, 1973), Herbert M. Parker Papers, University of Washington; "Liquid Waste Leak at Hanford Stopped Short of Water Table," *Nuclear Industry* 20 (July 1973): 34–35.

35. AEC Press Release, July 30, 1973, NRC Records, NRC Public Document Room; "The Great Escape," *Nuclear News* 16 (September 1973): 82–83; Gillette, "Radiation Spill at Hanford," p. 729.

36. *Tri-City [Washington] Herald,* August 9, 1973; Stanley M. Nealey and John A. Hebert, "Public Attitudes toward Radioactive Wastes," in *Too Hot to Handle? Social and Policy Issues in the Management of Radioactive Wastes,* ed. Charles A. Walker, Leroy C. Gould, and Edward J. Woodhouse (New Haven: Yale University Press, 1983), pp. 95–96; Gillette, "Radiation Spill at Hanford,"p. 728.

37. Howard W. Cannon to James R. Schlesinger, May 17, 1972, Mike O'Callaghan to United States Atomic Energy Commission, October 28, 1974, AEC Records, Department of Energy.

38. J. Samuel Walker, *Three Mile Island: A Nuclear Crisis in Historical Perspective* (Berkeley: University of California Press, 2004), pp. 31–34.

39. "Can Nuclear Waste Be Stored?" *Newsweek,* November 18, 1974, p. 56.

40. *Nucleonics Week,* November 14, 1974

CHAPTER 5

1. Robert Gillette, "William Anders: A New Regulator Enters a Critical Situation," *Science* 187 (March 28, 1975): 1173–75; J. Samuel Walker, *Three Mile Island: A Nuclear Crisis in Historical Perspective* (Berkeley: University of California Press, 2004), pp. 31–37.

2. U.S. Congress, Joint Committee on Atomic Energy, *Hearings on Storage and Disposal of Radioactive Waste,* 94th Cong., 1st Sess., 1975, pp. 23–33; U.S. Congress, House, Committee on Interior and Insular Affairs, Subcommittee on Energy and the Environment, *Hearings on Nuclear Waste Management,* 95th Cong., 1st Sess., 1977, p. 32; U.S. Congress, House, Committee on Science and Technology, Subcommittee on Fossil and Nuclear Energy Research, Development and Demonstration, *Hearings on Oversight: Nuclear Waste Management,* 95th Cong., 2nd Sess., 1978, p. 169.

3. House Subcommittee on Energy and the Environment, *Hearings on Nuclear Waste Management,* pp. 30, 123–30; Comptroller General of the United States, *Nuclear Energy's Dilemma: Disposing of Hazardous Radioactive Waste Safely (EMD-77-41),* September 9, 1977, pp. 23–36.

4. House Subcommittee on Energy and the Environment, *Hearings on Nuclear Waste Management,* pp. 123–29; Comptroller General of the United States, *Nuclear Energy's Dilemma,* pp. 23–26.

5. Joint Committee on Atomic Energy, *Hearings on Storage and Disposal of Radioactive Waste,* pp. 188–265.

6. SECY-75-526 (October 24, 1975), SECY-76–28A (February 6, 1976), SECY-76–191 (April 1, 1976), Records of the Nuclear Regulatory Commission (NRC), NRC Public Document Room, Rockville, MD. "SECY Papers" for the NRC served the same purpose as "AEC Papers" for the AEC.

7. Roger Strelow to the Administrator, August 11, 1976, Alvin L. Alm to Russell E. Train, August 30, 1976, Box 177 (Air and Waste Management), General Correspondence, Office of the Administrator, Record Group 412 (Records of the Environmental Protection Agency), National Archives, College Park, MD; Richard Livingston to Alvin L. Alm, n.d., Item 1501 (Nuclear Non-Proliferation 1945–1990), National Security Archive, George Washington University, Washington, DC; *Report to the President by the Interagency Review Group on Nuclear Waste Management (TID-29442)* (Washington, DC: National Technical Information Service, 1979), pp. 23–28; J. Samuel Walker, *Permissible Dose: A History of Radiation Protection in the Twentieth Century* (Berkeley: University of California Press, 2000), pp. 67–79.

8. SECY-76-238 (April 22, 1976), Marcus A. Rowden, "Nuclear Waste Management: Getting on with the Job," July 12, 1976, NRC Records, NRC Public Document Room; Joint Committee on Atomic Energy, *Hearings on Radioactive Waste Management,* 94th Cong., 2nd Sess., 1976, pp. 250–51.

9. William P. Bishop to the Commissioners, October 21, 1976, NRC Records, NRC Public Document Room.

10. SECY-76-238, NRC Records, NRC Public Document Room; Joint Committee on Atomic Energy, *Hearings on Storage and Disposal of Radioactive*

Waste, pp. 27–33; Joint Committee on Atomic Energy, *Hearings on Radioactive Waste Management,* pp. 281–85.

11. U.S. Congress, House, Committee on Government Operations, Subcommittee on Conservation, Energy, and Natural Resources, *Hearings on Radioactive Waste Disposal Problems,* 94th Cong., 2nd Sess., 1976, pp. 379–436; Walker, *Three Mile Island,* p. 13.

12. House Subcommittee on Conservation, Energy, and Natural Resources, *Hearings on Radioactive Waste Disposal Problems,* pp. 86–90, 379–421. Table S-3 is printed in the *Code of Federal Regulations,* 10 CFR 51.51.

13. NRC Press Release, August 13, 1976, Samuel J. Chilk, Memorandum for the Record, August 18, 1976, NRC Records, NRC Public Document Room; "Court Widens Licensing Needs," *Nuclear Industry* 23 (August 1976): 3–6.

14. Marcus A. Rowden to Commissioner Mason, August 16, 1976, NRC Press Release, October 13, 1976, NRC Records, NRC Public Document Room; U.S. Nuclear Regulatory Commission, *Environmental Survey of the Reprocessing and Waste Management Portions of the LWR Fuel Cycle: A Task Force Report (NUREG-0116),* ed. William P. Bishop and Frank J. Miraglia, October 1976.

15. NRC Press Release, November 5, 1976, Richard Cotton and Terry R. Lash to Marcus Rowden, November 8, 1976, NRC Records, NRC Public Document Room.

16. Ben Huberman to the Commissioners, February 10, 1977, Huberman to Sam Chilk, April 20, 1977, Chilk to Director, *Federal Register,* June 28, 1977, Ken Pedersen to Commissioner Ahearne, October 5, 1978, NRC Records, NRC Public Document Room; *Natural Resources Defense Council, et al. v. U.S. Nuclear Regulatory Commission,* 547 F.2d 633 (1976); *Vermont Yankee Nuclear Power Corporation v. Natural Resources Defense Council, Inc., et al.,* 435 U.S. 519 (1978).

17. Russell W. Peterson to William A. Anders, January 20, 1975, NRC Records, NRC Public Document Room.

18. SECY-75-37 (February 12, 1975), SECY-75-54 (February 24, 1975), NRC Records, NRC Public Document Room; *Wall Street Journal,* March 5, 1975; J. Samuel Walker, "Regulating against Nuclear Terrorism: The Domestic Safeguards Issue, 1970–1979," *Technology and Culture* 42 (January 2001): 107–32.

19. SECY-75-107 (March 19, 1975), SECY-75-171 (April 17, 1965), SECY-75-171A (April 28, 1975), NRC Press Release, May 8, 1975, NRC Records, NRC Public Document Room; Jim Cannon, Memorandum to the President, May 7, 1975, Domestic Council—Glenn R. Schleede Files, Box 30 (Nuclear Regulatory Commission 1975—General), Gerald R. Ford Papers, Gerald R. Ford Library, Ann Arbor, Michigan; "Pu Recycle Issue," *Nuclear Industry* 22 (May 1975): 3–4.

20. John A. Harris to the Commissioners, November 7, 1975, *Federal Register,* Notice on Mixed Oxide Fuel, November 10, 1975, NRC Records, NRC Public Document Room.

21. Transcript of Press Conference, November 12, 1975, NRC Records, NRC Public Document Room; Gus Speth, Memorandum Re. NRC Decision on Plutonium Recycle, November 13, 1975, Box 37 (Natural Resources Defense Council, Inc.), Union of Concerned Scientists Papers, Massachusetts Institute of

Technology, Cambridge, MA; "NRC Takes Bull by the Horns," *Nuclear Industry* 22 (November 1975): 7–8.

22. "Court Halts Interim License Plan," *Nuclear Industry* 23 (June 1976): 30–31; *Washington Post,* May 28, 1976; *Natural Resources Defense Council, Inc. v. U.S. Nuclear Regulatory Commission,* 539 F.2d 824 (2d Cir. 1976).

23. *New York Times,* June 19, October 4, 1976; *Washington Post,* June 2, 1976; Jimmy Carter, *Why Not the Best?* (Nashville: Broadman Press, 1975), p. 153; Jeffrey K. Stine, "Environmental Policy during the Carter Presidency," in *The Carter Presidency: Policy Choices in the Post–New Deal Era,* ed. Gary M. Fink and Hugh Davis Graham (Lawrence: University Press of Kansas, 1998), pp. 179–201; Michael J. Brenner, *Nuclear Power and Non-Proliferation: The Remaking of U.S. Policy* (Cambridge: Cambridge University Press, 1981), pp. 113–18.

24. *New York Times,* May 14, 1976; Brenner, *Nuclear Power and Non-Proliferation,* p. 113.

25. Glenn R. Schleede to Dick Roberts and others, November 3, 1975, Subject File—White House Central Files, Box 2 (AT-Industrial), James E. Connor to Brent Scowcroft and others, July 19, 1976, Subject File—White House Central Files, Box 1 (AT Atomic Energy), Schleede to Jim Cannon, November 18, 1975, Domestic Council—Glenn R. Schleede Files, Box 25 (Nuclear Energy 1975—General), "Collection of Items Already Proposed or Suggested for Possible Consideration in Nuclear Energy Section of an Energy Message, December 18, 1975, Domestic Council—Schleede Files, Box 13 (Energy 1976—Presidential Energy Message), Ford Papers.

26. Robert Fri to the President, August 13, 1976, Subject Files—White House Central File, Box 1 (AT Atomic Energy), Ford Papers; Brenner, *Nuclear Power and Non-Proliferation,* pp. 100–108.

27. Brent Skowcroft, Jim Cannon, and Jim Lynn to the President, September 15, 1976, Domestic Council—Glenn R. Schleede Files, Box 29 (Nuclear Policy 1976—Presidential Decision Memo), "Statement by the President on Nuclear Policy," October 28, 1976, Subject File—White House Central Files, Box 1 (AT Atomic Energy), Ford Papers.

28. Ron Fuller to Glenn R. Schleede, October 6, 1976, Domestic Council—Glenn R. Schleede Files, Box 27 (Nuclear Policy 1976—Background Material), "The Importance of Closing the Nuclear Fuel Cycle: A Statement of the Atomic Industrial Forum Review Group," October 1, 1976, Domestic Council—Glenn R. Schleede Files, Box 26 (Nuclear Policy 1976—Atomic Industrial Forum Statement), Ford Papers; *Wall Street Journal,* July 2, 1976.

29. Presidential Review Memorandum/NSC 15, January 21, 1977, National Security Archive; Frank Press to the President, March 21, 1977, Staff Offices—Science and Technology Adviser to the President (Press), Box 6 (Subject File—Nuclear Policies), Jimmy Carter Papers, Jimmy Carter Library, Atlanta, GA; Chris Fitzgerald, "Scrabble, Anyone?" *Nuclear News* 19 (December 1976): 27; Nuclear Energy Study Group, *Nuclear Power: Issues and Choices* (Cambridge, MA: Ballinger, 1977), pp. 22, 29–31; Brenner, *Nuclear Power and Non-Proliferation,* pp. 118–22.

30. "Statement by the President on Nuclear Power Policy," April 7, 1977, Staff Offices—Domestic Policy Staff (Eizenstat), Box 246 (Subject File—

Nuclear Power, Uranium), Carter Papers; Brenner, *Nuclear Power and Non-Proliferation,* pp. 132–47.

31. Marcus A. Rowden to the President, May 5, 1977, Stuart E. Eizenstat to Joseph M. Hendrie, October 4, 1977, Staff Offices—Domestic Policy Staff (Eizenstat), Box 246 (Subject File—Nuclear Power, Uranium), Carter Papers; *Nucleonics Week,* October 13, 1977.

32. SECY-77-553 (October 25, 1977), SECY-77-594A (December 7, 1977), "Mixed Oxide Fuel: Memorandum of Decision," May 8, 1978, NRC Records, NRC Public Document Room; "Completion of GESMO Evaluated by NRC," *Nuclear Industry* 24 (November 1977): 26–27; "GESMO Hearings Laid to Rest by NRC," *Nuclear Industry* 25 (February 1978): 34.

33. "ERDA Shifts and Delays Its Waste Storage Facility Program," *Nuclear Industry* 22 (April 1975): 34–35; *Nucleonics Week,* April 10, 1975; "Nuclear News Briefs," *Nuclear News* 18 (May 1975): 17.

34. U.S. Energy Research and Development Administration, *Nuclear Fuel Cycle: A Report by the Fuel Cycle Task Force (ERDA-33),* March 1975, pp. iv–12; "ERDA Acts on Waste Storage," *Nuclear Industry* 23 (February 1976): 6–8; "Views Differ on Waste Disposal," *Nuclear Industry* 23 (May 1976): 25–28.

35. U.S. Energy Research and Development Administration, *Alternatives for Managing Wastes from Reactors and Post-Fission Operations in the LWR Fuel Cycle (ERDA-76-43),* May 1976, vol. 1, pp. 1–18; ERDA Press Release, December 2, 1976, NRC Records, NRC Public Document Room; "The Solid Waste Problem," *Nuclear Industry* 23 (December 1976): 36–41; "ERDA Shifts and Delays Its Waste Storage Facility Program," *Nuclear Industry,* p. 34; Luther J. Carter, "Radioactive Wastes: Some Urgent Unfinished Business," *Science* 195 (February 18, 1977): 661–66.

36. "DOE Spent Fuel Plan Aired," *Nuclear Industry* 24 (November 1977): 5–6.

37. Carter, "Radioactive Wastes," *Science,* p. 666.

38. Department of Energy Press Release, October 18, 1977, NRC Records, NRC Public Document Room; Stu Eizenstat to James Schlesinger, October 17, 1977, Staff Offices—Domestic Policy Staff (Eizenstat), Box 246 (Subject File—Nuclear Power, Uranium), Schlesinger to the President, April 7, 1978, Staff Offices—Domestic Policy Staff (Eizenstat), Box 151 (Subject File—Breeder Reactor), Carter Papers; "DOE Spent Fuel Plan Aired," *Nuclear Industry,* p. 5.

39. "Plutonium: Questions and Answers," n.d., NRC Records, NRC Public Document Room; "Nuclear 'Defenseless' without Waste Solution," *Nuclear Industry* 25 (January 1978): 24–25; *New York Times,* September 27, 1977; Edmund Faltermayer, "Burying Nuclear Trash Where It Will Stay Put," *Fortune* 99 (March 26, 1979): 98–104; U.S. Congress, House, Committee on Interior and Insular Affairs, Subcommittee on Energy and the Environment, *Hearings on Nuclear Waste Management,* 96th Cong., 1st Sess., 1979, pp. 32–36, 119–40.

40. Stanley M. Nealey and John A. Hebert, "Public Attitudes toward Radioactive Wastes," in *Too Hot to Handle? Social and Policy Issues in the Management of Radioactive Wastes,* ed. Charles A. Walker, LeRoy C. Gould, and

Edward J. Woodhouse (New Haven: Yale University Press, 1983), pp. 95–106; *Nucleonics Week,* August 7, 1975; Carter, "Radioactive Wastes," *Science,* p. 661; Mira Engler, *Designing America's Waste Landscapes* (Baltimore: Johns Hopkins University Press, 2004), p. xiii.

41. Thomas Raymond Wellock, *Critical Masses: Opposition to Nuclear Power in California, 1958–1978* (Madison: University of Wisconsin Press, 1998), pp. 147–72.

42. Daniel F. Ford to Joan Konner, January 27, 1977, Box 37 (NBC-TV), Union of Concerned Scientists Papers; John A. Harris to the Commission, February 4, 1977, NRC Records, NRC Public Document Room; Atomic Industrial Forum, *Info: Special Report,* November 17, 1977, Box 8 (NBC Program: Danger—Radioactive Waste), Fred H. Schmidt Papers, University of Washington, Seattle; *Wall Street Journal,* July 26, 1976; Robert Kaper, "Lethal Seepage of Nuclear Waste," *Nation* 224 (March 5, 1977): 266–70; Richard Severo, "Too Hot to Handle," *New York Times Magazine,* April 10, 1977, pp. 15–19; "The Atom's Global Garbage," *Time,* October 31, 1977, pp. 62–63; "A Mixed Verdict on NBC Nuclear Waste Documentary," *Science* 198 (December 23, 1977): 1232–33; "Media Group Scores NBC Radwaste Documentary," *Nuclear Industry* 24 (December 1977): 28; *Washington Post,* March 13, 1978.

43. "Agencies Drawing Flak on Proposed Sites," *Nuclear News* 19 (August 1976): 111–12; "Delays Beset Radwaste Program," *Nuclear Industry* 23 (October 1976): 3–6; J.R. Wargo, "States Cut DOE Waste Options," *Nuclear Industry* 25 (April 1978): 12–14; Luther J. Carter, "Nuclear Wastes: Popular Antipathy Narrows Search for Disposal Sites," *Science* 197 (September 23, 1977): 1265–66. On the Waste Isolation Pilot Plant in New Mexico, see Chuck McCutcheon, *Nuclear Reactions: The Politics of Opening a Radioactive Waste Disposal Site* (Albuquerque: University of New Mexico Press, 2002).

44. Bertram Wolfe, "Perspectives on Nuclear Energy and Nuclear Waste Disposal," 1975, NRC Records, NRC Public Document Room; "Spent Fuel and Nuclear Waste: A Statement by the Atomic Industrial Forum's Study Group on Waste Management," October 18, 1978, Box 258 (Fuel Cycle, Waste), Victor Gilinsky Papers, Hoover Institution on War, Revolution, and Peace Archives, Stanford University, Palo Alto, CA.

45. "Report to the American Physical Society by the Study Group on Nuclear Fuel Cycles and Waste Management," *Reviews of Modern Physics* 50 (No. 1, Part 2, January 1978), pp. S1–S9, S138–39.

46. J.D. Bredehoeft, A.W. England, D.B. Stewart, N.J. Trask, and I.J. Winograd, *Geologic Disposal of High-Level Radioactive Wastes—Earth-Science Perspectives,* Geological Survey Circular 779 (Washington, DC: U.S. Department of the Interior, 1978); Luther J. Carter, "Nuclear Wastes: The Science of Geologic Disposal Seen as Weak," *Science* 200 (June 9, 1978): 1135–37; J.R. Wargo, "Waste Storage in Salt Faulted," *Nuclear Industry* 25 (July 1978): 8–12; *Washington Post,* August 26, 1978.

47. House Subcommittee on Fossil and Nuclear Energy Research, Development and Demonstration, *Hearings on Nuclear Waste Management,* pp. 341, 352–530; J.R. Wargo, "Radwaste Study Group Calls for More Study," *Nuclear Industry* 25 (April 1978): 9–11.

48. House Subcommittee on Fossil and Nuclear Energy Research, Development and Demonstration, *Hearings on Nuclear Waste Management,* pp. 341, 352–530; Walker, *Three Mile Island,* pp. 132–33.

49. Sheldon Meyers to Clifford V. Smith Jr., April 6, 1978, Joseph Fouchard to the Commissioners, October 18, 1978, NRC Records, NRC Public Document Room; "Nuclear News Briefs," *Nuclear News* 21 (November 1978): 23; J.R. Wargo, "Carter's Waste Plan Is Cautious," *Nuclear Industry* 25 (November 1978): 3–5.

50. Faltermayer, "Burying Nuclear Trash," *Fortune,* pp. 98–99; Wargo, "Carter's Waste Plan Is Cautious," *Nuclear Industry,* pp. 4–5; *Report to the President by the Interagency Review Group on Nuclear Waste Management,* pp. 6–7; U.S. Congress, Senate, Committee on Governmental Affairs, Subcommittee on Energy, Nuclear Proliferation, and Federal Services, *Hearings on Report of the Interagency Review Group on Nuclear Waste Management,* 96th Cong., 1st Sess., 1979, pp. 144–45.

51. Assistant Administrator for Air, Noise and Radiation to the Administrator, February 12, 1979, Box 37 (OANR), Intra-Agency Memorandums 1977–1983, Office of the Administrator, EPA Records; William J. Dircks to Commissioner Ahearne, October 19, 1979, NRC Records, NRC Public Document Room; J.R. Wargo, "White House Gets IRG Report," *Nuclear Industry* 26 (April 1979): 15–16; *Report to the President by the Interagency Review Group on Nuclear Waste Management,* pp. 35–46, 87–88.

52. Jim McIntyre and Stu Eizenstat to the President, September 5, 1979, White House Central File, Subject File (Atomic/Nuclear Energy), Box AT-3 (AT), Stu Eizenstat and Kitty Schirmer to the President, October 24, 1979, with handwritten response from Carter, Staff Offices—Domestic Policy Staff (Eizenstat), Box 247 (Subject File—Nuclear Waste), Carter Papers.

53. Office of the White House Press Secretary, Statement to the Congress of the United States, February 12, 1980, NRC Records, NRC Public Document Room; Al McDonald, Rick Hertzberg, and Bob Rackleff to Stu Eizenstat, February 8, 1980, White House Central File, Subject File (Health), Box HE8, Carter Papers.

54. John V. O'Neill, "Congress Indifferent to AFR Storage Needs; TVA to Store On-Site," *Nuclear Industry* 26 (August 1979): 10–14.

55. "It's Time to End the Holy War over Nuclear Power," *Fortune* 99 (March 12, 1979): 81; Stanley M. Nealy, Barbara D. Melber, and William L. Rankin, *Public Opinion and Nuclear Energy* (Lexington, MA: D.C. Heath, 1983), pp. 95–103.

CHAPTER 6

1. U.S. Congress, House, Committee on Government Operations, "Low-Level Nuclear Waste Disposal" (House Report No. 94-1320), 94th Cong., 2nd Sess., 1976, p. 3; "Low-Level Waste Debate Grows," *Nuclear Industry* 23 (September 1976): 22–25.

2. George T. Mazuzan and J. Samuel Walker, *Controlling the Atom: The Beginnings of Nuclear Regulation, 1946–1962* (Berkeley: University of California Press, 1984), pp. 366–68; U.S. Congress, House, Committee on Government

Operations, *Hearings on Low-Level Radioactive Waste Disposal,* 94th Cong., 2nd Sess., 1976, p. 19.

3. AEC Press Release, Draft, August 7, 1962, Terry D. Hufft to Glenn T. Seaborg, September 18, 1962, Nuclear Regulatory Commission (NRC) Records, NRC Public Document Room, Rockville, MD.

4. Committee on Government Operations, *Hearings on Low-Level Radioactive Waste Disposal,* pp. 363–65; U.S. Congress, Joint Committee on Atomic Energy, *Hearings on Radioactive Waste Management,* 94th Cong., 2nd Sess., 1976, pp. 261–63; Mazuzan and Walker, *Controlling the Atom,* pp. 277–303.

5. *Nucleonics Week,* November 13, November 20, 1969; *Chattanooga Times,* December 4, 1969.

6. Harold L. Price to the Commission, January 12, 1971, Lyall Johnson to C. Henderson, August 11, 1971, NRC Records, NRC Public Document Room; *Long Island Press,* July 25, 1971; *New York Times,* July 17, August 18, 1971.

7. Joint Committee on Atomic Energy, *Hearings on Radioactive Waste Management,* pp. 263–66; Committee on Government Operations, *Hearings on Low-Level Radioactive Waste Disposal,* p. 8.

8. Dixy Lee Ray to Kenneth Rush, June 26, 1974, AEC Press Release, September 12, 1974, NRC Records, NRC Public Document Room; *Nucleonics Week,* April 26, 1973, May 31, 1973, November 7, 1974.

9. *Louisville Courier-Journal,* April 20, 1975; SECY-75-232 (May 21, 1975), Kenneth R. Chapman to Julian M. Carroll, July 14, 1975, NRC Records, NRC Public Document Room.

10. Committee on Government Operations, *Hearings on Low-Level Waste Disposal,* pp. 26–133, 364.

11. "Low-Level Waste Debate Grows," *Nuclear Industry,* p. 22; Luther J. Carter, *Nuclear Imperatives and Public Trust: Dealing with Radioactive Waste* (Washington, DC: Resources for the Future, 1987), p. 73.

12. "Radwaste Worries Reduced," *Nuclear Industry* 24 (April 1977): 17, 33; Joint Committee on Atomic Energy, *Hearings on Radioactive Waste Management,* p. 268; Carter, *Nuclear Imperatives and Public Trust,* p. 104.

13. John A. Harris to the Commission, May 26, 1976, Lee V. Gossick to James D. Santini, August 9, 1976, NRC Records, NRC Public Document Room; "Contamination Removed from Nevada Desert Town," *Nuclear News* 19 (May 1976): 84; Joint Committee on Atomic Energy, *Hearings on Radioactive Waste Management,* pp. 271–72.

14. Committee on Government Operations, *Hearings on Low-Level Waste Disposal,* pp. 204–88; Committee on Government Operations, House Report No. 94–1320, pp. 1–9, 18.

15. Joint Committee on Atomic Energy, *Hearings on Radioactive Waste Management,* pp. 252, 256–57; Committee on Government Operations, *Hearings on Radioactive Waste Disposal Problems,* 94th Cong., 2nd Sess., 1976, p. 2.

16. *NRC Task Force Report on Review of the Federal/State Program for Regulation of Commercial Low-Level Radioactive Waste Burial Grounds (NUREG-0217),* March 1977, Joseph J. Fouchard to the Commission, September 28, 1978, NRC Records, NRC Public Document Room; "See More Low-Level Radwaste,"

Nuclear Industry 23 (December 1976): 55–56; "Radwaste Worries Reduced," *Nuclear Industry* 23 (December 1976): 17, 33.

17. SECY-78-256 (May 12, 1978), Bruce W. Johnson to Joseph M. Hendrie, August 4, 1978, NRC Records, NRC Public Document Room; J.R. Wargo, "Low-Level Waste Sites Cut," *Nuclear Industry* 26 (February 1979): 15, 32.

18. Robert G. Ryan to Commissioner Kennedy, July 13, 1979, NRC Records, NRC Public Document Room; *Inside N.R.C.*, August 27, 1979; John O'Neill, "Governors Criticize Low-Level Packaging," *Nuclear Industry* 26 (November 1979): 8–9.

19. *Christian Science Monitor,* November 1, 1979; "Proclamation by the Governor," October 4, 1979, NRC Records, NRC Public Document Room; U.S. Congress, Senate, Committee on Environment and Public Works, Subcommittee on Nuclear Regulation, *Hearings on Nuclear Waste Disposal,* 96th Cong., 2nd Sess., 1980, p. 421; U.S. Congress, House, Committee on Science and Technology, Subcommittee on Energy Research and Production, *Hearings on Low-Level Nuclear Waste Burial Grounds,* 96th Cong., 1st Sess., 1979, p. 8; O'Neill, "Governors Criticize Low-Level Packaging," pp. 8–9.

20. Low-Level: Sites Now Seen as Critical," *Nuclear Industry* 26 (October 1979): 12–13; *Baltimore Sun,* November 2, 1979; Subcommittee on Energy Research and Production, *Hearings on Low-Level Nuclear Waste,* pp. 7, 18, 40, 73–74.

21. *New York Times,* November 16, 1979; SECY-79-633 (November 27, 1979), NRC Records, NRC Public Document Room; Comptroller General of the United States, *The Problem of Disposing of Nuclear Low-Level Waste: Where Do We Go from Here? (EMD-80-68),* March 31, 1980, p. 4; Subcommittee on Energy Research and Production, *Hearings on Low-Level Nuclear Waste,* pp. 15–16.

22. Office of the White House Press Secretary, Statement to the Congress of the United States, February 12, 1980, NRC Records, NRC Public Document Room; *Congressional Record,* 96th Cong., 2nd Sess., 1980, pp. 33961–68; *Nucleonics Week,* December 18, 1980; Stephen Gettinger, "Congress Again Faces Nuclear Waste Crisis," *Congressional Quarterly* 43 (March 16, 1985): 484–88.

23. *Wall Street Journal,* March 31, 1981; SECY-81-98 (February 9, 1981), NRC Records, NRC Public Document Room; Gettinger, "Congress Again Faces Nuclear Waste Crisis," pp. 484–88.

24. U.S. Congress, House, Committee on Interior and Insular Affairs, *Hearings on Low-Level Waste Legislation,* 99th Cong., 1st Sess., 1985, pp. 1–2, 110–16; Council on Scientific Affairs, "Low-Level Radioactive Wastes," *JAMA* 262 (August 4, 1989): 669–74; *Nucleonics Week,* January 2, 1986; *Inside N.R.C.*, August 9, 1993; Gettinger, "Congress Again Faces Nuclear Waste Crisis," pp. 484–88. The NRC's regulations are printed in the *Code of Federal Regulations,* 10 CFR Part 61.

25. SECY-81-335 (May 27, 1981), Samuel J. Chilk to the Record, November 2, 1982, NRC Records, NRC Public Document Room; *Inside N.R.C.*, July 27, 1981; *New York Times,* October 24, 1982.

26. SECY-81-330 (May 26, 1981), Samuel J. Chilk to William J. Dircks, June 26, 1981, "Policy Statement on Low-Level Waste Volume Reduction," October 12, 1981, NRC Records, NRC Public Document Room.

CHAPTER 7

1. U.S. Atomic Energy Commission, *Everything You Always Wanted to Know about Shipping High-Level Wastes (WASH-1264),* September 1973, pp. iii, 2–30; Joseph M. Dukert, *Atoms on the Move: Transporting Nuclear Material* (Washington, DC: Energy Research and Development Administration, 1975), pp. 10–16; U.S. Congress, Senate, Committee on Commerce, *Hearings on Transportation of Hazardous Materials,* 93rd Cong., 2nd Sess., 1974, pp. 85, 111. Concern about the transportation of nuclear materials was not limited to shipments of radioactive waste. During the late 1960s and 1970s, the chances that terrorists or criminals could steal plutonium in transit and use it to make an atomic bomb generated a great deal of comment and controversy. This problem did not apply to waste shipments, however, because the plutonium in spent fuel was inaccessible without elaborate reprocessing procedures. For a discussion of efforts to protect shipments of nuclear materials from theft, see J. Samuel Walker, "Regulating against Nuclear Terrorism: The Domestic Safeguards Issue, 1970–1979," *Technology and Culture* 42 (January 2001): 107–32.

2. L.L. Zahn, C.L. Brown, and J.W. Langhaar, "Transportation of Radioactive Materials," in *Reactor Technology: Selected Reviews—1965* (Oak Ridge, TN: U.S. Atomic Energy Commission, 1966), pp. 249–319; U.S. Atomic Energy Commission, "Radiological Emergency Procedures for the Non-Specialist," January 1969, Nuclear Regulatory Commission (NRC) Records, NRC Public Document Room, Rockville, MD.

3. *Nucleonics Week,* August 19, 1971.

4. Harold L. Price to Commissioner Johnson, July 28, 1969, Atomic Energy Commission Records, History Division, Department of Energy, Germantown, MD; SECY-75-162 (April 14, 1975), NRC Records, NRC Public Document Room.

5. Clifford K. Beck to the Commission, January 18, 1973, SECY-R 661 (March 26, 1973), AEC Press Release, March 22, 1973, NRC Records, NRC Public Document Room.

6. Comptroller General of the United States, *Opportunity for AEC to Improve Its Procedures for Making Sure That Containers Used for Transporting Radioactive Materials Are Safe (B-164105),* July 31, 1973; John P. Abbadessa to Chet Holifield, August 29, 1973, NRC Records, NRC Public Document Room.

7. U.S. Atomic Energy Commission, *Environmental Survey of Transportation of Radioactive Materials to and from Nuclear Power Plants (WASH-1238),* December 1972, pp. 1–21.

8. SECY-R-625 (January 12, 1973), AEC Press Release, February 2, 1973, "Daily Digest of Rule Making Hearing: Environmental Survey of Transportation to and from Reactors," April 2, 1973, NRC Records, NRC Public Document Room; "Participants Critical of Various Aspects of Proposed Rule," *Nuclear*

Industry 20 (April 1973): 19–21; *Nucleonics Week*, April 5, 1973; J. Samuel Walker, *Three Mile Island: A Nuclear Crisis in Historical Perspective* (Berkeley: University of California Press, 2004), p. 14.

9. SECY-R-75-166 (November 26, 1974), Paul C. Bender to Director, Office of the Federal Register, December 30, 1974, AEC Press Release, January 6, 1975, NRC Records, NRC Public Document Room; "Transportation Hearing Completed in One Day," *Nuclear News* 16 (May 1973): 44–46; "Participants Critical of . . . Proposed Rule," *Nuclear Industry*, p. 20.

10. "Excerpt of SECY 2698," September 14, 1972, William R. Gould to Members of the Atomic Industrial Forum, June 25, 1974, NRC Records, NRC Public Document Room; "Excerpt frm. SECY-2931, February 8, 1973, AEC Records, Department of Energy; *Nucleonics Week*, April 18, 1974; Senate Commerce Committee, *Hearings on Transportation of Hazardous Materials*, pp. 225–33.

11. *Washington Post*, January 22, 1974; Senate Commerce Committee, *Hearings on Transportation of Hazardous Materials*, pp. 162–67, 373–99.

12. Senate Commerce Committee, *Hearings on Transportation of Hazardous Materials*, pp. 399–405.

13. "Extract from SECY-75-350," November 13, 1974, AEC Records, Department of Energy.

14. William Brobst, "Transportation of Nuclear Materials: The State of State Regulations," *Nuclear News* 18 (February 1975): 51–55.

15. *Nucleonics Week*, September 4, 1975.

16. Ibid.; Peter L. Strauss to Patricia Caruso, September 12, 1975, SECY-75–660 (November 12, 1975), NRC Records, NRC Public Document Room; "Washington Fights New York City's Ban on Nuclear Shipments," *Nuclear Industry* 23 (January 1976): 25–26; "Nuclear News Briefs," *Nuclear News* 19 (February 1976): 18.

17. Peter L. Strauss to the Commission, December 9, 1975, Kenneth R. Chapman to the Commission, March 17, 1976, "Preliminary Notification of Event or Unusual Occurrence (PNO-76-60)," April 2, 1976, NRC Records; "Washington Fights . . . Ban on Nuclear Shipments," *Nuclear Industry*, p. 26.

18. "Nuclear Transport: Who's Boss?" *Nuclear Industry* 23 (June 1976): 9–14; "Cost, Transport Ban Threat to Industry," *Nuclear Industry* 23 (November 1976): 26–28; John O'Neill, "Nuclear Freight Ban Rejected by ICC," *Nuclear Industry* 24 (October 1977): 3–5.

19. "ICC Backs Industry's Position," *Nuclear Industry* 24 (May 1977): 14; John O'Neill, "Lawsuits Boomerang, Railroads Feel Sting," *Nuclear Industry* 28 (May 1981): 3–5; O'Neill, "Nuclear Freight Ban Rejected," *Nuclear Industry*, pp. 3–5.

20. *Nucleonics Week*, June 26, 1975; "Shipping Cask Slams into Wall, Gets Scratched but Undamaged," *Nuclear Industry* 24 (March 1977): 14; "They're at It Again!" *Nuclear News* 20 (Mid-April 1977): 90B; ERDA Press Release, ca. May 24, 1977, attached to Photo No. 434-SF-79–57, National Archives, College Park, MD; U.S. Congress, Senate, Committee on Commerce, Science, and Transportation," *Hearings on Nuclear Waste Transportation Safety Act of 1979*, 96th Cong., 1st Sess., 1979, pp. 169–70.

21. Public Citizen's Critical Mass Energy Project, "The Uranium Accident of September 27, 1977: A Case for Emergency Preparedness Plans and the Adequacy of Transportation Standards," October 31, 1977, NRC Records, NRC Public Document Room; *Washington Post,* October 8, 1977.

22. Carlton Kammerer to the Commission, October 31, 1977, Critical Mass, "The Uranium Accident of September 27, 1977," NRC Records, NRC Public Document Room.

23. John O'Neill, "Industry Now Has Better Way to Challenge Transport Laws," *Nuclear Industry* 24 (June 1977): 8–9; *New York Times,* September 25, 1977.

24. John O'Neill, "DOT Airs Transport Debate," *Nuclear Industry* 24 (December 1977): 3–6; *New York Times,* November 11, 1977.

25. Howard K. Shapar to the Commissioners, April 13, 1978, U.S. Department of Transportation Press Release No. 44-78, April 5, 1978, NRC Records, NRC Public Document Room; John O'Neill, "New York Nuclear Traffic Ban Next Key Case for Shippers," *Nuclear Industry* 24 (October 1977): 6–7; O'Neill, "Nuclear Freight Rulings: For and Against the Industry," *Nuclear Industry* 25 (May 1978): 13–15.

26. Gerald K. Rhode to Joseph M. Hendrie, January 29, 1979, NRC Records, NRC Public Document Room; "New London Bans Shipments," *Nuclear News* 21 (June 1978): 120; Fred C. Shapiro, *Radwaste: A Reporter's Investigation of a Growing Nuclear Menace* (New York: Random House, 1981), pp. 196–97.

27. John O'Neill, "Nuclear Shipments—The Going Is Rough," *Nuclear Industry* 26 (November 1979): 3–8; John O'Neill, "Proposed DOT Rule Outlaws Bans on Nuclear Shipments," *Nuclear Industry* 27 (March 1980): 22–23; *Nucleonics Week,* October 4, 1979; *New York Times,* February 12, 1980.

28. SECY-80-305 (June 23, 1980), NRC Records, NRC Public Document Room; "The Talk of the Town," *New Yorker* 56 (June 30, 1980): 26–29; Shapiro, *Radwaste,* pp. 197–202.

29. SECY-80-305, NRC Records, NRC Public Document Room; *New York Times,* August 13, 1980; John O'Neill, "Transport Rule Finally Emerges, to Be Effective February 1982," *Nuclear Industry* 28 (February 1981): 24–27.

30. *Federal Register* 46 (January 19, 1981): 5298–5318; O'Neill, "Transport Rule Finally Emerges," *Nuclear Industry,* pp. 24, 26; Shapiro, *Radwaste,* p. 219.

31. *Nucleonics Week,* February 25, May 13, 1982, March 1, 1984; "Federal Judge Overturns DOT Transport Rule," *Nuclear Industry* 29 (March 1982): 19–20; John Maffre, "Court Reinstates DOT's Rule Preempting Local Nuclear Bans," *Nuclear Industry* 30 (September 1983): 16–17; Teresa A. Nichols, "DOE Releases Repository Candidates; DOT Issues Transportation Rulings," *Nuclear Industry* 32 (January 1985): 26–27; "Nuclear News Briefs," *Nuclear News* 26 (September 1983): 24.

CHAPTER 8

1. Roger J. Mattson to Keith Steyer, February 4, 1977, Ken Pederson to the Commission, October 11, 1977, Gary A. Robbins to Steyer, December 6,

1977, Nuclear Regulatory Commission (NRC) Records, NRC Public Document Room, Rockville, MD.

2. Jerome Nelson to Commissioner Gilinsky, October 17, 1977, James C. Malaro to Richard E. Cunningham and Sheldon Myers, February 8, 1978, NRC Records, NRC Public Document Room.

3. "Licensing Procedures for Geologic Repositories for High-Level Radioactive Wastes: Proposed General Statement of Policy," November 14, 1978, NRC Records, NRC Public Document Room.

4. SECY-79-580 (October 22, 1979), NRC Records, NRC Public Document Room.

5. *Nucleonics Week,* October 4, 1979.

6. John W. Wydler and Manual Lujan Jr. to Joseph M. Hendrie, November 20, 1979, John F. Ahearne to Wydler, March 18, 1980, Hendrie to Marilyn L. Bouquard, March 13, 1981, "Extract from Staff Requirements, Affirmation Session 81–4," February 5, 1981, SECY-79-580, NRC Records, NRC Public Document Room.

7. J. Samuel Walker, *Containing the Atom: Nuclear Regulation in a Changing Environment, 1963–1971* (Berkeley: University of California Press, 1992), pp. 205–10.

8. "10 CFR Part 60, Disposal of High Level Waste in Geologic Repositories, Subpart B—Performance Objective and General Technical Criteria," November 17, 1978, NRC Records, NRC Public Document Room.

9. Robert M. Bernero to John B. Martin, January 5, 1979, SECY-80-177 (April 4, 1980), Sheldon Meyers to Martin, April 24, 1981, NRC Records, NRC Public Document Room; JA [John Austin] to VG [Victor Gilinsky], May 6, 1981, Box 280 (Fuel Cycle, Waste Geologic Depositories), Victor Gilinsky Papers, Hoover Institution on War, Revolution, and Peace Archives, Stanford University, Palo Alto, CA; *Nucleonics Week,* October 4, 1979.

10. Roger Strelow to the Administrator, August 11, 1976, Alvin L. Alm to Russell E. Train, Box 166 (Office of Air and Waste Management), General Correspondence, Office of the Administrator, Record Group 412 (Records of the Environmental Protection Agency), National Archives, College Park, MD.

11. Renner B. Hoffman to Robert M. Bernero, March 1, 1979, Lee V. Gossick to Manager, Waste Environmental Standards Program, March 13, 1979, NRC Records, NRC Public Document Room.

12. Joseph M. Hendrie to Douglas M. Costle, June 22, 1979, John B. Martin to Edward F. Tuerk, May 4, 1981, NUREG-0804, *Staff Analysis of Public Comments on Proposed Rule 10 CFR Part 60 Disposal of High Level Radioactive Wastes in Geologic Repositories* (1983), pp. D-1 to D-42; NRC Records, NRC Public Document Room;

13. NUREG-0804, *Staff Analysis,* pp. 1–34.

14. *Nucleonics Week,* July 14, 1977. For background, see above, chapter 5.

15. *Nucleonics Week,* May 31, 1979; NRC Press Release, September 28, 1979, NRC Records, NRC Public Document Room.

16. Samuel J. Chilk, Memorandum for the Record, January 12, 1982, NRC Records, NRC Public Document Room; "Waste Confidence: Draft VG Preliminary Views," n.d., Box 272 (Fuel Cycle, Waste), "Waste Confidence Meeting,"

July 7, 1982, Box 276 (Fuel Cycle, Waste), Gilinsky Papers; Luther J. Carter, *Nuclear Imperatives and Public Trust: Dealing with Radioactive Waste* (Washington, DC: Resources for the Future, 1987), pp. 204–5.

17. "The Commission's Decision in the Matter of Rulemaking on the Storage and Disposal of Nuclear Waste (Waste Confidence Rulemaking)," August 22, 1984, NRC Records, NRC Public Document Room.

18. Office of the White House Press Secretary, Statement to the Congress of the United States, February 12, 1980, U.S. Department of Energy, *The National Plan for Radioactive Waste Management: Volume 1—Introduction and Highlights,* January 1981, pp. 1–1 to 1–7, NRC Records, NRC Public Document Room.

19. Department of Energy, *National Plan for Radioactive Waste Management,* pp. 1–2, 3–1 to 3–16; William J. Dircks to Commissioner Ahearne, October 19, 1979, NRC Records, NRC Public Document Room.

20. Comptroller General of the United States, *Is Spent Fuel or Waste from Reprocessed Spent Fuel Simpler to Dispose Of? (EMD-81-78),* June 12, 1981, pp. 1–38.

21. J. Samuel Walker, *Three Mile Island: A Nuclear Crisis in Historical Perspective* (Berkeley: University of California Press, 2004), pp. 7–11, 190–244.

22. G.A. Keyworth to Martin Anderson, June 29, 1981, Red Cavaney to James Baker III, September 9, 1981, Box 23 (Nuclear Power), George Keyworth Files, Ronald Reagan Library, Simi Valley, CA; John O'Neill, "Elections Cause Exhilaration," *Nuclear Industry* 28 (February 1981): 3–6.

23. *Nucleonics Week,* October 15, 1981.

24. Ibid.; John Maffre, "Nuclear: Some Forward Motion," *Nuclear Industry* 28 (November 1981): 8–10; Herman R. Hill to William A. Wilson, October 30, 1981, Box 23 (Nuclear Power), Keyworth Files.

25. Edwin L. Harper to Danny Boggs, March 24, 1982, WHORM: Subject File (AT Atomic/Nuclear Energy, ID# 073903PD), "Presidential Message to the Congress on Nuclear Waste," n.d., WHORM: Subject File (HE 007-03, ID# 044458CS), Ronald Reagan Papers, Reagan Library.

26. Andy Plattner, "Senators Jockeying to Keep Nuclear Waste Out of Their States; Debate Set to Begin," *CQ Weekly Report* 40 (April 17, 1982): 856–58. Luther J. Carter provides an excellent discussion of the debate over nuclear waste legislation in *Nuclear Imperatives and Public Trust,* pp. 195–230.

27. *Nucleonics Week,* December 18, 1980; John O'Neill, "Waste Bill Hits Snag, Dies in 96th Congress," *Nuclear Industry* 28 (January 1981): 8–9; O"Neill, "Congress Poised for Waste Bill," *Nuclear Industry* 28 (November 1981): 3–7 ff.; Carter, *Nuclear Imperatives and Public Trust,* pp. 199–204.

28. *New York Times,* April 29, 1982; Carter, *Nuclear Imperatives and Public Trust,* pp. 205–13.

29. Carlton Kammerer to the Commission, November 16, 1981, NRC Records, NRC Public Document Room; Andy Plattner, "Nuclear Waste Bill Faces Problems in House," *CQ Weekly Report* 40 (May 8, 1982): 1061–63; John O'Neill, "Senate Passes Waste Bill, Putting Pressure on House," *Nuclear Industry* 29 (June 1982): 10–13.

30. State Planning Council on Radioactive Waste Management, *Recommendations on National Radioactive Waste Management Policies: Report to the*

President, August 1, 1981, Box 26 (Nuclear Fuel—Waste), Keyworth Files; Eliot Marshall, "The Senate's Plan for Nuclear Waste," *Science* 216 (May 14, 1982): 709–10; Carter, *Nuclear Imperatives and Public Trust,* p. 201.

31. Jay Keyworth to Craig Fuller, April 22, 1982, WHORM: Subject File (HE 007-03, ID# 044458), Reagan Papers; U.S. Congress, House, Committee on Interior and Insular Affairs, Subcommittee on Energy and the Environment, *Hearings on Radioactive Waste Legislation,* 97th Cong., 1st Sess., 1981, p. 195; *Nucleonics Week,* January 8, 1981; Plattner, "Nuclear Waste Bill Faces Problems," pp. 1062–63; O'Neill, "Senate Passes Waste Bill," p. 10.

32. U.S. Congress, Senate, Report No. 97–282, *National Nuclear Waste Policy Act,* 97th Cong., 1st Sess., 1981, p. 63; Carter, *Nuclear Imperatives and Public Trust,* pp. 201–3.

33. Plattner, "Senators Jockeying to Keep Nuclear Waste Out of Their States," p. 858; O'Neill, "Congress Poised for Waste Bill," p. 27; Carter, *Nuclear Imperatives and Public Trust,* p. 202.

34. Frederick N. Khedouri to Edwin Meese III, February 4, 1982, WHORM: Subject File (AT Atomic/Nuclear Energy, ID# 044277CA), Reagan Papers; Plattner, "Nuclear Waste Bill Faces Problems in House," pp. 1062–63; Marshall, "Senate's Plan for Nuclear Waste," pp. 709–10; O'Neill, "Senate Passes Waste Bill," pp. 11–13; *New York Times,* April 29, 1982; Carter, *Nuclear Imperatives and Public Trust,* pp. 204–12.

35. Carl Walske to AIF Official Representatives, May 28, 1982, NRC Records, NRC Public Document Room; Alan Murray, "House Passes Comprehensive Nuclear Waste Legislation," *CQ Weekly Report* 40 (December 4, 1982): 2951–52; Plattner, "Nuclear Waste Bill Faces Problems in House," p. 1061; Carter, *Nuclear Imperatives and Public Trust,* pp. 212–23.

36. Lee Sherman Dreyfus to Robert Stafford, October 2, 1981, Bruce King, Robert List, Scott M. Matheson, and John Spellman to Stafford, April 16, 1982, S. 1662–97th–National Nuclear Waste Policy Act of 1981, Record Group 46 (Records of the United States Senate), National Archives, Washington, DC; Alan Murray, "Congress Clears Nuclear Waste Legislation," *CQ Weekly Report* 40 (December 25, 1982): 3103–4; John O'Neill, "After Four Years, a Waste Bill," *Nuclear Industry* 30 (January 1983): 6–7; Carter, *Nuclear Imperatives and Public Trust,* pp. 223–27.

37. Robert F. Bonitati to Marvin J. Boede, January 25, 1983, WHORM: Subject File (AT Atomic/Nuclear Energy, ID# 119456), Reagan Papers; O'Neill, "After Four Years, a Waste Bill," p. 7; Marshall, "The Senate's Plan for Nuclear Waste," p. 710.

38. Eliot Marshall, "Thirty Ways to Temporize on Waste," *Science* 237 (August 7, 1987): 591–92; Carter, *Nuclear Imperatives and Public Trust,* pp. 401–14.

39. Eliot Marshall, "Nevada Wins the Nuclear Waste Lottery," *Science* 239 (January 1, 1988): 15; Joseph A. Davis, "Nevada Senator Filibusters Nuclear-Waste Plan," *CQ Weekly Report* 45 (November 7, 1987): 2749–50; Joseph A. Davis, "Nevada to Get Nuclear Waste; Everyone Else 'Off the Hook,'" *CQ Weekly Report* 45 (December 19, 1987): 3136–38; *New York Times,* December 15, December 17, 1987.

40. *New York Times,* July 31, 2001; *Washington Post,* April 9, 2002; Rodney C. Ewing and Allison Macfarlane, "Nuclear Waste: Yucca Mountain," *Science* 296 (April 26, 2002): 659–60.

41. *New York Times,* February 16, July 10, 2002; *Washington Post,* March 26, 2002.

42. U.S. General Accounting Office, *Nuclear Waste: Uncertainties about the Yucca Mountain Repository Project (GAO-02-765T),* May 23, 2002; *New York Times,* July 10, 2002, August 10, 2005; *Washington Post,* August 10, 2005; *Los Angeles Times,* August 10, 2005; *Las Vegas Review-Journal,* August 10, 2005; Luther J. Carter and Thomas H. Pigford, "Proof of Safety at Yucca Mountain," *Science* 310 (October 21, 2005): 447–48.

43. *Energy Daily,* June 4, 2008; *Inside N.R.C.,* September 15, 2008.

Essay on Sources

There is a rich array of primary sources relating to efforts to deal with radioactive waste from the 1940s into the 1980s. Records of the Atomic Energy Commission were divided between the Energy Research and Development Administration and the Nuclear Regulatory Commission when Congress abolished the AEC in 1974. The NRC acquired AEC records on the regulation of commercial applications of nuclear energy. AEC and NRC regulatory documents on waste that are cited in the notes are available at the NRC's Public Document Room at its headquarters in Rockville, Maryland. The records of the AEC's military and promotional activities went to ERDA, and, in turn, to the Department of Energy when it was created in 1977. For access to documents in the custody of DOE that are cited in the notes, contact the DOE History Division. AEC records that DOE has transferred to the National Archives are available for research at the Archives building in College Park, Maryland. A wealth of information relating to AEC operations at Hanford, including waste, can be found on-line at the DOE Public Reading Room Catalog (http://rrcatalog.pnl.gov).

The papers of Abel Wolman at Johns Hopkins University in Baltimore, Maryland, are exceedingly valuable for studying radioactive waste issues from the late 1940s through the 1960s. The records of the National Academy of Sciences Committee on Waste Disposal and successors are essential for understanding waste questions during the 1960s. They can be examined at the National Academy of Sciences–National Research Council Archives in Washington, DC. On the Lyons, Kansas, controversy, the records of the Kansas State Geological Survey and the papers of Robert Docking at the Spencer Research Library,

University of Kansas, Lawrence, are indispensable. The papers of Robert J. Dole at the Dole Institute of Politics at the University of Kansas also contain important materials. The papers of Joe Skubitz at Pittsburg State University in Pittsburg, Kansas, include some useful documents. Unfortunately, they have very little on the Lyons affair between 1970 and 1972, when Skubitz was a leading figure in the debate. The papers of Victor Gilinsky at the Hoover Institution on War, Revolution, and Peace Archives at Stanford University, Palo Alto, California, are an excellent source of information on nuclear safety issues, including waste, during Gilinsky's terms as an NRC commissioner, 1975–84. The papers of Glenn T. Seaborg in the Manuscript Division of the Library of Congress, Washington, DC, cover a broad range of nuclear matters but do not contain a great deal of material on waste.

Several presidential libraries house records that shed light on the radioactive waste debate. Researchers can find some items of interest in the papers of Richard M. Nixon, currently housed at the Nixon Presidential Materials Project at the National Archives in College Park (scheduled for eventual transfer to the Nixon Presidential Library in Yorba Linda, California), and the papers of Ronald Reagan at the Reagan Library in Simi Valley, California. The papers of Gerald R. Ford at the Ford Library in Ann Arbor, Michigan, and the papers of Jimmy Carter at the Carter Library in Atlanta, Georgia, contain a great deal of valuable material on waste issues that became prominent during their administrations.

In addition, the following collections include at least some useful information on radioactive waste programs: records of the Joint Committee on Atomic Energy, a part of Record Group 128 (Records of the Joint Committees of Congress), and the U.S. Senate (Record Group 46), at the National Archives in Washington, DC; records of the Environmental Protection Agency (Record Group 412), and the Office of Science and Technology Policy (Record Group 359), at the National Archives in College Park; records of the Dupont Atomic Energy Division, Hagley Library and Museum, Wilmington, Delaware; papers of the Union of Concerned Scientists at the Massachusetts Institute of Technology, Cambridge; papers of Henry M. Jackson, Herbert M. Parker, and Fred H. Schmidt at the University of Washington, Seattle; and the papers of Chet Holifield and Craig Hosmer at the University of Southern California, Los Angeles. The files of the National Security Archive in Washington, DC, contain helpful materials on reprocessing, and the transcript of a fascinating oral history interview with M. King Hubbert is available at the Niels Bohr Library at the Center for the History of Physics, American Institute of Physics, College Park, Maryland.

There is little in-depth secondary literature on the history of commercial radioactive waste programs, but a few outstanding accounts have been especially useful to me. They are Luther J. Carter, *Nuclear Imperatives and Public Trust: Dealing with Radioactive Waste* (Washington, DC: Resources for the Future, 1987); Roy E. Gephart, *Hanford: A Conversation about Nuclear Waste and Cleanup* (Columbus, OH: Battelle Press, 2003); Fred C. Shapiro, *Radwaste: A Reporter's Investigation of a Growing Nuclear Menace* (New York: Random House, 1981); and Chuck McCutcheon, *Nuclear Reactions: The Politics of Opening a Radioactive Waste Disposal Site* (Albuquerque: University of New Mexico Press, 2002).

Index

Text: 10/13 Sabon
Display: Sabon
Compositor: BookComp, Inc.
Printer & binder: Sheridan Books, Inc.